Historical Transcendence
and the Reality of God

Historical Transcendence
and the Reality of God

A Christological Critique

Ray Sherman Anderson

With a foreword by Professor D. M. MacKinnon

WILLIAM B. EERDMANS PUBLISHING COMPANY
Grand Rapids

Published by special arrangement with Geoffrey
Chapman Publishers, an imprint of Cassell and Collier
Macmillan Publishers Ltd., London. First American
edition November 1975.

Library of Congress Cataloging in Publication Data:

Anderson, Ray Sherman.
    Historical transcendence and the reality of God.

    Bibliography: p.307
    Includes indexes.
    1. God. 2. Incarnation. I. Title.
BT102.A49   211   75-33737
ISBN 0-8028-3473-6

Printed in the United States of America

Contents

Part Two

Incarnation and Historical Transcendence

Part Three

Lived Transcendence and the Reality of God

In memory of
ALBERT SHERMAN ANDERSON

who touched the earth with gentle hands
and made me glad to be a son.

Foreword

There are three reasons why I am extremely glad to be able to commend Dr. Ray Sherman Anderson's book to the widest possible public. The first is that it is the work of a young man, who is concerned to explore certain fundamental questions in theology, and to do so by use of exceptionally wide-ranging discussion of relevant literature. No one is likely to agree with all Dr. Anderson's judgements; none will fail to gain from reflection on them, and none will fail to have their attention directed to work of which, apart from Dr. Anderson's most strenuous researches, they are unlikely to have heard. In particular he has had the advantage of reading the unpublished remains of the late Professor Donald Gregor Smith, whose sudden, premature death at the height of his powers in the autumn of 1968 deprived religious thought in the United Kingdom of a most original, even profound, writer and teacher. In Dr. Anderson's book considerable extracts from Professor Gregor Smith's unpublished writings are usefully quoted and discussed. Further it is important, and indeed fitting, that they are thus disclosed to the reading public not by a slavish disciple, but by a theologian whose work is leading him sometimes in very different directions to those followed by Professor Gregor Smith.

Secondly there is in Dr. Anderson's writing a nervous, restless quality, which together with the breadth and depth of his theological culture entices the reader to engage himself or herself with the issues with which he is concerned. His book is not an easy one; but it is never dull, even when its sense is as perplexing as it is provocative. While he would be the first to admit that he has done no more that make a contribution, the contribution which he has made is not one that any critic will easily dismiss as negligible.

Thirdly there is a particular field of Christian theology where (in my view) work is beginning to be done of fundamental significance, but where that work needs to be taken very much further. I am referring to the revival of the use of the concept of *kenosis* in the theology of the Incarnation, developed in close connection with the re-presentation of the doctrine of the Trinity, understood as the authentic Christian doctrine of God. The significance of this enterprise for the analysis of the notion of transcendence hardly needs statement. But its execution demands remarkable resources of historical knowledge, critical and constructive philosophical perception, theological insight and spiritual sensitivity. If I say that Dr. Anderson's study embodies a significant contribution to this work, I have given it high praise; but I have said no more than is due to his dedicated industry and effort.

D. M. MacKinnon

Corpus Christi College
Cambridge
17 June, 1975

Preface

Kierkegaard once told of being caught up into the seventh heaven, where the gods were all assembled, and told to make his wish for whatever he desired. Momentarily at a loss, he quickly recovered, and asked to 'always have the laugh on my side'. At which point, continued Kierkegaard, the gods began to laugh, and it could be concluded that the wish had been granted. For it would hardly have been appropriate for them to have gravely intoned: 'thy wish is granted!'[1] When one takes it upon oneself to write a serious book on the problem of the reality of God, the sheer presumption of the enterprise can only be mitigated by the secret hope that, in addition to an inexhaustible depth of mercy and kindness, the divine heart possesses an irrepressible sense of humour. It has been a source of constant comfort and encouragement to me through the academic exercise of preparing this manuscript to believe that God was not only keenly interested in my attempts to speak about the reality of his own being, but was pleasantly patient through it all, and as genuinely excited as I was at the end when his power and presence began to shine through the opacity of my magnum opus.

It is of particular satisfaction to me that the truths which have emerged through this exploration into God (in my judgement) sustain and illuminate the conclusions to which I had already been driven during eleven years of parish ministry. At the grave-side, in the hospital room, through shared tears and painful silences, out of the thousand hours, often terrifying and always lonely, of standing in the pulpit with the awful, and yet exciting weight of the WORD of God upon my lips and in my heart, I learned the theology of an Incarnate God—and taught it, recklessly and extravagantly. The classroom questions with their ready-made theological answers were never quite the right size and shape, and fell apart when trimmed to fit the particular human situation which demands an incarnational bread, and too often receives a theological stone.

I say this only to make it clear that when I speak of the 'kenotic community' and the 'ek-static community', this is not some new discovery for me, arrived at through the aseptic surgery of academic re-

---

[1] *Either/Or*, Anchor Books, New York, 1959, Vol. I, pp. 41, 42.

search and reporting. These are first of all places and faces that would not recognize the terminology, but embody the reality of that which the language herein only reaches through the tortuous paths of disciplined thought. And the 'thresholds' of lived transcendence each have names for me, of persons who first taught me to know the reality of a God who makes himself concrete through historical existence. To this extent, the greater part of this book works beneath the surface of those realities which I discovered first of all through the agony and ecstasy of living on the raw edge of faith, where vulnerability is one's only strength and transparency of humanity one's only truth.

If then there are foundations here, upon which others may build and upon which my own commitments may rest with deeper assurance and conviction, my first gratitude is for those who have already believed and are living these truths, and who gave me the courage and the will to dig deeper into their foundation structure, even at the price of leaving their love. This work represents, in substance, the thesis presented for the Ph.D. degree at the University of Edinburgh. So here, too, I must express my appreciation to my academic supervisors and teachers, Professor Thomas F. Torrance and Canon Roland Walls. It was Canon Walls who recognized at the very outset the truth of what I was trying to say with stammering words, and who drew from the well of his own life with God to encourage me and to inspire me. He turned what could have been a wearisome task into an adventure in which he participated with delightful surprise and wise counsel. I owe a particular debt of gratitude to Professor Torrance, whose brilliance of mind and tenacity of theological purposefulness show me how far I have to go to bear the title of theologian, but whose devotion to Christ and love of the truth make me want to settle for nothing less. I gratefully acknowledge that whatever in this book, despite its limitations and shortcomings, touches the truth, I owe to the inspiration of these two men who not only are teachers, but believers. The imperfections, and even errors, of course, are my responsibility alone. It is, above all, a human document. And if it is genuinely so, I am satisfied that it speaks truly of God.

Ray S. Anderson

Westmont College
Santa Barbara
January, 1975

Introduction

It is a particularly happy time in which to write, when the issues have become so sufficiently polarized that the rational way makes more sense than the radical. One can acknowledge the contribution of radical theology in creating the extreme by which the truth is put into perspective, and yet, feel grateful that theology once again seems to have a centre instead of ragged alternatives. And by a centre, I mean at least the clear outlines of the fundamental task for theology—a task not only implicit in the subject of theology itself, but made explicit by the gaping seam in the fabric of this generation's faith.

'If any factor marks our generation, it is the almost total loss of an intelligible rationale for a transcendent alternative to the secular reduction of reality.'[1] Like all generalizations, this one of Carl Henry's is built on a simplistic assumption that bears examination. The fact that a secular ideology reduces reality to a sub-human level would be contested by many theologians. But it has become increasingly clear that some who were themselves architects of a 'secular theology' now question the adequacy of radical secularity.[2] What is most important in Henry's observation is his pin-pointing of transcendence in its relation to reality

[1]Carl F. H. Henry, 'The New Consciousness', *Christianity Today*, October 8, 1971, pp. 28-29.
[2]Cf. R. G. Smith, *Secular Christianity*, Collins, London, 1966, who speaks of a 'tide of secularism' which has caused 'the general reduction of all modern societies to the unitary level of secularism' p. 138. Cf. also his book, *The Free Man*, Collins, London, 1969, where he suggests that secularism is 'inherently self-destructive'. p. 36; he also goes on to speak of the 'waiting answer to the ultimate question which arises at the end of the secularist road' p. 41. Cf. also, pp. 147ff. In this respect, one should also consider the words of Paul van Buren, *Theological Explorations*, SCM Press, London, 1968, who says, 'Now that the hot air has leaked out of the recent "death of God" balloon, and as we push the flaccid remains to the back of the drawer reserved for mementos of our more foolish exploits, it may be said that behind all that journalistic nonsense lay an important issue ... a rediscovery in our time that man's question about God ... does not long admit of clear and simple answers', p. 6. However, it must be said that van Buren, unlike Smith, has no interest in the transcendence of God as a viable beginning towards those answers.

as the crucial issue for contemporary theology, and, indirectly, his call for
an intelligible rationale expressing this relationship. This, I believe,
marks the way forward, and establishes at the same time the precise
purpose of this book. What is meant by the terms 'transcendence' and
'reality', of course, remains to be determined.

In formulating my thesis, I have qualified both the words 'transcendence' and 'reality' in such a way as to define more clearly the way
in which they are to be determined. 'Historical transcendence and the
reality of God' is a construction which states the problem in the sharpest
possible way, but also includes the element of a single rationale in which
to work it out.[3] Admittedly, historical transcendence is a somewhat
odd combination of words, and some might say, an apparent confusion
of language games.[4] The formulation is based on the thought of Ronald
Gregor Smith, who may well have been the first to recognize and attempt
to develop Dietrich Bonhoeffer's fragmentary remarks concerning transcendence and worldliness into a specific theology of transcendence as
historical experience.[5] Thus, while I shall take up the matter of trans-

---

[3]The problem which remains to be defined refers to the loss of a meaningful concept of the transcendence of God in terms of an historical understanding of
existence. This loss includes both an 'experienced' loss in the 'silence of transcendence' and a conceptual, or theological, loss in the non-objectiveness of God.

[4]The use of language in the sense that it is restricted to a particular action,
so that the 'language game' is the language and actions into which it is woven.
Thus, the meaning of a word is said to be determined by its use in language. The
concept comes from L. Wittgenstein, *Philosophical Investigations*, Basil Blackwell,
Oxford, 1953, pp. 3ff. Cf. also the concept of 'odd language', or the impropriety
of language situations' as suggested by I. T. Ramsey, *Religious Language*, SCM
Press, London, 1957, pp. 49ff. While I accept the general principle that language
can have a function that appears to be 'logically odd', I maintain that the phrase
'historical transcendence' has an inner logic which holds the key to the rationale
of the transcendence of God.

[5]While Gregor Smith, to my knowledge, only uses the phrase 'historical transcendence' once in his published writings (*J. G. Hamann*, Collins, London, 1960,
p. 98), his first theological work published included a chapter entitled 'This-worldly
Transcendence', an obvious development of Bonhoeffer's concepts of 'worldliness'
and transcendence. Cf. *The New Man*, SCM Press, London, 1956, pp. 94ff. Smith
says that transcendence and history 'are woven together in an inextricable web
which is itself the one single reality for Israel'. *Ibid.*, p. 28. For the same idea,
cf. *Secular Christianity*, pp. 121-122; *The Free Man*, p. 151; and *The Doctrine of
God*, Collins, London, 1970, pp. 126, 135. The specific references in Bonhoeffer
concerning transcendence and worldliness are found in his *Letters and Papers from
Prison*, The Macmillan Company, New York, 1972. The Enlarged Edition. pp.
282, 379, 381. This was first published in 1951, only five years prior to Smith's
book in which the historical aspect of transcendence was developed in the form
of a theology of 'this-worldly transcendence'. Cf. John A. T. Robinson, *Honest
to God*, SCM Press, London, 1963, who says that Smith's book was a 'pioneering
attempt' to make Bonhoeffer's concept of worldliness relevant to contemporary
theology (p. 26). The history of the term 'historical transcendence' in theological
literature then, as I am using it, for all practical purposes, goes back only to

cendence where Gregor Smith left it with his untimely death, the point of reference which will determine the scope of this book will be rooted firmly in the theological thought of Dietrich Bonhoeffer. So that, by historical transcendence, I mean no more than that which is denoted by the use of the general concept since Bonhoeffer, but no less than the full significance of the 'inner logic' of this concept as an explication of the reality of God.

When I suggest that a phrase such as 'historical transcendence' has an 'inner logic', I mean that the phrase is referential in its meaning, not to the existential self-understanding of the one who attempts to comprehend it, but to the reality which 'stands behind' the phrase, the reality to which the phrase points. I also intend to signify, that this reality has an intrinsic intelligibility of its own which imposes its rationality upon the subject comprehending it.[6] The 'intelligible rationale' of the transcendence of God is thus to be discovered in historical transcendence, and not conferred upon it through some kind of self-understanding.

While it will be necessary at the outset to examine the matter of why both transcendence and the reality of God have become problematical, I do not intend to take up every question 'flying around in the air' concerning this topic. Immanuel Kant has reminded us that there are absurd questions which produce in incautious listeners absurd answers, and which he likened to 'one man milking a he-goat and the other holding a sieve beneath'.[7] Rather, my examination will attempt to expose the fundamental issue involved in the problematic of transcendence, history and the reality of God, and then to take up that issue critically from the perspective of a Christological standpoint. The concept of transcendence will be used to expose the inner logic of the Incarnation in such a way that the reality of God imposes upon us its own intrinsic historicality. It must be made clear that this will not be a study of transcendence as much as an explication of the dynamic of the Incarnation, with transcendence as the working tool. Which is to say, it will attempt to be an exercise in theology rather than in metaphysics.

1956, and certainly not further than 1951. This does not mean that the concept is restricted to Bonhoeffer's last writings, but as I shall show later on, is to be found expressly stated in his very first theological work published in Germany in 1930.

[6]The concept of 'inner logic' has been taken from the thought of T. F. Torrance, who has shown that with the presupposition of a Creator, the created world of reality has a 'rationality' given to it, which 'imposes' itself upon the mind of one who seeks to understand it according to this 'inner logic'. Cf. *God and Rationality*, Oxford University Press, London, 1971: '... we let our knowledge of things and events in their own states be illuminated by the intelligible relations directly forced on our recognition by the things and events themselves.' p. 104. Cf. also, pp. 94ff. 99ff, 169ff.

[7]*The Critique of Pure Reason*, trans. by Norman Kemp Smith, Macmillan and Co., London, 1929, p. 97.

This might be as good a time as any to lay to rest the 'bug-a-boo' of metaphysics! I am well aware of the problem caused when a system of metaphysics becomes a 'given' in theology which imposes its categories of thought upon the subject of theology itself. And one can only applaud Kant's massive efforts to invalidate speculative metaphysics as a delusion. But even more can we appreciate his final conclusion:

> We can therefore be sure that however cold or contemptuously critical may be the attitude of those who judge a science not by its nature but by its accidental effects, we shall always return to metaphysics as to a beloved one with whom we have had a quarrel.[8]

For all of the distaste which metaphysics has bred in the minds of contemporary theologians, most would have to confess to its being a lover's quarrel. Right up to the last, Gregor Smith sought to escape its embrace, and yet complained of an inadequacy of concept to work out a rationale of faith.[9]

The particular problem that metaphysics, as a reflective activity of man, has posed for theology has been the relationship of thought and being. Whether thought and being have been equated, as they were since Aristotle, or separated as they have been since Kant, it is still the nature of being that preoccupies the metaphysician, as well as the theologian. The traditional doctrine of God based upon a particular metaphysic raises serious questions for many theologians today, a fact confirmed by Professor Donald MacKinnon:

> Few of us find it easy to accept ... the principle on which the doctrine of the analogy of being depends, that is, the conception of being as an analogically participated transcendental ...[10]

[8]*Ibid.*, p. 664.

[9]Cf. R. G. Smith, *The Doctrine of God*, p. 175. The fact that Smith was aware of his ambiguity towards the problem of metaphysics is revealed in a letter to Mr. Peter Baelz, Dean of Jesus College, Cambridge, dated 19th July, 1968, from which I cite the following: 'I am conscious of my own efforts to discredit "metaphysics" and I still think that I was not utterly wrong—though my colleague Allan Galloway has always said that I was using metaphysics in order to try and do without metaphysics. My own intention, as I now see it, was to develop a metaphysic of faith—or, more simply, to understand faith on its own terms.' *Collected Papers*, Glasgow University Library.

[10]*Borderlands of Theology*, Lutterworth Press, London, 1968, p. 214. Cf. here, Schubert Ogden, 'Theology and Objectivity', *The Journal of Religion*, Vol. 45, July 1965, pp. 175-195, who says: '... it is the deep doubt whether there either can or should be any such metaphysical justification [sc. of theological statements] that is one of the chief underlying conditions of much recent theology.' p. 190. Ogden does not share this scepticism concerning metaphysics, and suggests that metaphysical thought is going through a decisive transformation, and now shows signs of having a future as well as a past. Ogden holds that the particular metaphysic represented by process theology shows the most promise. *Ibid.*, p. 191.

Introduction

Among the more notable attempts to overcome metaphysics, or better, to 'get behind' metaphysics, is the attempt of Martin Heidegger, who defined metaphysics as 'anthropomorphy—the shaping and viewing of the world in accordance with man's image'.[11] Such a metaphysic, according to Heidegger, leads inevitably to the question of what kind of ultimate ground there is for Existence (*Dasein*), and the answer is—nothing.[12] Man cannot ground himself in the Cartesian sense in his own thought, for thought is grounded in nothing.[13] Heidegger finds in the thought of Plato, signs of the first 'humanization' of truth; by shifting the emphasis from *aletheia* to *idea*, Plato made philosophy human, that is, relative to the perceptions and judgment of the human subject. Thus, Heidegger traces a line running directly through Aristotle, Aquinas, Descartes, Hegel, and finally, culminating in Nietzsche as a 'will to power'.[14]

Heidegger's alternative to metaphysics is found in what he terms 'back tracking (*der Schritt zurück*). 'The "back track" starts with what has not yet been thought, from difference as such, to proceed towards what is yet to be thought.'[15] It is the 'unthought' essence behind metaphysics which reveals itself to thought. This is the 'fundamental ontology' which does not yield itself to thought, but rather, comes to thought as Being, as the 'unthought'; so that one could say, for Heidegger, 'man does not use

[11]*Nietzsche*, Vol. II, Verlag Günther Neske, Pfullingen, p. 127. Cited by L. Versényi, *Heidegger, Being and Truth*, Yale University Press, New Haven and London, 1965, p. 72.

[12]In Heidegger's early writings, the term *Dasein*, a combination of *da*: here, there, with *sein*: to be, being, is his term for man. The traditional meaning of existence, life, became more specialized in Heidegger's thought to mean man's existence as being quite of its own kind. This is 'being concerned with its being'. *Dasein*, as 'thrown' into the world, without any concept of a 'thrower', was grounded transcendently in itself. *Dasein* is grounded in nothing outside of itself. *Dasein* held out into nothing, reaches the ultimate end of metaphysics—nothing. The nothing to which *Dasein* transcends is not at *Dasein's* disposal, but comes upon *Dasein* as vague dread. The turning point in Heidegger's thought comes when the nothing which emerged when metaphysics sought to ground *Dasein* outside of itself, ceases to be nothing, and Being dawns. There is now a decisive shift of emphasis from *Dasein* to being, which gives itself to *Dasein*, which now corresponds to the claim of being. See Martin Heidegger, *An Introduction to Metaphysics*, trans. by Ralph Manheim, Yale University Press, New Haven, 1959, pp. 9, 18-19; and, *On the Way to Language*, Harper and Row, New York, 1971, p. 30. Cf. also, L. Versényi, *Heidegger, Being and Truth*, pp. 3ff; James M. Robinson and John Cobb Jr., *The Later Heidegger and Theology*, Vol. I, Harper and Row, New York, Evanston, and London, 1963, pp. 7ff, 13ff. The rendering of *Dasein* by 'Existence' is an attempt to avoid the use of technical terms; where it seems crucial that Heidegger's concept of *Dasein* be especially noted, I will place the German word in parentheses following the translation 'Existence'.

[13]Robinson and Cobb, *The Later Heidegger and Theology*, p. 12.

[14]L. Versényi, *Heidegger, Being and Truth*, pp. 52ff, p. 60.

[15]M. Heidegger, *Essays in Metaphysics*, Philosophical Library Inc., New York, 1960, p. 43.

language, language uses man'.[16] What is at stake here for Heidegger is whether Existence is to be grounded in its own authentic being, or in the wholly other 'being', which on its own initiative brings mankind's Existence (*Dasein*) into authentic existence.

Despite the complexity and even obscurity of Heidegger's thought, made no less so by this superficial sketch, one thing becomes quite clear: Heidegger's rejection of metaphysics makes it impossible to speak to a 'rationale' with regard to the transcendence of God and historical existence. One is reduced to virtual silence, where only the poet speaks, or rather, is 'spoken through' by the 'holy'.[17]

It is for this reason that I cannot accept Heidegger's definition of metaphysics, nor his project of overcoming metaphysics. Although, it must be said, Heidegger's concept of the 'ontological difference' between Being and beings is too important to be ignored, and will be taken up at the appropriate point in the book itself with regard to historical transcendence.

I will instead propose my own definition of metaphysics in order to make it 'clear precisely where I stand with respect to the role of metaphysics in theology: I call metaphysics the problematic of the concrete man's bond with the absolute.[18] I do not accept the fact that metaphysics is merely a projection of human thought, or a distortion of authentic being which can be eliminated. Rather, metaphysics is a 'problematic' constituted by the two fundamental poles of reality—the concrete and the absolute; one could also say, the concrete and the transcendent. Or, it may be said to consist simply of the old question of the 'one and the many'. When either of these poles is reduced into the other, as Idealism absorbs the concrete into the absolute subject, or, as Realism absorbs the absolute into the concrete object, the reality of existence is either tyrannized by a system or tormented by a science.

What I call the problematic' of metaphysics is irreducible, and constitutes an action, of which thought is the subordinate and not the primary element. This is what makes the reality of personal existence problematic. It is problematic to thought, as reflection abstracts from the action, but has an inner rationality of relation through action. It is only in the act of a personal agent that the problematic of the concrete man's bond with the absolute can be expressed. The problematic is irreducible because the concrete pole of existence is the primary, though conditioned, one, while the absolute pole is the subordinate, though

---

[16]M. Heidegger, *On the Way to Language*, p. 124.

[17]Robinson and Cobb, *The Later Heidegger and Theology*, p. 45.

[18]Martin Buber calls the concrete man's bond with the absolute a metaphysical presupposition, while I call it the problematic of metaphysics itself. Cf. *Between Man and Man*, Collins, London, 1969, p. 199.

unconditioned one.[19] It is because of this that the so-called subject/object way of thinking following Descartes came to grief over the problem of relating spirit to matter, or thought to being; once the thinking subject had been isolated as the primary substance of reality, there was no way of comprehending the reality of an object as a 'thing in itself', as Kant so brilliantly revealed.[20]

I have introduced the problem of metaphysics at this point to make it clear that my position in no way can be termed anti-metaphysical.[21] The equation of metaphysics with philosophy, and for that reason ruling both out in the name of 'pure' theology is unreal. As Wittgenstein once said, 'Philosophy is a battle against the bewitchment of our intelligence by means of language'.[22] Metaphysics can never be 'overcome' in philosophy because philosophy is itself the problematic constituted by the two poles of existence—the concrete and the absolute.[23] However much one might wish to reduce this problematic into either a pure system of thought, with its own direct relation to absolute being (ontology), or into a pure science with its direct relation to concrete being (empiricism), the

[19]For the conception of action as the primary element in a structure of reality, with reflection as its necessary but subordinate element, see John Macmurray, *The Self as Agent*, Faber and Faber, London (1957), 1966, pp. 128ff. When Macmurray says, 'The particular metaphysical assertion which I have in mind is that the world is one action' (*ibid.*, p. 217), he comes very near to expressing what I mean by the concept of metaphysics. This is why I have said that the problematic is irreducible in metaphysics—it cannot be abstracted from the act into a reflective activity. I will take up Macmurray's concept of the *Self as Agent* in detail in developing the rationale intrinsic to the relation of transcendence and history. For an application of Macmurray's concepts of action to the subject/object dualism implicit in contemporary theology, see Robert J. Blaikie, *'Secular Christianity' and God Who Acts*, Hodder and Stoughton, London, 1970, *passim*. For the validity of starting with a problematic concept of reality, see also Macmurray, *The Self as Agent*, pp. 27ff., where he argues that it is unreasonable to abandon the problems to preserve the method, or to create new problems to fit the forms—the problems, or the problematic, as I would put it, are the 'given factors of reality'.

[20]Cf. David Jenkins, *The Glory of Man*, SCM Press, London, 1967, pp. 62ff. See also, R. J. Blaikie, *'Secular Christianity' and God Who Acts*, pp. 19ff, 151ff, for a discussion of the subject/object dualism following Descartes.

[21]I wish to make it clear that the use of a metaphysical structure is a procedural necessity, which is continually subjected to revision by the 'problematic' itself. Cf. D. Bonhoeffer: 'To object that categories of a generally metaphysical nature have been employed ... is to overlook the necessity of a certain formal 'pre-comprehension' as a standpoint from which questions—even if wrong ones—can be framed, whose answer is subsequently returned by revelation together with a fundamental correction of the question.' *Act and Being*, Collins, London, 1962, p. 174.

[22]L. Wittgenstein, *Philosophical Investigations*, p. 47 (109).

[23]L. Versényi, *Heidegger, Being and Truth*, p. 168.

structure of reality itself refuses to surrender either pole.²⁴ It was to the
everlasting credit of Kant that he devised a rational schematic which
included the problematic without a reduction of it. What Kant could not
achieve, and this because he accepted the Cartesian starting point of the
'I think', was the conception of the absolute in personal terms. Thus, Kant
was left with a formal dualism of theory and practice. He could give no
account of the dimension of the personal because there was no 'categorical'
way in which the object of thought could become a subject and disclose
itself.²⁵

The problematic which constitutes the structure of metaphysics is not
the dualism of the subject/object sort (Cartesian), nor of the pheno-
menal/noumenal sort (Kantian), but a genuine *duality* in which concrete
and absolute are interacting realities. This distinction is fundamental to
my thesis that there is an 'inner logic' to the problematic of history and
transcendence. I will endeavour to show that the bond, while it remains
a problematic because it cannot be reduced is, nonetheless, a positive
relation effected by the reality of God as an agent who acts. This means,
in effect, that the transcendence of God is his action, and that this action
has an 'intelligible rationale' intrinsically contained in the interaction,
which is the problematic of historical transcendence.

It is in this sense that I call metaphysics the problematic of the concrete
man's bond with the absolute.

The development will follow out the procedure implied in this preliminary statement. In Part One I shall take up in turn the problem of
transcendence and the problem of the reality of God, in order to
establish the true dimensions of the problematic involved in the concept
of historical transcendence. I will then examine the theology of historical transcendence, in the thought of Ronald Gregor Smith, but
particularly in Dietrich Bonhoeffer, to demonstrate how this problematic
was essentially grasped, and expressed as the problematic of the Incarnation. It is at this point that I will seek to establish the validity of the
Christological basis for the critique of historical transcendence and the
reality of God.

In Part Two I will proceed to work out the inner logic of the Incarnation through an analysis of the concept of *kenosis*.²⁶ This inner logic,

²⁴Cf. Donald MacKinnon: '. . . the issue of attaching the unfamiliar vision to the
familiar description remains; the attachment of the strange to the usual, of the
final to the relative.' *Borderlands of Theology*, p. 214.

²⁵J. Macmurray, *The Self as Agent*, pp. 66ff.

²⁶*Kenosis:* a term used in Christian theology from the third or fourth century
to describe the idea expressed in Philippians 2:7, where Christ is said to 'empty
himself' (ἑαυτὸν ἐκένωσεν). The word *kenosis* was apparently used in patristic
literature as a synonym for the Incarnation, but with a special emphasis on the
humiliation or condescension of the Son of God (II Corinthians 8:9). In modern
theology, it has a wider connotation—namely, that Christ surrendered or re-

I will maintain, expresses transcendence as an action of a personal agent, an action which imposes its categories of understanding upon our rationality. These categories have both an ultimate and a penultimate pole of reality, which constitutes the problematic, but also the possibility of faith.

Part Three then follows, not as an appendage of practical application, but as the heart of the book itself. For as the bond of historical transcendence is the reality of God conceived in action, only an act of 'lived transcendence' can express it. It can be 'thought' only in terms of its problematic, but it can be expressed only in terms of an act. This act, as an act of faith, receives its 'shape' and 'style' in the world through the inner logic of historical transcendence—that is, it is incarnational.

I will assume that the reasonable results of Biblical criticism leave us with a creditable record of the person and acts of Jesus Christ lying behind the experiences and theological concepts of the first Christian community. While not denying the validity of historical criticism as a necessary and continuing exercise of Biblical scholarship, it seems clear enough to me that the documents of Scripture confront me with both the act and being of God through the historical life of Jesus of Nazareth. For this reason, I will not undertake a critical analysis of the field of biblical criticism in order to account for those incidents in the life of Jesus which seem alien to the laws of natural science, or to contemporary existential self-understanding.

To this extent, I must reject the assumptions of historical positivism that demand the excision from Scripture of all material not amenable to universal laws of existence deduced from common experience. I choose rather to deal with Scripture as a whole, including that which is alien to my understanding, hoping thereby to be more of a radical listener than a radical critic.[27] So also the unity of Scripture, which I presuppose, does not appear to me as a unity in the religious sense, as though its rationality grew out of a process of religious consciousness, but here also it is true: 'The unity of Scripture is audible rather than visible.'[28]

I am convinced above all, following David E. Jenkins, that real theology must not only be an emerging theology, but an open theology;

stricted himself in the use of divine attributes in order to become man. Cf. S. E. Johnson, *Kenosis, The Interpreter's Dictionary of the Bible*, Abingdon Press, New York, 1962, Vol. 3, p. 7.

[27] Cf. E. Käsemann, 'Zum Thema der urchristlichen Apokalyptik', *Zeitschrift für Theologie und Kirche*, Vol. 59, February 1962, who says quite significantly: 'The cardinal virtue of the historian and the beginning of all meaningful hermeneutic is for me the practice of hearing, which begins simply by letting what is historically foreign maintain its validity and does not regard rape as the basic form of engagement.' p. 259.

[28] Kornelis Miskotte, *When the Gods are Silent*, Collins, London, 1967, pp. 108, 127.

so open, that one cannot be accused of wrongly distorting the secular possibilities in asserting divine realities;[29] so open also, that one does not become guilty of taking the world too seriously, and 'murdering the child in us'.[30] Because theology has to do with a relationship of givenness, in which God confronts us from the outset as subject as well as object,[31] theology is itself a commitment as well as a quest. Again, David Jenkins has put it as plainly as I myself would want to say it:

> ... in this connection we have to be quite clear that it is impossible to do theology apart from a spiritual discipline which is related to worship and prayer. If you want the cash value, if I may be allowed to use that term, of the word 'God', you can get nowhere near it without worship and prayer, and I cannot see how any theology can be done except by men who worship and pray. But even that means, or that means more than ever, that we are confronted here with necessary brokenness ... there is a commitment here without which there can be no real theology, and this demands brokenness, and because theology demands brokenness, there is no real tension between commitment to theology and open theology.[32]

I would only add that brokenness in theology denotes a living theology, where neither God nor man can be exhausted of meaning or possibility.

Knowing as I do a commitment to a living God with whom I am confronted in Jesus Christ, knowing it as I say, as that which could not be broken even in brokenness, I turn now to probe the depths of my commitment as much as the dimension of his reality. Whatever here is strange, it is not he; he is not the alien to be overcome, the opposition is within me—my commitment is to the one who 'does the truth'.[33]

[29]*Living with Questions*, SCM Press, London, 1969, p. 157.

[30]K. Miskotte, *When the Gods are Silent*: 'Just as Christ was not a smasher of things (*Kaputtmacher*), as Blumhardt said, so theology dare not carry to extremes the Western tendency to murder the child in us.' p. 202.

[31]I will take up at a later point just in what sense God can be spoken of as objective. It certainly does not mean here that God is merely an object in the sense of 'being to hand' (*Vorhandensein*).

[32]D. Jenkins, *Living with Questions*, p. 158.

[33]'... the opposition party we must always look for in ourselves ... the objections which we have to fear lie in ourselves. We must seek them out ...' I. Kant, *The Critique of Pure Reason*, p. 618. Cf. also, Aristotle: '... truth or falsity is as follows—contact and assertion are truth ... and ignorance is non-contact.' And again, 'For falsity and truth are not in things—it is not as if the good were true, and the bad were in itself false—but in thought.' *Metaphysics*, The Works of Aristotle translated into English, Vol. III, The Clarendon Press, Oxford, 1908, pp. 1051b (20), 1027b (25). For somewhat the same idea see John Macmurray, *Freedom in the Modern World*, Faber and Faber, London, (1932), 1968: 'So long as we think something is real we can never know that it is not.' p. 126.

Part One

The Crisis of Transcendence
for the Doctrine of God

Chapter I

The Crisis of Transcendence

1 'The Lost Lane-end Into Heaven'

Which of us has known his brother? Which of us has looked into his father's heart? Which of us has not remained forever prison-pent? Which of us is not forever a stranger and alone? O waste weary of loss, in the hot maze, lost, among bright stars on this most weary unbright cinder, lost! Remembering speechlessly we seek the great forgotten language, the lost lane-end into heaven, a stone, a leaf, an unfound door. Where? When?[1]

Who will dare to relativize this loss? Our wise men tell us that man is the 'shepherd of being',[2] but is this wisdom to one who has lost the sound of his sheep? Can language die, and with it perish the way back to a remembered loss?[3] 'The gods are silent; *hear* the silence of the gods.'[4]

In this silence, that becomes unbearable, the very whisper of the word 'god' becomes a scream. Nor can this shattering stillness be silenced by the familiar voice of man raised to its highest pitch. No word will ever be sufficient to banish a Wordless god, who has never been known, but can never be forgotten.

And why are we so sure that no crime is being committed in allowing this unborn Word to die? To be sure, there are no longer the happy dances in which the figures are gods, and 'secularized man no longer engages in this sacred play'.[5] But can one accept without examination

---

[1]Thomas Wolfe, *Look Homeward, Angel!*, Charles Scribner's Sons, New York, 1930, from the Frontispiece.

[2]A concept of Heidegger, *Über den Humanismus*, Klosterman, Frankfurt am Main, p. 29.

[3]For Heidegger, the path of language is from Being to human words, and is the actual dimension in which being takes place. Cf. *On the Way to Language*, pp. 111ff.

[4]K. Miskotte, *When the Gods are Silent*, p. 7. 'We must say that the gods are silent. The idea is still in the air, but is mute. The shape lingers on the horizon, but is suffused in a silent fog. The words still resound, as in a strange, unknown language or like a song from childhood; but they no longer tell the mystery to us latecomers.' *Ibid.*, p. 9.

[5]*Ibid.*, p. 2.

the claim that it makes no difference for modern man to be without God in the world? And if our poets dare to name what our theologians presume to ignore, all the more reason to listen.

Who will dare to relativize this loss? What I mean to ask is, who will presume to reduce the dimension of the loss constituted by the silence of the gods from an absolute loss to a relative one? What is at stake here is the nature of the crisis itself. If the crisis is only a 'poeticized' version of man's essential existential anxiety, then nothing has really been lost, man simply has not yet come to terms with his own being—he has not yet become 'god'.

There is a way of relativizing the loss, and it has many forms. Its social form appears in the appeal to *co-humanity*. The 'lost lane-end into heaven' is considered to be a shadow which one should 'jump over', or better yet, ignore. We are told here that the words of Jesus constitute 'an invitation to forget all about gods and to concentrate our attention on our neighbour ... for only in a friend—not in a shadow, however exalted the name we give it—shall we meet the unexpected, the imponderable that astonishes and recreates us'.[6] But when the absolute demand of love is relativized to one's neighbour without the word 'god' as the middle term in that relation, it becomes little more than a union of selfishness.[7] Admittedly, the word 'God' casts no more than a 'shadow' upon the experience of co-humanity, but could not one speak here of a 'concrete shadow' which points us unavoidably to the unuttered Word in the language of human love?

The existential form of a relativized loss appears as *self-understanding*. In the face of the utter meaninglessness of the 'silence of the gods', modern man assumes that it is his responsibility to give meaning to his experience. This 'theology of meaningfulness' makes all religious language referential to man's existential self-understanding. Therefore, talk 'about God' is really to be understood as talk about the possibilities of man's own existence. As man awakens to new dimensions of self-understanding, the 'forgotten language' is remembered in the sense that the self acquires its authenticity in the full grasp of its existential situation. The absurdities of existence are overcome through the decision of the self to confer meaning upon them by 'authentic existence'.[8] The lost lane-end into

[6]Werner and Lottie Pelz, *God is No More*, Victor Gollancz, London, 1964, p. 35.

[7]S. Kierkegaard, *Works of Love*, Oxford University Press, London, 1946: 'Worldly wisdom believes that love is a relationship between man and man; Christianity teaches that love is a relationship between man—God—man, that is, that God is the middle term ... what the world honours and loves under the name of love, is a union of selfishness ...' pp. 87-88.

[8]A leading exponent of the hermeneutic of 'self-understanding' is Schubert Ogden. Cf. his *Christ Without Myth*, Harper and Brothers, New York, 1961, pp. 137ff.

heaven is now discovered to be the 'back door' of man's own home, but one can just as well go in at the front.[9] Such a relativizing of the loss does shift the emphasis from the meaningless object to the subject, *provided* an interpreter is present to change the language into acceptable currency.[10] One cannot doubt the seriousness with which Rudolf Bultmann wishes to preserve the 'offence' of the gospel or to make modern man aware of the real transcendence of God, but in the final analysis, he must be said to have relativized the loss of transcendence to man's self-understanding.[11] The problem of relativizing in this sense could be termed 'solipsism', which Wittgenstein defines as 'turning all statements into descriptions of my inner life ...'[12]

When a relativized loss of transcendence appears in a cultural form it emerges as a *new paganism*. The equation of paganism with atheism is a common misunderstanding. Far from being atheism, paganism is the expression of a strong and vital faith in the presence of the gods.[13] One of the interesting phenomena in the emergence of youth movements is the rediscovery of paganism. The god of the pagan is a 'superstar', endowed with mythical powers and yet 'familiar' in the sense of participating in the pleasures, sorrows and activities of finite creatures.[14] The new paganism is a cultural way of relativizing the loss of 'holiness' in a technological society; it is an attempt to breathe the joy of life into the unanimated corpse of dying humanity. It is a recovery

[9]Cf. Kenneth Hamilton, *Revolt Against Heaven*, Eerdmans, Grand Rapids, 1965. who says: '... van Buren, having bowed deity out at the front door, has smuggled it in again through the back door. He has banished the supernatural, but he has found room for the transcendental.' p. 163.

[10]For a trenchant critique of the assertion that 'statements about God can actually be understood as statements about man', cf. Kenneth Hamilton, *Revolt Against Heaven*, pp. 23ff. Hamilton terms the theology of 'self-understanding' a 'theology of meaninglessness', taking the phrase 'theology of meaningfulness' as a designation for his own alternative. I have chosen to retain the phrase 'theology of meaningfulness' as a description of self-understanding, because of its intent to confer meaning upon existence through self-affirmation.

[11]R. Bultmann, *Jesus Christ and Mythology*, SCM Press, London (1958), 1966: '... if we hold that we can speak of all such matters [sc. God's action as redemptive event] only when we are concerned with our personal existence, then it can be said that faith is a new understanding of personal existence. In other words, God's action bestows upon us a new understanding of ourselves.' p. 73. While Bultmann attempts to defend himself against the problem of relativizing the transcendent act of God by appealing to a distinction between the terms existential understanding (*das Existentielle*) and existentialistic understanding (*das Existential*), this distinction is irrelevant because what is involved here is a 'new way of understanding' which *determines* whether or not an event can be called an act of God. This effectively relativizes a 'forgotten language' into a 'meaningful one', to refer back to our starting point.

[12]L. Wittgenstein, *Philosophical Investigations*, p. 12.

[13]Cf. K. Miskotte, *When the Gods are Silent*, p. 8.

[14]*Ibid.*, p. 8.

of the sacred earnestness of holy play. 'Jesus Christ Superstar' is an impotent god but a larger-than-life man who becomes the focal point of a generation's disillusionment with a society that has lost its soul.[15] The great theological irony of the twentieth century is that so-called modern man, with his sophisticated secular world-view, is rapidly creating a culture which is relativizing the loss of transcendence through the occult, the tribal, quasi-religious community, and the folk hero.

The ancient gods will return, but with new faces. Only their power over men and their laughter over the sins of world history will be the same. They will come back.[16]

But when the gods become silent, it only reveals their eternal silence— they never do speak. They never have. The tragedy of the new paganism as a cultural relativization is not the return of the gods, but their eternal silence. Hidden in this most recent cultural form, the speechlessness of the gods will break out in ever more terrifying silence, and only then will their votaries discover how deeply they have been betrayed.

It may not be possible to sustain a distinction between a cultural and a religious form of relativization, for Miskotte tells us that '... "Christianity" as a religion presents to us a face marked with all the signs of an ultimately impenetrable silence'.[17] And yet, I would maintain that one aspect of a particularly religious form of relativizing is the *worship of transcendence,* even as silence.[18] I could have said—particularly as silence. For religious consciousness has an unlimited capacity for expansion when it is a 'one way street'. That is, the nature of such a consciousness is primarily that of response; not as response to a direct call, but response as an 'openness toward the infinite'. One could say then, that the experience of 'loss' only intensifies the religious consciousness, so that the 'response' itself is heightened.

Religious consciousness is a particularly effective way of relativizing the loss, because the loss is never allowed to objectify itself. The religious symbol, be it an ecstatic utterance, a credal statement, or a piece of furniture in the temple, constitutes an objectification of the religious experience itself, so that the loss of a God who *speaks* is relativized into many forms of religious language. But if it is true, that '... man's religion is ultimately a "round about road to himself by way of the

---

[15]Just such an interpretation of the popular reception of the rock opera *Jesus Christ Superstar,* by contemporary youth, is made by Gilbert Meilaender, Jr., in which he deals with it as a phenomenon of 'new paganism.' Cf. 'The New Paganism', *Christianity Today,* September 24, 1971, pp. 4-6.
[16]Janko Janeff, cited by K. Miskotte, *When the Gods are Silent,* p. 8.
[17]*Ibid.,* p. 11.
[18]P. L. Berger, *A Rumour of Angels,* Allen Lane, The Penguin Press, London, 1970, p. 108.

symbol of the god" ',[19] this form of relativization is the very worst, because it throws man back upon himself. If a point comes when the religious symbolization is inadequate, the religious man cannot turn against his gods who have suddenly become silent, but only against himself for failing to sustain his 'response'. It is for this reason that Miskotte has told us that when Christian faith is relativized into Christian religion, it has a 'face marked with all the signs of an ultimately impenetrable silence'.[20] In this case, religion becomes the face of the silent gods, but it is also the face of the religious man. This is the ultimate expression of a relativized loss.

Who will dare to relativize such a loss? The question becomes instead, who will dare *not* to relativize it. Who will dare to radicalize the loss! Who will dare, like Job, to take up his position, give heaven its ultimatum, and demand an *answer*:

> Oh, that I had one to hear me! (Here is my signature! let the Almighty answer me!)
> Oh, that I had the indictment written by my adversary![21]

It becomes increasingly clear that the loss which cannot be relativized without a fundamental betrayal, can only be radicalized. The relativizers are themselves to be relativized.[22] Only thus will a new freedom to question emerge. The demise of the supernatural, with its empirically supported rationale, has produced a crisis of unprecedented dimension. The crisis is a crisis of silence. It is a crisis of transcendence. What is at stake is a fundamental assumption about reality, not this or that historical variation of it. If the crisis dare not be relativized, what remains then but to radicalize it?[23]

I feel led to choose this alternative. Not because I am at all sure that it will lead to the rediscovery of the supernatural, or even to the overcoming of the crisis itself, but as a start, I see it to be an overcoming of triviality.[24] The pervading tendency of—for lack of a better term—

[19]K. Miskotte, *When the Gods are Silent*, p. 3.

[20]*Ibid.*, p. 11.

[21]Job 31:35. All Scripture citations, unless otherwise indicated, are from the Revised Standard Version.

[22]Cf. P. L. Berger, *A Rumour of Angels*, p. 59.

[23]'There is just as good an empirical foundation for this assumption [sc. the demise of the supernatural] as for other generalizations.' P. L. Berger, *A Rumour of Angels*, p. 18. This, of course, does not establish the assumption, it merely corroborates my assertion. With regard to my statement that the crisis, which I will call a crisis of transcendence, is unprecedented, I adduce the support of K. Miskotte, who says, 'One can say—with reservations, because we cannot fathom the depths of unbelief in the soul of other times and places—that such an experience of the absence of God as that which we see today in the way of the Gentiles never existed before.' *When the Gods are Silent*, p. 319.

[24]Cf. P. L. Berger, *A Rumour of Angels*, p. 119.

post-Barthian theology, has been to trivialize the fundamental existence of man. I do not intend to document this generalization; it is simply my judgment that the reducing of man's ultimate concerns to his existential possibilities, all in the name of authentic existence, has in fact reduced revelation to self-understanding and transcendence to 'intimations of immortality'.[25]

To radicalize the loss must mean at least this: to insist that the loss is a real loss of speech. Which means to settle for nothing less than a *word* which comes to us and which we do not have to utter ourselves. There is this advantage in beginning with the poet rather than the theologian—the poet does not trivialize in order to triumph. If the talk is to be of a real loss, let us at least seek a name for the terror which overtakes us. But what does it mean to seek out a name? Wittgenstein reminds us that '... only someone who already knows how to do something with it can significantly ask a name'.[26] It is one thing to speak of the 'silence of the gods', but quite another to seek after a name. The question is, do we already know how to do something with the name we seek?

There are dark times in everyone's life, times when the terror of being alive comes swooping down like an evil thing, compassing the poor mind with unimaginable tortures, shaking questions from its wings before which the established habits cower and shrink away, and leaving the victim exhausted and apathetic. If these times come only once or twice in a man's life then it is possible still to continue with the accustomed things, or if that time first breaks through the crust of routine at the crucial moment of death, then it does not matter that the routine is smashed for ever. But to one who is studying for the ministry these times come not once, or twice, but again and again, storming him like a black wave breaking on an island fortress, till his

[25]While I can appreciate the candour with which P. L. Berger has struck out for a 're-discovery of the supernatural', and his protest against the trivialization of a non-supernatural theology, I cannot agree when he finds hope in what he calls 'the signals of transcendence', which seem to be occurring within empirically given situations. Cf. *A Rumour of Angels*, p. 70. These 'signals of transcendence' appear to be human 'protypical' actions which point beyond to supernatural reality; among others, he lists as signals of transcendence: man's propensity for order (p. 71); the argument from play, 'the playful universe' becomes eternity, i.e., it is 'timeless' (p. 76); the argument from hope (p. 80); the argument from damnation, i.e., outrage produces a curse of supernatural dimensions (p. 84). I will maintain that the real loss, and thus the real crisis, is produced, not by a lack of 'pointers' beyond to the supernatural, but that given these pointers, the 'gods remain silent'; what becomes incredible, is that there are no 'pointers', no speech, no actions of the beyond concretizing themselves in our world. Not to grasp this, is to miss the crucial point in the crisis of transcendence.
[26]*Philosophical Investigations*, p. 15 (31).

defences are battered in and he is utterly exposed to the mercy of the attack.[27]

What is significant in these words, is not that they were said, but who it was that said them. They are the words of Ronald Gregor Smith, who struggled to understand the transcendence of God as much as any man, and who was abruptly summoned from this world in the midst of this very task, and among whose final words left to us we have these: 'So our task must be to lift the Name of God out of the dust again and to set it over the hour of our responsibility.'[28] But the words that speak of the 'times of terror' were not written near the end, but at the beginning, thirty years earlier, as a young divinity student. And while the words are written as one who, in preparing for the ministry, now sees this preparation to be a relativizing of the Spirit, they speak of the way in which we already know what to do with the name:

And the pity of it is that from the first day of preparation the young man is deprived of the only succour he might have: the terror of the Spirit's visitation. When He comes to him in the night—while the applause of teachers and comrades is still ringing in his ears—and whispers dread simple questions in his ears, then all this training has taught him to deny the rightness of these questions. This is mere melancholy, this is useless idealism, this is not how souls are saved. And he turns to his books again, and if he cannot sleep, helps himself with an anodyne, and slays the ghost which came in the guise of the Spirit. But that ghost is truly the Spirit.[29]

The importance of these words must not be allowed to be absorbed

---

[27]R. G. Smith, 'Preparing for the Ministry', *Collected Papers*, August 31, 1938. This three-page essay, apparently unpublished, was '... written by one who has spent the last eight years preparing for the ministry, and has now decided to abandon his intention.' *Ibid.* As a matter of fact, Gregor Smith did not follow through with this statement, but the following year accepted the position of minister of the Lawson Memorial Church at Selkirk, Scotland, a position which he held until 1944. Smith was managing Director and Editor of SCM Press in London from 1950 to 1956, and from 1956 until his sudden death in September of 1968, he was Professor of Divinity at the University of Glasgow.

[28]*The Doctrine of God*, p. 161.

[29]R. G. Smith, 'Preparing for the Ministry', p. 2. Smith concludes his essay: 'The young man who abandons this fight is doing the weak thing. But if he does not abandon it, he must be prepared to face a living death and a martyrdom of the spirit untold in the lives of the saints. For he is no saint, yet he must fight the fight which only the Spirit can win ... it is a fight whose strength is weakness, whose life is the utter nonentity of the man. For the life of it is the Spirit, always and only the Spirit.' *Ibid.*, p. 3. One cannot read the above document without realizing that here is the key to a man who could never relativize this encounter with the transcendence of Spirit, and however deep his involvement in history and in humanity, he attempted to give that Spirit a language in which to speak.

into the development of a theme. A certain note has been struck here which is vital to the full dimension of this book. Perhaps it is this that I mean by the radicalization of the loss. This placing of ourselves in a position to hear the name, to be no less vulnerable in the middle when questions are asked, and at the end when conclusions are drawn, than now at the beginning.

The fact is, and I have not been totally unaware of it, that up to this point there has been a certain vagueness to the discussion as to just what is meant by this 'loss' which dare not be relativized. The 'lost lane-end into heaven' has only been grazed by such references as the 'loss of language', the 'silence of the gods', the 'ghost which came in the guise of the Spirit'. It seems to me that these all have been pointing to one thing, despite their obliqueness, and that is a crisis of reality which becomes a crisis concerning the NAME of the reality which speaks to us—or does not. But I shall simply call it a crisis of transcendence at this point, and proceed to an examination of how the crisis can be understood. The first question is: is it any longer possible to use the language of transcendence at all in speaking of God?

2 'Trembling in the Presence of the Gods'

It must be admitted at the outset that the language of transcendence may have already indeed 'died the death of a thousand qualifications'.[30] One has only to make a cursory study of transcendence in the literature of theology alone, to become depressed at the way in which the concept has been 'drawn and quartered' by those who wish to save it for the vocabulary of faith, but who cannot stomach all of its content; and some, on the other hand, who would rather discard it, but cannot resist poking at its carcass in some kind of horrible fascination, like a boy with a dead snake. There is the unmistakable aura of mystery here, a primitive shiver, as though in encroaching upon the transcendence, one has 'grazed the gods' in passing—and one wonders.

It seems to be everyone's right to define 'modern man' for himself these days ... when we have done so, however, few of us seem to have had in mind the man who trembles, be it but once in his life, 'in the presence of the Gods'. Is it because we have not so trembled ourselves that we wish to make that man's peculiar gift—or curse—available to us on our own terms? ... I am certainly willing to grant that some of the strange ones of this world have wrestled with a sense of limitation and out of this struggle have been led to speak of the

---

[30]'A fine brash hypothesis may thus be killed by inches, the death of a thousand qualifications.' A. Flew and A. MacIntyre, *New Essays in Philosophical Theology*, SCM Press, London, 1955, p. 96.

gods ... I suggest that we use a sense of wonder, rather than limitation, as the point of departure.[31]

Paul van Buren, in his typically straightforward way, suggests that we leave the 'strange ones' to their fascination with the marginal experiences of life, while we 'ordinary' ones look for the extraordinary in our own back yards. Or rather, when we are struck with a sense of wonder, *any* ordinary thing can become extraordinary in our eyes. And this, van Buren suggests, might well be a better concept, or even a better word, than transcendence.[32] Without accepting van Buren's concept of a 'way of seeing' as the fundamental meaning of transcendence, it must be admitted that he has raised an important question: is the word 'transcendence' the word we want when thinking about the word 'God'?[33] Should the word be left to those who 'tremble in the presence of the gods', while we seek another word to speak of God?

Two things must be made clear at this point. First, the language of transcendence must be tied in with a proper level of reality.[34] An alteration of language cannot produce a change in reality—it only reflects a change in the subject's *view* of reality. What van Buren proposes, in changing the language of transcendence to that of the extraordinary, is a concept of reality which is purely relative to the way in which one sees things.[35]

Secondly, one's view of the reality to which a particular word serves as a pointer, may necessarily be changed by the emergence of some new aspect of the reality itself. This means that the language of transcendence, as a pointer to the reality of God, will undergo a shift in meaning as the reality of God discloses itself in a new way. In other words, it is possible that a way of speaking will no longer be appropriate to a reality which can now be perceived in a way radically different from a previous perception—in which case, language can be altered, or,

[31]Paul van Buren, 'Is Transcendence the Word We Want?', *Theological Explorations*, pp. 164, 169.

[32]*Ibid.*, pp. 170, 174; van Buren, who relies heavily upon the linguistic philosophers for his reconstruction of the language about God, shares also their limitations, as R. Hepburn says, '... the linguistic philosopher's metaphysics tends to be an imaginative aid to the comprehending of the familiar, not to the discovery of the unseen.' *Christianity and Paradox*, Watts, London, 1958, p. 9.

[33]Paul van Buren, *Theological Explorations*, p. 174.

[34]Cf. T. F. Torrance, *God and Rationality*, p. 76.

[35]Cf. *Theological Explorations*, pp. 171ff, where van Buren confesses his difficulty in establishing the grounds for seeing something in a certain way. While admitting that there are some 'ways of seeing' (e.g., that of Hitler) whose grounds cannot be called 'good', he is not anxious that the justification for a certain way of seeing be found any place else than in the subject. This is the crucial problem for theology today, says van Buren. And indeed it is, although one must say that van Buren makes little progress towards a solution.

a constructive qualification made in the meaning of the traditional language used. It then becomes a matter of how much qualifying a language can endure without 'dying the death of a thousand qualifications'.

I do not intend here to take up the complex problem of linguistic analysis. But certain clarifications need to be made to establish the grounds for my own 'way of seeing' things. Because, as Wittgenstein said, 'Philosophical problems arise when language goes on holiday'.[36] The problematic of language impinges upon the problematic of metaphysics itself. Namely, the problematic of the concrete man's bond with the absolute.[37]

There is a subtle, but crucial distinction to be made here between what Ian Ramsey calls a 'discernment situation' which can occur only in language that is logically 'odd',[38] and what Miskotte calls the 'strangeness' of the event character of God's manifestation, that is, in the concrete form of the NAME, *which* is not merely human projective language.[39] A disclosure situation of a religious nature, according to Ramsey, is merely 'evoked' by language, and thus religious language has a necessarily 'odd' character about it. The 'ultimate posits'[40] which claim man's commitment can only be discerned in language which has a logical impropriety about it. Thus, for Ramsey, religious language has an evocative logic, and not a descriptive logic. It is not referential to reality as such, but is a 'projective' function of the human mind by which words are thrown upon the 'screen of language' to elicit a response or commitment from the subject towards a non-concretized ultimate.[41] Miskotte, on the other hand, takes the 'anthropomorphism' of religious language, in which the actions of God are spoken of as occurring in concrete human history, as not mere projection of human thought to evoke religious experience, but as the concrete expression of the Name, that is, of God himself. In this sense, language, even religious language, has a referential meaning to a concretized absolute *independent* of a

---

[36]*Philosophical Investigations*, p. 39.

[37]Cf. above, pp. 9ff.

[38]Ian T. Ramsey, *Religious Language*, *passim*. Ramsey stands in the tradition of the British empiricists, Russell and Ayer, the linguistic philosophers, Wittgenstein and Hare, but more particularly within the apologetical philosophy of Joseph Butler, from whom he drew his two principle concepts of discernment and commitment. Ramsey then works out an application of this principle of discernment-commitment in terms of religious language; that is, language about God, biblical language, and language about the doctrine of God. However, it would appear that this kind of 'religious language' can say no more about God than man discerns in the language itself.

[39] *When the Gods are Silent*, pp. 127ff.

[40]The word 'God' is, for example, an 'ultimate posit'.

[41]I. T. Ramsey, *Religious Language*, pp. 47-48.

discerning subject. The 'strangeness' of religious language is thus determined by the 'strangeness' of the concrete reality behind it.[42]

Because my sympathy lies with the latter assumption, and not with the former, in speaking of the uniqueness of God, I choose to retain the word 'transcendence'. Rather than having the word deadened by the use of such qualifiers as 'discernment situation', the word can be given new life by allowing the reality to which it refers to disclose itself anew. I am fully aware of the difficult task that exists in bringing about a significant shift in the ordinary meaning of the word, but such a task properly belongs to a living theology.[43]

It is not an easy task to arrive at a suitable agenda for the discussion of transcendence. If there is a 'hidden agenda' in the concept itself, it will have to be teased out.

From an etymological consideration, 'to transcend' originally meant to climb over or across some obstacle. It then came to mean, in a figurative sense, the experience of being overwhelmed or surpassed. Then in a somewhat curious shift of meaning, it came to represent that which could not be crossed over. In being stopped by an object too great to be surmounted, one is said to have come up against something 'transcendent', that is, too great to be transcended. The term is now used almost exclusively in the sense of going beyond something, or an extension beyond the limits of something. The abstract noun 'transcendence', is owned in common by Aristotelian scholastics, moral philosophers, existentialists, personalists and theologians. In each case, 'transcendence' means something different.[44]

To continue the search for the 'hidden agenda' within the concept of transcendence, it would seem helpful at this point to consider several 'models' of transcendence, particularly models constructed from the

[42]K. Miskotte, *When the Gods are Silent*: 'We are free to speak of symbols, primary and secondary symbols, and also of saga and legend, and even of myth. But if these are understood as projections of human experience and not as the concrete form of the Name, not as the precipitate of the meeting with YHWH which is initiated, established by Him, then the qualification of this event as a history of God with men again goes to ruin.' p. 129.

[43]Cf. T. F. Torrance: '... an alert theology has an all-important role to play, in constructive as well as critical activity, in demanding and carrying through a significant shift in the meaning of ordinary terms to cope with the new insights and in creating new forms of expression opposite to new truth where the adaption of old forms of speech and thought does not prove adequate.' *God and Rationality*, p. 19.

[44]Cf. G. F. Woods, 'The Idea of the Transcendent', *Soundings*, A. R. Vidler (ed.), Cambridge University Press, Cambridge (1962), paperback reprint, 1966, pp. 45-65; esp. pp. 55ff. Cf. also, Thomas D. Parker, 'How Can We Think of God——Another Look at Transcendence', *McCormick Quarterly*, Chicago, Vol. 20, January, 1967, pp. 79-96, esp. pp. 85ff. Also, see D. Cairns. *God Up There?* The Saint Andrew Press, Edinburgh, 1967, pp. 25ff.

theological perspective as an attempt to speak of the transcendence of God.

One such model of transcendence is based on analogy. As G. F. Woods says, 'Both transcendence and immanence are rather curious analogies describing what is and what remains in being.'[45] For example, a ball floating in water can be immanent in the water only because it retains its distinction from water. In one sense, the ball transcends the water, and in another is transcended by the water. The analogy works both ways. What is important here in considering the analogical nature of transcendence, is that transcendence is not a particular, invisible feature of each visible being. Transcendence is not some kind of 'hidden thing' behind each observed thing, but is the presence of the thing itself with respect to something not identical with it, but in relation to it.[46] This 'analogy of being' as a principle of transcendence enables Woods to come to the final conclusion that:

> In our experience of the changing, we have also a curious experience of the unchanging. I believe that we are gradually driven towards an awareness of some being, which is variously styled pure, absolute, or transcendent. The conclusion is being itself.[47]

Unfortunately, Woods comes to the very conclusion which he wished to avoid when he said earlier, 'It is plain that we cannot simply use the word "transcendent" and assume without more ado that it always has the same meaning.'[48] A 'pure, transcendent being' may be no more than a ball in water—or God. The analogy cannot lead past a certain indifference.

Another model of transcendence which is akin to the model of analogy is that of causality. The essence of this model is the principle of priority, the priority of cause over its effect. The word 'cause', by itself, means priority. To cause something, is to make it happen. The cause does not necessarily need to precede the effect, it can be coterminous with it, in which case the causal priority is a priority of efficacy.[49] Thus, God's *real* existence is posited prior to, or efficient in, the observed effects, or causes and effects of creatures. The idea that actuality is prior to potency is as old as Aristotle:

> ... it is clear that actuality is prior to potency ... for from the potential the actual is always produced by an actual thing ... there is always

[45]'The Idea of the Transcendent', p. 57.
[46]*Ibid.*, pp. 59-60.
[47]*Ibid.*, p. 63.
[48]*Ibid.*, p. 61.
[49]Cf. R. H. King, 'Models of God's Transcendence', *Theology Today*, July 1966, Vol. 23, pp. 200-209, esp. p. 201.

a first mover, and the mover already exists actually.[50]

What is at stake in this model of transcendence, is the *independence* of a cause from its effect, prior to the necessary connection between the cause and the effect. In this model, the actuality, or transcendence, is not conditioned in its priority by immanence, that is by the connection of a contingent world with its transcendent priority:

Just as a man is only a man and not a father unless he has children, so God is wholly transcendent and in himself not a creator unless he creates. And as a man, in order to have children, must first be independent in himself of his children, so God, in order to be an immanent creator, must also be transcendent in himself.[51]

The principle of priority as a model of transcendence leads inevitably to the abstraction of transcendence as 'being in itself', about which nothing can be known. For the only access to such transcendent being is through its connection with a contingent world, and that connection is its immanence, not its transcendence.

Robert Neville has shown that the conflict between Descartes and Leibniz over the priority of will in the creator (Descartes) as against the priority of understanding (Leibniz) was over this very problem of transcendence. Descartes argues that 'supreme indifference in God is the supreme proof of his omnipotence'.[52] On the contrary, argued Leibniz, 'Indifference arises from ignorance, and, the wiser a man is, the more determined he is towards the most perfect....'[53] What Leibniz was saying, is that there could be no intelligence beyond the intelligence imbedded in the act of creation. To posit a supreme will prior to this intelligence is to posit ignorance.

Neville goes on to demonstrate that the same issues are at stake in the concept of transcendence as held by Paul Tillich and Charles Hartshorne. Process theology, as advocated by Hartshorne, holds that God is transcendent in the understanding of the intelligible world as a totality, which is a model of transcendence following the argument of Leibniz against Descartes. On the other hand, Tillich is following Descartes in positing the transcendence of God in the 'ground of being', and therefore is reduced to symbols in speaking of this 'unknowable' being.[54]

[50]Aristotle, *Metaphysics*, p. 1049b.
[51]R. C. Neville, 'Some Historical Problems about the Transcendence of God', *Journal of Religion*, Vol. 47, January 1967, pp. 1-9, esp, p. 6.
[52]*Ibid.*, p. 6.
[53]*Ibid.*, p. 3.
[54]*Ibid.*, pp. 6ff. What Tillich actually says is that finite man '... implicitly asks the question of ultimate reality; he must assume, as every Christian believer must, that in the symbols of his ultimate concern the answer to the question of ultimate

The model of transcendence based on priority as the transcendent element in causality comes to grief against the same 'supreme indifference' as the analogical model. A cosmology which is conceived along philosophical lines can only yield an impersonal 'idea' of transcendence. It really does become a matter of indifference!

A cosmology conceived along the lines of personalism offers still another model of transcendence. It is transcendence experienced as 'encounter' and has been ably presented by David Cairns, drawing heavily upon Brunner.[55] Cairns offers as an alternative to the cosmic dualism supernatural/natural—in which the supernatural drains all the reality out of the world and history—a creature/creator duality of relation modelled on the principle of love. The operative principle for this model is faith.[56] The content of transcendence is what God has revealed of himself through his mighty works and his word.[57] 'Here we are not allowed to remain

reality is implied.' *Biblical Religion and the Search for Ultimate Reality*, James Nisbet and Co. Ltd., London, 1955, p. 59. Also, 'The freedom of the creature to act against its essential unity with God makes God transcendent to the world . . . a distinction between . . . the ground of being, which transcends all polarities and finite being, which is subjected to them [exists] . . .' *Ibid.*, pp. 75, 80. On the other hand, Hartshorne says, '. . . God is not pure being but total actual being of a given moment, with achieved determinations. Thus God is being in both its opposite aspects: abstract least common denominator, and concrete de facto maximal achieved totality.' *The Divine Relativity*, Yale University Press, New Haven, London (1948), 1969, p. 88.

[55] David Cairns, *God Up There?*, pp. 25ff, 108.

[56] Cf. Kenneth Hamilton, *Revolt Against Heaven*, p. 49, where Hamilton divides transcendence into two categories: one in which a conceptuality is used, based on some specified cosmology, and the other in which faith is the principle, with no cosmology in particular relevant to it. 'Transcendence as a concept used in discursive thought is of service only within a cosmological system. Therefore, although metaphysical transcendence may well provide a God whose very nature is to be the Wholly Unconditioned, such a God is at the same time an earthbound God, a deity whose reality hangs upon a metaphysician's reasoning; and if that reasoning turns out to be faulty, this God simply disappears.' *Ibid.*, p. 52, Cf. also Edward Farley, *The Transcendence of God*, The Epworth Press, London (1958), 1962, pp. 36ff, who makes a distinction between 'metaphysical transcendence' and 'Kerygmatic transcendence'; the latter is a situation in which, when the gospel is proclaimed, a faithful response is a 'confession' of a transcendent God, not a rational assertion. 'Kerygmatic transcendence is "existential" not "essential" transcendence.' *Ibid.*, p. 39. Farley sees the conflict between these two concepts as the 'theological impasse for modern theology'. Farley himself takes a mediating position, offering a concept of transcendence based upon the 'analogy of grace'. *Ibid.*, pp. 217ff. Farley's weakness is in his structuring of the problem of transcendence as an 'impasse' and hoping to mediate the impasse without letting go completely of either a metaphysical or confessional transcendence. Farley's study of transcendence, therefore, while comprehensive, is not particularly helpful. He fails to get to the fundamental problem and consequently struggles helplessly with the impasse.

[57] D. Cairns, *God Up There?*, p. 97.

spectators, God affirms his transcendence by calling for our free yet obedient response.'[58] The true correlative of divine transcendence thus, is human response to the encountering of God in his works and his word. Cairns thus is able to preserve the notion of 'beyondness' in this model of transcendence without ending with the 'supreme indifference' inherent in the analogical and causal models. Precisely the opposite—God's transcendence is known in faith as supreme concern.

What is not completely clear in this encounter model, is how one conceives of the 'limits' *within* the personal which constitutes the reality of transcendence. The Buberian concept of the I-Thou relation, which Brunner built into his personalistic theology, and which Cairns accepts for himself, would appear to posit transcendence as a factor *of the relation*, that is, of the human relation, rather than beyond it.[59]

In order to seek clarification of this, we need to turn to yet another model of transcendence, reflecting also a personalist cosmology, which can be called the intention-action model.[60] The operative word in this model is not faith, but act. 'The being of a person is being-in-act,' says Karl Barth.[61] The intention is revealed in the act itself, and if it can be established that the intention of a person can be identified with the person's *essential* self, then the act is an act of transcendence.[62] If a person does not act, he cannot be known except as an object in an impersonal way, that is, as an 'It' in Buberian language. This 'Itness' would appear to be the limit which must be overcome, or transcended, if knowledge of the other as a 'really other' self is to be possible. But this is an illusion inherent in the nature of the personal itself.

For example, in attempting to relate to another person, we know

[58] *Ibid.*, p. 98.

[59] This is precisely the criticism Gregor Smith makes of the Buberian model of I-Thou transcendence; cf. *The Doctrine of God*: 'On the one hand I-It is a permanent condition of I-Thou and provides objectivity and continuity. On the other hand the person-to-person relation paradoxically is present in its fuller potentiality when the hinterland of the personal relation offers a reality which is not personal. This non-personal reality is spirit, the reality of the between.' pp. 165-166. Also, 'I myself would say that we begin neither with "I" and the other "I", but with the situation of Spirit in which "Thou" and "I" are interwoven.' *Ibid.*, p. 174.

[60] I am indebted to Robert King, 'Models of God's Transcendence', pp. 205ff, for the phrase "intention-action". King develops this model of transcendence as one exemplified by Karl Barth. I am not so much concerned here to enter into a critique of Barth's concept of transcendence as "God's freedom" to be and act with love for man, as I am to explore the question of where an ultimate "limit" falls in the intention-act of a personal encounter.

[61] K. Barth, *Church Dogmatics*, T. & T. Clark, Edinburgh, 1932-1962, II/1, p. 271.

[62] I will not attempt at this point to prove the assertion that the intention of a person is primarily located in his action. It will be taken up later when I work out the concept of historical transcendence as a kenotic act. For an able treatment of this concept see J. Macmurray, *The Self as Agent*, pp. 152, 197ff, 220.

that there is a barrier, a 'limit' which must be passed before real knowledge of the other and real communion can take place. Without examining this further, it would be natural to assume that the barrier is constituted by the fact that we are separated by the time-space condition of objectivity, which prevents us from 'immediately' knowing the other self. We must move through the symbolic world of sounds (language), pictures (gestures) and sensations (touching) in order to know something other than us to be a *person*.[63] We do this as a matter of course. We do not think of speech as mere 'noise', assuming we know the language, but simply hear the sounds as 'he' or 'she' in the act of speaking. The 'hiddenness' of the other as self—I shall call it spirit—is only known mediately through the symbolic language of the objective world—that is, the body. Some psychologists, for example, have taken a special interest in what is called 'body language', the revelations which the self unconsciously makes through certain movements or attitudes which the body of a person assumes.

But now if we carefully ask the question—what constitutes the ultimate limit which must be crossed for there to be knowledge of the other person at the level of spirit, that is, of the inner self?—we should have to answer, I believe: the ultimate limit is spirit. It is the inaccessibility of the other as spirit that constitutes the ultimate limit. To speak of transcendence, therefore, in the mode of the personal, is to speak of a limit which is constituted by spirit itself which must be crossed over.[64] To

---

[63]I am fully aware of the oversimplification of this illustration. Some might argue that in the area of parapsychology there are evidences of non-symbolic contact of persons of an immediate nature. I am not concerned here to deny or defend this as a possibility. In any event, it does not affect the point I am making, as shall become evident.

[64]Gordon Kaufman gives an unusually able exposition of the ultimate limit with which transcendence is concerned in his essay, 'On the Meaning of "God": Transcendence Without Mythology.' *Harvard Theological Review*, Vol. 59, April 1966, pp. 105-132. Kaufman's main point is that the ultimate limit is best conceived as a personal limiting known in the intercourse and interaction of personal wills (p. 122). Thus, the limit is not one of a physical or organic nature, which would require an impersonal transcendence, but is one drawn from ordinary language which deals with inter-personal relations. It is the 'will' of the other person, not his physical presence, which constitutes a restriction or barrier to relation; thus, Kaufman claims, God can transcend man in a quasi-personal way through a transcending will. Unfortunately, Kaufman does not see the problem of identifying transcendence with inaccessibility: 'Now it is clear that this image of inaccessible transcendence and freedom made known and effective through the explicit acts of communication and power—through words and deeds—is built up analogically from the model of the *hiddenness* and *transcendence* and freedom of the finite self, who also can ... hide himself from his fellows and remain inaccessible, except as he chooses to manifest himself through acts and words.' p. 124 (Italics mine). If Kaufman is saying that the act of transcendence is the finite self 'hiding himself from his fellows', he is left without any way of speaking of

speak of body as the limit which must be crossed in order to encounter the hiddenness, or transcendence of spirit is a serious misunderstanding of transcendence as a mode of personal existence.

Failure to understand this important distinction led Schleiermacher to model the transcendence of God along the lines of pure self-consciousness. Schleiermacher 'overcame' the objective realm of the ethical and empirical by placing transcendence in self-consciousness, and thereby assumed that he had passed over the limit which separated him from immediate communion with God.

... the *whence* of our receptive and active existence, as implied in this self-consciousness, is to be designated by the word 'God', and this is for us the really original signification of the word.[65]

It was through the immediate intuition of consciousness that Schleiermacher 'felt' the transcendence of God as the *whence* of his personal existence. Schleiermacher's model for transcendence was the self, but not the self as an agent who is known in his act, but the self as self-consciousness, prior to act.

Accepting for the moment the assertion that the ultimate limit for transcendence is the boundary of spirit, not the limiting factors of finitude, of what practical value is this distinction? For 'person', as we know ourselves to be, is not simply spirit or body functioning independently of the other, but a concrete union of the two in a single reality. When someone injures a portion of my body they have hurt *me*! And when my spirit is wounded through a cruel insult, *I* suffer. Is the mystery of the 'hidden' self in the concrete person, a 'third' entity which constitutes the 'relation' of the two, or is it spirit itself? This is a question which I will raise, but not attempt to answer.[66] My concern here in this examination of the limits

transcendence as a concrete form of reality. It is this precise problem which I am endeavouring to expose, first of all, and then to solve. To suggest that spirit constitutes the limit with which transcendence is concerned, is not the same as saying that spirit is to be equated with either hiddenness or transcendence.

[65]Friedrich D. E. Schleiermacher, *The Christian Faith*, T. & T. Clark, Edinburgh, 1928, p. 16.

[66]This is the kind of question raised and discussed by Kierkegaard. 'Man is spirit. But what is spirit? Spirit is the self. But what is the self? The self is a relation which relates itself to its own self, or it is that in the relation (which accounts for it) that the relation relates itself to its own self; the self is not the relation but (consists in the fact) that the relation relates itself to its own self.... In the relation between two, the relation is the third term as a negative unity, and the two relate themselves to the relation, and in the relation to the relation; such a relation is that between soul and body, when man is regarded as soul. If on the contrary the relation relates itself to its own self, the relation is then the positive third term, and this is the self.' *The Sickness Unto Death*, Oxford University Press, London, 1941, pp. 17, 18. Cf. also, *The Concept of Dread*, Princeton University Press, Princeton, 1944, pp. 39ff. Without attempting an exposition of

which transcendence overcomes is the fundamental distinction between a restriction set by finite conditions and that set by the conditions of the inner self, however it is psychologically constituted. There is, however, a crucial problem in the matter of how spirit, or self, is concretized. It is here, I suspect, that we will begin to see the emergence of the 'inner logic' contained in the problematic of the concrete man's bond with the absolute.

If, as is commonly assumed, transcendence is the hiddenness of spirit *beyond* the limit of concreteness, then we make contact with the transcendent self by passing beyond its concrete manifestations to spirit itself. Here, the movement of transcendence, if we could call it that, is *away* from concreteness towards the more absolute spirit of person. It is this basic assumption which lies behind the kind of language that speaks of God being 'transcendent of the world, but immanent in it'. The assumption being that the transcendence of God is the hiddenness of Spirit relative to the world contingent to it.[67]

However, if one takes as an assumption the notion that the ultimate limit to be overcome is that which constitutes spirit itself, then the movement of transcendence would be from spirit *towards* concreteness. This would mean that concreteness as we think of it in terms of personal existence is not a 'limit', but is the act of transcendence itself. That is, it is spirit concretizing itself as action. So that, when we are 'up against' the concreteness of the 'other', we are not up against a symbol, or a barrier which must be 'transcended', but we are up against spirit itself.[68] But this

Kierkegaard's thought, I will only say that I understand him to mean that the spirit, as the self, is not the divine in man, nor is it a third element in a trichotomous concept of man, and still less a neutral bridge which joins soul and body, but it is 'self-consciousness, which is already activity, that is inwardness; thus, spirit is not the abstraction of the personal, but the concretion of it as inwardness becoming act. Cf. *The Concept of Dread*, pp. 127ff. For a very helpful and quite exhaustive study of Kierkegaard's concept of spirit, see George Price, *The Narrow Pass—A Study of Kierkegaard's Concept of Man*, Hutchinson and Co. Ltd., London, 1963, pp. 36ff.

[67]Even John Macmurray, who made it clear that he considered that transcendence in personal relation was the act by which a personal agent moved beyond himself into relation with the 'other', finds himself saying, 'God, therefore, as the infinite Agent is immanent in the world which is his act, but transcendent of it.' *Persons in Relation*, Faber and Faber, London (1961), paperback, 1970, p. 223. However, in a personal conversation recently with Professor Macmurray, he admitted that he has not attempted to work out a concept of transcendence along theological lines, and agreed that, consistently developed from his concept of the person as agent, God's self-transcendence would be his act in the world, as the infinite Agent.

[68]One must say then, that Gregor Smith's attempt (cf. above, p. 38, n. 1) to locate the transcendence of God 'between' the I and Thou in impersonal spirit, is hardly adequate, because it seems to posit a third dimension somewhere in the experience of faith which is not an intention-act of concrete experience. It is becoming questionable that one can attempt to locate transcendence in any

too is by way of anticipation, and remains to be carefully worked out.

The more immediate gain has been the emergence of the 'hidden agenda' by which the discussion of transcendence can now proceed. Rather than considering the various models of transcendence, with an attempt to sort the different theological varieties into their appropriate category, it has now become quite clear that the limit which van Buren wished to avoid, where the strange ones 'tremble in the presence of the gods', is the limit which marks off spirit from spirit. Van Buren has relativized this limit, and thus rightly can hardly talk of transcendence, much less of God.[69]

Transcendence has its own agenda which allows no relativizing of limits. We are up against the 'wholly other' in speaking of the transcendence of God—because we are up against Spirit. This, and this only, is 'out-and-out transcendence'. It now remains to be seen just how fruitful this concept will be.

3 'Can Spirit Survive—In the Last Analysis?'

At the outset, it does not appear to be a promising conclusion. Just what, or who, is this 'wholly other'? Having radicalized the silence of transcendence for modern man into an 'objective' silence, which is more than the echo of inwardness, dare we give it a name? If the ultimate limit, which may or may not be transcended, is said to be spirit, is there such a thing as Spirit? We may well have come to the position of the man who went to the market to buy some fruit, only to be told that it was not available. There were oranges and apples, there were offered to him peaches, cherries and grapes. But the customer rejected them all—he wanted fruit, at any cost! Now what was offered to him *was* indeed fruit, but he was forced to the conclusion that *fruit* could not be bought.[70]

---

kind of 'betweenness' with an I-Thou polarity, and at the same time in its concreteness of reality. What is at stake, of course, is a way of establishing the concreteness of God's transcendence. This will be examined in greater detail in Chapter III.

[69]'Men have had difficulty speaking of God, I suggest, not because God was beyond this world and our experience, but precisely because they were speaking of this world of human experience, a world of experience in which at least the strange ones of this world have known at least some "ordinary" situations in such a way that words failed them. Until theology has learned just this sort of speechlessness, may the gods or God save us from another doctrine of God. That is what I mean by asking whether "transcendence" is the word we want.' *Theological Explorations*, p. 181.

[70]This parable is told by Heidegger, who credits Hegel with its original form. *Essays in Metaphysics*, p. 59. Cf. also Aristotle: '... universal causes ... do not *exist*. For the *individual* is the source of the individuals. For man is the cause of man universally, there *is* no universal man....' *Metaphysics*, p. 1071a.

It is possible to name that which does not actually exist, and if the 'wholly other' is merely a universal name for a particular *kind* of otherness, our words will have insufficient value to make a purchase. There is a warning here: 'The language of "transcendence", the thought of God as a personal being, wholly other to man, dwelling apart in majesty —this talk may well collapse into meaninglessness in the last analysis.'[71]

There are arguments which could be adduced against this collapse into meaninglessness, even at this point, but I hesitate over the phrase, 'in the last analysis.' Does this mean that there is some 'trump card' hidden in the deck, so that when the final hand is played out for the transcendence of God, the trick is taken 'in the last analysis' by an unexamined assumption?

Or, to change the metaphor, is the 'last analysis' actually the first roof timber to be laid across the gap between two standing walls, so that the most unskilled observer can call out to the carpenter: 'I say, old boy, it's too short you know, you apparently miscalculated the distance!'

In any event, the warning is clear; once the loss of transcendence has been radicalized, the full distance needs to be calculated, every card turned over. What really are we up against in speaking of a limiting spirit which is wholly other to the spirit of man?

The full implications of the course I am taking are made quite clear, I believe, in a penetrating essay by Leslie Stevenson, in which he seeks to demonstrate the logical fallacy of 'out-and-out transcendence'.[72] Stevenson establishes a basic theme of logic and works it out in the form of several variations, one of which he directly relates to the problem of transcendence. Stated informally, the theme is this: given the existence of *many* individual realities, one cannot logically assume *one* reality common to them all. That is, there may or there may not be one reality commonly related to the many; what the theme affirms is that when the one common reality is *not* given in actuality, one cannot logically infer it from the many.

[71]Ronald Hepburn, *Christianity and Paradox*, p. 193-194. Karl Barth, who has made such an impression with his talk of God as 'wholly other' to man, quite candidly admits that it is not an altogether felicitous phrase: 'It is nevertheless true that it was pre-eminently the image and concept of a "wholly other" that fascinated us and which we, though not without examination, had dared to identify with the deity of Him who in the Bible is called Jahweh-Kyrios. We viewed this "wholly other" in isolation, abstracted and absolutised, and set it over against man, this miserable wretch—not to say boxed his ears with it—in such fashion that it continually showed greater similarity to the deity of the God of the philosophers than to the deity of the God of Abraham, Isaac, and Jacob.' *The Humanity of God*, Collins, London, 1961, Fontana Library edition, 1967, p. 41.
[72]Leslie Stevenson, 'Immanent Transcendence', *Religious Studies*, Cambridge University Press, Vol. 6, No. 1, March, 1970, pp. 89-98.

An illustration which Stevenson himself uses makes the logical theme clear enough. In a normal series of whole numbers which can proceed infinitely, such as 1-2-3-4-5, and so on, it cannot be logically assumed that there is actually a single number larger than all whole numbers which are possible, that is, an infinite whole number. Yet it is true that for any given number, there can be a larger one.[73] This, of course, is the old philosophical problem of the 'one and the many'. The value of Stevenson's formulation of it is found in its application to the problem of transcendence.

If we substitute 'spirit' for whole numbers, the logical theme asserts that an infinite number of 'spirits' existing in a transcending relation to each other does not provide a logical basis for the inference that there is one spirit 'wholly other' to all spirits.[74] This Stevenson calls a logical fallacy.[75]

The concept of divine transcendence, Stevenson maintains, as a concept of an infinitely supreme being, transcendent to *all* finite beings, violates 'well established philosophical principles of significance'.[76] It is a logical fallacy. And, apart from the interests of value, 'There is no good reason for thinking that the notion of God has any important regulative utility for thought about the world.'[77]

However, if one does not proceed on the basis of pure theory, but does take a system of values into consideration, Stevenson suggests that the 'illusory transcendent concept', though it has no objective validity, can be useful as a regulative image, or model. What Stevenson means here, is that we can be helped along the way towards an ever increasing

---

[73]*Ibid.*, p. 90. Stevenson calls the proposition that there is a particular number larger than all other numbers in an infinite series a *Platonic* type of proposition. The proposition that in the ordinary unextended system of whole numbers, there is none larger than the rest, although it is true that for any given one there is a larger one, he calls an *Aristotelian* type of proposition. While Stevenson says that he does not consider these designations as inappropriate philosophically, he does not attempt to justify the names as used in this connection. The point which Stevenson makes is that, while one cannot proceed logically from an Aristotelian type of proposition to a Platonic type, the reverse is obviously possible. *Given* a single whole number which includes all other whole numbers in an infinite series, all numbers could logically be said then to be related. What Stevenson also makes clear, is that, while one cannot proceed logically from an Aristotelian type assertion to a Platonic one, this does not rule out the possibility that the Platonic one exists—we simply have no logical way of affirming it.

[74]I am using the word 'spirit' here, of course, in the sense defined above as the 'inaccessible self' which constitutes the uniqueness and particularity of a concrete person.

[75]Again, it must be made clear that Stevenson does not mean that it is impossible for the 'wholly other' to exist, but that it is a logical fallacy to infer its existence out of the world.

[76]*Ibid.*, p. 97.

[77]*Ibid.*, p. 96.

achievement of an ethical ideal by 'picturing' this ideal as a transcendent, objective one. The notion of a transcendent God, even if illusory, can serve as an inspiration to the individual continually to 'transcend' his limitations.[78] This concept of the transcendent ideal, Stevenson calls 'out-and-out transcendence'.[79] Thereupon, he concludes: 'My suggestion is that in the crucial theological contexts, the principle of out-and-out transcendence is strictly false or non-significant.'[80]

Now it seems that this would be a good place to stop and draw a breath. I am not sure that this line of thought has taken us to the 'last analysis', but it does seem a pretty fair measurement of the 'gap'. While the logical theme is in no way a new one, it does seem to me that Stevenson has cleared up the language of transcendence in a very respectable way. The categories of 'out-and-out transcendence' and 'immanent transcendence', while somewhat clumsy, I think are rather plain. If, that is, one is committed to the use of the word 'transcendence' at all.

The 'out-and-out' kind of transcendence is plain talk for saying that there is an ultimate reality which has its own existence independent of and beyond a contingent and finite world. That is, it is a concept of a fixed point outside of the process by which all moving points take their reckoning. The 'immanent' kind of transcendence, on the other hand, conceives no fixed point external to the contingent world, but transcend-

---

[78]*Ibid.*, pp. 96-97. What Stevenson is here suggesting is very similar to Kant's notion that theoretical concepts of supersensible beings are empty in themselves, and yet useful in a practical sense to regulate the moral law. '. . . thus the application to the supersensible solely in a practical point of view does not give pure theoretic reason the least encouragement to run riot into the transcendence.' I. Kant, *Critique of Practical Reason*, trans. by Thomas Abbott, Longmans Green and Co., London, 1909, p. 147 (175). The difference between Stevenson and Kant at this point, of course, is that Kant held that the concept of a causality free from empirical conditions was theoretically possible, even though empty (*ibid.*, p. 146). Stevenson denies that it is theoretically possible at all.

[79]'Immanent Transcendence', p. 97.

[80]*Ibid.*, p. 97. The conclusion of Stevenson's essay follows: 'I suggest that Christian theologians and apologists have traditionally insisted on the concept of transcendence in its out-and-out form because they felt that it is a guarantee of vital existential truths. Progress in logic (since Frege) enables us to see that it is not strictly necessary as a logical guarantee, for the Aristotelian-type proposition expresses those existential truths literally. Progress in epistemology (Since Kant) shows us that the concept of out-and-out transcendence is strictly illusory, since it involves the use of concepts where the conditions for their meaningful application are not satisfied. Whether the ideal of out-and-out transcendence is needed as a psychological guarantee of existential truths is, I suppose, an empirical question which a philosophical paper cannot answer.' p. 97. I will only comment here, that Stevenson's thoughtful essay has only shown the limits of logic, not the impossibility of theology, in speaking about a reality which is actually given as an out-and-out reality of transcendence.

ing relationships within the process of infinite possibility. Immanent transcendence could be likened to the 'transcending' rock just above the head of a mountain climber by which he pulls himself a few feet higher. When he overtakes (transcends) that point, there is another one always above him. Immanent transcendence includes all of the possibilities of an infinite series of events as well as an infinite self-transcendence of this series. What it does not include, is the possibility of an 'other' spirit (self) independent of the infinite series. Or, if it is included, it becomes a regulative 'model' used to give assurance to the contingent reality of finite existence.

There are three questions which I wish to formulate out of this discussion: (1) How can we continue to speak of the objective reality of God 'wholly other' to man in the sense of 'out-and-out transcendence'? (2) Can we continue to speak of the transcendence of God at all if the concept is being used as a regulative model to give psychological guarantee to existential truths? (3) In the 'last analysis', does not the greater share of the talk of God's transcendence in contemporary theology collapse into 'immanent transcendence?'

I raise the first question only to say that I consider it to be the fundamental question for this book, and that it will constitute the theme of Chapter II. Before proceeding to take up this question, I will deal briefly with the other two questions in order to press home the radical nature of this 'last analysis'.

In dealing with the last question first of all, I must immediately qualify the phrase 'the greater share of the talk of God's transcendence in contemporary theology'. It lies beyond the scope of this book to make such an exhaustive examination in order to substantiate the assertion contained in the question. Although I am inclined to think that the assertion is generally valid. Instead, I will take up the question in this form: in the last analysis, do not some claims made by contemporary theology for divine transcendence collapse into 'immanent transcendence'? And I will answer this in the affirmative by citing some examples.

As a leading exponent of process theology,[81] Charles Hartshorne

[81]Process theology cannot be precisely defined, as it has many exponents with differing emphases. There are, however, fundamental assumptions shared in common, taken basically from the process philosophy of A. N. Whitehead, particularly as put forth in his Gifford Lectures of 1927-28, published as *Process and Reality*, Macmillan, New York, 1929. Some of these assumptions include: a concept of the cosmos which includes God as the exemplification of all principles (p. 52); a concept of reality which sees becoming as the dynamic and creative determining of being (p. 34); a dipolar concept of the the process of becoming in which both the physical and mental poles of reality prehend (i.e., to grasp something in such a way that the prehender is affected by what he prehends) the data of existence (p. 54); the positing of a 'subjective aim' for each entity which is given

attempts to maintain both the transcendence and immanence of God in
terms of the dipolar nature of process philosophy. That is, while there
is an abstract or fixed concept of divine being, there is also, in process
theology, a concept of an absolute relativity of God in terms of his
becoming, his concrete relativity to all that is in the process of becoming.
The divine absolute is a 'divine object in the divine subject and for the
divine subject'.[82] Consequently, Hartshorne can say, 'At long last we
can be existentialists in theology, without denying the serene independence
of that in God which is bound to be embodied in existence.'[83] It becomes
clear, however, that the 'serene independence' is not in any way to be
construed as God's out-and-out transcendence, but rather, it is the least
common denominator of divine subjectivity inherent in all subjectivity
as such:

> In this aspect, God is not pure being but total actual being of a given
> moment, with all achieved determinations. Thus God is being in both
> its opposite aspects: abstract least common denominator, and concrete
> de facto maximal achieved totality.[84]

Without attempting to caricature Hartshorne's position, but simply as an
attempt to understand him, this concept could be likened to the relation
of a recipe to the baking of a cake. The process of mixing and baking the
cake includes both the abstract form of the initial intention and the concrete reality of the cake, in whatever stage or state it may happen to be.
In this sense, one could not say that God is the recipe which determines
the baking of the cake, one cannot even say that God *is*, except that at
any stage in the process, God becomes the totality of what has come to
be.[85] It follows, then, that one can only speak of what God's *consequent*

to it by God, and which becomes the principle by which the entity's 'self creation'
is actualized (p. 374): the principle of divine relativity, in which God, in his
consequent nature is determined by the sum total of all actualities which he prehends (p. 524).
    [82]Charles Hartshorne, *The Divine Relativity*, p. 87.
    [83]*Ibid.*, p. 87.
    [84]*Ibid.*, p. 88.
    [85]To take the analogy of the cake one step further, the recipe is little more
than an 'initial intention' which determines that *some* cake is baked, or partly
baked. In process thought, the original initial intention given to each entity, which
makes it a 'society' of events, can be modified by the actual achievement of the
entity itself. The initial intent serves to insure that the entity reaches the 'best
possible' concretion within its limitations. The concept 'God' has no final content
until the 'baking is done'; but then, when there is no more 'baking', the 'adventure
of God' is at an end anyway. 'If there should come a time when there would be
no more "making", then the adventure of God would be at an end.' B. Loomer,
'Christian Faith and Process Philosophy', *The Journal of Religion*, Vol. 29, 1949,
pp. 181-203, esp. p. 201.

being will become when concretized through a totality of concrete actualities.[86]

Now this would appear to be a rather straightforward presentation of what we have termed 'immanent transcendence'. All of the possibilities of an infinite series are included, but reality as such is restricted to those possibilities actually concretized. But then we come up against a rather curious twist in process theology, a concept of God which greatly resembles the *Platonic* type of proposition as defined by Stevenson:

> It is open to us to adopt a sweeping and consistent programme of attributing to God the supereminent form of every property capable of such a form.[87]

Something of the same can be found in the thought of Schubert Ogden, who has taken up the process line of thought to a considerable degree:

> As the eminent Self, by radical contrast, God's sphere of interaction or body is the whole universe of nondivine beings, with *each one of which* his relation is unsurpassably immediate and direct.[88]

Now while it is true that process thought generally has 'turned Plato on his head' by making the transcending 'forms' relative to their concretion in actual entities, nevertheless the positing of an 'eminent Self' as an abstraction drawn by inference from concrete selves is a logical fallacy, according to Stevenson, and has no value. *Unless* it is being used simply as a regulative model to guarantee the existential truths inherent in the process. In which case, the proper question to ask process theology is: can we continue to speak of a transcendent God at all when the word is used in this sense? Bernard Loomer, himself an advocate of process theology apparently thinks not:

> In process thought the universe is actually 'in the making', and God is incomplete in his concrete nature. If there should come a time when there would be no more 'making', then the adventure of God would be at an end. The only escape from this conclusion seems to be in terms of a basically transcendental God. This alternative is categorically denied by process philosophy.[89]

As a further example of the question as to whether or not contemporary

---

[86]Cf. Schubert Ogden, *The Reality of God and Other Essays*, SCM Press, London, 1967, who says: 'Rather, he [God], too, is understood to be continually in the process of self-creation, synthesizing in each new moment of his experience the whole of achieved actuality with the plenitude of possibility as yet unrealized.' p. 59.

[87]C. Hartshorne, *The Divine Relativity*, p. 124.

[88]S. Ogden, *The Reality of God*, p. 60. My emphasis.

[89]B. Loomer, 'Christian Faith and Process Philosophy', p. 201.

talk of the transcendence of God does not, in the last analysis, usually collapse into immanent transcendence, I would like to refer to the concept of transcendence in what might be termed 'onto-theology'. This concept has its roots in the fundamental ontology[90] of Heidegger's thought. It can be found in Tillich, although Tillich's thought is much too complex and eclectic for him to be classified as strictly following Heidegger's ontology. John Macquarrie has perhaps a greater appreciation, if not understanding, of Heidegger than Tillich, and calls his own theology: existential-ontological theism.[91] One must also take into account Heinrich Ott, who represents the most recent and most controversial focus of ontological theology, especially with respect to Heidegger's later concepts.

Heidegger's concept of Being forces the language of transcendence to the limit, where grammar is stretched to the breaking point. 'The Being of entities "is" not itself an entity,' says Heidegger.[92] Thus, ontology, as a way of speaking of the fact that God 'is', can no longer carry the additional freight of Heidegger's thought. God *is* not in the sense that other entities can be said *to be*.[93] Following Heidegger at this point, Tillich advanced the theological assertion that 'God does not exist. He is being-itself beyond essence and existence.'[94] Because traditional theology had conceived of God as a being—that is, one who *is*—Tillich could only show the inadequacy of such a concept by stating that God was the 'Ground of all being', and that he can only be referred to as 'the God above the God of theism'.[95] Kenneth Hamilton criticizes Tillich's concept of the transcendence of God—'the God above God'—as sheer immanence:

The perspective is one of immanence, for, although the definitions

---

[90]The phrase 'fundamental ontology', is the technical term which expresses Heidegger's distinction between traditional ontology which defined man in terms of the way *things* are, and an ontology based on a concept of *Dasein*, which asserts that man is a being of quite his own kind, which in its being is concerned *with* its being and *is* this being. Cf. Robinson and Cobb, *The Later Heidegger and Theology*, p. 7.

[91]John Macquarrie, *God and Secularity*, Lutterworth Press, London, 1968, p. 98.

[92]M. Heidegger, *Being and Time*, trans. by John Macquarrie and E. Robinson, SCM Press, London, 1962, p. 26.

[93]The ontological problem actually surfaces here in grammar. For *onta* (things which exist) is a substantive formed from the participle of the greek verb *einai*, 'to be'. It is at this point that the grammar of 'being' begins to fall apart, when God cannot be said 'to be' and yet it is said that he is the 'Being beyond being', or the Being who is the 'ground of being'. See the essay by Heidegger, 'On the Grammar and Etymology of the Word "Being"', *An Introduction to Metaphysics*, pp. 52-74.

[94]Paul Tillich, *Systematic Theology*, University of Chicago Press, Chicago, 1951, Vol. I, p. 227.

[95]P. Tillich, *The Courage to Be*, Collins, London, 1962, p. 183.

of God advanced may contain the word *transcendent*, they actually refer to a deity immanent within experience and transcendent only as a ground of experience.[96]

It is doubtful that Hamilton has really grasped the thought of Tillich at this point, and for this reason his criticism misses the mark. It seems clear that Tillich's concept of 'God above God' has reference to that which is inaccessible to human experience, and as such is posited as transcendent to being. '... the God who is *a* person is transcended by the God who is the Personal-Itself, the ground and abyss of every person.'[97] Thus, when Tillich says that man stands between 'being and non-being', it is a way of saying that man stands in the 'abyss' before the divine transcendence.[98]

Thus man continues to ask the question of ultimate reality, that is, of transcendence, but, says Tillich, '...he must assume, as every Christian believer must, that in the symbols of his ultimate concern the answer to the question of ultimate reality is implied.'[99] There is no question but that Tillich posits an 'out-and-out' transcendence, but it can only be a symbolization of that to which man's question about ultimate reality points. Again, like process theology, the ontology of Tillich appears to be no more than a regulative 'symbol' of ultimate reality to give man the 'courage to be'. Without the regulative function of the symbol, Tillich's language of transcendence collapses into immanent transcendence. Hamilton's criticism is right, but for the wrong reason.

Macquarrie, on the other hand, turns the fundamental ontology of Heidegger into a new style natural theology, which can rightly be termed philosophical theology. Man, says Macquarrie, in 'his *quest* for the sense of existence is met by the *gift* of a sense of existence.'[100] Being, for Macquarrie, becomes 'holy being', which seems to call to the self from one side of an extended line between being and non-being. It is 'faith in being' which is the religious man's proper response to the call of 'holy being'.[101] Macquarrie has gone further than Tillich in making 'holy being' an autonomous, seeking, and purposive reality. He is clearly speaking of the transcendence of God in his concept of 'holy being'. Crucial to his concept, is the notion that 'holy being' discloses itself as a *gift* to the one who believes 'in being'. We can best understand what Macquarrie means by the transcendence of 'holy being', in turning back to Heidegger:

[96]*Revolt Against Heaven*, p. 100.
[97]*Biblical Religion and the Search for Ultimate Reality*, p. 82.
[98]*Ibid.*, p. 58.
[99]*Ibid.*, p. 59.
[100]*Principles of Christian Theology*, SCM Press, London, 1967, p. 75.
[101]*Ibid.*, pp. 104ff.

Being transcends and covers, while revealing itself, what is encountered in open presence by such enthrallment. Encounter means seeking refuge in open presence, thus, being sheltered in presence, being an existent.... Being exhibits itself as revealing enthrallment and Existence as such manifests itself as an encounter fleeing into unmasked presence.[102]

Thus, when Macquarrie talks of the transcendence of God, it is in Heidegger's sense of a 'path' on which man who is in quest of authentic being is surprised and enthralled by the gift of being itself.[103] It has all the marks of a delightful rendezvous, but unfortunately, on this shrouded passageway, we cannot determine whether it is the embrace itself that matters, or *who* does the embracing![104]

There is also the suspicion that if one does *not* go looking down that passageway of transcendence, there will be no 'holy being' left waiting somewhere along that lonely path. For, in fact, though Heidegger posits an ontological difference between Being and beings, that is, the 'transcending enthrallment' really does come to meet the 'encounter seeking refuge', this is an event with a nucleus of one reality, not two.[105]

The collapse of this kind of language of transcendence is clearly pointed out by Bultmann, in his criticism of Heinrich Ott for taking over Heidegger's 'square'[106] and saying that it is completed by the divine on one side as the Transcendent.[107] Bultmann argues that this is an 'immanent transcendence'. What Bultmann seems to fear is that if God is

---

[102]*Essays in Metaphysics*, p. 57.

[103]For Heidegger, the terms 'passage' (*Übergang*) and 'encounter' are corresponding concepts. 'Passage' is equivalent to transcendence; it is an 'event-bound path', by which, through language, man takes the 'step back' from metaphysics to meet the 'unthought'. *Ibid.*, p. 60.

[104]'To know the world in its depth, and to know ourselves in the depth is already to know something of the mysterious transcendence that embraces the world and ourselves and that promises a meaning and wholeness that we could not otherwise find.' J. Macquarrie, *God and Secularity*, p. 70.

[105]Cf. Robinson and Cobb, *The Later Heidegger and Theology*, pp 57ff.

[106]Heidegger's concept of the square is taken from the idea that a thing is a meeting, an assembling having four sides, which he characterizes as earth and heaven, the divine and the mortal. The 'thing' which assembles as the square constitutes the world; e.g., 'A bridge, "assembles" two shores at this point, provides passage for the flood water coming from the storm in the sky, provides the mortals passage on their way, and as it arches them over the stream points them up to the divine. The bridge assembles the square, makes place for it.' *Ibid.*, pp. 59ff.

[107]Heinrich Ott, who wrote his doctoral dissertation under Karl Barth on a critique of the theology of Rudolf Bultmann, seeks to bring Bultmann in his theological position closer to Barth, by appealing to what he called the 'newer Heidegger'. It was Heidegger's later thinking in which he gives priority to being over *Dasein* that suggested to Ott that the philosophy of Heidegger would now be more acceptable to Barth. As Barth's successor to the chair of Dogmatics at the

merely one side of a square, opposite to man, which is formed when a 'thing' assembles, the reality of transcendence will be drained out into the 'historicness' of the event.[108] One can share Bultmann's concern at this point without conceding that his own concept of divine transcendence is completely adequate. But I will not attempt to demonstrate that at this point.

The fundamental weakness in all onto-theology appears to be the weakness inherent in Heidegger's thought itself. Having cut off the top (out-and-out transcendence), Heidegger attempts to separate what is left into two movements with only one centre of reality. Each person has his own 'path of transcendence'; there is no *one* reality which stands in a relation of freedom to these many events. In the last analysis, then, this too is immanent transcendence.

The two general examples of process theology and existential-ontological theology have been shown to have real difficulty in sustaining a dimension of transcendence in terms of the reality of God. Both Ogden and Hartshorne find it necessary to bring in a definite 'theistic' concept in the form of a personalized God to prevent their process thought from collapsing into a radical immanence. Heidegger, of course, cannot even speak of God, because it would be a violation of his non-metaphysical attempt to understand being. And yet, he labours to the limits of language to take the initiative for being away from *Dasein* and give it to Being. Both Tillich and Macquarrie sense the dangers of an 'immanent theism' where God is merely a very big but unfortunately invisible person, and so opt for an non-theistic concept of divine transcendence expressed in categories of impersonal being. But which, apparently, has no face, or, to speak facetiously, even a 'backside' like the God of Moses,[109] and so can have no real Name, but only a symbolic representation as a qualification of being, as 'ground of being' and 'holy being'.

Because the fundamental problem in these examples has been their inability to make good a *reality claim* in their use of the word 'transcendent' with respect to God, I want to examine one other attempt in which this claim is expressly made.

University of Basel, Ott's theological position can be seen, to some extent, as a new alternative for Barthians. See Robinson and Cobb. *The Later Heidegger and Theology*, pp. 30ff. Also, cf. Ott's essay, 'What is Systematic Theology?', *ibid.*, pp. 77-111.

[108]This criticism of Bultmann's, is recorded in a conversation with R. Scherer, cited by Heinz-Horst Schrey, 'Die Bedeutung der Philosophie Martin Heideggers für die Theologie', *Martin Heideggers Einfluss auf die Wissenschaften*, (Heidegger Festschrift, Bern: A. Francke AG. Verlag, 1949), p. 16. Cited by Robinson and Cobb, *The Later Heidegger and Theology*, p. 62.

[109]Exodus 33:23.

In a very incisive essay on the nature of divine transcendence, Thomas D. Parker succinctly sets forth his argument:

> Clearly, it is insufficient simply to establish the meaning of a category such as transcendence without making a reality claim for that which is transcendent. God is not 'the Transcendent' as such. If God is a name for that which is beyond us and which addresses us in such a way that we respond in faith, we must speak of God as a transcendent *reality*. This takes us beyond mere analysis of concepts, and places us in a position of making a claim. To speak of God as a reality is to talk about the One who meets us at our limits and supports us within those limits. Such speech supposes that a genuine encounter with God has taken place and that man is not alone with his faith and its (illusory) object.[110]

Precisely. It is the *kind* of reality which the word 'transcendent' claims to represent that concerns us in this examination. Parker gives us reason to hope that the reality of God intended by his transcendence is the reality of one who is really 'other' to man, one whose reality does not need the assistance of qualifiers. Parker continues: 'Men must be able to encounter an "other" outside themselves in a way that is decisive for their self-activity in order to be confronted by God as a transcendent reality.'[111] We now have the three basic concepts with which Parker proceeds to build his language of transcendence: transcendence, reality, encounter. Transcendence must be understood as a reality claim for that which is other to man, rather than simply as a qualifier for an eminent dimension to human existence. But the *kind* of reality claim which is made for divine transcendence is the crucial step needed to make the language work. For Parker, the reality claim is established through encounter. And it is at this point that one becomes apprehensive.

Transcendence, for Parker, as a purely formal term, has no content. The content 'remains to be supplied by the context in which it is used'.[112] The context, it turns out, includes an understanding of what is transcended. This understanding is properly called immanence, and serves as the correlate to transcendence, not merely in a formal way, but in a material way. So that for Parker, 'An entity which has nothing that relates it to another entity is not transcendent to it.'[113] The fact that Parker conceives of this in more than formal terms is revealed by his further assertion that ' "God" is transcendent in his relationship to human beings, and not otherwise.'[114] It is the encounter which one has with the

[110]How Can We Think of God? Another Look at Transcendence'. p. 88.
[111]*Ibid.*, p. 90.
[112]*Ibid.*, p. 86.
[113]*Ibid.*, p. 86.
[114]*Ibid.*, p. 94.

reality of God through faith, prayer and worship that provides the necessary material context for the reality of divine transcendence. It is this existential-encounter which Parker construes as immanence, which together with the corresponding dimension of transcendence, constitutes the 'reality claim'. It now becomes clear just what the implications of this 'encounter-transcendence' are for the real 'otherness' of God:

> If transcendence contains a hidden but real reference to what is transcended, it cannot (logically) ever indicate a 'wholly other' or non-immanent reality. It must always appear in relation to something immanent, i.e. to that reality whose limits it surpasses in some way or another.[115]

This, of course, is exactly what Stevenson has said. You cannot logically separate a reality from the series in which it is immanent and call it an absolute reality. Starting from *within* an infinite process of reality, you cannot posit a reality which is not constituted by the process itself. If you do, no matter what you *name* it, it is an illusion. It is not surprising to discover that Parker sees as significant the fact that the word 'God' 'Names the ultimate source of the life of the community of faith as the ultimate source and end of all creaturely life.'[116]

His reality claim turns out to be the *name* which believers give to the transcendental dimension of their faith experience. The name itself is risked upon the validity of the concept:

> Transcendence, reality, and encounter, then, are three concepts that appear to be required if we are to speak of 'God' as a *name* for an 'other' whom we meet as that which supports and limits our existence as Christians and as human beings, and to which we respond in faith and love. If these three concepts are meaningless in a secular-technological world, then all talk of 'God' which names a reality beyond ourselves is ruled out along with all traditional theology.[117]

[115]*Ibid.*, p. 86. I think that it can be shown that Parker's 'logic' of transcendence has some of the characteristics of the Cartesian subject/object dichotomy. For Parker, the formal concept of Transcendence is empty without immanence. That is, the concept of the 'other' as 'beyond' can only have meaning if it is related to the subject, the one who 'thinks' the other. The immanence, which is the necessary context for the reality of the transcendent, is really the subjectivity of the self, so that transcendence can have no real 'subject' qualities of its own, but is always the 'object' beyond the subject. I would question all similar immanent-transcendent constructions on the same basis, and suggest that the actual relation of an 'other' to man's own 'otherness', can only be the action of a subject, and thus is transcendence, not immanence. This will be shown in Part Two when transcendence is explicated as the act of an agent.
[116]*Ibid.*, p. 82.
[117]*Ibid.*, p. 90.

But if, as Parker assumes he has demonstrated, the three concepts are not excluded by a secular style of life, then '*Analytically, neither transcendence nor its implicates are ruled out as useful concepts by the secular style of life.*'[118]

This is a very clever piece of reasoning! The three concepts, as Parker has worked them out, are all fashioned out of the context of man's existential life of faith, and thus they cannot be logically excluded from a secular life style. Given Parker's premise that both the form and content of transcendence as a reality of God are part of the context of faith-existence, it *should* analytically follow, that the realities which faith-existence encounter cannot be ruled out of such a life style! The fact that his final appeal is to the *usefulness* of the name 'God' as a transcendental reality of faith-existence, seems to me to indicate quite clearly, that, whether or not Parker is aware of it, his compulsion to continue to speak of a reality of God as a real 'otherness' beyond man's existence is primarily a regulative image to give psychological guarantee to existential truths. Strip away this, and Parker's language of transcendence collapses into 'immanent transcendence', much as Stevenson indicated.

I should like to make it perfectly clear at this point that my purpose has been to carry out the 'last analysis' in certain claims for the transcendence of God. I am well aware that if, and this is to anticipate, there is a reality which is 'wholly other' to man, and who has *named himself* in historical reality as 'God', then it is likely that our only way of speaking of God would be through a relational knowledge of him. That is, the context of which Parker speaks is not altogether irrelevant to our knowledge of God's reality. However, at this particular stage of my argument, this context must be submitted to the rigour of the 'last analysis' to determine at least what difference there would be in a God who is 'named' by man and one who could name himself. That is, to show the difference between 'out-and-out transcendence' and 'immanent transcendence'.

I must also explain that it would be a misunderstanding to conclude from the examples which I have selected for examination, that there are no claims for a transcendent God which do not collapse into immanent transcendence. Of course, I have selected those claims for transcendence which seemed to me to collapse, in order to support an affirmative answer to the question raised: in the last analysis, do not some claims made by contemporary theology for divine transcendence collapse into 'immanent transcendence?[119]

Now what has become obvious is that if there are any claims of divine transcendence which do not collapse into mere immanent trans-

[118]*Ibid.*, p. 92. Parker's emphasis.
[119]See above, p. 25.

cendence, they must be those which, in fact, are claims of out-and-out transcendence. And whether or not these claims can be sustained is a question which will be taken up in the following chapter. What has also become obvious is that all claims for divine transcendence which are not claims for a 'wholly other' God in an out-and-out sense, must, in the last analysis, now give some answer to my second question, which I will now discuss: Can we continue to speak of God at all, if the concept is being used simply as a regulative model to give psychological guarantees to existential truths?[120]

I consider this question to be the basic one for this chapter, and the one which exposes in the clearest way the crisis of transcendence which I have been exploring. Nor is it simply a rhetorical question, but it is one that must be taken with seriousness and faced with resolution. I suspect that many have come up against it and experienced a failure of theological nerve. Alistair Kee is not one of these.

In his book, *The Way of Transcendence*, subtitled, 'Christian Faith Without Belief in God',[121] Kee makes a distinction between faith and belief. The former he holds to be commitment taken by man in the face of his ultimate concern for life, the latter is a religious belief in God. While faith can be the result of a man's decision, belief cannot—one either believes in God or does not. As a result, in a secular age, when belief in God has become problematic, such belief cannot be assumed to be the presupposition for one's Christian faith. To demand faith is one thing, Kee concludes, but to demand belief is impossible, because changing one's belief is not something which can be brought about by an act of will.[122] Kee's concern in writing his book is to further a secular faith in Christ without going by way of belief in God:

> The future of Christianity is not viable unless we can find a way of presenting it which includes the old doctrine of God, but does not demand belief in God as a prior condition of becoming a Christian.[123]

I must confess that I find Kee's argument at times confusing, and at points absurd. But he consistently hews to one line, and that is categorical elimination of God as a reality of transcendence for man. When he states that he wishes to 'include the old doctrine of God' in his a-theistic Christian faith, this can best be explained by quoting him with regard to the content of the doctrine of God for Israel as recorded in the Old Testament:

[120]See above, p. 25.
[121]Penguin Books, Middlesex, England, 1971.
[122]*The Way of Transcendence*, p. ix.
[123]*Ibid.*, p. x.

It is not the history of something done to them or shown to them,
but rather the course of their growing awareness of the true nature
of the world, and of social and individual existence. It is the history
of Israel's understanding of transcendence.'[124]

Here we see the convergence of two concepts in Kee's thought: the
experiencing of life's ultimate concerns, which he calls 'secular transcendence'; and, the embodiment, or incarnation of whatever *expression*
was given to these concerns, which he calls the doctrine of God. These
experiences of secular transcendence were at one time expressed as 'God
concepts', but that was only a cultural and religious form of self-
expression. The *same* realities of secular transcendence were expressed
in an eminent way in the life of Jesus. 'What Jesus inherited was
the ancient convenant choice, which we have interpreted in terms of
transcendence.... "Jesus is the very incarnation of the way of transcendence".... Jesus Christ is the norm of what is entailed in the way
of transcendence.'[125] It thus follows that:

> Christian faith means commitment, with ultimate concern, to that
> which came to expression in Jesus Christ; Christian theology is the
> systematic reflection on what is entailed in commitment, with ultimate
> concern, to that which came to expression in Jesus Christ.[126]

Because Kee assumes that 'God' was the *name* religious people at one
time gave to the reality which they experienced in a faith-existence type
of encounter, he concludes that, not only is that now shown to be a mis-
naming of the reality, but that it is no longer useful as a regulative
model.[127] His position, then, is precisely the one suggested as the inevitable and necessary consequence of a concept of a transcendent God
used merely as a regulative model: in the last analysis, can we continue
to speak of the transcendence of God at all? Kee's answer is no, we
cannot, and need not.[128]

Kee looks at all modern attempts to redefine transcendence in terms
of a concept of God and judges them to have failed, and their failure, in

[124]*Ibid.*, p. 213.
[125]*Ibid.*, pp. 208, 211, 218.
[126]*Ibid.*, p. 193.
[127]*Ibid.*, p. 203.
[128]The question as to why Kee continues to hang on to the word 'transcendence'
can only be answered by his continuing emphasis on the 'two ways' of secular
life. These two ways, he finds, correspond to the way of the Gentiles and the
way of the people of Israel in the Old Testament. The Gentiles took the way of
immanence, Israel the way of transcendence, which was the way of covenant
(*ibid.*, pp. 202ff). While Kee admits that this is an historical oversimplification,
it serves for him as a model to illustrate a lower and higher way of secular life.
The higher way—the way of transcendence—is the way of ultimate concern
expressed as a value judgment that 'things are not as they seem'. *Ibid.*, pp. 228ff.

his eyes, is precisely the point at which they insert a theistic condition into their explication of Christian faith.[129]

While Kee's position cannot really be taken seriously as a viable alternative in the discussion on the crisis of transcendence, it is highly significant for two reasons: (1) it exposes the inconsistency of a certain type of contemporary theology which can neither face up to the demands of out-and-out transcendence, nor relinquish the use of transcendence as a regulative image to guarantee the reality of existential truths. In a certain sense, Kee's thought represents the *reductio ad absurdum* of a theology without the transcendence of God. (2) Kee has brought the crisis of transcendence into clearer focus by sharpening up the alternatives. His dismissal of Bonhoeffer, in an extended footnote, as useless for contemporary theology because of his unreserved commitment to the transcendence of God, confirms my own conviction that the use of Bonhoeffer to advance a secular theology without a transcendent God was, in fact, a misuse. And, to turn Kee's conclusion around, I would suggest that Kee has helped us to see that to return for a closer look at Bonhoeffer's concept of transcendence may 'be the only way forward for 'theology now'.[130]

It is time to pick up some threads left hanging in the rough fabric of this chapter. The crisis of transcendence is a crisis of reality—a crisis which I have stubbornly radicalized into a real loss of transcendence, felt like the loss of a warm body in the face of a chill wind, upon which moves the silence of the gods. The lost lane-end into heaven seemed to appear momentarily—the ghost was kept alive in order not to

---

[129]In Kee's eyes, the most radical theology merits the somewhat derisive epithet 'reformist'. Heidegger is suspect at the point that being becomes Being (*ibid.*, p. 33). Tillich relapses when he speaks about 'God above God' (p. 35); Macquarrie becomes hopelessly involved with theism when he changes 'holy being' to 'Holy Being' then finally calls it 'God' (p. 50). When it comes to the prophets of secular theology, Kee finds them all to be false prophets. Bishop J. A. T. Robinson and Harvey Cox are at best 'reformers' who can only speak to those who already find it possible to believe in God (pp. 64ff). The 'Death of God' theologians are 'irresponsible' for promising so much and at the end resuscitating the corpse (pp. 78ff); Altizer is an un-repentant Barthian, whose 'anticipation', at the end, of the God who was known earlier, betrays his hankering after theism (pp. 94-95). Paul van Buren, whose position Kee considers to be the most consistently radical, and which he terms 'reductionist', finally is revealed to have a 'positivism of the head but not of the heart'. Though he has given up the word 'God', he has not given up the concerns of theology (pp. 183ff).

[130]'Bonhoeffer, for all his talk about the false "religious premise" ... based his work on the simple religious premise of the existence of God. Although he recognized that, increasingly, fewer and fewer people would be able to believe in God, he made no attempt to interpret Christianity without reference to belief in God. ... It is for this reason that Bonhoeffer has been entirely ignored in this book ... this may be the only way forward for theology now.' *Ibid.*, pp. 186-187, n. 3.

slay the spirit. This was not theology—or was it?

The hidden agenda of the language of transcendence was patiently teased out, and behold it was spirit!—the inaccessible 'other', with no umbilical cord of flesh or mind, so that one could ascend, hand over hand, to emerge within. But spirit is a 'hard' reality in a world of soft shadowy bodies, or so it seemed in the first discovery. The question was, what would survive the insouciant gesture of the last analysis?

And so the 'thousand qualifications' were taken from the living thing and refiled under the categories of 'adjectives', 'nouns' and 'modifiers', so that only the verb was left—and now the *act* remains. And, yes, vulnerability is there too. The gap is wider than would be thought appropriate to any reasonable conclusion. No comfort here in the friendly 'limits' of human finitude, beyond which reality swims in unnecessary shape or form. *Within* these limits, not beyond them, we must speak of 'hard reality', as real as a leaf, a stone, an unfound door—but at the same time of Spirit.

This is the 'problem of God'.

Chapter II

The Problem of God

1 'The Problem of the Absolute Difference'

'The general form of propositions is: This is how things are.'—That is the kind of proposition that one repeats to oneself countless times. One thinks that one is tracing the outline of the thing's nature over and over again, and one is merely tracing round the frame through which we look at it. A *picture* held us captive. And we could not get outside it, for it lay in our language and language seemed to repeat it to us inexorably.[1]

Lying in our language, one syllable, like Melchizedek—without father or mother or genealogy—the word 'God' compels our constant fascination and our greatest frustration. It holds us captive, this picture, and defies our struggles to either walk away, or get behind it to touch its being. It is, as Gregor Smith confessed, a tormenting problem.[2]

But it would be a mistake to conclude that our disquietude with the word 'God' is a torment of language itself. That would lead us to the very kind of exercise against which Wittgenstein has warned us. Though it must be added that in writing these words, he inscribed a fitting epitaph to be placed over his own labours. The problem is not: what kind of assertion are we making when we say 'God exists as the Wholly Other'; but rather: how can we make any assertion *at all* about a reality that is 'wholly other'?[3]

Not everyone will accept the logic of transcendence which was pursued in Chapter I to the exclusion of all relativization, which led in the last

[1]L. Wittgenstein, *Philosophical Investigations*, p. 48.
[2]'The question which has so long tormented me, in what way we may speak of God as personal, and in what way impersonal (or as Being), may well be the kind of question that admits of no answer.' *The Doctrine of God*, p. 166.
[3]It should be made clear here that I am not using the expression 'wholly other' in the sense of a profound religious feeling of the numinous, of the *mysterium tremendum* with its creaturely 'shudder' in the *feeling* of a Wholly Other, as Rudolf Otto expounds the idea. Cf. *The Idea of the Holy*, Oxford University Press, London (1923), 1926, pp. 12ff, 25ff. My designation of God as the 'wholly other' will be expounded in terms of an active transcendence of Spirit, not a felt transcendence of religious consciousness.

analysis to the reality claim that only Spirit, as wholly other to man, could be the transcendence of God. Doubtless there are arguments which are compelling to some, by which they understand transcendence to be linked more plausibly to the reality of self-understanding. I do not say that they are held captive by the picture of transcendence, unable to get outside of it. I only say that I have examined their arguments and, in the last analysis, find them unsatisfying. Unsatisfying, not to an aesthetical, nor even to a logical intuition, but unsatisfying as a language of transcendence when up against the reality of Spirit, which makes claims upon me that I cannot relativize to my own existence. The question of the 'wholly other' is a question which can be anticipated and rejected, so that it does not actually arise as a problem. But that would mean that one could use a particular methodology to determine answers, not to seek out the right questions.[4] The question of the 'wholly other' seems to me to be the right question to ask, despite its 'torment', because it is a question of the reality of God.[5]

While it was the answer that tormented Gregor Smith, he possessed the gift of a particular lucidity in stating the problem:

> To find a way of asserting simultaneously the absolute difference of God from everything else, and his relation to everything else, without diminution of the difference, is without any doubt the key problem for theological thought today.[6]

One cannot put it more plainly than that. And I shall follow this formulation of the problem of God as the working outline for this chapter, taking up first of all the question of the absolute difference of God from everything else.

The assertion that God exists, and that his existence is a reality to be understood quite independently of other existing beings, seems to be a quite straightforward type of proposition. The idea of God as an existent (*das Seiende*) among other existents, while producing considerable metaphysical speculation, was not considered *an impossible* idea in metaphysical thinking up to our so-called modern period.[7]

---

[4]Cf. John Macmurray, *The Self as Agent*: 'I can formulate a series of questions to be answered through a process of reflection, and decide the order in which they shall be asked. What I cannot do is to determine in advance the answers that I shall get. These have to be discovered. For this reason the success of reflective activity depends largely upon a methodology—upon a systematic ordering of attention.' pp. 172-173.

[5]Kenneth Hamilton makes the point that Barth's criticism of liberalism was so devastating because it attacked its theory of reality. Over against faith in immanence, Barth set the declaration that God was Wholly Other—transcendent. *Revolt Against Heaven*, pp. 94-95.

[6]R. G. Smith, *The Doctrine of God*, p. 89.

[7]The 'modern period' in philosophic thought is generally assumed to have begun

The metaphysical presupposition that a divine being had its 'place' in the cosmos, toward which the Ptolemaic spheres were stepping stones, became untenable in the face of the irresistible humanism of the Renaissance. With Boccaccio, Montaigne, and Erasmus, a new view of reality emerged that was neither hierarchical nor sacramental. So that, with Renaissance humanism and Newtonian cosmology, the very notion of God became more difficult to comprehend.[8] The final mood of the Enlightenment was one of immanence, stressing both the continuity of the cosmos in which the idea of God had its place as a regulative principle, and the autonomy of *human* ideals and virtues in virtual identification with the idea of God.[9]

It was the great French philosopher, René Descartes, in the middle of the seventeenth century, who produced the foundation principle—'I think, therefore I am'—which changed the general pattern of philosophical thinking. From this principle emerged the concept that it is the process of thought itself which distinguishes between what is objective and what is subjective in experience. The activities of the self in spontaneously providing the form in which the object is to be determined, left reality with no objective basis for its determination. As a result, man is conceived of as a subject or 'mind' who thinks *about* the objective world, from which he distinguishes himself. Once the dichotomy between the subject and object had been introduced, and primacy given to the thinking subject, there was no way to hold reality together in the sense of an interaction between the mental and physical realms.[10] It is not difficult to find the fundamental problem emerging here of a concept of God as an 'existent', that is, as an object about which man as subject could think.

with the Renaissance, and more specifically, with the thought of Descartes. H. H. Rex, while oversimplifying the issue, nevertheless makes a quite valid point when he says: 'We live on this side of a rupture which divides the whole history of mankind into two sections; the one extending from the cavemen to the men of the Renaissance, and the other covering this post-Cartesian world of ours. On the surface it may seem preposterous to lump the cavemen, Plato and Michelangelo into one class, and the rest of us into another. And yet, so long as we fail to appreciate the full magnitude of this fact, we have understood very little about the nature of the modern secular world.' *Did Jesus Rise From the Dead?*, Blackwood and Janet Paul, 1967, p. 75. Cited by R. J. Blaikie, *'Secular Christianity' and God Who Acts*, p. 23. On the other hand, Heidegger asserts that the original Greek concept of reality as 'truth disclosing itself', was 'humanized' by Plato when truth was subordinated to an idea. Thus Heidegger draws a line from Plato through Aristotle, Aquinas, Descartes, Hegel, culminating in Nietzsche. Heidegger's own attempt to 'overcome' metaphysics is then an attempt to recover the original Greek concept of reality. Cf. Versényi, *Heidegger, Being, and Truth*, pp. 54ff.
[8]Cf. Edward Farley, *The Transcendence of God*, pp. 15ff.
[9]*Ibid.*, p. 19.
[10]Cf. J. Macmurray, *The Self as Agent*, pp. 31ff, and R. J. Blaikie, *'Secular Christianity' and God Who Acts*, pp. 16, 20ff.

But it remained for Immanuel Kant to make the final separation between thought and being. Kant concluded that the fatal error of idealism was its abstraction from empirical reality into a unity of consciousness, whereby thought could be grounded in itself.[11] Pure reason, said Kant, can only be extended to objects of possible experience, and can never be extended beyond the object of sense perception, that is, to know 'things in themselves'.[12] It was this 'infinite chasm' between the world of sense experience (phenomenal world) and the world of things as they really are in themselves (noumenal world), which Kant introduced to rid dogmatic metaphysics of its distortions and to silence objections to religion and morals. Thus Kant could say that he 'denied knowledge to make room for faith', by restricting the categories of pure thought to empirical realities.[13]

In his second critique, of Pure Practical Reason, Kant expounded a 'rational faith' which was expressed in terms of the moral law. It now becomes clear why he posited the absolute disjunction between things as they are in themselves and as they appear in sense experience. By placing the source of the moral law in the pure principles of reason, that is, in the noumenal, he has made faith inaccessible to reason, and therefore inaccessible for verification. If I act by inclination, I act as a member of the phenomenal world, basing my actions upon what can be empirically determined from the world of experience. But, if I act from duty (that is, in faith), I act as a member of the noumenal world, by conforming to a rule of reason.[14] It was in the freedom from determinism, which the noumenal world of things in themselves offered, that Kant located his idea of God. The result of this 'dis-objectifying' way of speaking of God is that God becomes a mere notion of morals, a notion which only has objective reality in terms of man's practical fulfilment of his moral duty. While Kant would accept the theoretical possibility of God's existence 'in himself', he held that it only had a regulative value as a principle of reason challenging man to objective moral action.[15] What Karl Jaspers was later to say was true already for Kant:

God is no object of knowledge, not conclusively inferable; yet the collapse of all proofs leaves no void, but an inexhaustible, ineffable consciousness of God.[16]

[11]I. Kant, *Critique of Pure Reason*, pp. 375, 377.
[12]*Ibid.*, p. 91.
[13]*Ibid.*, p. 29.
[14]J. Macmurray, *The Self as Agent*, pp. 53ff, 65.
[15]I. Kant, *Critique of Practical Reason*, p. 89.
[16]Cited by H. Gollwitzer, *The Existence of God as Confessed by Faith*, SCM Press, London, 1965, p. 68.

The Problem of God 43

In these strands of modern philosophic thought, we find revealed
quite conclusively the source of the contemporary problem for theology,
and why, given these metaphysical presuppositions, talk of God existing
as the Wholly Other is condemned to failure by the very nature of the
reality by which we seek to designate God. Heinrich Ott formulates the
problem of the absolute difference of God in this way:

> God, as the Lord and Creator, as the 'Wholly Other', can never be
> an object. No objective assertions may be made about him, such as
> are made about objects which we find in the world. As a consequence,
> theological thinking and speaking presents a special case, in that
> it is condemned to failure, as it were, by the very reality with which
> it concerns itself, because it can take no other form than the objective.
> Thus the theologian (and also the preacher) must continue to speak
> objectively. There remains no other choice for him—except to keep
> silent. He must take upon himself this frustration of his speaking
> and must understand his speech as indirect communication, or, to put
> it more precisely, an objective indication of an utterly nonobjective,
> existential act of faith, about which otherwise no more could be
> said.[17]

Out of the dilemma created by this formulation of the problem of
God, a somewhat tortured third alternative has arisen, without basically
questioning the assumptions upon which the dilemma arose. God is protected from an objectifying type of thinking by not ascribing 'being'

[17]Heinrich Ott, 'The Problem of Non-Objectifying Thinking and Speaking in
Theology', *Journal for Theology and the Church*, Vol. 3, 1967, p. 112. It must
be made clear that Ott has formulated this statement of the problem as the
typical problem for theology today. He does not feel that the reasoning back of
this way of stating the problem really hits the essence of the matter, although Ott
himself does not want to say that God is an object, nor that human speaking
of God is not frustrated by the reality of God himself. What Ott offers as an
alternative is a theologized version of the later Heidegger, in which Ott seeks to
overcome the subject/object dichotomy by getting behind it to an 'object-less'
objectivity. Heidegger says that 'back tracking' to the essence of metaphysics
releases the object of thought into its 'object'—the opposite may then remain
object-less. *Essays in Metaphysics*, pp. 56-57. It is this kind of object-less thinking which Ott calls faith: '...the intelligible enactment of human self-understanding which takes account of itself not in the consciousness of the objectifiable,
but only in the special objectivity of the symbol.' 'The Problem of Non-Objectifying Thinking and Speaking in Theology', p. 151. What Ott is after is a new
kind of objectivity which can be achieved by taking Heidegger's concept of
the ontological difference between Being and being as an 'object-less' reality
which is actually 'opposite' to man (*Dasein*), but which cannot be thought, and
therefore is not caught in the subject/object dilemma. The inherent problem of
Ott's position is the fact that 'object-less' objectivity is essentially non-cognitive,
and therefore offers no rationale for the reality of God.

44   *The Crisis of Transcendence for the Doctrine of God*

to him, as that would imply that he is an existent (*das Seiende*) along with other existents and, as such, an 'object' of thought. And yet, this alternative would seek to avoid pure subjectivism by speaking of the 'experienced non-objective reality of God'.[18]

In somewhat the same way, Gregor Smith attempts to speak of God as 'impersonal Being', and of 'impersonal Spirit' which lies between the I and the Thou, and by this indicates his desire to avoid this very dilemma.[19] The very concept of the personal, which for a time seemed so promising as an analogical way of speaking of the reality of God, has more recently tended to be seen as inadequate, precisely because it seems to 'objectify' God. The reasoning behind this is simply that as all human personal relation includes a dimension of relation as I-It, as well as I-Thou, we have no concept of person which does not include the objectification of the other as an It.[20] And we are not really helped much by Martin Buber's suggestion that if God 'was not a person in Himself, He, so to speak, became one in creating man, in order to love man and be loved by him—in order to love me and be loved by by me'.[21] This raises more questions than it answers, and is best regarded as a rather curious way of speaking, to say the least.

One attempt to escape this impasse has been made by Fritz Buri, who suggests that 'personhood', *being* itself, is non-objectifiable:

In the enactment of responsible personhood a leap is made, a leap

[18]Cf. Paul van Buren, who says: 'It seems, however, that neither Ogden nor Bultmann has other human beings in mind when they speak of "experienced nonobjective reality". They seem to mean "God", or the "Transcendent",... This extremely odd use of the word "experience", which is ordinarily used of that which can be sensed in some way, suggests a confusion of categories, a mixing of language-games.' *The Secular Meaning of the Gospel*, Penguin Books, Middlesex, 1968, pp. 73-74. Van Buren, of course, has caught the impropriety of accepting the assumptions of a dichotomy between sense experience and the noumenal world and yet attempting to form a synthesis.

[19]'I still think that there is a third alternative, which is neither that of an objectifying metaphysic nor that of an immanentist process view of history.... Man is not simply a doer, he is primarily a receiver. He receives the reality which is possible in each encounter.... This reality is neither himself nor the other; but in its entirety it lies between the two. There is a hinterland here which cannot be explicated.' R. G. Smith, *The Doctrine of God*, p. 177; cf. also, pp. 165-166.

[20]Cf. Ronald W. Hepburn, *Christianity and Paradox*, pp. 24-59, who questions the adequacy of the personal encounter model for a doctrine of God precisely because all I-Thou is also I-It. The problem which a 'two-level ontology' of the personal (i.e., material and spiritual) raises for theology is discussed by Johannes Körner, 'Die transcendente Wirklichkeit Gottes', *Zeitschrift für Theologie und Kirche*, Vol. 63, 1966, pp. 473-495, esp. pp. 491-492.

[21]*Eclipse of God*, Harper and Row, The Cloister Library, New York, 1952, p. 60.

out of objectivity into non-objectivity. Personhood in its enactment is and remains non-objectifiable.[22]

Thus, for Buri, it is not simply a question of how one can speak of the being of God without objectifying being, but in *no* sense can being, even the being of persons, be 'conditioned' by objectivity. Only when man enacts his being in the form of responsibility does he become 'personal being'. He finds his foundation for a language about the unconditioned being of God, as wholly other, in the unconditioned reality of all personal being:

> What is at stake for us is neither a demythologized Christ, nor a Christ without myth, nor a Christ without God. Instead we seek to validate the responsibility of man in the unconditionedness of his non-objectifiability as the foundation of our discourse about God. We seek to do this... in a theology of responsibility.[23]

There is a Voice which calls man to responsibility, according to Buri. This voice is transcendence, that is, it is unconditioned by the objective world in which it takes its form. 'God', Buri concludes, 'is the mythological expression for the unconditionedness of personal responsibility.'[24] It is clear that Buri is making an attempt to escape the dilemma of a subject/object dichotomy by advancing his notion of 'enactment' as the non-objective and unconditioned reality of being. But what is not clear, is how Buri can actually make a distinction between the reality of God and the reality of man. There seems to be only one reality, that of the non-objectifiable dynamic of personal being, in which the enactment of responsibility (faith) is at the same time a representation of the Voice (God). Buri does not wish to relativize the Voice by conditioning it with objective personal being.[25] But as a result, he relativizes the reality of God to the enacted-faith of the existing subject. Buri cannot speak of the 'voice' apart from the enactment of responsible personhood. Because he has made this enactment of personhood 'non-objective', that is, unconditioned by the historical,

---

[22]'How Can We Still Speak Responsibly of God?', *McCormick Quarterly*, Chicago, January, 1968, Vol. 21, pp. 185-197, esp. p. 191.

[23]*Ibid.*, p. 192.

[24]*Ibid.*, p. 193.

[25]'We hold fast to the *persona Dei loquentis* not in the form of a proof for the existence of God or by using any kind of *analogia entis*. Then it would again be a question of false objectification and relativization. However, we do hold fast to it in the form of an *analogia fidei*. Here by faith is meant nothing else than the unconditioned knowledge-of-one's-responsibility as it occurs in enactment.... Responsible personhood is that being in which the *personare* occurs, the sounding forth and the penetration of the voice of the unconditioned.' F. Buri, *Ibid.*, p. 194.

contingent form in which it appears, he feels that he has made it possible to speak of the reality of God in a non-objective way.

Gollwitzer's comment with regard to this kind of an existentialist call-and-response theology is highly appropriate: ' "God" is admitted by that postulate to be a hypostatization which dissipates when examined more closely.'[26]

Gollwitzer himself is not happy with the concept of God as person. He feels that this can all too easily be understood as an objectification of God in the sense of 'being to hand' (*Vorhandensein*), that is, at the disposal of human thought the same as other persons.[27] Nor is he happy with an attempt to 'transcend' theism by 'swallowing up' God in the relation and reducing the subject/object dichotomy into its single pole of human subjectivity:

> Those who say 'encounter' must not shrink from also saying 'object', and thus from speaking of an objectivity of God; nor must they seek to banish the subject-object pattern from theology lock, stock and barrel, but must carefully state the sense in which they wish to transcend it and the sense in which it remains. For indeed in its simplest form it means no more than the confrontation of two factors, one of which is the addressee of the activity proceeding from the other.[28]

Gollwitzer thus suggests his own 'third alternative' to the problem originally set out by Ott. In criticizing Herbert Braun for failing to make a distinction between the speculative theism of the ancient world and the Biblical witness to God in theistic terms, and thus attempting to posit the reality of God 'beyond theism and atheism', Gollwitzer states that 'To describe the Bible's faith in God as "theism" is as inescapable as it is inappropriate.'[29] It is inescapable; for the God who acts in the history of the world, in order to enter into a 'worldly' relation with his people, has actually encountered man 'person to person.' However, to call such Christian faith 'theism' is inappropriate for it subsumes faith and God under the general category of religion as a special case. Thus Gollwitzer will not surrender a concept of God's objectivity, though he carefully qualifies it from signifying an objectivity in the Cartesian sense of an 'objective entity' at the disposal of man's thought. 'He [God]

[26]H. Gollwitzer, *The Existence of God*, p. 63.

[27]"God is not a person—not at any rate in the sense that by describing him thus we could classify him under a category of entities known to us and in that way make him conceivable to us. As he does not come under any other general concept, including that of the gods, so he does not come under that of person either. *Deus non est in genere*, ... "God is not one of a kind." God is God...." H. Gollwitzer, *Ibid.*, p. 163.

[28]*Ibid.*, p. 48.

[29]*Ibid.*, p. 43.

does not belong in the list of what is, not even at the head of it as the "highest Being", the *summum ens*.'[30]

Gollwitzer, instead, speaks of God as the *subject* who confronts us in the midst of our earthly historical reality, and though such a concept is anthropomorphic, *all* our concepts are anthropomorphic, and thus no concept is adequate for speaking of God. The reality of God is his reality as subject who stands over against us.[31] God is the Thou that stands apart from us in the encounter with him. And with this notion, Gollwitzer can speak of objectivity as the *Gegenständlichkeit* of God. It is 'objectiveness' in the sense of one reality standing in a relation of being opposite to (*gegen*) the other.

In the midst of the tortured qualifications which surround the question—does God exist?—it is more than a little refreshing to hear Gollwitzer say: 'It is a sensible question and we do it an injustice, to our own detriment, if we at once impute to it the foolish sense of asking about the being of God like that of a thing in space.'[32] God exists as the reality of the Subject who addresses me, through his concrete acts in history of an anthropomorphic character. The concept of God as 'wholly other', is handled by Gollwitzer with a certain delicacy. In the sense that God is the Subject who stands apart from me in the speech-act in which he discloses himself to man, he is totally other. But this can never be known in a disinterested way, nor asserted as a neutral statement of fact. In other words, it cannot be an indicative statement, but only a vocative utterance. To say that God is the Subject who stands in a relationship of absolute otherness to me, is to confess that my situation has already been changed by that reality. It is, therefore, basically a 'faith statement.'[33]

In pondering Gollwitzer's argument, which surely must be one of the most adequate statements about the existence of God we have in contemporary theology, I have the feeling that Gollwitzer may be slightly 'terrorized' by the ghost of a subject/object type of thought. His concern to qualify an act of God as an inescapable but inappropriate anthropomorphism seems to betray an anxiety caused by a glance over his shoulder in the direction of Descartes.[34]

[30]*Ibid.*, p. 204.
[31]*Ibid.*, p. 204.
[32]*Ibid.*, p. 240.
[33]*Ibid.*, pp. 213ff.
[34]This seems to be borne out in Johannes Körner's critical essay on the Gollwitzer-Braun debate, 'Die transcendente Wirklichkeit Gottes'. Körner argues that Gollwitzer's attempts to speak of God's existence in himself, as a given reality prior to and apart from his relation to man, is virtually meaningless. The reason is that Gollwitzer has already bracketed off knowledge of God from a general and universal type of reality by suggesting a special, or theological ontology of God's existence (p. 489). If, as Körner suggests, 'Man stands, therefore,

Why should an objective act in the sense of a concrete space-time reality be considered an 'Objectifying' way of speaking at all? Even if one is speaking of an act of God? Perhaps, only if one goes on the assumption that thought is the primary reality of being and actually has an objective act at its disposal, that is, to determine it by thinking it as *IT*. Gollwitzer's reliance on 'existence-utterance' to speak of the reality of God as wholly other, does not really escape the subject/object dilemma, but rather presupposes it.

The hidden problem which I am attempting to tease out into the open is made more explicit by Schubert Ogden in his essay on 'Theology and Objectivity'.[35] Ogden's purpose is to examine the 'non-objectifying' concept as it is used in the assertion that all theological utterances about the existence of God must be non-objectifying. Ogden suggests that the natural 'home' of the German infinitive *objektivieren* and its English equivalent 'to objectify', is a certain strand of post-Kantian philosophy which divides cognitive awareness into two classes: (1) 'The original, internal cognitive awareness of our own existence in relation to the manifold reality encountering us', and (2) 'Our derived, external perception of reality distinct from ourselves as the object of our ordinary sense experience.'[36]

Theological utterances, says Ogden, properly belong to the first class of cognitive awareness, while empirical assertions of a scientific nature are cognitive statements in the second sense. Therefore, concludes Ogden, theological statements about God are strictly non-objectifying, as they are existence-utterances, and as such, are not verifiable in the objective forms of science.[37] Ogden assumes that there would be general agreement with this conclusion, not only among existentialist theologians, but with the vast majority of contemporary theologians as well. Ogden further asserts that 'there is a difference *in principle* between the thinking and speaking of science and the thinking and speaking proper to theology....'[38]

originally in a *hermeneutical* relation to God' (p. 489), no statements at all can be made about him apart from that relation. What Körner suggests, therefore, is that Gollwitzer's position logically implies a limitation of all knowledge about God to the concrete reality of the person of Christ. 'The word "God" is consequently a formal concept, to which as such, no personal reality reaches ... the designation "God" which comes forth in an incessant way, is to be attributed no personality of its own alongside of Jesus Christ.' (p. 494, my translation). The point of Körner's argument, as it relates to this discussion, is not his own conclusions, but the fact that he has detected, in Gollwitzer's desire to avoid 'objectifying' ways of speaking of God as personal, a more radical dichotomy between objective and existential reality than Gollwitzer would like to admit.

[35]*Journal of Religion*, pp. 175-195.
[36]*Ibid.*, pp. 177-178.
[37]*Ibid.*, p. 178.
[38]*Ibid.*, p. 178, my emphasis.

Ogden's further clarifications of the sense in which one may speak objectively of the existence of God, in no way overturns the assumption made by the above distinction, but takes place within it.[39] It seems clear to me, that this is precisely the situation with Gollwitzer as well. His alternative way of speaking of God's objectiveness (*Gegenständlichkeit*) is tortured by the same restrictions imposed upon him by his assumption, without examination, of the distinction which exists *in principle* between internal and external cognitive awareness.

If there is one point at which modern theology seems to lose its nerve, it is precisely when it comes to questioning the split in our culture between pure science and social science.[40] T. F. Torrance interprets this split as a radical disjunction between explanation (*Erklären*) and understanding (*Verstehen*).[41] This is the distinction which Ogden says exists *in principle* between internal and external perception. When explanation is split off from understanding, each cognitive process suffers distortion:

We recall that human concepts have a bi-polar structure through correlation with the object and correlation with the subject. If this polarization of conceptuality gets broken up we are apt to fall into a false dichotomy between the conceptual and the non-conceptual, construing the latter as a non-knowing relation to the object, and placing the former entirely within the power of our active reason.... This is the development, taking its rise from the radical dualism of post-Cartesian philosophy, which has worked itself out in Neo-Protestant thought into the kind of agnosticism that is so familiar to us today.[42]

The very core of rationality (that is, a cognitive relation to reality) is the capacity to respond appropriately to the nature of that which objecti-

[39]Within the existential form of cognitive awareness, Ogden makes a further distinction between an *existentielle* (existential) and an *existential* (existentialistic) perception. The latter form is objectifying as it has to do with existence only indirectly. It objectifies by creating a universal 'doctrine' of existence. Ogden would accept this as a valid way of speaking 'objectively' of God. On the other hand Ogden rejects the non-cognitive way of speaking about God represented by the reduction of the logical statements to statements about historical perspective (e.g. van Buren): 'Whatever else Christians have usually supposed themselves to be doing in proclaiming their faith, whether in personal confession, prayer, preaching, or teaching, they surely believed they were somehow responding cognitively to a divine reality radically different from themselves, in whose gracious initiative and approach alone their proclamation has its basis and object.' *Ibid.*, p. 186. Thus, Ogden wants to continue to speak about *God*, not about 'discernment-situations' in which the word 'God' can be replaced by a 'blik'. But he also wants to avoid the dilemma he accuses Bultmann of falling in to, that of making faith dependent upon an historical particularity concerning Jesus of Nazareth.
[40]Cf. T. F. Torrance, *God and Rationality*, p. 104.
[41]*Ibid.*, p. 104.
[42]*Ibid.*, p. 20.

fies itself to us.[43] Therefore, a difference 'in principle' between theological and scientific knowledge, with the former held to be non-objective while the latter is objective, is an irrational assertion. It is a failure of theological nerve to accept this philosophical assumption without question. It remains, of course, to be seen what kind of rationale inherently exists in the relation of God as 'wholly other' to man.[44] But one cannot turn back from the attempt to discover this rationale on the assumption that such an attempt is 'condemned to failure, as it were, by the very reality with which it concerns itself,...'[45]

The basic problem which determined, at least at the outset, the shape of this part of the chapter, was the problem of how to assert the absolute difference of God from everything else, but simultaneously, assert his relation to everything else. It has become clear that Gregor Smith's statement of the problem contains an unusually keen grasp of the dilemma facing modern theology. For Gollwitzer, as we saw, was able to state quite consistently the absolute difference of God, but not *from everything else!* He could only express the absolute difference in terms of a relation which faith had already recognized. Of course Gollwitzer could say that faith enables one to *say* that God is related to everything else and thus is absolutely different in that relation. This is what Körner calls the original 'hermeneutical relation to God' which God sovereignly makes clear through his Word of creation.[46] But that seems to be cheating a bit. What Gregor Smith clearly had in mind was the kind of assertion that was indicative, not merely a vocative existence-utterance. The 'simultaneous' aspect of the formulation cannot be made the hinge on which the absolute difference turns inward towards the relation of faith. That is, a mere reciprocity between God and man of a transcendent sort which really does not also turn towards history.

If Gregor Smith took the 'absolute difference' with utter seriousness, he took the 'everything else' with no less radical a concern. 'The category

---

[43]*Ibid.*, p. 52. Cf. also, J. Macmurray, *Reason and Emotion*, Faber and Faber., London, 1935, who says: 'The capacity to love objectively is the capacity which makes us persons. It is the ultimate source of our capacity to behave in terms of the object. It is the core of rationality.' p. 32.

[44]Cf. R. J. Blaikie: 'The ultimate problem of modern theology ... is not really the problem of God and His existence, as is often said, it is the problem (which theology shares with all modern thought) of *action* and its rational possibility: the problem, therefore, of how the existence of *persons* can be rationally acknowledged.' *'Secular Christianity' and God Who Acts*, p. 181. I feel that Blaikie is essentially correct here. It seems to me that only in a concept of person as agent, can the two poles of subjective and objective be distinguished without breaking the rational bond between them. This will be taken up in Part Two.

[45]H. Ott, 'The Problem of Non-Objectifying Thinking and Speaking in Theology', p. 112.

[46]J. Körner, 'Die transcendente Wirklichkeit Gottes', p. 489.

of history must include God,...'[47] Or, as he put it in another way, God must include history.

It is the second part of this formulation that must occupy us now—the absolute difference *from everything else*. The inner logic of the problematic does seem to lie in the concept of simultaneity, but that must not be used too soon to escape false dilemmas. Even as the problem of the 'wholly other' has been shown to be, not an intrinsic dilemma posed by the nature of the reality itself, but rather, one part of a problematic with an essentially rational core, the problem of the 'everything else' must be examined to see why it appears to have no place for the 'wholly other'.

2 'The Problem of "Everything Else"'

The angels keep their ancient places;
Turn but a stone, and start a wing!
'Tis ye, 'tis your estranged faces,
That miss the many-splendoured thing.[48]

There are some who would say that no stone has been left unturned. The earth is familiar and polluted; the moon has felt the shadow of man, suffers his footprints silently. The planets yield their secrets to unblinking metallic eyes at low altitudes. We know the temperature of the sun, the specific gravity of the stars, the way to the heavens—and back. Once upon a time, the sound of divinity could be heard upon the night air, men heard the voices of the gods, devils and angels mingled freely, though mysteriously, with the goings on of flesh and blood people. But now, is it true—that the world has become deadly serious, and 'secularized man no longer engages in this sacred play'[49]

There is, it is true, a new way of looking at the earth since Nietzsche. There is a certain 'profaneness' to the cosmos, which seems at least honest in its pretentions, even if it is 'dread-full' in its implications. History, Bultmann tells us, has closed its gates to the intervention of forces from beyond, and man has closed the temple of the self against unknown forces acting from within.[50] The stories of God acting on the stage of history and communicating from heaven with man on earth have now become mythological because they are impossible.[51] 'Modern' man now

[47]*The Doctrine of God*, p. 166.
[48]Francis Thompson, 'The Kingdom of Heaven', *Selected Poems of Francis Thompson*, Burns and Oates, London, 1907, pp. 132-133.
[49]K. Miskotte, *When the Gods are Silent*, p. 2.
[50]'Modern men take it for granted that the course of nature and history, like their own inner life and their practical life, is nowhere interrupted by the intervention of supernatural powers.' R. Bultmann, *Jesus Christ and Mythology*, p. 16.
[51]The word 'mythological' is here used in the technical sense that Bultmann speaks of myth: 'The whole conception of the world which is presupposed in

knows that there are no angels hiding behind stones, no space in the cosmos where a divine being resides, and no supernatural act which breaks the closed continuum of human history.

This is not the place to dispute such 'knowledge', or even to question the existence of so-called modern man.[52] The question germaine to this discussion is this: is there, in fact, a correlation between this modern 'profaneness' of the world and the concept of God as 'wholly other' in his transcendence?

To this point, we have consistently followed the path which led to the assertion that the reality of God can be only the reality of one 'wholly other' to man. Our path began with the claim that the loss of such transcendence is a *real* loss, not simply a striking symbolization of an existential mood, the logic of the language of transcendence has insufficient power to place a transcendent reality at the *limits* of human thought and experience without, at the same time, placing it within the process enclosed by the limits. Not even a sacred god-like figure at the limits of our existence can be a comfort any longer—there is an *absolute* difference between the ghost of a god and the Spirit. For the Spirit is itself the limit which no self-transcendence can reach, and yet whose reality must not be ghostly, but real, and independent of the indirect light coming from other realities. This led us to accept the assertion of Gregor Smith, that the reality of God means his 'absolute difference from everything else'.

It seems difficult to escape the conclusion that with the absolute difference of God from everything else, it is no longer possible for 'everything else' to remain sacred in any sense of the word. The utter profaneness of the cosmos is demanded by the assertion of God's absolute otherness. That is, the dialectic of the sacred and the profane at the phenomenological level can no longer be considered to be a struggle to hold on to the reality of God. Rather than pointing to a loss of God, the loss of the sacred from the world is itself a form of 'god-

the preaching of Jesus as in the New Testament generally is mythological; i.e. the conception of the world as being structured in three stories, heaven, earth and hell; the conception of the intervention of supernatural powers in the course of events; and the conception of miracles, especially the conception of the intervention of supernatural powers in the inner life of the soul, the conception that men can be tempted and corrupted by the devil and possessed by evil spirits.' *Jesus Christ and Mythology*, p. 15.

[52]For an analysis of the 'modern man' construct as a presupposition of contemporary theology, cf. Arnold Loen, *Secularization—Science Without God?*, SCM Press, London (1965), 1970, pp. 160-165. Loen suggests that, while there is no such figure as 'modern man', there is a presupposition of reality as the 'self cohesion of effects' common to much modern thought. This presupposition, Leon maintains, is in direct antipathy to the one of the Gospel, so that no 'change in the categories' of Biblical thought will suffice to communicate the reality of God to the reality of modern man who holds this basic assumption.

lessness' which follows from taking seriously the absolute difference of
God from the world. And it is this form of 'godlessness' which demands
to be taken seriously as a profaneness which points to the reality of God.[53]
If this indeed' is the inescapable answer to the question concerning
the apparent correlation between the concept of God as 'wholly other'
and a concept of the utter profaneness of the world, then it is an answer
which must be accepted as a further step in exposing the inner logic
of historical transcendence. The 'problem of everything else', as I have
put it, is the problem of how to understand the utter profaneness of
the world as pointing to the reality of God. This is the hidden problem
in the problem of the so-called 'secular theology'. It will not be my
intention to give an exhaustive survey of secularism as a cultural and
historical phenomenon.[54] Rather, I shall attempt to show that a failure
to understand this problem by historical theology delayed an authentic
secularity and at the same time precipitated a false secularism. The

[53]Cf. D. Bonhoeffer: 'There is the godlessness in religious and Christian clothing,
which we have called a hopeless godlessness, but there is also a godlessness
which is full of promise, a godlessness which speaks against religion and against
the Church. It is the protest against pious godlessness in so far as this has corrupted the Churches, and thus in a certain sense, if only negatively, it defends
the heritage of a genuine faith in God and of a genuine Church.' *Ethics*, Collins,
The Fontana Library (1949), 1970, p. 103. This concept of godlessness, or the
loss of the sacred, as pointing to the reality of God, should be distinguished from
the theory of Thomas J. J. Altizer, who suggests for theology a positive *coin-
cidentia oppositorum*, in which profaneness radically accepted becomes the radically
sacred. That is, in the midst of a negative and profane mood of existence, the
possibility of a certain ecstatic break-through occurs which he understands as
an incarnation of the sacred within history. Cf. *Mircea Eliade and the Dialectic of
the Sacred*, Westminster Press, Philadelphia, 1963, p. 15. Altizer's view is one of total
immanence, and rather than pointing to the reality of God, leads to the apotheosis
of irrational spirit in the name of the sacred.
[54]For a short survey of the history of secularism, together with an attempt to
classify the different meanings of the term in contemporary usage, cf. Larry
Shiner, 'The Concept of Secularization in Empirical Research', *The Journal for
the Scientific Study of Religion*, VI, 2, Fall, 1967, pp. 207-220. Cf. also, his essay,
'Toward a Theology of Secularization', *The Journal of Religion*, Vol. 45, 1965,
pp. 279-295. Martin Stallman gives an excellent discussion of the history of the
term 'secularization' in his book, *Was ist Säkularisierung?*, J. C. B. Mohr, Tübingen,
1960, pp. 5-17. Cf. also, Friedrich Gogarten, *Verhängnis und Hoffnung der
Neuzeit*, Siebenstern Taschenbuch Verlag, München und Hamburg (1958), 1966;
especially his distinction between secularism and secularity, pp. 134-148. Peter
L. Berger treats secularism as a sociological phenomenon rather than a scientific
or rational one, *A Rumour of Angels*, pp. 30ff; cf. also, his book, *The Sacred
Canopy—Elements of a Sociological Theory of Religion*, Doubleday, Garden
City/New York, 1967, pp. 105ff. For a treatment of secularism from the stand-
point of the language of the Bible, see Arnold Loen, *Secularization—Science
Without God?*, pp. 150ff. Gregor Smith gives a very fine exposition of the
history of the word 'secular' in *Secular Christianity*, pp. 135ff.

meaning of this distinction shall become clear, I trust, as the discussion proceeds.

It is generally agreed that the first serious confrontation between Christian faith as represented in the theological formulations of a first century cosmology was the crisis of Gnosticism. The thought forms in which Christian faith were first expressed were inherited, at least to some degree, from the Hellenistic world, where a rather sharp cleavage existed between the idea of a thing, which was considered the real, and the material event of a thing, which was only its image. The highly developed intellectual system of the Gnostics attempted to bridge this gap through an ascending construct of created beings.[55]

When some early Christian 'apologists' took up these concepts and synthesized a 'theological gnosticism', the Church was forced to articulate its fundamental understanding of the Incarnation.[56] Despite the brilliant attempts of Irenaeus in the second century and Athanasius in the fourth century, by the fifth century the dogmatic theology of the Church had lost its grip on history as testified to by the prophets and as fulfilled in Jesus Christ. Instead, it affirmed the world as the good and reasonable creation of God, with the help of Stoic ideas of the cosmos and their immanent teleology. So that it would be fair to say:

> In this way the world was re-naturalized to the order of creation and the redemptive action of God was supernaturalized to the order of redemption, and so the relationship between the two orders and natures, the natural and the supernatural, the reality of the world and the reality of God, became the discursive problem.[57]

[55]Our most detailed knowledge of the complex system of thought known as Gnosticism comes from the writings of Irenaeus, Bishop of Lyons during the last quarter of the second century, who wrote a treatise consisting of five books under the title *Adversus haereses*; see *Irenaeus Against Heresies*, Ante-Nicene Christian Library, Vols. I and II, T. and T. Clark, Edinburgh, 1868. Valentinus was the foremost advocate of Gnosticism from a Christian standpoint. The Christian Gnostics were generally concerned with the salvation of the inner, spiritual man. Man's true self, the Ego (*nous*) must be liberated from the darkness of this world and the prison of the flesh. Man's true self, according to the Gnostics, derives from the world of light, from above, and only through *gnosis*, which is brought to man from above, can man be freed and receive salvation. The Gnostic teachers combined a highly speculative and complicated system of emanations from the Primordial Father (Paroarche) with an allegorical and typological use of the Bible to construct their 'theology'. Cf. J. T. Nielsen, *Adam and Christ in the Theology of Irenaeus of Lyons*, Van Gorcum & Co., N.V., Assen, The Netherlands, 1968, pp. 2ff. The significance of Gnosticism, at this point, is its attempt to solve the problem of God's absolute difference from everything else, and yet, his relation to everything else.

[56]Cf. T. F. Torrance, *Theological Science*, Oxford University Press, London, 1969, pp. 17ff.

[57]Hans Schmidt, 'The Cross of Reality?', *World Come of Age*, R. G. Smith (ed.), Collins, London, 1967, p. 252.

The interaction of God with the world became 'unthinkable' in the intellectual thought forms which separated concept from image. However, through a synthesis of Plotinian (Neoplatonic) notions of real and timeless truths existing as concepts, and Ptolemaic notions of the spheres of space, a 'Christian cosmology' emerged. Taking shape through the thought of Augustine, this view of reality can best be described as that of a sacramental universe, by which natural and physical events were considered to have meaning only as they pointed beyond themselves to a supernatural and spiritual realm of timeless truths. In this way, the gap between the reality of God and the world was bridged by a doctrine of infused grace, mediating between the supernatural and natural worlds. In the twelfth century, this medieval synthesis reached its highest expression in the thought of Thomas Aquinas, who introduced Aristotelian notions of metaphysics, binding concept and image together with a doctrine of analogy. All knowledge of God was conceived to be indirect, arising out of discursive thought which inferred the reality of God by analogy from the phenomena of sense experience.[58]

With the Reformation came the collapse of the medieval synthesis and the breaking asunder of the *corpus christianum*. The resulting segments —the *corpus Christi* and the world—constituted a unity which could be held together only by faith in the Lordship of Christ, who rules the two kingdoms. It was not Luther's intention to shatter the unity of the church, but to reach a higher synthesis than that of deity and nature, a synthesis of faith, in obedience to Word alone.[59] The world was given a new significance as the object of God's attention, thus possessing a reality of its own by virtue of the grace of the Creator.

If in the former outlook the world was interpreted in its attraction towards God, in the latter it was interpreted in God's action upon the world. In the former the danger lay in a world-denying movement (particularly apparent in monasticism and its sharp contrast between the religious and the secular), but in the latter the danger lay in a tendency to allow attention to the world to induce forgetfulness of God (as in modern secularism).[60]

Thus, in the seventeenth century, a new crisis emerged; with nature freed of divine 'final causes', the age of science could begin. Experimental inquiry, which sought to discover the intrinsic laws of nature, replaced the old methods of logical abstractions which forced eternal patterns of thought upon the process of nature. But with the new method came a new form of an older problem:

[58]Cf. T. F. Torrance, *Theological Science*, pp. 18, 66ff.
[59]Cf. D. Bonhoeffer, *Ethics*, pp. 94ff.
[60]T. F. Torrance, *Theological Science*, p. 67.

The Reformer's biblical faith in God had radically removed God from the world. The ground was thereby prepared for the efflorescence of the rational and empirical sciences, and while the natural scientists of the seventeenth and eighteenth centuries were still believing Christians, when faith in God was lost all that remained was a rationalized and mechanized world.[61]

As a result, continues Bonhoeffer, 'The people deemed that they had now come of age, that they were now capable of taking in hand the direction of their own internal and external history.'[62]

The origin and existence of secularism as a threat to the reality of God is usually traced to the events briefly summarized above, culminating in man's grasp for autonomy, and the absolute independence of the world from divine intervention. Only faith could hold God and the world together, and with the loss of faith, secularism had the field to itself.[63] It is this particular assumption that our initial assertion calls into question. For, if there is a correlation between God's absolute difference from the world and the utter profaneness of the world, the alternatives of secular or sacred can be only an oversimplification, and most certainly, trivialization of the problem.

There is an almost hidden clue to what we are searching for in something which Bonhoeffer says in this connection: 'The revolt of the natural against grace contrasts sharply here with that reconciliation of nature with grace which is found in the Roman heritage.'[64] The key seems to lie in the two concepts of revolt and reconciliation. Both imply a disjunction between two spheres of reality, which have some intrinsic antipathy to be overcome, or else they shall be split apart. This seems to be the situation Bonhoeffer has in mind:

> The division of the total reality into a sacred and a profane sphere, a Christian and a secular sphere, creates the possibility of existence in a single one of these spheres, a spiritual existence which has no

---

[61]D. Bonhoeffer, *Ethics*, p. 96.

[62]*Ibid.*, p. 100.

[63]This seems to be the assumption of Robert J. Blaikie, *'Secular Christianity' and God Who Acts, passim*, who can find only a pejorative significance in the word 'secular', as it points, in his opinion, to the presumptuous positivism of rationalism following the Enlightenment, where the action of God was excluded *a priori* from the plane of history. He thus groups all forms of secular theology in one category, without taking seriously the implications which the profaneness of the world seems to suggest. This is what Arnold Loen calls the 'fearful' approach to secularization. 'This [approach] sees secularization as a fateful destiny which has overtaken thought, condemning the wonders of creation to be increasingly eroded and robbed of their glory by scientific thinking and technical practice.' *Secularization*, p. 11.

[64]D. Bonhoeffer, *Ethics*, p. 91.

part in secular existence, and a secular existence which can claim autonomy for itself and can exercise this right of autonomy in its dealings with the spiritual sphere.[65]

If the autonomy of natural existence over and against a supernatural existence is the root of secularism, then that root must be traced back beyond the 'revolt' to the point at which the original reconciliation was fashioned. The question which must be examined a bit more in depth is: does the 'revolt' of secularism against the supernatural, by which human nature demands its own autonomy, point towards an artificial disjunction imbedded in the reconciliation itself? I suspect that it does. And I believe that this can be at least pointed out, without being diverted from the central issue with which this chapter is concerned.

It has already been suggested that Augustinian cosmology, with its attempt to bridge the gap between the supernatural and the natural, produced a form of infused grace. Because the nature of man was considered to be, in itself, an intractable substance, possessing no qualities of divine reality, the grace of God was conceived of as a supernatural 'addition' to nature, superseding its pure temporality, and infusing into it a reality of relation with the divine. The 'natural' man was, in this system of thought, separated from God by a religious deficiency which could be made up only by the added grace. This supernatural gift could, of course, be appropriated (or infused) only in a sacramental manner. The material symbols being the image of the *real*, or spiritual, grace.[66]

This is the 'reconciliation' to which Bonhoeffer referred, when he alluded to the relation of nature and grace in the Roman heritage. But this then is what the 'revolt' of secularism has exposed—the addition of grace to human nature is, in principle, secularist. That is, it posits a specific 'autonomy' to human nature which can be overcome only by divine grace. The infusion of grace in a supernatural way alters the natural man so that he becomes a religious man. However, hidden within this reconciliation, sulks the autonomous natural man! And secularism is one way of seeking the recovery of this autonomy by denying the addition of supernatural grace, and, at the same time, asserting man's freedom to follow his own interests and find his own destiny. The root of secularism in this sense, then, is a Christian anthropology which makes a distinction between human nature and religious nature. Once the dis-

---

[65]*Ibid.*, pp. 196-197.

[66]Cf. T. F. Torrance, *God and Rationality*: 'Once a gap between the conceptual and the non-conceptual has been posited in this way, it will not do to appeal to "infused grace" which in a roundabout way is said to give objective and intelligible content to faith in spite of the alleged "non-evidence" of the divine Being. Far from getting rid of the fatal dualism it derives from the Augustinian tradition, it reinforces it by interposing a "supernatural" order between God and the created world.' p. 21.

58   *The Crisis of Transcendence for the Doctrine of God*

tinction has been made in terms of natural versus supernatural nature, the possibility is opened up, as Bonhoeffer said, for existence in a single one of these spheres.[67] This is the autonomy of secularism which finds its root in the attempted reconciliation, not in the revolt.

This root can be traced as far back as Athanasius; although it should be made clear that Athanasius generally overcame the Hellenistic dichotomy between the sensual and the intelligible worlds in his exposition of the Incarnation. It was, perhaps, something more than an incautious use of language, that allowed Athanasius to say:

> ... he has made all things out of nothing by his own Word, Jesus Christ our Lord ... the race of men, and having perceived its inability, by virtue of the condition of its origin, to continue in one stay, he gave them a further gift.... But if they transgressed and turned back, and became evil, they might know that they were incurring that corruption in death which was theirs by nature.[68]

The 'further gift' to which Athanasius alludes was that of the *logos*, man's created rational nature. Undoubtedly Athanasius was thinking in terms of a logical and not a temporal priority, but it is clear that this still leaves room for a certain autonomy of nature, which, though basically corruptible and destined for death, nonetheless, can assert itself independently of God.[69]

From this point, there are two ways which can be followed: (1) the religious man can seek to develop the 'gift of grace', and repress his created nature through forms of asceticism and spiritualism. Athanasius had certain affinities for this, despite his later emphasis on the reality of the human nature in the Incarnation in his polemic against the Arians.[70] Or, (2) the secular man can seek to recover the original

[67]*Ethics*, p. 196.

[68]Athanasius, *The Incarnation*, trans. A. Roberson, N. Nutt, London, 1891, p. 6 (III. 3,4).

[69]One could possibly object at this point, that 'nature' for Athanasius was 'corrupt, fallen nature', and thus could really possess no independent existence from God, but rather, in its corruption even more dependent. But my argument here is based on Athanasius' concept of the 'further gift'. If this gift was given to a created race of men, as Athanasius suggests, whether it was given to fallen or unfallen nature is beside the point which I am making. If the 'further gift' was something other than the gift of God himself, in gracious relation, it was then a created grace, subsequent to, and mediating between, the relation of Creator and creature. We are not far from an Augustinian doctrine of grace here.

[70]Cf. J. A. B. Holland, *The Development of the Trinitarian Theology of Athanasius, in His Conflict with Contemporary Heresies*, unpublished Ph.D. thesis, New College Library, Edinburgh, 1963. Holland asserts that Athanasius' handling of Christ's suffering, i.e., that the Logos 'hands over body for suffering', was directly taken over by the Western Church and produced asceticism and extreme dualism between the physical and the spiritual. Holland also claims that there is a

'autonomy' of human nature by stripping off the religious, authoritarian concepts of theism. The addition of grace as a supernatural 'plus' is considered a form of heteronomy by man in his striving for autonomy. The fact that this second alternative surfaced most clearly through the overthrow of religious authoritarianism at the time of the Renaissance and the Enlightenment, presents the illusion that it is a new stage of man's maturity, when in actuality, it is simply the corresponding distortion to spiritual asceticism. At its worst, secularism may be simply the bastard child of bad theology. At its best, it seems to point us to the right kind of question to ask if we are to understand the 'problem of everything else', which has been stated earlier to be the problem of how to understand the utter profaneness of the world as pointing to the reality of God.[71]

Gregor Smith liked to speak of an 'ultimate secularism' which must be reached, which he defined as '. . . the waiting answer to the ultimate question which arises at the end of the secularist road.'[72] The difference is, Gregor Smith was looking to the end of the secularist road which lay ahead; I prefer to look back to that end of the road which lies at the beginning. I think, however, we are looking for the same thing.

It would seem that this would be a good point to take up the question raised earlier concerning a failure of historical theology which not only delayed an authentic secularity, but precipitated a false secularism.[73] I have endeavoured to show, at least in part, how the latter problem developed. Secularism, I would now assert, as a revolt against the 'heteronomy' of a supernatural order imposed on the natural, a revolt in which reality is now conceived to be the cohesion of a self-subsisting universe, is a mis-conceived reality founded upon a half-truth.

The half-truth is the assertion that the making of a religious man out of a natural man by the addition of supernatural grace confuses both the reality of man and God. Secularism is an instinctive revolt against this 'inhuman' supersession of genuine human interests.[74] However, and here is why it is only a half-truth, I would say that a concept of reality which conceives the independence of man from God to be a self-subsisting reality, is a misconceived notion of true humanity. It was

direct correlation between the Christology of *De Incarnatione* and the ascetical movements in Egypt and Syria. See pp. 122, 218.
[71]See above, p. 90.
[72]*The Free Man*, Collins, London, 1969, p. 41.
[73]Cf. above, p. 92.
[74]Cf. Lionel S. Thornton, *The Incarnate Lord*, Longmans, Green & Co. Ltd., London, New York, Toronto, 1928: 'The true law of the new organism is therefore hostile to all supersessions of human interest. Where these supersessions have occurred in Christian history they have been violations of the true genius of Christianity. In the reactions of history supersession has been followed by movements for the emancipation of human interests.' p. 442.

this mis-conception which Gregor Smith saw so clearly, and which caused him to look for a more authentic secularity which did not supersede genuine human interests by a spurious claim for autonomy in the name of freedom.[75] With consummate eloquence, Kornelis Miskotte says the same thing:

> It is true that in a legitimate sense we can say that faith has its own autonomy, that it is personal and chosen in freedom, that the Word of God exercises an authority which not only engenders freedom but, being inherent in it, carries with it, creates, and preserves freedom. But 'somewhere' there must be a point where the criterion of truth does not lie with me; 'somewhere' (but this point is actually the qualitative 'all') there will be a point where it will not be a matter of agreement between my thinking and what has been thought. 'Somewhere' my thinking will be called upon to allow itself—in joy—to be brought into conformity with what God has thought about me. 'Somewhere', when we ask ourselves whether the givenness of God satisfies our religious 'needs', we shall come to the end of our tether. 'Somewhere' —unless we give up this *hubris* altogether—we shall have to see that if we follow the current method, we arrive at nothing more than a psychological fact, a thought or a feeling or a conjecture which pretends to be super-psychological. 'Somewhere' man must definitely submit: he must let himself be told that he is not autonomous, that he cannot be either a creator or a judge of the universe. 'Somewhere' he will have to grasp, not so much in ecstasy as in sober apprehension of truth, the privilege of understanding that he is understood and known and chosen.[76]

We are now left to deal with the first consequence attributed to a failure of historical theology—the delay of an authentic secularity. This authentic secularity is what previously has been termed the 'utter profaneness of the world' determined by the absolute difference of God from everything else.

This has been spoken of by some as the de-divinization of the cosmos which was effected in an absolute form through the Incarnation. By this it is meant, not that the living God was at first present in the world and has withdrawn from it, but that the *idea* of a divinity inextricably involved with the natural world has been driven from the consciousness of man. Miskotte holds that this can already be found to be the im-

---

[75]'So my question here is, Is secularism because it is tied to a view of the world (relativist, immanent, perfectionist yet pessimistic) not inherently self-destructive? Has it not an inadequate view of man's being, so that in all that it so powerfully plans for man it actually leaves out his limited and conditioned being, as the presupposition for his unlimited aspirations?'. *The Free Man*, p. 36.

[76]K. Miskotte, *When the Gods are Silent*, p. 15.

plication of the emergence of the faith of Israel: '... when Israel's faith was awakened, the gods were unmasked as being nothing more than the utter silence, the total taciturnity which they had always been.'[77]

Arnold Loen defines secularization as 'the historical process by which the world is de-divinized'.[78] But then he goes on to say that when put to the test, the definition melts away when one tries to grasp it. Despite the fact that there is substance to the idea that, in a social and historical sense, the consciousness of man has altered with regard to the presence of a divine being in the world—that is, the essentially sacred character of life—secularization conceived as mere de-divinization misses the mark.[79] The kind of profaneness which has its reality as a correlate of the absolute difference of God from everything else, does not result from 'radically removing God from the world', as Bonhoeffer liked to put it.[80] What Bonhoeffer wants to affirm is that with the Incarnation of God in Jesus Christ, God was radically removed from everything else by virtue of his being radically present in the man Jesus.[81] It is true that the Incarnation, properly understood, made it impossible to *think* of God as being immanently involved with the world in any other way than through Jesus Christ. It was the authority of this Word which shattered the medieval synthesis and freed the world from its sacramental role and gave it a rationality of its own as a created reality.

But what is absolutely crucial at this point is to see clearly what the Incarnation can hide if it is used primarily as a point of reference for a new way to *think* the relation of God to the world. The reason for the deliberation with which we have approached the problem of historical transcendence, avoiding a head-long rush to the Incarnation, will, I believe, become clear now. We are not seeking a rationale to justify a way of seeing the world, either as secular or sacred. Instead, we have been forcing the rationale of historical transcendence to expose its own inner logic.

The formulation of this rationale resolved itself into the assertion of God's absolute difference from everything and, simultaneously, his

---

[77]*Ibid.*, p. 10.

[78]*Secularization*, p. 7.

[79]Loen asserts: 'What secularization cannot mean within the biblical framework is de-divinization (although it could mean de-demonization—hence the ambivalence of secularization).' *Ibid.*, p. 9.

[80]'The Reformer's biblical faith in God had radically removed God from the world.' *Ethics*, p. 96.

[81]Bonhoeffer says: 'History became a serious matter' with the Incarnation of God in Jesus Christ, so that 'through the life and death of Jesus Christ it does for the first time become truly temporal.' *Ibid.*, p. 89. The truth of this should not obscure the fact that history has always been a serious matter, when the absolute difference of God has been affirmed. It was the Incarnation that made it possible to see this in its ultimate sense.

relation to everything else, without diminution of the difference. Because the absolute difference of God carries the implication of utter profaneness on the part of the world, there exists a rationale to this relation *apart* from the Incarnation. This is not to say that it can be expounded apart from the Incarnation. But what I am trying to make clear here, is the priority of reality to the epistemological structures by which it is grasped. The Incarnation must not be conceived as a bridge thrown over a chasm—that would be to substitute an enigma in place of a dilemma—but rather, the Incarnation has a rationality which is given to it by the very structure of rationality which exists in the relation of Creator to creation. If the opposite is held—that the Incarnation confers a rationality upon the Creator-creature relation—this rationality will then reside ultimately as a construct of the mind in the subject which considers the Incarnation. This was Kant's conclusion, and his dilemma.

Because there is a correspondence between the absolute difference of God from the world and the utter profaneness of the world, the failure of historical theology to grasp the reality of the world produced, in an illegitimate sense, the half-truth of secular theology. Which, while it could grasp the profaneness of the world, could not grasp it in reality, for the reality of that profaneness is the correlate of God's absolute difference. As a result, and not surprisingly, the radical secularists are ultimately concerned with some new form of the sacred.[82]

What now remains to be seen, is just how this correlation expresses itself in such a way that a *real* relation between God and everything else is possible. That is, we are now ready to take up Gregor Smith's problem of how to make these assertions 'simultaneously'. This is the problematic of historical transcendence.

3 'The Problematic of Historical Transcendence'

The eternal spirit speaks of eternal responsibility.... This is grace, which thus liberates the spirit and repairs the broken trackless ways: not an effluence, but an act; not a treasury of merits, but a person: not a right, but an utter, and utterly surprising, inrush of life: it is the life of the eternal person in act.

And this is forgiveness: not a theory, but an event; not a hope but a meeting; not an isolated experience, but a life: the life of the human person is met by the eternal spirit.[83]

[82]See above, p. 53, n. 53 for Altizer's concern with the sacred. Cf. also, Alistair Kee, whose sole purpose is to deny the transcendence of God and to speak solely of secular transcendence, yet who continues to speak of the sacred in a euphemistic way as 'a mystery beyond our ultimate concern.' *The Way of Transcendence*, p. 232.
[83]Ronald Gregor Smith, 'History is Personal', *Collected Papers*, p. 7.

There is a certain theme belonging to the problematic of historical transcendence which is the unique contribution of Ronald Gregor Smith. That theme is spirit, and its reality is act. The man, who was neither secularist nor traditionalist, who defied all attempts to 'pin him down' with some gummed label indicating a particular theological species, this man who moved always just slightly ahead of the winds of doctrine which blew others off course, never did discover a theological haven where he could finally drop anchor—but his sails never limped from lack of the Spirit's wind.

He would be uncomfortable with my assertion that the transcendence of God, in the last analysis, could only mean that God was 'wholly other' to the world. He could never say that much for himself, though he could not speak of less than an absolute difference between the spirit of the world and God as Spirit. I suspect that old fears, instilled in earlier days of dogmatism, caused him to keep the Spirit always within a *relation* of difference; to speak of the 'wholly other' was unreal for him. And thus I would guess that, while he could state with lucidity the problematic of historical transcendence, this self-imposed limitation made it impossible for him to work out its rationale.[84]

Because I have said that the spirit is a 'hard' reality in the problematic of the concrete man's bond with the absolute,[85] and that the limits with which transcendence has to do is the limit of spirit, the problematic of historical transcendence seems to me to form itself around the notion of spirit as act.

It is this idea which emerges in flashes of inspiration in Gregor Smith's life-long dialogue with Spirit.

We have already heard passionate, and almost angry, tones in his first utterance on the 'terror of the Spirit's visitation', written in 1938 at the conclusion of his studies as a divinity student.[86] The conflict between theology and the Spirit became an unbearable suffering which caused him at the time to come to the very brink of aborting a mission he had accepted

---

[84]'I believe that it is meaningless to assert, over against the secularized world, that the God of the Christians is "wholly other". The importance of the intention behind this assertion is clear: it is the attempt to give God his glory, to preserve his otherness, to indicate his absolute difference from creation. But it is meaningless, because an assertion about the 'wholly otherness' by its own definition excludes any relation or knowledge of what is *wholly* other.' R. G. Smith, *The New Man*, p. 66. My answer to this would be that a difference which is conceived as a modality of relationship only, is no more than immanent transcendence. I would, however, agree, as I have already indicated, that there is a 'hermeneutical horizon' of relation to God which conditions all of our *statements* about God, but which does not relativize his reality to our own.

[85]See above, p. 38; see also, the definition of metaphysics as 'the problematic of the concrete man's bond with the absolute', Introduction, p. xviii.

[86]See above, p. 8.

and believed in since childhood. But in his youth he had received more than a call to the ministry, he had received a strange and almost melancholy summons of the Spirit. So powerful was this experience, that whenever the two threatened to come into collision, there was never any doubt which he would choose to follow. Speaking of his experience as a boy, Gregor Smith writes:

> I believe that the most authentic experience of all my childhood and boyhood was the one that was repeated many times, as I sat at the back of the aisle, in Corstorphine Church, and especially on a summer Sunday's evening. The sun struck low then across the cool paving-stones, its living beams poured in from the ancient quiet churchyard. That old lovely church, with its roof of great mossy flagstones, always had for me both externally and within its quiet walls, a quality of mystery, and surprise, and suspense, of dim uncanny powers; it remains for me as my first solid and positive experience—dare I say of Christianity? .... I can see now that at that time I was always watchful, expectant, waiting for something surprising to happen, for the sudden voice which should make everything clear, swing back the curtains, and let the hidden glory be disclosed.... And I still think that nothing of what is afterwards learned of any religion, Christianity not excepted, has any substance of gracious life unless first, and always, there flows in on the spirit this awareness of life, of mystery and glory, of power and terror, of invitation and of judgment.[87]

What is significant in Gregor Smith's own mind, is his consciousness of 'being acted upon' by Spirit. How much greater this was than merely an overwrought imagination of an impressionable boy will become clear in even a cursory study of his later concepts concerning history, transcendence, and, of course, Spirit. So we are not surprised that in this attempt to work out a theology of history he can say: 'The eternal spirit ... is the life of the eternal person in act.'[88] This is more than poetry, or a vague sense of the numinous, it is a fundamental structure of reality which, while taking several forms, will serve him as a hermeneutical horizon for the rest of his life.

In 1943, his first published work appeared under a pseudonym, called *Still Point*.[89] This book, written out of his first, and only, experience as a parish minister, shows his struggle to keep the 'spirit of life'

---

[87]From an unpublished manuscript with no title, written about 1944, *Collected Papers*.

[88]See above, p. 62, n. 83.

[89]*Still Point*, Ronald Maxwell (R. G. Smith), Nisbet and Co. Ltd., London, 1943.

from slipping over into sheer pantheism.[90] But always there is the 'music from beyond' which acts upon him, confronting him with a reality, which in its sharpness of perception and hardness of spirit, is undeniably other:

> I found myself wandering in a bleak valley, where all the work that men had ever done, and all that they had ever hoped and desired, was laid out for my wondering gaze. It was magnificent, but not terrible: for of it all there was nothing that lasted, no, not one single thing: but everything passed away, reaching in the end dust and death. And nothing was perfect, but through all things reached the terror of time. And I was afraid. Then suddenly I was compelled to look up from what lay there, and like a hidden light casting a faint glow, like a glory not revealed but only glimpsed, there high and lifted up I saw another power and another hope. But this too was terrible, though magnificent: for though high, and remote from those broken things, it was also low, down where the indescribably haunting notes of the violoncello can only hint of majesty and sweetness; so that through it all, even through that glimpsed high glory, there ran the melancholy and the majesty of man's destiny. The gods walked there, but I caught only the echo of their laughter, and it sounded in my ears like weeping.[91]

The two inseparable strands of reality, which were later to take the form of transcendence and history, are clearly visible in this panegyric on Spirit. There is the glimpsed glory, high and lifted up, and then there is the same glory, low and melancholy as man's destiny. Even at his highest point of numinous experience, Gregor Smith was becoming more and more inextricably involved in the concrete.[92]

The Spirit now becomes more visible for him as the Spirit of history. He was soon to describe history as 'the conspiracy and public covenant, between God and man; and neither man nor God is fettered'.[93] But history in this sense of 'conspiracy' is not something which man does,

[90]'But "real life is on the yonder side of convention", as Dr. Jung has said. Thus it is only ... by setting aside, or passing beyond, such dead cold classifications as this point about Wordsworth's "pantheism" that here, as everywhere, the ever-present Spirit may be approached by the seeking soul.' *Ibid.*, p. 13.

[91]*Ibid.*, pp. 72-73.

[92]Two years after writing *Still Point*, Gregor Smith, in commenting upon his own perspective at the time of its writing, said: '*Still Point*, without being a falsification, is the nearest I was able to reach, in modern circumstances, to Herbert's exposition of the priestly life. It is notable, and ominous, that there is almost nothing in it about living people. The sentiment in it could not pass the test of meeting ordinary human beings. It is abstracted from our total situation in its miseries and splendours.' 'Turning Point', *Collected Papers*, p. 17.

[93]*The New Man*, p. 93.

but what happens to him. He so identified spirit and history at this stage that instead of spirit, he could say that it was history which presents the claim of God's presence upon us.[94] Those who later found it frustrating and confusing to attempt to grasp Gregor Smith's concept of history failed to see that, for him, history is but the concrete form of man's dialogue with Spirit.

But with the publication of his book, *The New Man*, in 1956, Gregor Smith was already moving towards a concept of Spirit as freedom.

In the historical situation of man, then it is necessary to recognize that freedom and obedience both have their place.... The doctrine of the Holy Spirit in an integral unity with a full doctrine of the Word has always been the laggard in the armoury of Christianity. For it is in this teaching that the explosive and revolutionary quality of Christianity is seen at its most potent: the teaching, namely, which affirms man and his history as leading through grace into unimagined spheres of truth and freedom.[95]

With more of an emphasis now on Kierkegaard's dialectic of reality, Smith can talk of the presence of God within history, and so resolves the earlier problem of a virtual identification between God and history. The spirit is the gift of freedom to man which enables him to have a real history of possibility. 'The Protestant spirit', says Gregor Smith, 'needs to be characterized rather in terms of a living encounter with the Holy Spirit, with responsibility and freedom towards and in history.'[96]

It was his dialogue with the Spirit which carried Smith through the shoals of secularity, while so many of his contemporaries were stranded on the sands of secularism. After almost ten years, and with the publication of his book, *Secular Christianity*—which scarcely could be called a genuine secular theology, although not a few questioned its Christianity—it was apparent that Gregor Smith was on to something else. He was still saying that 'history is what happens to you',[97] and 'transcendence is what happens to us',[98] but Spirit now has become the Spirit of powerlessness. We are deep into Bonhoeffer at this point, where Smith has found at last the depth of passion and vision of the world to match his own spirit. It is interesting to note that during the development of his

[94]"The Word of God is God's being in its actuality, its actuality is uttered, expressed, established, brought into relation with us. And this is not a static or abstract thing, to which we then ascribe a certain category of transcendence, but it is the presence of God in history. History as a present claim upon me.' R. G. Smith, 'Lectures on Apologetics', *Collected Papers*, p. 120.

[95]*The New Man*, pp. 59, 60-61.

[96]*Ibid.*, p. 75.

[97]*Secular Christianity*, p. 86.

[98]*Ibid.*, p. 121.

thesis in *Secular Christianiy*, the dialogue with the Spirit has virtually dropped out of sight, only to surface at the very end in his epilogue on Prayer:

> Only by way of the utter desolation of Christ's historical being on the Cross is prayer possible at all. It is thus the impossible possibility which is only found in the utmost mystery of the Spirit being with us and speaking for us. There is no place for anxiety if faith holds fast, in the power of the Spirit, hoping against hope, believing against unbelief. So the conclusion is that the Spirit is the only power in the world. But this Spirit is power in powerlessness. 'Only a suffering God can help.'[99]

Only when he is at last sure that he can speak of the Spirit in the powerlessness of being utterly involved in history does Gregor Smith dare at last speak openly of the Spirit as the Spirit of God. There is a deep breath drawn at the end of *Secular Christianity*, which tells us that once more Gregor Smith has put one way behind him and is ready to launch out on a new one.

We should not then be surprised that his final work, which was in preparation as the Princeton Lectures when he died, was to be titled *The Doctrine of God*. The words 'spirit, speech, word, and history', are after all, he says, ways of indicating reality. Spirit is God.[100] So at last he is able to state the terms of the problematic of historical transcendence. It is not man's engagement with history, nor his quest for freedom, and not even his experience of co-humanity.[101] But it is a problematic in which God has a reality which is absolutely his own, which is Spirit acting upon us within history, not above it, or in addition to it. And yet, for Gregor Smith, it remained a problematic for which he had no clue. His life-long dialogue with the Spirit ended with an inexplicable silence:

> This reality [sc. between the I and Thou] is neither himself nor the other: but in its entirety it lies between the two. There is a hinterland here which cannot be explicated. I meet the other: we enter into our common reality. We neither acquire the other, nor do we possess the reality. We participate in it.[102]

There are two things worth noting at this point. First, the concept of a spirit which acts upon man in his utter worldliness, which is the characteristic, not only of Gregor Smith's theology from beginning to end, but also of his life, constitutes the problematic of historical transcendence, even though he was unable to explicate it. Secondly, once Gregor Smith

[99]*Ibid.*, p. 209.
[100]*The Doctrine of God*, pp. 136ff, p. 144.
[101]*Ibid.*, p. 144.
[102]*Ibid.*, pp. 177-178.

68   *The Crisis of Transcendence for the Doctrine of God*

found in Bonhoeffer the concepts of this-worldly transcendence, which became the garment with which he clothed the nakedness of spirit-act, he went no further in exploring the significance of Bonhoeffer's earlier writings, which were profoundly Christological. To my knowledge, neither his published nor his unpublished writings reveal a substantial reference to, and certainly no direct use of, any work of Bonhoeffer prior to his *Ethics*. I think it would be fair to say that he considered Bonhoeffer to make a radical break with his earlier Christological thought, so that only in *Ethics* and the fragmentary letters from prison is Bonhoeffer considered to be relevant for Gregor Smith's purposes. This use of Bonhoeffer is generally consistent with most modern attempts to continue the programme of religionless Christianity as sketched out by Bonhoeffer, primarily in his *Letters and Papers From Prison*. His earlier works have never been taken with the seriousness, with which his later, more fragmentary thoughts were received.[103]

This is not only a serious misunderstanding of Bonhoeffer, which I hope to demonstrate in Chapter III, but was a fatal mistake for Gregor Smith. In choosing to follow Bultmann's 'paradoxical identity' rather than Bonhoeffer's Christology, he was left without a means of explicating the 'hinterland' of God's reality as Spirit act.[104] For this reason, we cannot really follow Gregor Smith's concept of historical transcendence further than this. He has left it in a timeless 'holding pattern', circling, but never landing. I would at least hope to get it on the ground, and for his sake, I trust, in one piece.

I want to take up now one final point in regard to the correspondence which exists between the assertion of God's absolute difference from everything else, and his relation to everything else. The question upon which the problematic turns, and the rationale of which eluded Gregor Smith, is how an absolute difference can be *simultaneously* a real relation. Here then is the distinction between what I call a problematic and a paradox. If the absolute difference of God is an assertion that is made on the basis of the modality of the relation itself, a paradox results which

---

[103]One of the first, and probably the one most responsible for linking Bonhoeffer's concepts with those of secular theology, was Bishop John A. T. Robinson in his book *Honest to God*; cf. especially pp. 75-91. Cf. also, Paul van Buren, *The Secular Meaning of the Gospel*, pp. 15ff. For a discussion of the 'new start' taken by Bonhoeffer, and also of the relationship of his later concepts to his earlier works, see the biography, *Dietrich Bonhoeffer*, Eberhard Bethge, Collins, London, 1970, pp. 757ff.

[104]The phrase 'paradoxical identity' refers to a theological reality which can be seen by the eye of faith coinciding with an historical reality, without breaking the 'skin' of history, so to speak. In Bultmann's sense, historical events can also have an eschatological significance which is only grasped by existential self-understanding and uttered as a kerygmatic statement. Cf. R. G. Smith, *The Doctrine of God*, p. 153. See also, R. Bultmann, *Jesus Christ and Mythology*, pp. 79ff.

can only be mediated by a dialectical movement. That is, by asserting the truth of both as a faith-assertion without reducing the paradox to one or the other of the terms.[105]

This is what Gollwitzer attempted, by speaking of a new kind of objectivity (*Gegenständlichkeit*) conceived as encounter, and this is what Gregor Smith resorted to in the last analysis, conceived as spirit-act. But in both cases, a dialectic is involved in which faith supports *both* assertions simultaneously. It is the concept of simultaneity built into the formulation by Gregor Smith which determines its paradoxical nature, and betrays its subjectivizing tendency. For this attempts to resolve the reality of both God and man into a *single* assertion of reality. And when this is done by the human subject, the only way to preserve the other pole of reality is through paradox.

A problematic, on the other hand, is a correspondence which has an intrinsic rationality which is given to the relation by a reality not inferred from the relation itself. When I defined metaphysics as the problematic of the concrete man's bond with the absolute, I was suggesting that, while there is a meaningful correspondence between freedom (spirit) and necessity (body) in terms of human existence, the *rationale* of that relation cannot be inferred from the relation itself, but must be given to the relation by spirit, and that only in act—that is its problematic. Human action as a correspondence between body and spirit, or freedom and necessity, is rational, meaningful action, but in abstracting from the action, it will always remain problematic. But it is never paradoxical, because the reality of existence does not depend upon the simultaneous assertion of freedom and necessity.

Clearly, it must then be spirit which acts, because only spirit is free to act. This is the core of rationality in the problematic of human relation. The action of the other can never be infallibly inferred out of the relation, because it is the act of spirit, not the body. In this way, one could say that the rationale of a human relation is given by spirit, which transcends its limit and moves beyond itself to act in some way towards the other.

Therefore, to say that God is absolute in his difference from man is to say that he is Spirit. Correspondingly, then, that which is not God, but wholly other—we have called this utter profaneness—exists in a rationality of correspondence given to it by the freedom of God; I repeat,

[105]For an evaluation of the concept of paradox as Kierkegaard used it, see Alastair McKinnon, 'Believing the *Paradoks*: A Contradiction in Kierkegaard?' *Harvard Theological Review*, 1968, pp. 633-636. McKinnon argues that Kierkegaard did not mean by paradox a logical contradiction, but that which was *self*-contradictory, and thus, existential, dialectical, systematically incomprehensible, and historically dependent. But this throws the weight of faith even more upon the self as the Subject, and misses what I believe to be the important truth in a problematic— namely, that the rationality of a relation with God is given by God to the relation.

it is given and cannot be inferred out of the relation. This important distinction is clearly shown by Barth:

> ... the absoluteness of God—that which makes it a genuine absoluteness—does not derive primarily from the mode of his relationship to the world. For this very reason, He can enter into a real relationship with the latter.[106]

Once we have determined that the nature of Spirit in transcendence is action, and that this action is that which constitutes a real relation, the *interaction* between God and the world is the core of rationality which we discover in the relation, not what we project upon it. What Gregor Smith failed to see, despite the fact that he always conceived spirit as that which acted upon man, was that the rationale of that relation was not lost by speaking of God's absolute difference, but instead, could only be given to it by God's act of freedom—and that act is the transcendence of God. Miskotte is right when he says:

> It is precisely the act-character of God as being that determines the fact that God distinguishes himself *in* the world *from* the world. It is the reverse side of the fact that he elevates himself above Being.[107]

The act-character of God's being, which Miskotte calls the reverse side of his freedom from the world—that is, his absolute difference from everything else—constitutes for us a 'hermeneutical horizon' beyond which we cannot go, but which is a *real* horizon because its rationality is not conferred upon it by the world with which God interacts, but by the God who acts.

Consequently, we can say that, instead of God's absolute difference being diminished in any way by his interaction with the world, it is made more real and explicit, because this 'worldly' act is God's transcendence; it is the act of Spirit, which constitutes a *real* relation between God and the world. And here Gollwitzer also has it right:

> ... the theologians of the ancient church rightly considered it of decisive importance that the humanity of Jesus ... should be understood as the appearing of God himself, as God's own incomparable act of self-manifestation.... that God does not conceal himself behind the concrete symbol in some unapproachable aseity.[108]

Everything now points to the question of how the transcendence of God as spirit-act concretizes itself, and how its inner rationality can be explicated.

---

[106] K. Barth, *Church Dogmatics*, II/I, p. 309.
[107] K. Miskotte, *When the Gods are Silent*, p. 143.
[108] H. Gollwitzer, *The Existence of God*, pp. 166-167.

From the beginning our quest has been for a certain kind of concreteness of spirit. In the first chapter the crisis of transcendence was radically determined, in the last analysis, to be a crisis of spirit. It is spirit which is 'wholly other' and which has limits which cannot be placed by any kind of inference out of existence, and which cannot be overtaken by any kind of logical leap. The transcendence of God is his absolute difference from everything else.

In this chapter, the implications of that assertion have been traced, particularly with respect to the correspondence between the absolute otherness of God and the utter profaneness of the world. Rather than an irrational chasm existing between God and the world, there was discovered the possibility of a rationale in the assertion that Spirit transcends its own otherness with act, and in that act, gives reality and meaning to the correspondence. The Spirit-act is the problematic of historical transcendence. Which means that the reality of God is problematical to human knowledge apart from the concretion of Spirit in historical form.

You will ask what is meant by historical, but we cannot speak of that as yet. For now, we can only speak of a stone, and a leaf and an unfound door. These have the texture of spirit, if we dare to know it. And yes, this too: '... no theology of divine transcendence has any right to call itself Christian that does not see the very transcendence of God in terms of the crown of thorns.'[109]

That can only have been said since Bonhoeffer. What did he know that we still seek to understand?

[109]D. M. MacKinnon, *Borderlands of Theology*, p. 126.

Chapter III

The Theology of Historical Transcendence

1 'After the Fall and a World Come of Age'

But love, is love enough? What love, what wave of pity will ever reach
this knowledge—I know how to kill? ... Or is it possible that this is
not bizarre ... to anyone? And I am not alone, and no man lives
who would not rather be the sole survivor of this place than all its
finest victims! What is the cure? Who can be innocent again on this
mountain of skulls? I tell you what I know! My brothers died here
—but my brothers built this place; our hearts have cut these stones!
And what's the cure?
    Or is that exactly why she hopes, because she knows? What burn-
ing cities taught her and the death of love taught me: that we are
very dangerous! ... Is the knowing all? To know, and even happily,
that we meet unblessed; not in some garden of wax fruit and painted
leaves, that lie of Eden, but after, after the Fall, after many, many
deaths. Is the knowing all? And the wish to kill is never killed, but with
some gift of courage one may look into its face when it appears, and
with a stroke of love—as to an idiot in the house—forgive it; again
and again ... forever?[1]

The common denominator that links a Jewish author, who dramatizes
the outrage of Nazi atrocities against humanity, with a particular
Christian theologian, who was a victim of the same holocaust of hate
and horror, should not be too difficult to discern. Especially when the
theologian is Dietrich Bonhoeffer.
    In his search for a spirit of mature responsibility in man's contem-
porary involvement with the world, Bonhoeffer turned to a faith which
was willing to recognize and embrace the godlessness of the world, and
to accept the community of a common guilt as the 'whole thing' which
a religious form of life can never grasp.[2] To Miller's rhetorical question,
'Who can be innocent again on this mountain of skulls?' Bonhoeffer

---

[1]Arthur Miller, *After the Fall*, Penguin Books, Middlesex, England; first
published in 1964, Penguin reprint, 1968, pp. 119-120.
[2]Cf. E. Bethge, *Dietrich Bonhoeffer*, p. 782.

would respond with another question, 'Who can be religious again when God has been edged out of the world and onto a cross?'[3] While Miller sees that innocence is no longer possible because of every man's complicity in one man's inhumanity, Bonhoeffer sees that it is religion which is impossible because of God's complicity in the godlessness of all men:

Man is summoned to share in God's sufferings at the hands of a godless world. He must therefore really live in the godless world, without attempting to gloss over or explain its ungodliness in some religious way or other.[4]

But beyond this common denominator, there is a world of difference. Bonhoeffer's 'world come of age' is far more than a blind idiocy in the name of human hope. For in a stroke of brilliance, as profoundly theological as it was powerfully dramatic, Bonhoeffer turned the 'helpless idiot' into the power and reality of a suffering God—the curse becomes the cure:

To that extent we may say that the development towards the world's coming of age outlined above, which has done away with a false conception of God, opens up a way of seeing the God of the Bible, who wins power and space in the world by his weakness. This will probably be the starting-point for our 'secular interpretation'.[5]

Tempting as it is to pursue the clues which would reveal more clearly the outlines of Bonhoeffer's concept of 'world come of age', which, along with his concepts of 'religionless' Christianity and 'this-worldly' transcendence, constitute the major themes in his prison letters, that exercise would detract us from the real purpose of this exploration of Bonhoeffer's theology.[6] Furthermore, the greater share of the literature on Bonhoeffer tugs on these fragments sticking up out of the rubble of his thought hoping to unearth a whole body, or at least an arm or a leg to graft on to their own dismembered theology. Their attempts have not been all that encouraging. The fact that it is quite possible, contrary to the hasty assumptions of some, to find in Bonhoeffer's earlier writings definite theological antecedents for most of his later, more 'radical' concepts, is not as helpful as it would appear to be.[7] This indeed does

---

[3]Cf. D. Bonhoeffer, *Letters and Papers From Prison*, p. 360.
[4]*Ibid.*, p. 361.
[5]*Ibid.*, p. 361.
[6]For attempts to explicate the concept 'world come of age' in Bonhoeffer's thought, see Wm. Hamilton, 'The Letters are a Particular Thorn', *World Come of Age*, R. G. Smith (ed.), pp. 145-152; E. Bethge, *Dietrich Bonhoeffer*, pp. 769-774; R. G. Smith, *Secular Christianity*, pp. 176-184; John A. Phillips, *The Form of Christ in the World*, pp. 145-181.
[7]For example, Bonhoeffer's statement in his *Letters and Papers From Prison* on the nature of this-worldly transcendence can be found in very much the same

establish the fact that Bonhoeffer's concepts of 'religionless Christianity' and 'world come of age' arise more out of his theological orientation than a phenomenological assessment of the actual character of the world, a point which I shall take up later on in this chapter; but what this does not do, is clarify for us the nature of his theological assumptions.

The question which we want to put to Bonhoeffer concerns the degree to which he grasped the fundamental problematic of historical transcendence as it has been exposed thus far, namely the correspondence of the reality of God and the reality of the world, which has as its rationale the transcendence of God as Spirit concretely given to the relationship out of the freedom of God. The problematic of this rationale is that it cannot be inferred out of the relationship by the human subject, but can only be known concretely as the transcendence of God. This is what I have called historical transcendence.

The very nature of the problematic as it has been revealed so far in the discussion, demands that its rationale be theological. When I assume that this is axiomatic, I presuppose that the argument thus far has excluded the possibility of any rationality inherently existing in the relationship of God to the world, other than that which is given to it by God. That is, the relationship has a transcendent source for its intrinsic reality.

The question which we are left with, and this is the second question which must be put to Bonhoeffer, is: how can the theology of historical transcendence and the reality of God be explicated without reducing the problematic to either an irrational or rational subjectivism, but at the same time reveal its inner logic? These two questions will be set aside for the moment in order to take a closer look at the basic theological assumptions in Bonhoeffer's thought.

Stated in the broadest possible terms, Bonhoeffer's problem was that of uniting the reality of God with the reality of the world.[8] Rejecting the dualism implicit in thinking of reality as two distinct and static spheres, Bonhoeffer, rather, conceived the reality of God and the reality of the world as two levels of reality with genuine interaction between them.[9] In his very first work, *Sanctorum Communio*, which was written in 1927

form in his first work, *Sanctorum Communio*, written in 1927 and first published in 1930. Cf. *Letters and Papers From Prison*, p. 282, with *Sanctorum Communio*, p. 33. For a discussion of the way in which Bonhoeffer's later concepts are prefigured in his earlier writings, cf. E. Bethge, *Dietrich Bonhoeffer*, pp. 793ff. Bethge argues quite convincingly that there is a fundamental unity to Bonhoeffer's thought; he is less convincing, to my mind, in showing us the relevance of Bonhoeffer for the present crisis of transcendence.

[8]Cf. R. G. Smith, *World Come of Age*, p. 14. Hans Schmidt concurs in this assessment of what Bonhoeffer set out to do, although he judges him to have failed. See his essay, 'The Cross of Reality?', *World Come of Age*, p. 236.

[9]*Ethics*, p. 196. Cf. also, T. F. Torrance, *God and Rationality*, who suggests that this was the key to Bonhoeffer, pp. 75, 83.

at the age of twenty-one, as his doctoral thesis at the University of Berlin, Bonhoeffer developed the form and structures of the Church as the community of revelation. 'Christ existing as the Church' was his key thought, uniting the sociological reality of the Church as a community embodying a 'collective person' through 'objective spirit' with the transcendental reality of God revealed in Christ.[10]

The inherent tensions of the argument in *Sanctorum Communio* were picked up and developed in his second work, *Act and Being*, which was written as his qualifying thesis for a lectureship at the University of Berlin in 1930. While he now leaves behind his concern with the sociological categories which comprise the reality of the Church as an empirical community, he continues his theme of the Church as the community of revelation which mediates between the sheer contingency of a theology of act and the static and objectifying givenness of a theology of being. The philosophical foils for his argument were the transcendentalism of Kant and the ontology of Heidegger, but in a positive sense, he is seeking to unite the concept of revelation which he found in Karl Barth with the reality of man in community, thus giving continuity and concreteness to revelation without making it an entity which man possesses by his ideas or his institutions. Revelation *is* the community established by the Word and Spirit of God—Christ existing as the Church.[11]

The Christology which was implicit in Bonhoeffer's early theology became more explicit following 1933 with his lectures on Christology at the University, in which we can trace a movement from the rigid Ecclesiology of Christ existing as the church to 'Christ the transcendent person'.[12] But the theme is still the concreteness of revelation in Christ, and in his book *The Cost of Discipleship* (1937),[13] concreteness becomes expressed as obedience to the person of Christ expressed in a life of discipleship and communal existence. The period of 1933 to 1939 appears to have brought Bonhoeffer's own life and thought into tension. His Christology, rooted in the concept of the church as the empirical community of revelation, was placed at the service of the newly formed Confessing Church in its struggle against the Nazi controlled State Church.

---

[10]*Sanctorum Communio*, pp. 84-85, 65-66.

[11]Cf. J. A. Phillips, *The Form of Christ in the World*, pp. 57ff, 65ff.

[12]'If we look for the place of Christ, we are looking for the structure of the "Where?" within that of the "Who?" We are thus remaining within the structure of the person. Everything depends on Christ being present to his church as a person in space and time.... The nature of the person of Christ is to be temporally and spatially in the centre. The one who is present in Word, sacrament and community is in the centre of human existence, history and nature. It is part of the structure of his person that he stands at the centre.' D. Bonhoeffer, *Christology*, pp. 61-62.

[13]SCM Press, London (1937), 1969.

While at the same time, his life and teaching in connection with the Confessing Church's seminary at Finkenwalde and the communal and semi-monastic experience with the *Bruderhaus* gave him a chance to explore an alternative and more dynamic Christology centring on the person of Christ.[14]

After 1939, and his forced separation from the church struggle by the Gestapo, a new phase in Bonhoeffer's thought arises, marked by his work on *Ethics* and culminating in his imprisonment and the *Letters and Papers From Prison*. During this period he was thrust into intimate relationship with men of varying political, cultural and religious convictions, primarily through his involvement with the German intelligence service as a plain-clothes agent and as part of the conspiracy to assassinate Hitler. The problem of the reality of God and the reality of the world, which he had seen as essentially a problem of how revelation could be concretely experienced through relationship with Christ, now becomes the problem of how Christ can be thought of as the Lord of the non-religious and the totally worldly community. It now becomes a problem, not so much of the concrete space which revelation occupies within the world, but of how the whole of worldly life can be subjected to Christ, to revelation.[15]

I have briefly outlined the movement of Bonhoeffer's theological thought through successive stages to show the consistency of his orientation to the fundamental problem of the relationship between the reality

[14]For a very fine summary and evaluation of this period and the two Christologies of Bonhoeffer, see John A. Phillips, *The Form of Christ in the World*, pp. 73ff.

[15]An indication of the way in which Bonhoeffer's life and thought was being transformed during this period can be found in an excerpt from a letter he wrote to E. Bethge on the train home from Stockholm in June of 1942: 'Again and again I ponder my activities, which are still so strongly concerned with the worldly sector. I am surprised that I can and do live without the Bible for days—if I forced myself, it would be auto-suggestion rather than obedience. I know that such auto-suggestion could be and is a great help; it's just that I am afraid of falsifying a genuine experience and of receiving, in the last resort, no genuine help. Then, when I open the Bible once again, it is new and rewarding as never before, and I want eagerly to preach again. I know that I have been through periods which were much richer "spiritually". But I can feel in myself the resistance growing against everything "religious". Often to the point of an instinctive horror—and that surely isn't a good thing either. I am not naturally religious. But I do return again and again in my thoughts to God and Christ: the genuine things, life, freedom and mercy mean a great deal to me. It's just that the religious clothing is so uncomfortable. Do you understand? All these are not new thoughts or views, but because I think that something new is about to burst in upon me, I am letting things run their course without resisting. This is how I understand my present activity in the wordly sector. Please forgive these confessions, the long train ride is at fault.' *Gesammelte Schriften*, Munich, 1958-66, Vol. II, p. 420. Cited by J. A. Phillips, *The Form of Christ in the World*, p. 128.

of God and the reality of the world. Bonhoeffer demonstrates a remarkable facility for overhauling his own conceptual tools without losing sight of the central task for theology. What some take to be inconsistency and even discontinuity in his thought, can be otherwise understood as the adjustments necessary to a consistent outworking of his basic theological assumptions. There would, of course, be room for disagreement as to precisely what these assumptions are, but not, I think, with the assertion that one's basic assumptions to a large extent determine his response to a particular situation and problem. I would argue that there are at least three interrelated assumptions which comprise the heart of Bonhoeffer's theology.

The first assumption can be stated in the form of a proposition: *The intrinsic coherence of the reality of Creator and creation is concretized in community.* The basic problem, says Bonhoeffer, 'is the relation between the person, God, and social being.'[16] Social being is not what Bonhoeffer means by community. Rather, community is the relation between man and God *concretized* as social being. This concept of community gives a theological dimension to the very core of human social relations. For this reason, Bonhoeffer has no hesitation about taking over sociology as the concrete reality of revelation, for he views sociology as the science of the original and essential nature of sociality.[17] He can also state it in another way: 'There is no sociological concept of the church which does not have a theological foundation.'[18]

The proposition unfolds in this manner: the person in his concrete life, wholeness and uniqueness, is willed by God as the ultimate unity by which social relations are formed.[19] For this reason, the social dimension of community, which is the dimension of concreteness, is also the theological dimension, because authentic personhood is only constituted by the direct involvement of God as divine person:

> For Christian philosophy the human person comes into being only in relation to the divine person which transcends it, opposing and subjugating it.[20]

God, therefore, is not a reality 'added to' the social relation, but the reality of God constitutes that relation; consequently, God, man and community intrinsically cohere in the concrete social relation.

Two important implications of this basic assumption need to be mentioned at this point, without further elaboration. One is the archetypal structure of social relations in religious community. 'Our first

[16]*Sanctorum Communio*, p. 36.
[17]*Ibid.*, p. 19.
[18]*No Rusty Swords*, Collins, London, 1970, p. 28.
[19]*Sanctorum Communio*, pp. 36-37.
[20]*Ibid.*, p. 31.

thesis is that, from the standpoint of its genesis, the concept of religion as a whole is taken from social life: If a man were not a social being he would not have any religion.'[21] While this does not seem especially significant at this stage in Bonhoeffer's thought, the fundamental assumption which made man's religious life adventitious to his social life was later to surface in more radical language as the 'non-religious' interpretation of Biblical terminology and 'religionless' Christianity.[22]

The second implication of this basic assumption concerns the way in which Bonhoeffer ties in the world as a physical reality to the essential community of man and God:

> Without God, without his brother, man loses the earth. In his senti-
> mental backing away from dominion over the earth, man has always
> lost God and his brother. God, our brother, and the earth belong
> together.... From the beginning the way of man to the earth has
> only been possible as God's way to man.... Man's being-free-for God
> and the other person and his being-free-from the creature in his
> dominion over it is the image of God in the first man.[23]

Implicit in the communion of God and man is a rationale for man's relationship to the world. Again it only needs to be noted here that this evidence of latent possibilities for a theology of worldliness can be discovered in Bonhoeffer's basic theological assumption.

Only one further aspect of the proposition needs to be shown—how the reality of God is concretized in community. While carefully guarding his concept of spirit from the 'universal spirit' common to the thought of German Idealism,[24] Bonhoeffer asserted that spirit is presupposed by community and that human 'spirituality' and sociality was originally willed by God as a common reality. In taking up the problem of the relation between man's spirituality and sociality, Bonhoeffer says: 'We shall show that man, as spirit, is necessarily created in a community, and that his general spirituality is woven into the net of sociality.'[25] The problematic, then, of social relation at the concrete level, is that of spirit, and the extent to which spirit transcends the other as spirit within this relation.

> In knowing myself as 'I', I lift myself out as a unity from the vegeta-
> tive spiritual state of the community; and simultaneously the being of

---

[21]*Ibid.*, p. 93.

[22]Cf. *Letters and Papers From Prison*, pp. 328, 359.

[23]*Creation and Fall*, SCM Press, London, 1959, p. 38.

[24]'The I is a person so far as it is spirit. Spirit, however, as Kant says, is the highest principle of form, comprising and overcoming all material, so that spirit and the universal are identical and the individual loses its value.' D. Bonhoeffer, *Sanctorum Communio*, p. 27.

[25]*Ibid.*, p. 44.

the 'Thou' as the other self-conscious spirit rises up for me. We could turn this round and say that in recognising a Thou, an alien conscious spirit, separate and distinct from myself, I recognise myself as an 'I': I become aware of my self-consciousness.[26]

Because Bonhoeffer has already said that 'The other man presents us with the same problem of cognition as does God himself',[27] the relation of God to community is also through spirit, but always spirit in its concrete form. But what is the concrete form of spirit?

Body is the existence-form of spirit, as spirit is the existence-form of body.... The human body is distinguished from all nonhuman bodies by being the existence-form of God's Spirit on earth.[28]

We have now closed the circle, as far as Bonhoeffer is concerned. Concrete personal being arises out of the concrete social situation, but only if God is in that situation creating an absolute barrier in the form of the concrete 'other' person—this barrier is the transcendence of Spirit.[29] The community, then, is the body which becomes the existence form of the divine Spirit.

The first basic assumption of Bonhoeffer's theology has been stated as the proposition: the intrinsic coherence of the reality of Creator and creation is concretized in community. As a corollary to this proposition, a second assumption can be stated as follows: *the normative character of basic ontic relationships*. There are two questions which immediately arise concerning just what this assumption means: the question of what constitutes an ontic relationship and secondly, that for which the relationship is normative.[30]

Let us see if what Bonhoeffer means by an ontic relation cannot be made a bit more lucid by interpreting it with respect to some of his other statements. First of all, Bonhoeffer says that it is revelation which

---

[26]*Ibid.*, p. 47.

[27]*Ibid.*, p. 37.

[28]D. Bonhoeffer, *Creation and Fall*, p. 46.

[29]*Sanctorum Communio*, p. 31. It is worth noting at this point, the way in which the problematic of the concrete man's bond with the absolute is reflected in Bonhoeffer's basic theological assumption. The person cannot abstract himself from the concrete social relation and remain in contact with the divine absolute. Absolute spirit is only known through concrete relation. Bonhoeffer's rejection of religion as 'individualistic' and 'metaphysical' (see *Letters and Papers From Prison*, p. 285) can be seen as his concern to maintain this bond with the absolute, that is, not to reduce the problematic to an abstraction of pure subjectivity.

[30]'It is the basic ontic relations which provide the norm for all empirical social life. This is of the greatest significance for a concept of the church. ... This brings us once again to what was said at the beginning of our inquiry, about the normative character of basic ontic relationships. In the sphere of Christian ethics it is not what ought to be that effects what is, but what is effects what ought to be.' D. Bonhoeffer, *Sanctorum Communio*, pp. 26, 146.

places the I into truth, that is, gives an understanding of God and self.[31] The fact that one cannot 'place himself in truth' is a fundamental concept for Bonhoeffer. This follows from his rejection of German Idealism which drew all reality into the self-conscious 'I'. Bonhoeffer follows Barth at this point, by asserting that it is the Word of God which places man into truth, not man's understanding of that Word:

> What offends Christian thought in any autonomous self-understanding is that it considers man capable of bestowing truth on himself, of transporting himself into the truth by his own resources, since it is reasonable to suppose that the 'basis' of existence must somehow be within truth (likeness to God).... Is it merely by chance that the profoundest German philosophy finishes in the I-confinement of the All? No, the knowledge it represents is likewise a self-placing into truth—for the world of the I untouched by grace is confined to the I—though not the truth of God's word, because it simply 'is' not in this truth.[32]

This also applies when man attempts to set his own limits, even transcendental ones, for limits set by 'I' remain with the power of the 'I'. My own being then, cannot define its own limits nor place itself in reality. Therefore, a purely ontological exploration of reality (concern with being) is considered by Bonhoeffer to be a retreat from the ontic dimension of personhood: 'The abandonment of the ontic by retreat upon the ontological is considered inadmissible by revelation.'[33]

Now what kind of a relationship is it that 'places' one's being in truth? It can only be a relationship which limits my being and defines it by confronting it in an I-Thou relationship. And this, we have already seen, can only take place at the level of concrete sociality. A non-ontic relation would then be a relation which does not concretely limit and define man as personal being before God:

> The being of an institution is incapable of affecting the existence of man *qua* sin; it cannot stand over against man, be objective (*gegenständlich*) in the full sense. That is only possible in the real meeting with another person.[34]

As a further explanation of what it means for a person to be 'placed in truth', and thus, of an ontic relation, Bonhoeffer's exposition of the creation story can be cited. The prohibition which God gave to Adam, is seen by Bonhoeffer to indicate to Adam his creatureliness and his

---

[31]Cf. *Act and Being*, p. 80.
[32]*Ibid.*, pp. 71-72.
[33]*Ibid.*, p. 74.
[34]*Ibid.*, p. 111.

freedom, which can only be understood as freedom for God. Thus, Bonhoeffer continues,

> this prohibition must have made the grace of the Creator only more visible to Adam. But this very being addressed in his creatureliness and freedom made the distance between the Creator and the creature more distinct, and thus at the same time it must have emphasized the creature's own being. In the creation of woman from Adam's rib, Adam's own being as creature is intensified in a way he had never imagined. The limit within which he lives has now taken on bodily form.... Man's limit has drawn nearer to him and has become all the more sharply defined,... with the creation of woman, man's limit has entered into the midst of the created world.[35]

An ontic relationship can thus be said to do two things: It confronts man with the limit of his being and concretely places him in personal relation to God. Therefore, it follows that a social relationship is ontic only because the divine person confronts the persons in relation at the concrete social level. The converse, of course, would also be true for Bonhoeffer: a relationship with God is ontic only because it is concretized in social relation. What is fundamental for Bonhoeffer's concept of an ontic relationship is that through a concrete situation, the person is placed in a relationship of truth with respect to God. What is not clear at this point, is how Bonhoeffer can draw his ontic boundaries between Christ existing as community and Christ in the world.[36] But this, as we shall see, was not exactly clear to Bonhoeffer either in the light of subsequent events.

We must now come back to the original form of our second assumption: the normative character of basic ontic relationships. The word 'normative' is the operative word in this statement. The full weight of the assumption hangs on the content that Bonhoeffer gives to this word. Again, we can only draw conclusions from the larger context in which

---

[35] *Creation and Fall*, p. 75.

[36] Bonhoeffer's thinking at the outset was clearly restricted by his concern for the problem of the church as the concrete form of Christ in the world. When he does relate his thinking to the relation of the church to the world, he arrives at a difficult and somewhat ambiguous conclusion: 'Revelation, then, happens with the communion; it demands primarily a Christian sociology of its own.... man in reality is never *only* the single unity, not even the *one* "claimed by the Thou", but invariably finds himself in some community, whether in "Adam" or in "Christ". The Word of God is given to mankind, the gospel to the communion of Christ, ...' *Act and Being*, p. 122. I think that it can be said, even at this point, that the 'normative character of basic ontic relationships' had already gone beyond this artificial distinction, a fact that Bonhoeffer did not realize until he was forced beyond this boundary himself during the war.

Bonhoeffer uses it, as well as from the basic assumption already taken into consideration.

Bonhoeffer has already put forth his claim that a person is only totally a person in community. An atomistic concept of person would violate the 'norm' by which person is determined. But within empirical social relations, in which persons are apparently in community, only an ontic relation—a relation in which the person is placed into truth— carries the structure of true community. That is, only then can one say that Christ is existing as community. This, then, would seem to be the meaning of 'normative' when used with regard to ontic relation- ships. In concrete social situations, only relationships which have the character of placing persons into the truth of relation with God are considered normative, and is the standard by which all other concepts of personal reality are measured.

This seems to be the way in which we are to understand the use of this basic assumption by Bonhoeffer in his attempt to defend his concept of Christ existing as the church in the face of arguments that the empirical church is often far from a perfect or ideal community:

> For the church is Christ existing as the church. No matter how dubious its empirical form may be, it remains the church so long as Christ is present in his Word. Thereby we acknowledge that God has willed the church's historical life, in the sense that it is intended to perfect itself. The Body of Christ is just as much a real presence in history as it is the standard for its own history. This brings us once again to what was said at the beginning of our inquiry, about the normative character of basic ontic relationships. In the sphere of Christian ethics it is not what ought to be that effects what is, but what is that effects what ought to be.[37]

Bonhoeffer is still operating at this point with the traditional Lutheran marks of the church, the Word and the sacraments. Where these are faithfully proclaimed and experienced, man is being placed in the truth despite any imperfections in the form of the church, and especially is he being placed in the truth if he knows himself as sinner. As a result, Bonhoeffer's assumption of the normative character of basic ontic re- lationships and the traditional marks of the church coincide. What Bonhoeffer has not faced at this stage is the possibility of a basic ontic relationship outside the boundary of the church, and especially, beyond the boundary of a religious community. The moment that can become a possibility, the normative character of that ontic relationship will cause it to stand independently of the traditional marks of the

[37]*Sanctorum Communio*, p. 146.

church. Unquestionably, it was this basic assumption which gave Bonhoeffer some of his most creative insights near the end, but also which caused him his greatest perplexity.

And the reason for the perplexity is to be found in a third basic assumption which I believe is the most fundamental one for his theological thought: *God is identical with himself in his revelation.*

> The concept of revelation presupposes that God is identical with himself in his revelation. Otherwise it is not strictly a question of revelation but of manifestation, or an idea. To say that God becomes man thus makes it necessary to say that Jesus Christ is identical in being with God.[38]

Taken by itself, this assumption of Bonhoeffer's is no radical departure from the classical statements of orthodoxy concerning the relation of God to Jesus Christ. The council of Chalcedon established the dogma that one was up against God himself in Christ, not merely a representation of God. Bonhoeffer was also following Luther at this point, who liked to say, 'You should point to the whole man Jesus and say, "That is God".'[39] But it is another remarkable citation from Luther that reveals the direction of Bonhoeffer's thinking with regard to the identity of God himself in his revelation:

> It is the honour and glory of our God (*unseres Gottes Ehre*), however, that, giving himself for our sake in deepest condescension, he passes into the flesh, the bread, our hearts, mouths, entrails, and suffers also for our sake that he be dishonourably (*unehrlich*) handled, on the altar as on the Cross.[40]

What Bonhoeffer has done, is to create, in effect, a theological syllogism with this latter assumption as the minor premise: Christ is the revelation of God existing concretely as community; God is identical with himself in his revelation; therefore, man is up against God himself in the church as the community of revelation.

> In revelation it is a question less of God's freedom on the far side from us, i.e. his eternal isolation and aseity, than of his forthproceeding, his *given* Word, his bond in which he has bound himself, of his freedom as it is most strongly attested in his having freely bound himself to historical man, having placed himself at man's disposal. God is not free *of* man but *for* man. Christ is the Word of his freedom, God is *there*, which is to say: not in eternal non-

---

[38]D. Bonhoeffer, *Christology*, p. 102.
[39]Cited by Bonhoeffer, *Christology*, p. 81.
[40]Luther, W. A. 23, 157. Cited by D. Bonhoeffer, *Act and Being*, p. 81.

objectivity but ... 'haveable', graspable in his Word within the Church.[41]

What Bonhoeffer does not take up, is the question of *how* the divine Word is made identical with the historical community, but in the face of this question, neatly paraphrased Luther by saying, 'You shall point to this word of man and say, "That is the Word of God".'[42]

What was later to cause a great deal of perplexity for Bonhoeffer is already apparent when one considers his three basic theological assumptions in their relationship to each other.[43] His christological syllogism which identified the reality of God with the church as community does not really take into account the full force of his second basic assumption: the normative character of basic ontic relationships. For, as I have already indicated, this assumption cannot be contained within the traditional ecclesiastical boundaries, and carries Christology further into the world than even Bonhoeffer realized at the time. This becomes clear when he says,

> existence either is or is not actually encountered by revelation, and this happens to it, as a concrete, psychophysical whole, on the 'borderline' which no longer passes through man as such, or can be drawn by him, but is Christ himself.[44]

This borderline 'at the centre' of man's existence has its antecedent in Bonhoeffer's concept of the 'barrier' which limits the individual's existence by placing him in an ethically responsible relation to the concrete other as Thou.[45] In *Creation and Fall*, Bonhoeffer speaks more explicitly of the limit at the middle:

---

[41]*Act and Being*, pp. 90-91.
[42]*Christology*, p. 53.
[43]The perplexity to which I refer is expressed by Bonhoeffer in his *Letters and Papers From Prison*: 'What do a church, a community, a sermon, a liturgy, a Christian life mean in a religionless world? How do we speak of God—without religion, ... In what way are we "religionless-secular" Christians, in what way are we the ἐκ-κλησία, those who are called forth, ... What is the place of worship and prayer in a religionless situation?' pp. 280-281.
[44]*Act and Being*, p. 80.
[45]'This brings us close to the problem of reality, of the real barrier, and thus of basic social relations. It is a Christian recognition that the person, as a conscious person, is created in the moment when a man is moved, when he is faced with responsibility, when he is passionately involved in a moral struggle, and confronted by a claim which overwhelms him. Concrete personal being arises from the concrete situation.' *Sanctorum Communio*, p. 31. Rejecting the 'idealist' concept of person as a metaphysical abstraction and a dialectic of the mind, Bonhoeffer defines 'person' in terms of the ethical, which, for him, is always concrete and always involves the necessity of the 'other'—of the Thou. 'The Christian person arises solely from the absolute distinction between God and man;

Man's limit is in the middle of his existence, not on the edge. The limit which we look for on the edge is the limit of his condition, of his technology, of his possibilities. The limit in the middle is the limit of his reality, of his true existence.[46]

It is this particular Christological concept, then, that finds its expression in the *Letters and Papers From Prison*:

Here again, God is no stop-gap; he must be recognized at the centre of life, not when we are at the end of our resources; ... in our activities, and not only in sin. The ground for this lies in the revelation of God in Jesus Christ.[47]

A second theological syllogism can now be formulated out of Bonhoeffer's basic assumptions, using the third assumption in this case, as the major premise: God is identical with himself in his revelation; basic ontic relations are normative for the revelation of Christ; therefore, man is up against God himself when Christ meets him at the centre of an ontic relationship.

The three basic assumptions, therefore, appear to produce the so-called 'two Christologies' which John A. Phillips has identified as a point of tension in Bonhoeffer's thought—Christ existing as the church and Christ existing as the personal centre and boundary of individual existence in the world.[48] But it must be asked: how can there be two Christologies if one begins with Christ? This points to the need for a critique of Bonhoeffer's theology of historical transcendence from the Christological perspective.

One is forcibly reminded at this point, of the words which Arthur Miller placed in the mouth of his leading character in *After the Fall*:

What burning cities taught her and the death of love taught me: that we are very dangerous! ... And the wish to kill is never killed, but with some gift of courage one may look into its face when it appears, and with a stroke of love—as to an idiot in the house—forgive it; again and again ... forever?[49]

Is this the kind of ontic relationship with reality that places one in the truth of God, and thus is normative? Is the knowing all—as Miller says—or does some other, inexplicable thing have to be present before Christ

only from the experience of the barrier does the self-knowledge of the moral person arise. The more clearly the barrier is recognized, the more deeply the person enters into responsibility.' *Ibid.*, p. 31.
[46]p. 51. Bonhoeffer's emphasis.
[47]p. 312.
[48]*The Form of Christ in the World*, pp. 73ff, p. 83.
[49]p. 120.

is there? There is no easy answer—but it is the kind of question that Bonhoeffer would have liked.

2 'Closing the Circle of Transcendence'

The recognition of the world's coming of age is, with Bonhoeffer, neither philosophy nor phenomenology, but the knowledge of God, i.e. 'theology', and that is a knowledge that seeks to follow God where he has already preceded us. That is why Bonhoeffer's statement about the world come of age, is first and last a theological statement.[50]

With his customary self-assurance, that would have been insufferable in anyone who lacked his great humanity, Bonhoeffer dismissed Bultmann's efforts at demythologizing the New Testament as no more than the liberal approach, in the final analysis; 'whereas', Bonhoeffer continued, 'I seek to think theologically'.[51]

It was Bultmann's dependence upon the ontology of Heidegger that led Bonhoeffer to conclude that he was probably 'sailing in the channel' of German idealism after all, and that the projection of faith along the lines of authentic potentiality through the self-understanding of *Dasein* was not theological thought because it failed to make room for revelation.[52] Theology, as we have seen, did not mean for Bonhoeffer a particular way of seeing the world or human existence with respect to God; it was never *Weltanschauung*, but rather the core of reality resulting from man's being placed in the truth through revelation:

> Revelation, which places the I into truth, i.e. gives understanding of God and self, is a contingent occurrence which can only be welcomed or rejected in its positivity—that is to say, received as a reality—but not elicited from speculation about human existence as such.[53]

There is, then, a distinct correspondence between a theology of historical transcendence and the problematic of historical transcendence. For the reality which gives meaning to historical existence is the reality of God in concrete relation to the world as its creator and redeemer, and

[50]Bethge, *Dietrich Bonhoeffer*, p. 771.
[51]*Letters and Papers From Prison*, p. 285.
[52]'... ontology is unable to advance beyond an intramundane metaphysic in its concept of God, so long as it purports to discover possibilities in man of understanding himself, and God via himself—in other words self-'projection on the lines of his authentic potentiality.' (Heidegger)—and so long as the world and its idea of God are both contained within the I; but that means, so long as there is failure to make room for a revelation, i.e. to form theological concepts of act and being.' *Act and Being*, p. 69.
[53]*Ibid.*, p. 80.

yet that reality of relation is problematical because it is theo-logical and not anthropo-logical. It is contingent in its positivity, as Bonhoeffer said, and can never be inferred out of the relationship itself.

We are now ready to take up the two questions which were set aside at the beginning of this chapter: (1) the degree to which Bonhoeffer has grasped the fundamental problematic of historical transcendence, and (2) how the theology of historical transcendence and the reality of God can be explicated without reducing the problematic to either an irrational or rational subjectivism, but at the same time reveal its inner logic.

In considering the first question, we should have clearly in mind the nature of a problematic and particularly, the nature of the problematic of historical transcendence as it has been defined in the second chapter. A problematic, in distinction from a paradox, is a correspondence which has an intrinsic rationality which is given to the relation by a reality not inferred from the relation itself.[54] The reality of the relation is known concretely and its rationality must always be that which is explicated out of concreteness and not conferred upon the relation by thought alone. To avoid confusion, it should be remembered that the 'problematic' aspect of this kind of relation only indicates the insufficiency of reflective thought to 'hold' the reality in its grasp, it does not imply a questionable character to the reality itself.

The question then of the relation of the reality of God to the reality of the world is said to be problematical in precisely this sense: there is a real relation between God and the world at the concrete (or ontic) level sustained by God's interaction with the world from his freedom. This interaction actually intensifies the 'profaneness' of the world and gives it a reality of its own, but the rationality, or the inner logic of this reality cannot be abstracted from the reality of God, that is, his transcendence in the form of concrete interaction. This transcendence is the theology of historical transcendence and properly belongs to the second question.

Perhaps the best way to pursue the question of Bonhoeffer's grasp of this problematic of historical transcendence would be to examine the argument of a man who holds that Bonhoeffer has failed in his attempt to bring the reality of God and the reality of the world together. Bonhoeffer failed in his theological task of uniting the reality of God and the reality of the world, says Hans Schmidt, 'because the problem of *history* in all its depth remained hidden from him'.[55] Schmidt charges that Bonhoeffer's thought remained imprisoned in the classical Western tradition of the doctrine of the two natures, and that consequently 'Bonhoeffer's oft-emphasized "seriousness of historicity" corresponds to the "serious-

---

[54] See above, p. 69.
[55] 'The Cross of Reality?', *World Come of Age*, p. 219.

ness" of his "Christian doctrine of sin", not however to taking history seriously as a reality effected by God's Word.'[56]

It is Bonhoeffer's alleged depreciation of history as a sphere of genuine human responsibility for progress and change that Schmidt seizes upon in his criticism:

> The thought of a possible positive historical change of social 'givens', even a discovery and development of new possibilities of social realization being given as man's responsibility, is unable to emerge in this transitory, dualistic scheme of the social process.[57]

Bonhoeffer has virtually abandoned history to its 'godlessness', says Schmidt,[58] and 'merely sanctioned the *status quo* of an abstractly conceived reality of Creation for the *time* between the Fall and the Last Judgment, as the end of the reality of this world'.[59] Instead of overcoming the 'thinking in two spheres', as Bonhoeffer thought he had done, Schmidt accuses him of an 'historically unmediated, dialectical union between God and man, Creation and salvation, time and eternity ... which we find in this paradoxical relationship between penultimate and ultimate'.[60]

The crucial insight we need into an understanding of Schmidt's critique of Bonhoeffer comes through his charge that Bonhoeffer has seriously misunderstood 'our world' as a world come of age, that is, as a world which has been forsaken by God and left to its own autonomous self-sufficiency until the end of time.[61] This, says Schmidt, is a betrayal of the reality of the world for the sake of the reality of God. What Schmidt wants to affirm, is that what is needed is a 'conversion to the world' in order to affirm its reality for the sake of Jesus Christ, along with the prophets, evangelists and apostles, as the history of God with man.[62]

> In contrast to this, did not Bonhoeffer's acknowledgement of the so-called 'world come of age' remain imprisoned, in spite of everything, in *the* tradition which, according to his own conviction, had already run its course? ... Because for Bonhoeffer this world appeared to be left to its own resources precisely through the word of God, God could no longer be thought of by him as the one who does his work in and with the world, but only as its last limit.[63]

In arriving at some evaluation of Schmidt's criticism of Bonhoeffer, it must be admitted at the outset that he has exposed many of the problems in Bonhoeffer's theology. He has clearly seen the tension in Bonhoeffer's

[56]*Ibid.*, pp. 246, 224-225.
[57]*Ibid.*, p. 224.
[58]*Ibid.*, p. 244.
[59]*Ibid.*, p. 233.
[60]*Ibid.*, p. 231.
[61]*Ibid.*, p. 241.
[62]*Ibid.*, pp. 252-253.
[63]*Ibid.*, p. 253.

thought between the reality of God in the world and the reality of God in the church, what Phillips called his 'two Christologies'. Schmidt has also shown, and rightly I think, the failure of Bonhoeffer to say what it meant *for the world* for Christ to transcend it in suffering, and for God to concretize himself in his revelation in the world. He has also pointed out the difficulties of a theology of the cross without a profound understanding of the Incarnation itself. There is room for a valid critique of Bonhoeffer's Christology here, as I have already indicated.

Nor can one fault Schmidt for showing that Bonhoeffer interpreted the reality of the world in terms of the reality of God, that is, taking a specifically theological view of sociology and of history. What is debatable though—and here is where the lid can be lifted on the problematic of historical transcendence—is Schmidt's argument that this necessarily implies a dialectical concept of the relation between God and the world. Ronald Gregor Smith, in his introductory essay to the volume in which Schmidt's essay appears, comes to Bonhoeffer's defence at this point by insisting that Schmidt has missed the 'subtlety of the dialectic with which Bonhoeffer seeks to hold together the reality of the world and the reality of God'.[64] Now this is not very helpful, in my estimation. If one wishes to avoid a situation, a subtle dialectic is as much a problem as for a woman to be slightly pregnant. Smith, of course, does not wish to avoid the concept of dialectic at all, and in attempting to exonerate Bonhoeffer ends up substantiating the criticism.

I would argue, on the other hand, that Schmidt has mis-read Bonhoeffer at this point, because he has interpreted as a dialectic what is, in fact, a problematic. Because Schmidt himself feels that man's ultimate freedom is a freedom 'for history' rather than 'for God', he can only interpret a distinctly theological assumption as dialectical, and thus, unhistorical. Bonhoeffer, on the other hand, sees man's historical reality as truly problematical because it is a reality which is *willed* for man by God, and thus is intrinsically theological.

What is missing from Schmidt's argument is any reference to the place of revelation in Bonhoeffer's construct of historical reality. Because he interprets Bonhoeffer as 'thinking' the relation between the reality of God and the reality of the world, he reduces the actual problematic of a real relationship to mutually exclusive realities—which he imputes to Bonhoeffer.[65] When Bonhoeffer concluded that a world which had come of age was characterized by 'godlessness' (which, by the way, he termed a hopeful godlessness as distinguished from a hopeless godlessness),[66] far from this being an abandonment of the world in order to take up the theme of the reality of God, it was an ontic reality which

[64]*World Come of Age*, p. 18.
[65]'The Cross of Reality?', *World Come of Age*, p. 232.
[66]*Ethics*, p. 103.

Bonhoeffer understood as a 'placing of the world in truth' by the revelation of Christ:

> Thus the world's coming of age is no longer an occasion for polemics and apologetics, but is now really better understood than it understands itself, namely on the basis of the gospel and in the light of Christ.[67]

It is difficult to see how Schmidt could come to his conclusion that Bonhoeffer arrived at a concept of the world 'coming of age' through a 'serious misunderstanding of the man who is freed to be responsible for the world, a misunderstanding which lives from the denial of history and which prematurely justifies the reflection of the apparently autonomous reason'.[68] Unless, of course, we conclude that Schmidt has simply failed to grasp the basic theological assumptions implicit in Bonhoeffer's thought in which two levels of reality, not two spheres, are locked together through God's interaction with the world. This interaction taking the form of revelation concretizing itself as a limit in the centre of man's existence, continually places man in the truth of relation to God—and this, for Bonhoeffer, was the true meaning of man's history. The argument between Schmidt and Bonhoeffer is not merely the problem of history, what is at stake is a fundamental theological assumption concerning the nature of reality.

John A. Phillips has also criticized Bonhoeffer for failing to give serious consideration to the problem of history and faith. Specifically, he charges that Bonhoeffer failed to enter into serious conversation with the problem of historical relativism as represented by Troeltsch because of his axiomatic assumptions concerning the finality of revelation as over against religious consciousness.[69] While granting that Bonhoeffer tended to dismiss as irrelevant problems which he had already by-passed with his basic assumptions, one might ask, nevertheless, why should the axiomatic assumptions of Troeltsch concerning the irrelevance, if not the impossibility, of revelation be considered a normative truth against which other alternatives are forced to argue their existence? It is significant that Bonhoeffer's historical transcendence (revelation) was directed towards and could include the reality of history, while Troeltsch's historical religious-consciousness could offer no real freedom or hope for history, and yet, had no place for revelation as an act of God. If God brings history under judgment through the finality of a revelation of himself in Christ (a thought which Schmidt has difficulty in accepting), he thereby makes possible a radical redemption for history, and herein is the possibility of its real freedom. A 'conversion to history' such as Schmidt sug-

[67]*Letters and Papers From Prison*, p. 329.
[68]'The Cross of Reality?', *World Come of Age*, p. 237.
[69]*The Form of Christ in the World*, pp. 173ff.

gests, is actually a form of 'historical solipsism' in which the fundamental reality of history as that which is made possible by God is ignored.

But it appears that we are wandering off course in pursuing this particular argument any further. The question which must now be answered is: has Bonhoeffer grasped the fundamental problematic of historical transcendence? My answer to this is a qualified—yes. Two important aspects of the problematic are clearly present in Bonhoeffer's basic theological assumptions, and seem to carry through despite the sometimes fragmentary style of his thought. First, he assumes that there is a correspondence between the reality of God and the reality of the world which has an inner logic, or rationality of its own which cannot be inferred out of the relation, but which is given to the relation by God. This is sustained by his concept of revelation. While this is basically a Christological relation for Bonhoeffer, he makes it clear that he considers the original Creator-creature relation to have been established with this inner logic of grace.[70] This is fundamental to what has been said earlier about the Incarnation being more than a solution to the problem (assumed by some) of a gap between Creator and creature which left an inexplicable enigma to be resolved by an inexplicable paradox of the God-man.

Second, the revelation of God which is concretized in the relation is the transcendence of God, so that a basic ontic relation with this concretized revelation is a relation directly with God. Thus, while the relation between God and the world remains problematic in the sense that man cannot place himself into the relation, but must be placed into its truth, there is no gap and no dualism between the two levels of reality which requires mediation by means of a dialectic. The reality is *in* the relation, not in the grasping of it.

My qualification is in the extent to which one could say that Bonhoeffer completely understood this in terms of a problematic, and, therefore, the extent to which his 'Christological shorthand', taken over considerably from Luther,[71] obscured and even relativized his insights into the nature of the problematic itself. However, I am convinced that dimensions of the problematic are fundamentally there in his thought, so that a valid theology of historical transcendence can be discussed on these terms. After all, if, as asserted earlier, it is axiomatic that the rationale of the problematic of historical transcendence be theological, Bonhoeffer offers us the most hope of an answer to our second question.

The question is: given the problematic, how can the theology of historical transcendence be explicated without reducing the problematic

---

[70]*Creation and Fall*, pp. 73ff.

[71]For a discussion of the relationship of Bonhoeffer's Christology to Luther, cf. Regin Prenter, 'Bonhoeffer and the Young Luther', *World Come of Age*, pp. 161-181.

to either an irrational or rational subjectivism, but at the same time reveal its inner logic? It might be said that Bonhoeffer tackled this very question in his book *Act and Being*. For it was his express purpose in that work to recover the 'inner logic' which united revelation as act to revelation as being, but which had been broken apart when revelation had been volatilized as non-entity, on the one hand, through transcendental metaphysics (Kant—and Barth as well, thought Bonhoeffer) and, on the other hand, swallowed up as entity in being itself (Heidegger):

> There is no hiding the fact that the identification of entity and revelation failed to make articulate any genuine ontology. It arose on that frontier of thought where the compulsion of inner logic broke down and the paths of transcendentalism and ontology diverged, the latter suspending thought itself in being, which therefore also transcended the entity.[72]

What Bonhoeffer sought to articulate, was revelation concretized in community, as the mediating way. In doing this, Bonhoeffer criticized Barth for his sheer 'actualism' of revelation in which God was always related contingently to time and space—thus revelation became timeless and non-objective.[73] Bonhoeffer saw this as a violation of the concrete man's bond with the absolute, and one might say, a reduction of the problematic in such a way that the reality of concrete, temporal existence was itself violated. This could also be said to be the thinking behind the 'positivism of revelation' attributed to Barth by Bonhoeffer in his prison letters.[74]

On the other hand, Bonhoeffer criticized Gogarten, and indirectly, Buber, for absolutizing man's encounter with the human 'Thou'; this, asserted Bonhoeffer, is mere reciprocity—the I and Thou 'placing' each other into truth without God and without revelation.[75] This too was a way of reducing the problematic of historical transcendence by sacrificing the transcendence of God.

The question of how to avoid either of these tendencies, was for Bonhoeffer essentially a question of the theology of being:

> Theological concepts of being must have precisely this as their ontological premise, that the Is can in no way be detached from the concrete definition.[76]

To say that God *is* in relation with the world, is, therefore, to say some-

[72]*Act and Being*, p. 112.
[73]*Ibid.*, p. 83.
[74]Cf. *Letters and Papers From Prison*, pp. 286, 328.
[75]*Act and Being*, p. 88.
[76]*Ibid.*, p. 68.

thing about God's concrete reality. The question thus became for Bonhoeffer a Christological question—for this was the concrete definition of God in his relationship with man. 'There are bounds only to concrete man as a whole, and their name is Christ.'[77] The believing community became the concrete existence of Christ, and, for Bonhoeffer, the articulation of the inner logic in the problematic of historical transcendence.

So far we have followed Bonhoeffer's attempt to work out a theology of historical transcendence in the face of what he considered to be threats to the intrinsic reality of the relation between God and the world. What remains to be shown is the way in which his theology of historical transcendence led to his conclusion concerning the 'worldliness' of christianity and the 'religionlessness' of the world. I will argue, that, contrary to the view of some, these latter concepts were not theological premises of Bonhoeffer's thought. That is, they were not a basic theological assumption chosen in opposition to the 'religious' premises of 19th century theology.[78] This important distinction can be illustrated by an examination of the difference in the concept of the religious premise between Bonhoeffer and Barth.

For Barth, the religious *a priori*, which had become the theological premise of Bonhoeffer's former teacher at Berlin, Reinhold Seeberg,[79] seemed to be an inescapable element in human consciousness and the highest human possibilty, which, nonetheless, must be overcome by grace.[80] On the other hand, for Bonhoeffer, religion is a sheer historical

[77]*Ibid.*, p. 32.

[78]This is the conclusion also drawn by Hiroshi Obayashi in his essay, 'Implicit Kantianism in Bonhoeffer's Conception of "Religionless Christianity",' *The Northeast Asia Journal of Theology*, September, 1970—March 1971, pp. 107-126. 'The present author's judgment is that even the so-called "maturity" and "religionlessness" of the world are not premises of Bonhoeffer's theology. It is precisely his theological orientation which leads to his other concepts.' p. 109.

[79]Cf. J. A. Phillips, *The Form of Christ in the World*, p. 42. According to Seeberg, the religious *a priori* was 'the intrinsic capacity for becoming aware of the being and activity of the supramundane God, and accordingly, for receiving the content of his revelation, as divine into the soul'. *Ibid.*, p. 43.

[80]'The image of God is always that reality of perception or thought in which man assumes and asserts something unique and ultimate and decisive either beyond or within his own existence, by which he believes himself to be posited or at least determined and conditioned. From the standpoint of revelation, man's religion is simply an assumption and assertion of this kind, and as such is an activity which contradicts revelation,' Karl Barth, *Church Dogmatics*, I/2, p. 302. Also, 'Religious dogma, ritual, faith and personalities are phenomena which do not have to be alien or unsympathetic, but which may well be basically integrated with its picture of human reality in both past and present.' *Ibid.*, IV/3, p. 621. It is clear that Barth speaks of religion as the refuge which man takes in his disobedience to God; nonetheless, Barth says, '. . . an escape to religion, to adoring faith in a congenial higher being, is the purest and ripest and most appropriate possibility at which he grasps in his sloth, and cannot finally cease from grasping as a slothful man.' *Ibid.*, IV/2, p. 406.

94   The Crisis of Transcendence for the Doctrine of God

accident, and as was suggested earlier, is adventitious to a theological understanding of the basic ontic relation between God and man. Bonhoeffer denied the reality of the religious *a priori* altogether. His basic theological premise would not allow for the religious premise, but instead, demanded an absolute disjunction between religion and revelation. 'Not religion, but revelation, not a religious community, but the church: that is what the reality of Jesus Christ means.'[81] Now it is true that Barth could just as well have said that, but he would never have meant the same thing by it as Bonhoeffer. What Bonhoeffer meant as the implication of this statement is that a 'religionless' world is the direct corollary of a theological assumption concerning the reality of human existence. Barth could never have really understood or affirmed a religionless world, because the very religious nature of the world was the negative pole of his dialectic of grace:

> The religious relationship of man to God which is the inevitable consequence of his sin is a degenerate form of the covenant-relationship between the Creator and the creature. It is the empty and deeply problematical shell of that relationship. But as such it is a confirmation that God will not be mocked, that even forgetful man will not be able to forget Him.... He has to bear witness to the Word of God and seal the fact that he can not be without God in this way, in the form of religion.[82]

Bonhoeffer introduced the religious question in *Creation and Fall* as the question put in the mouth of the serpent which aroused man's intention to go behind God's Word and inquire after the profundity of the true God who could be understood out of man's own being.[83] The religious question, then, can be seen as a way of reducing the true problematic by taking possession of the rationale of God's Word. This concept of religion, which Barth calls a 'deeply problematical shell', is actually a non-problematical way of understanding the reality of God according to the definition which we have been using. Bonhoeffer's understanding at this point appears to grasp the essential nature of the

---

[81]D. Bonhoeffer, *Sanctorum Communio*, p. 112.
[82]K. Barth, *Church Dogmatics*, IV/I, p. 483. It may be well to note at this point, that I consider Bonhoeffer's theology of historical transcendence more helpful in this exposition than Barth's, and for this reason, Barth has not been taken into consideration to the extent that one might expect. This is not to deny that Barth does have much to contribute, especially concerning the inner logic of the Incarnation, which we will take note of at a later point, but I find that Bonhoeffer's criticism of Barth concerning his "positivism of revelation' and lack of temporal structure of reality for revelation to be fundamentally valid. See the essay by Regin Prenter, 'Dietrich Bonhoeffer and Karl Barth's Positivism of Revelation', *World Come of Age*, R. G. Smith (ed.), pp. 93-130.
[83]p. 66.

relation between revelation and history better than does Barth's. It was, therefore, because of his basic theological premise that Bonhoeffer finally concluded that the world was religionless and 'mature', *not* because he was accurately describing the contemporary cultural-historical situation. He is not proclaiming a phenomenological fact, but making an assertion which is intrinsically included in his basic theological assumption.[84]

The conclusion, therefore, is that the structure of historical transcendence which loomed so large in Bonhoeffer's thought in the correspondence with Bethge and published in *Letters and Papers From Prison*, particularly in the concepts of the transcendence of God as the 'beyond in our midst' and 'the neighbour who is within reach',[85] is a theology of historical transcendence, as Bethge himself has already indicated.[86] Consequently, I would have to say that Bonhoeffer did indeed explicate this theology without reducing the problematic of historical transcendence, and thus retained its inner logic. To support this affirmation, I will attempt to show briefly that a correct interpretation of Bonhoeffer must understand his so-called 'two Christologies' as neither parallel developments which had to be tenuously reconciled at the end (J. Phillips) nor a subtle dialectic in which God is both absent and present in the world through a secular faith (R. G. Smith), but rather, it must be understood as a *circle of transcendence* which is closed through the 'worldliness' of the community of Christ.[87]

The explanation for this, it seems to me, lies in a closer look at a common assumption concerning Bonhoeffer's thought. Namely, that the concreteness of transcendence which Bonhoeffer sought in the world beyond the boundary of the community of belief was a movement *towards* the transcendence of God—that the movement of worldliness was necessary in order to concretely meet Christ there. I believe that this interpretation of Bonhoeffer is mistaken and creates a dichotomy in his thought which he himself did not sense. The perplexity which Bonhoeffer did sense was not an 'internal' perplexity concerning his own theological

[84]I am indebted to the essay by H. Obayashi for the structure of this argument concerning the distinction between Barth's and Bonhoeffer's religious premise. Obayashi argues quite convincingly that Ebeling has misunderstood Bonhoeffer at this point, assuming that the concept of the 'maturity of the world' and the 'religionlessness' of the world are the premises of Bonhoeffer's theology. 'Implicit Kantianism in Bonhoeffer's Conception of "Religionless Christianity"', p. 109.

[85]pp. 282, 381.

[86]*Dietrich Bonhoeffer*, p. 771.

[87]William J. Peck ('The Significance of Bonhoeffer's Interest in India', *Harvard Theological Review*, 1968, pp. 431-450) makes the interesting suggestion that Bonhoeffer was seeking to discover the faith of an 'Abraham' by going to India, and that his prison cell became his 'India', from which he saw the unity of Christ and the world (p. 449). Thus, Peck argues against the unity of Christ and the world shattering the unity of Bonhoeffer's thought by positing two unreconciled Christologies.

assumptions, but what it would mean to take them seriously in terms of a world come of age, that is, to understand the world better than it understood itself.

The basic assumption of Bonhoeffer which seemed to have the greatest force in ranging beyond the ecclesiastical boundary to his Christology was, as we saw, the normative character of basic ontic relationships.[88] It did seem at first that this was incompatible with his other assumption that Christ exists as the believing community, and that revelation only concretizes itself in that community. But at that point, the assumption of our interpretation of his two theological premises was that the normative character of ontic relations was to establish the concrete reality of Christ existing as community. Obviously, this set up an 'either-or' situation between the believing community and the world. If one knows the reality of Christ through an ontic relation with the world—with one's neighbour—then the church has been superseded as the *place* where revelation is concretized.

However, if we re-think that problem, and now suggest that the normative character of the ontic relationship is not to *find* Christ concretely, but to *be* Christ concretely in the world, the problem is resolved and new possibilities open up for our understanding of the theology of historical transcendence. There seem sufficient grounds to conclude that Bonhoeffer never departed from his fundamental assumption that God reveals himself concretely through Christ, and that Christ *is* the community established between believers through Word and Spirit.[89] This is not a reality

---

[88]See above, pp. 79ff.

[89]Cf. E. Bethge, *Dietrich Bonhoeffer*, pp. 737ff. André Dumas (*Dietrich Bonhoeffer: Theologian of Reality*, SCM Press, London, 1971) argues convincingly that the key to the unity of Bonhoeffer's thought is the concept of 'structure' (*Gestaltung*) conceived along the lines of an incarnational Hegelianism. Jesus Christ, for Bonhoeffer (says Dumas), is the responsible structure of reality in ontological dimensions which reveal the eternal reality of God through the reality of 'everydayness' (pp. 30ff). This 'ontology of an incarnate transcendence', according to Dumas, carries with it a concreteness which marks Bonhoeffer's thought from beginning to end (pp. 116-117). Therefore, it is not surprising to find that Dumas holds, that of all interpretations of Bonhoeffer, that of Heinrich Ott is closest to the central purpose of Bonhoeffer himself, for, as Dumas says, 'Ott has correctly grasped Bonhoeffer's central purpose, which was to understand follow the structuring presence of God in reality by means of the christology of the incarnation, and to overcome the dualism of metaphysics and inwardness by an ontology of presence and openness.' (p. 276). What Dumas sees as the weakness of Bonhoeffer's incarnational ontology is the lack of a well developed eschatological dimension which would keep the structure of incarnational reality from identifying God so intimately with reality that there was a danger of the incarnation ceasing to be the word of revelation *to* reality and of being transformed into the ongoing structure of reality (pp. 234-235). Despite the valuable insights of Dumas, he seems to have missed the problematic in Bonhoeffer's historical transcendence, which (in my estimation) preserves the eschatological dimension.

which stands apart from the world and demands a privileged place, but it is part of the total logic of historical transcendence which includes the world as well. Consequently, historical transcendence has a circular movement and not a punctiliar one, that is, it does not complete itself in a point of belief, but closes itself in a continued act of historical transcendence. The church, says Bonhoeffer (though he had no formula for its identification in mind) 'must get out of her stagnation. We must move out again into the open air of intellectual discussion with the world, . . .'[90] But it is clear that he had more in mind than mere intellectual discussion with the world:

> I therefore want to start from the premise that God shouldn't be smuggled into some last secret place, but that we should frankly recognize that the world, and people, have come of age, that we shouldn't run man down in his worldliness, but *confront him with God* at this strongest point, . . .'[91]

Confronting the world with God is an ontic relationship for Bonhoeffer, and thus must mean that the Christian closes the circle of historical transcendence by moving out of his 'secret place', where he knows Christ as community, and *becomes* Christ in the world. It is this movement which exposes the intrinsically non-religious character of Christianity, for the 'secret discipline'[92] must complete itself in worldliness, not by becoming worldly, nor merely 'non-religious', but by taking the place of Christ in the world. Thus the 'secret discipline' is not in a dialectical relationship with the worldliness of Christianity—that is, saying both a 'yes' and a 'no' to the world.[93] Rather, as the concretizing of revelation through identification with Christ, historical transcendence presses towards the closing of the circle by a transparent, and Bonhoeffer would say, powerless life in the world.[94]

The concept of 'sharing in the sufferings of God' and 'only a suffering God can help'[95] should then be understood as the closing of the circle,

---

[90]*Letters and Papers From Prison*, p. 378.

[91]*Ibid.*, p. 346. My emphasis.

[92]For the references to the 'secret discipline' in Bonhoeffer, cf. *Letters and Papers From Prison*, pp. 281, 286. The secret discipline (*Arkandisziplin*), says Bethge, is the guarantee of an identity between the believer with Christ through a life with Christ in which the world does not share. *Dietrich Bonhoeffer*, pp. 783ff.

[93]J. A. Phillips, e.g., interprets secret discipline and worldly life in this dialectical way. *The Form of Christ in the World*, p. 283.

[94]The extent to which one could say that the church can be defined apart from this 'closing of the circle of transcendence' is difficult to assess at this point, without confusing the line of argument concerning an interpretation of Bonhoeffer. However, this will become an important question in the final section of this book.

[95]Cf. *Letters and Papers From Prison*, p. 361.

and not as an open-ended posture of reaching out for transcendence through suffering. It is only in the exposure of oneself to the world in this 'suffering way' that one can transcend the world in the way in which Christ transcended it, through the confrontation of its 'anti-logos' with the Logos of Christ.[96]

The crucial element in this circle of historical transcendence, of course, is the reality of revelation. When that is removed, the problematic falls apart and the remaining dimensions of worldliness and inwardness are only dialectical elements of human and social experience. Revelation, one could say then, is the rationale of historical transcendence and is that which makes it possible to close the circle.

It is for this reason that I have concluded that Bonhoeffer does offer a theology of historical transcendence which can be explicated out of the problematic without reducing the problematic, because the explication of it (closing the circle) carries within it the rationale of the problematic (revelation).

The circle of historical transcendence was closed by Bonhoeffer in a way that was entirely consistent with his theology and his life. His final, normative, ontic relationship was with the hangman, who slipped the noose around his neck. This was normative, not merely for Bonhoeffer, but for the world. It was the ultimately non-religious word which had been incarnated as the penultimate. The world was being transcended again by the 'suffering God'—the circle is closed.

3 Précis

Along the somewhat tortuous ascent, which words have a way of winding around the plain truth of reality, the spirit craves a place of respite from the stupefying clamour of discussion—this is one of them.

Some things can be best seen in retrospect. The eye can link up in a glance the necessary (or unnecessary) turns which were taken in what seemed once to be an endless tacking across the face of a trackless sea of words. The truth must often be pushed up to eye level by a bushel of anonymous words, and even a self-evident thought occasionally needs to be trapped in the entrails of an argument.

From this distance, it seems surprising that it took so long to arrive at the place of absolute otherness, or that it seemed so precarious a precipice at the time. It feels quite comfortable now, to give the name God to the one who is free to approach me from his own reality. And the world did not seem suddenly to grow pale and colourless when robbed of its divinity. Human blood, after all, is no less red when un-doctored by some divine preservative. Profane, I think, was the word used

[96]Cf. D. Bonhoeffer, *Christology*, pp. 29ff.

to describe a world which is held together by muscle and not by magic. It is not a good word, and better forgotten, when it is remembered that human is *his* word.

But yes, that means that human reality is his *Word*, and that there is no network of ideas nor an ocean of feelings connecting our skins to his skinlessness. There is *nothing* to keep him close or to hold him safely at a distance, but his Word—and his Spirit. And yet, this is not his transcendence, we said, but his reality—he is God. The limit which determines his absolute difference from everything else is Spirit, and his transcendence is the act of his Spirit which places our world in its truth by his Word.

Of the three coins to be carried with us from the realm of this part to the next, this is the *first*: the transcendence of God is his act upon us and with us, and this is what we mean when we say that it is always historical transcendence.

And this is the *second*: the reality which binds God and the world together is the same reality which binds spirit and act together, it is the reality of spirit which enters into the concrete situation and becomes the act—this is the rationale of historical transcendence, but also its problematic. This means that there is no 'relation' between God and the world which is a separate entity—a thing (*die Sache*) which can be an object of thought—but the relation is always the concrete knowledge of God himself which is constitutive for that which is thought out of the act. There is then a language and a meaningful utterance which issues from historical transcendence, and which makes possible what we call theology.

So here is the *third*: the theology of historical transcendence is the explication of the incarnating and incarnate Word. It is always more than a christological assumption which seeks to smother out the life of other assumptions. The Incarnation cannot be merely an alternative way of articulating a world-view, but is itself the inner logic of historical transcendence coming to complete utterance in Jesus Christ.

We have learned some of this from Bonhoeffer, although one could have wished for a broader scope to his basic christological assumption. By that I mean, a deeper insight into the relation of the Incarnation to the inner logic of historical transcendence. Bonhoeffer had a firm grasp on the theology of historical transcendence, and to that extent, the transcendence of God. But his vulnerability was the lack of a rationale by which he could have shown *how* the circle of transcendence was closed by 'sharing in the sufferings of God at the hands of a godless world'.

This vulnerability may well be the 'tender muscle' in the thigh of a reasoning man, which cannot bear the full weight of the reality of God: but even in this sense, the vulnerability then ought to expose the structure of reality which nonetheless sustains faith—this too is a form of rationality.

The task then, which lies ahead, is to seek to expose this structure of reality which lies in the Incarnation. The inner logic of an incarnating Word will have to be shown in the historical transcendence of God as attested in the life and experience of the people of God before the time of Jesus Christ. The Incarnation itself, then, will be considered, primarily through an examination of the concept of *kenosis*—the condescending act in which God becomes man, and confronts man. But always we will be looking for the way in which the circle of historical transcendence can be closed:

'So that the world may know that thou hast sent me
and hast loved them even as thou hast loved me.'

(John 17:23)

Part Two

Incarnation and Historical Transcendence

Chapter IV

The Inner Logic of Incarnation

1 'Exploration into God'

The human heart can go to the lengths of God,...

....

Thank God our time is now, when wrong
Comes up to face us everywhere,
Never to leave us 'till we take
The longest stride of soul man ever took.
Affairs are now soul size.
The enterprise
Is exploration into God.[1]

More uncanny than the *mysterium tremendum* which lurks in the
grotesque shapelessness of the startled imagination, is the event-full
intimacy of a familiar face. More disturbing than the unknown intentions of a stranger, are the knowing footsteps of an approaching friend.
More awe-full than a disembodied spirit, is the flesh of an incarnate
God.

Not to understand this, is to allow the rationale of this book to turn
a corner and disappear completely. For the fact is, there is no way to
extend logical assumptions—cantilevering argument upon argument—
in such a way that we can construct coherent connections within and
between realities other than we are. This in no way implies a sacrifice
of the intellect, nor an epistemological dichotomy between subject and
object (contrary to Kant), but it does imply that rationality is a capacity
to behave objectively in terms of the object—as we are confronted by
it.[2]

But this also implies that we can only really be confronted by the
coherence of another reality. Incoherence has no power of confrontation, and thus carries with it neither an ultimate demand upon us nor
an immediate possibility for the communication of truth. It is in the
exposing of ourselves to the coherence of truth as it exists over against

[1]Christopher Fry, *A Sleep of Prisoners*, Oxford University Press, London, 1951,
p. 49.
[2]Cf. John Macmurray, *Reason and Emotion*, p. 32.

us, that we are rendered most defenceless—for in seeking to discover, we cannot avoid being discovered.

At one point, Bonhoeffer was troubled by a quotation he attributed to Giordano Bruno: 'There can be something frightening about the sight of a friend; no enemy can be so terrifying as he.' 'Can you understand that?', Bonhoeffer asked Bethge; 'I'm trying hard, but I can't really understand it. Does "terrifying" refer to the inherent danger of betrayal, inseparable from close intimacy (Judas?)?'[3] It would be interesting to discover what Bethge's answer was, and whether or not Bonhoeffer was satisfied with it, but there is no further reference to the subject in the correspondence. It surely must be that the 'terrifying' possibility of an encounter with a friend—certainly a strange idea at first thought—is not in the possibility of betrayal, but in revelation. We touch the highest mystery when we come up against the known, or the knowable, not the unknown or the unknowable. For this is the mystery of 'coming up against', it is the 'uncanny' moment when we *know* something or someone. When it dawns upon us that we are loved freely and intelligently by another; where the inner logic of that love is undeniably present, not in our own needs, but in the other's actions, not even in our own spirit, but in the other's body. And thus it is here that we come up against the transcendence, not the beyond, the infinite, which extends out from us, but the 'nearest to hand', the flesh which carries in it the logic of spirit.

But we can only say that this kind of logic is theo-logic because of the Incarnation, because the 'Word became flesh and dwelt among us.' (John 1 : 14). There is no Logos of God apart from the Logos of flesh— of course this is unproved! How could one prove it?[4] It comes as a terrifying, and yet utterly comforting word to us out of our own history. It is the terrible coherence of the Logos-flesh which confronts us in Jesus Christ, and which presses upon us the logic of the reality of God. It is no longer a matter of whether or not we can find coherent answers to our questions about God—it is the coherence of the question which confronts us that demands our attention, if we are willing to know the truth.

This is the methodological clue by which the exploration may now

[3]*Letters and Papers From Prison*, p. 375.

[4]I should like it to be clearly understood that the statement—there is no Logos of God apart from the Logos of flesh—is an *a posteriori* christological statement cast into the discussion at this point without qualification as an axiomatic assertion of the non-formalizable relation of God to his concrete self-expression in the world. This statement does not exclude, though it does not consider, the existence of the Logos of God 'prior' to the Incarnation. It is the kind of statement meant to break through the rigidity of a semantic barrier that one can compare to the stroke of an artist's brush which is meant to lift the imagination towards a trans-conceptual reality.

proceed. The exploration of historical transcendence, as indicated at the conclusion of the previous chapter, is into the inner logic of the incarnating and incarnate Word. As such, it is an exploration into the logic of God woven into the fabric of his history with man. But having said this, we are immediately confronted with—*confronted with!*—the organic connection which seems to exist between the man Jesus as the Incarnate Word and the 'Israel of God' as a history of incarnating Word.

The postulate of the New Testament proof from Scripture is this: Jesus' human Being was, both as a whole and in detail, 'formed' in the light of what it was God's will to do with Israel and what he is now realising.... Therefore God's action in and through Jesus, too, is only to be 'understood' on the basis of the Word in the Old Testament.... God's action in the Old Testament is not just something added to the Jesus-event by way of confirmation and corroboration, that is to say, with a cognitive significance, but it has a causative, axiomatic importance for Jesus, and therefore forms a constitutive part of this event itself.[5]

This organic connection, of course, can only be given an axiomatic value at this point. But, as T. F. Torrance has shown, axiomatic thinking is the kind of thinking forced upon us by the intrinsic structure of reality itself, and is the only kind of thinking which allows us to penetrate to the inner intelligibility of things, in nature or in God.[6] It is precisely this *kind* of thinking that enables us cognitively to grasp the inner coherence of reality which is itself problematical to straightforward logical deduction. For what really happens, is not that we grasp the truth through the sheer power of intellect, organizing bits and pieces into a whole, but we are grasped in our whole person by the inescapable reality of truth as it confronts us. Methodologically, therefore, the axiomatic assumption of an organic connection between Jesus and Israel is the 'whole thing' which confronts us. The axiom permits us to examine the connections rather than being forced to construct them. It should also be noted, however, that axioms are never fixed principles but only

[5]C. H. Ratschow, *Der angefochtene Glaube*, Gütersloh, 1957, p. 70; cited by G. von Rad, *Old Testament Theology*, Vol. II, Oliver & Boyd, Edinburgh, 1965, p. 331, n. 16.

[6]*God and Rationality*, pp. 99ff. Cf. also, Norman W. Porteous, 'The Old Testament and Some Theological Thought Forms', *Scottish Journal of Theology*, 1954, pp. 153-169: 'It is my own personal conviction that a theology of the Old Testament, properly so called, is possible only through some kind of participation, so that we come to take the God of the Old Testament quite seriously as God.... It is through participation that understanding and discrimination come. In a Biblical Theology there is bound to be an axiological element; the judgment of value cannot be excluded.' p. 168.

methodological tools, and are therefore always open to correction as the inherent structure of reality discloses itself and conforms our minds to its own truth.[7]

It now becomes possible to show why our exploration of historical transcendence will carry us beyond Gregor Smith, and to a certain extent, further than Bonhoeffer was able to go. When Smith rejected both the alternative of Bultmann (transcendence without myth, i.e., through existential self-understanding) and the alternative of Tillich (transcendence as myth, i.e., as symbol), he asked:

> Is there not a simpler answer to our problem of expressing God's action as a historical one without destroying the beyondness, the otherness, the transcendence, which is the very heart of God's being? Is this transcendence necessarily to be expressed at all in conceptual language? ... Is the Incarnation itself not to be recognized as itself providing, bringing with it, its own mode of being understood? Is there not what we may call the interior logic of faith, to be found in the event of Christ as God's final revelation? It seems to me that the givenness of Christ is something which should be seen as carrying with it certain unavoidable implications for our thinking about both history and transcendence.[8]

Right on target, I would say; the only question is—will there be any real penetration? Unfortunately not, for Smith continues:

[7]This concept of axiomatic thinking, which seeks the 'inner logic' of the Incarnation through penetration of the connections between Israel and Jesus, can be distinguished from what James Barr calls a 'purist' stance which seeks to avoid all presuppositional liabilities to error through a totally 'internal' relation to the Bible. *Old and New in Interpretation*, SCM Press, London, 1966, pp. 171ff. I would argue that axiomatic thinking differs from the 'purist' stance in at least three ways: (1) the seeking of an 'inner logic' to something does not involve the avoidance of error through an antithetical type of reasoning which sets Hebrew thought against Greek, presuppositional thinking against non-presuppositional thinking, or philosophy against theology. But rather, is a kind of thinking which seeks 'real meanings' intrinsic to 'real contacts' between God and man. As Barr himself says: 'In that God works towards what happens in Christ, he works towards it in situations of actual contact with God, and the form by which we can enter into some understanding of the contact is the text which is the reflex produced by the contact.' (p. 155). (2) Axiomatic thinking is not a 'method', but the seeking of the true meaning of a situation as given in its original context. Once again, cf. Barr, pp. 143-144. (3) Finally, axiomatic thinking centres upon the explication of evidences rather than an analysis of presuppositions. Or again, as Barr says, 'Its centre lies in the use of evidence and not in the influence of presuppositions.' (p. 187). While I am not implying that Barr would agree with all that I mean by the 'inner logic' of the Incarnation, I think that I have shown that it is more consistent with the directions of his own exegetical approach than that which he labels with the rubric 'purist' in a pejorative sense.

[8]R. G. Smith, 'Lectures on Apologetics', *Collected Papers*, pp. 114-115.

The answer which is contained in the interior logic of the Incarnation is that God is disclosed in and through the ordinary situations of our life and nowhere else. We encounter transcendence not as a theory of understanding the universe but as the very nature of our encounter with things and persons in this world.[9]

One has the feeling that Gregor Smith desperately *wanted* to grasp the inner logic of God's action with man through history and so avoid speculative metaphysics with its abstract *ideas* of God. He hit upon the right place, but it was, after all, only a glancing blow. The interior logic of the Incarnation was always hidden from him because he sought instead the interior logic of faith.[10] The Incarnation was, for him, a paradigmatic event through which he sought to give validity to the concreteness of life-situations.[11]

The Incarnation *can* be seen as a way of relating God to the world and the world to God in a way that gives meaning to contemporary man. This has a particular kind of logic to it, for it appears to establish a correspondence between two kinds of disparate realities—that of God and the world. But it is this kind of thinking which reduces the Incarnation to a 'timeless event' which, though inaccessible itself, serves as a regulative principle for either a religious—or a non-religious—interpretation of faith. Thus, even for Bonhoeffer, the 'inner meaning' of the Incarnation was more an operative principle for the placing of his own life and time in perspective than it was an axiomatic penetration of God's transcendence in the world. For this reason, his profound assertion that 'only a suffering God can help', while christologically valid, lacks the inner logic which a deeper penetration of the Incarnation would

[9]*Ibid.*, p. 116.
[10]Concerning the Incarnation Smith says: 'The power of that event can be properly faced only in the logic of that event itself, ... we call the way of meeting and accepting it *faith*.' *The New Man*, p. 109.
[11]'In this kind of a situation, in the relation with a friend, we may see the category of transcendence at work. Transcendence is otherness in with-ness, it is a living relation in the given situations of our life. In the life of Jesus we meet with the same kind of thing. We do not know God in his inapprehensible Otherness, for about that we cannot speak at all.' R. G. Smith, 'Lectures on Apologetics', *Collected Papers*, p. 119. Unfortunately, the substance of Smith's exposition of the inner logic of the Incarnation is 'in the life of Jesus we meet with the same kind of thing'. This is what I mean when I say that he saw in the human life of Jesus the paradigm for the transcendence of 'historical suffering love'. This remains true despite his final attempts to avoid this kind of philosophical extrapolation: 'Is Christ then just the illustration of the way in which a philosophical puzzle can be solved? Not at all: but he is the way in which historical human experience points to the only source of transcendence, viz., historical suffering love.' 'Princeton Lecture Notes', March 20, 1968, *Collected Papers*.

have yielded.[12] However, it must be said that Bonhoeffer was moving closer and closer to a grasp of the organic connection between Jesus and the Old Testament.[13] There is good reason to think that the most profitable push one can take from Bonhoeffer is in this direction.

For reasons that ought to be obvious, an exploration of the organic connection between God's act in Jesus and God's act in Israel cannot pretend to take up the difficult, but important, question of the relationship of the Old Testament to the New, or even, for that matter, the complex critical and theological questions which pertain to a proper theology of the Old Testament. The concept of an organic connection does, in itself, go a long way towards establishing a genuine unity between the Old and New Testaments. But the pertinent question for this chapter is not the question of the unity of the Testaments but the coherence of God's history with man. Because axiomatic assumption of an organic connection between Jesus and Israel emerges from a consideration of God's action with Israel as a redeemed community and his act in Jesus as the redeemer, the proper subject of the recorded testimonies concerning this history is not the religion of Israel, nor the faith of Israel, and not even a history of 'revelation', but the living Word of Jahweh—the God who names himself in his actions with and for his people. If this may be said to be the basic assumption on which we are to proceed, it should be noted that it can be supported by at least some recent Old Testament theologians.[14] It only needs to be emphasized that

[12]'The reality of God discloses itself only by setting me entirely in the reality of the world, and when I encounter the reality of the world it is always already sustained, accepted and reconciled in the reality of God. This is the inner meaning of the revelation of God in the man Jesus Christ.' D. Bonhoeffer, *Ethics*, p. 195.

[13]'My thoughts and feelings seem to be getting more and more like those of the Old Testament, and in recent months I have been reading the Old Testament much more than the New. It is only when one knows the unutterability of the name of God that one can utter the name of Jesus Christ; ...' *Letters and Papers From Prison*, pp. 156-157; cf. also pp. 336, 374.

[14]Cf. G. von Rad, *Old Testament Theology*, Vol. I, Oliver & Boyd, Edinburgh, 1962: 'Never, in these testimonies about history, did Israel point to her own faith, but to Jahweh. Faith, undoubtedly finds very clear expression in them; but as a subject it lies concealed, and can often only be grasped by means of a variety of inferences which are often psychological and on that account problematical. In a word, the faith is not the subject of Israel's confessional utterances, but only its vehicle, its mouthpiece. And even less can the 'history' of this world of faith be the subject of the theology of the Old Testament.... So too the idea of a 'religion of Israel', that is, the idea of the faith as an entity, appears more problematical still as a result of the investigation of the history of tradition in our own time.... If, however, we put Israel's picture of her history in the forefront of our theological consideration, we encounter what appropriately is the most essential subject of a theology of the Old Testament, the living word of Jahweh coming on and on to Israel for ever, and this is the message uttered by his mighty acts. It was a message so living and actual for each moment that it accompanied her on her journey through time, interpreting

if we are to consider God's action with Israel a 'pre-history' of the Incarnation, this does not mean reading back into the Old Testament christological ideas and imposing them upon the text; and still less does it mean abstracting from the Old Testament a set of systematic principles which can be added to the Incarnation. This would be a violation of the methodology already chosen, in that a structure of reality would then be imposed on the object of our study rather than allowing the inherent structure of that reality to confront us. This would also be to ignore the fact that these exegetical methods so common to the 19th century have largely given way to a theology of the Old Testament which focuses on the interconnection of revelation by Word and event.[15]

itself afresh to every generation, and informing every generation what it had to do.' pp. 111-112. Cf. also, T. C. Vriezen, *An Outline of Old Testament Theology*, Basil Blackwell, Oxford, 2nd revised edition, 1970: 'In the Old Testament He reveals Himself by entering into an immediate relationship with Israel, His people, as the God of Salvation, and, as such, as the Creator, Sustainer and Recreator of the world. In Jesus Christ, whom the New Testament affirms to be the Way, the Truth and the Life, God proceeds with his work in Israel. The revelation of God in Jesus Christ is so closely linked with the prophetic testimony of the Old Testament, not only historically but also intrinsically and fundamentally, that when the Christian Church proclaims Jesus of Nazareth to be the Messiah she cannot do without the Old Testament revelation.' pp. 22-23.

[15]Cf. G. von Rad, *Old Testament Theology*, Vol. II: 'The larger context into which we have to set the Old Testament phenomena if they are to be meaningfully appreciated is not, however a general system of religious and ideal values, but the compass of a specific history, which was set in motion by God's words and deeds and which, as the New Testament sees it, finds its goal in the coming of Christ. Only in this event is there any point in looking for what is analogous and comparable.' p. 369. While James Barr would challenge the assertion that revelation through historical event is the dominating motif of the Israelite tradition (*Old and New in Interpretation*, pp. 65ff.), G. Ernest Wright, on the other hand, insists that one cannot separate God's activity as Word (speech) from his activity in event: 'An event is expressed by means of a subject conjugating a verb. Neither the subject nor the verb will be analysed as an entity in itself; it is the former realizing itself through the latter, giving to the latter its tense, its time.' 'Reflections Concerning Old Testament Theology', *Studia Biblica et Semitica*, H. Veenman & Zonen N.V., Wageningen, 1966, p. 383. While not wishing to enter into the complex problem of the primacy of either Word or event in their inter-relation, I wish to assume as axiomatic, the intrinsic connection of divine Word to historical event, in order to investigate the structure of God's self-expression by which he is known as the *subject* of Israel's history. To this extent, I would share Barr's criticism of any equation of revelation with history, although I must immediately add that I cannot share Barr's apparent preference for 'balanced exegesis' over revelation as history. Cf. *Old and New in Interpretation*, p. 101. What Barr has not done, at least to my satisfaction, is to come to grips with the problem of what it means to say that God is the subject of Israel's history. This in essence, is the judgment made by G. Ernest Wright in his evaluation of Barr's attempt to challenge the relation of revelation to history. *The Old Testament and Theology*, Harper and Row, New York, 1969, pp. 47ff.

It is in the explicit assertions which Israel makes about Jahweh that we can discover the fabric of God's history emerging through a Word which is at the same time event. It is in the 'telling' of these deeds of Jahweh, or what Kornelis Miskotte calls 'narrative philosophy',[16] that the living truth is carried on, to be appropriated by each succeeding generation, and to be incorporated into the new deeds and the situations which Israel experiences. The inner logic of these acts, indeed of the history itself, remains inaccessible to the systematician. But here the theologian—thus arises the true science of dogmatics—must transpose himself into a way of thinking which is open to the acts of God.

Concerned as we are with the inner connections of God's action in and with human existence, which appear to point towards the structure of Logos becoming flesh, it now remains to be seen just how this structure is exposed prior to what we call the Incarnation—the 'Word becoming flesh.' Because God, as the subject of Israel's testimony to his deeds, expresses himself concretely as divine Logos through the historical act of word-event, we should expect to find in God's self-communication, his self-revelation, and even in his self-condescension a logic and language which help us to *think* our way into the Incarnation and expose its inner rationale.

The Humanity of God in His Self-Communication

The cluster of events which constitute the spine in the living body of Israel's history with God can be quite easily plotted as: the call of Abraham and the founding of a particular people; the exodus from Egypt; the giving of the Law at Sinai; the conquest of the land of Canaan; the establishing of the monarchy; and the exile. At the far end, one can take note of the table of Nations (Genesis 10) following the flood epic and the confusion of languages at Babel (Genesis 11), and assign them some relevant connection as rudimentary skeletal forms embedded in the pre-history of Israel. And at the near end, one might wish to add the return from exile and the rebuilding of the temple. But every spine has its practical limits, and for the sake of precision, let us consider the six at the centre as sufficient to grasp the narrative at its core.[17]

At the heart of these narratives which testify to God's action in calling, redeeming and establishing a people for himself in the world, lies the reality of divine self-communication. It is God himself who appears to

[16]*When the Gods are Silent*, p. 206.
[17]There are at least two 'canonical' records of the saving acts of God which include the events from the calling of Abraham to the conquest of the land. Deuteronomy 26:5-9 and Joshua 24:2ff. However, James Barr, who questions the value of such *kerygma*-type statements, places little weight upon these passages as being representative of normal Old Testament Literature. Cf. *Old and New in Interpretation*, p. 74.

Abram (Genesis 17:1), who confronts Moses as Jahweh, the God of
Abraham, Isaac and Jacob (Exodus 3:15), who speaks the Law from
Mt. Sinai in the wilderness (Exodus 19:3ff.), and it is God who will
give himself to the task of claiming the promised land (Exodus 34:10ff.).

The Old Testament has many names for God, some of which they
no doubt shared with other ancient near-east religions. But beyond
these names, the God of Israel has a special name which belongs uniquely
to the self-communication of God through these special acts with and
for his people. This unutterable name of YHWH (Jahweh) is *given* to
Israel as the concrete reality of their God who is totally other than all
other gods, and yet who is the God of Abraham, Isaac and Jacob:

> Then Moses said to God, 'If I come to the people of Israel and say
> to them, "The God of your fathers has sent me to you", and they ask
> me, "What is his name?" what shall I say to them?' God said to
> Moses, 'I AM WHO I AM.' And he said, 'Say this to the people of
> Israel, "I AM has sent me to you."' God also said to Moses, 'Say
> this to the people of Israel, "The Lord (YHWH), the God of your
> fathers, the God of Abraham, the God of Isaac, and the God of Jacob,
> has sent me to you": this is my name for ever, and thus I am to be
> remembered throughout all generations.'[18]

It is the concrete Name of God which takes Israel beyond the realm of
religion and frees them from 'the silence of the gods'. The 'nameless'
Name—I AM WHO I AM, or, I WILL BE WHAT I WILL BE—is
not a name that can be used so as to *designate* one god among the
gods, but *is* the reality of God himself:

> The primary meaning is that the God of Israel withdraws himself
> from all conjuration; he cannot be conjured up with this nameless
> name and be made subservient to an ulterior purpose. But more
> specifically (and this concerns us directly), Israel is referred to the
> *action* that proceeds from YHWH, to what he undertakes to do, the
> long journey he takes with Israel from Egypt to the Promised Land
> and from there into the exile and the Diaspora, the 'days' and the
> 'deeds' which are the days and the deeds of God.[19]

Embedded within the narrative of these days and deeds, is the reminder
to God that he has given *himself* to Israel by acting through the power
of his Name; thus Moses argues, 'Remember Abraham, Isaac, and
Israel, thy servants, to whom thou didst swear by thine own self.'
(Exodus 32:13). The guarantee of Israel's nearness to God and of his

[18]Exodus 3:13-15.
[19]K. Miskotte, *When the Gods are Silent*, p. 121. Miskotte's parentheses. For
a detailed explanation of the origin and significance of the Tetragrammaton
YHWH, see *Ibid.*, pp. 119ff., 214ff.

nearness to help was in the fact that he had 'given himself away' in giving his Name to them in these mighty acts.[20]

This self-communication of God through what we may call a Name-act, marked Israel off from all others, but also served to place the reality of God *in* the world even as he was marked off *from* the world. Thus, Israel could only know its God by starting from the concrete act, not from the universal idea of the godhead. They were always called back—and calling God back!—to the deeds and days in their history. The formula was always 'The Lord is God'—Jahweh is *Elohim* —and this formula is irreversible. That is, one cannot start from the general concept, or idea of the godhead, and proceed to define Jahweh. Jahweh is only known in his self-communication, and this self-communication *is* God.[21]

The significance of this for an understanding of the transcendence of God should be immediately apparent. When we start from the infinity of God and attempt to reach his particular reality, we destroy the decisive character of the encounters of God in a concrete sense and end up with the theological ambivalence which is characteristic of the silence of the gods. When we start from the omnipotence of God's being, we are merely stating a theory, and can then find no place for the deeds and the days which place him in ontic relation with our history. When we start with the equivalence of the so-called communicable attributes, e.g., righteousness and mercy, we have lost the context of the saving and sustaining work, that is, we have lost the reality of God in his self-communication.[22] It is the 'narrative philosophy' of Israel's testimony

---

[20]'According to ancient ideas, a name was not just "noise and smoke": instead, there was a close and essential relationship between it and its subject. The subject is in the name, and on that account the name carries with it a statement about the nature of the subject or at least about the power appertaining to it. For the cultic life of the ancient East, this idea was of quite fundamental importance.... Thus the name Jahweh, in which, one might almost say, Jahweh has given himself away, was committed in trust to Israel alone. The heathen do not know it (Psalm 74:6). In it and in it alone lay the guarantee of Jahweh's nearness and of his readiness to help, and through it Israel had the assurance of being able at all times to reach his heart (Exodus 33:19; 34:6—small wonder that at all times she looked upon the name as a holy reality of a quite special kind (on occasion coming almost to the point of understanding it in a material way).' G. von Rad, *Old Testament Theology*, Vol. I., pp. 181, 182-183.

[21]Cf. K. Miskotte, *When the Gods are Silent*: 'We have already referred to the key saying: YHWH is *Elohim*! This is not reversible. The proper name YHWH defines the (seemingly) more general name, which actually is rather to be regarded as an epithet ("Know that the Lord is the Godhead," Psalm 100:3). The nameless Name is understood through the acts which occur and will continue to occur in the carrying and fulfilling of the covenant. Thus, "the Almighty" is an epithet which is to be understood on the basis of the proper name YHWH. The "primitiveness" bars the way to any ontologizing.' pp. 215-216.

[22]*Ibid.*, p. 218.

to the mighty deeds of God which gives Israel's history an ontic connection with the reality of God. The uniqueness of this against all other religious concepts of God sets Israel apart as the *place* where the transcendence of God is concretized in the saving acts of faith.[23]

But here we can see how subtle the inner logic of this historical transcendence really is! The obvious response is: yes I see! Israel's history is an objective reality with God concretely placed in the centre. But *how* does the infinite enter into the finite, or the Name into an act, without tearing the fabric of historical reality itself?

The Hebrew man was frustratingly innocent of the kind of ruthless, penetrating (it assumes!) questioning so familiar to the typical Western mind, represented by the all-too-knowing sort of demand: if you had been there with a camera, could you have taken a picture of God? Instead, the narrator tells us: 'And God said to Noah ... "Make yourself an ark of gopher wood."' (Genesis 6:13); 'When Abram was ninety-nine years old the Lord appeared to Abram, and said to him....' (Genesis 17:1); 'And Moses hid his face, for he was afraid to look at God.' (Exodus 3:6); 'And he gave to Moses, when he had made an end of speaking with him upon Mount Sinai, the two tables of the testimony, tables of stone, written with the finger of God.' (Exodus 31:18).

There seems to be no particular problem for the Hebrew narrator in recording these theophanies: when a face shines, a hand moves, and a voice speaks out of the fire, it never occurs to him to ask the question 'how?', but rather 'who?'. It is worth noting that the very features which are most offensive to so-called enlightened thinking appear to be implicit in the proclamation of God's self-communication to and with man. The foreignness of this kind of language, and thinking, becomes a fundamental block to our *hearing* the narrator:

[23]This uniqueness of historical consciousness on the part of Israel with regard to the acts of God, is asserted by G. Ernest Wright in his reply to the criticism of James Barr. Cf. *The Old Testament and Theology*, pp. 47ff. However, Bertil Albrektson (*History and the Gods*, CWK Gleerup, Lund, Sweden, 1967) not only attempts to show that a *heilsgeschichtlich* perspective is entirely lacking in the traditions of Israel's history (p. 84), but also, that the idea of historical events as divine revelation was common theology for all ancient Near East religions (p. 114). Albrektson concludes that the distinctiveness of Israel's tradition was the *content* of its Word-revelation, not its mode (p. 120). In particular, the distinction is to be found in the way in which Israel allowed the idea of divine activity in history to influence its cultic life (p. 116). I would think that one could accept much of what Albrektson has shown as a caution against building too much on a *heilsgeschichtlich* tradition in Israel's history, although he is not entirely convincing in his assertion that Israel's chroniclers totally lacked this perspective. On the other hand, when Albrektson says that Israel's distinctive was not in a different concept of history from its neighbours, but in a different concept of the deity (p. 96), we are back to the fundamental thing which I am seeking to explore as the key to the inner logic of Incarnation.

Anybody who simply cannot 'put up with' the incarnation will also not know what to do with YHWH, who speaks and hears, who wounds and heals, who comes down and visits us, who walks in the garden and confuses the language of the tower builders, who accompanies his people in pillars of cloud and fire, who sits enthroned on the cherubim and precisely as such is the God of Heaven and earth, of whom it is said that heaven and earth cannot contain him and that in the face of this God the nations are like a drop from a bucket and counted as the dust on the scales.[24]

What Miskotte says here is true enough, but it could as well have been put: 'Anybody who simply cannot "put up with" YHWH, who speaks and hears ... will also not know what to do with the incarnation.' For the point which I wish to enlarge upon here is precisely the fact that the inner logic of the Incarnation is organically connected to the relation of Jahweh to Israel. To dismiss the anthropomorphisms which are at the very heart of the narrative of God's history with Israel as primitive and naïve religious conceptions, is to cut the heart, and the logic, out of the Incarnation. Difficult as it is to give a consistent account of just what Israel meant by the anthropomorphic language of its testimony to God, and its testimony to the 'appearances' of God to certain individuals as a human-type figure, the difficulty cannot be resolved by appealing to the 'Oriental mind' as against a 'Western' tendency to think more in abstractions. Though T. C. Vriezen inclines toward this solution, he attempts to keep his balance by insisting upon the reality of Israel's *immediate* relationship to God through the anthropomorphism:

... the fact that the Old Testament speaks so widely of God in this sense must somehow be connected with experiencing God in images familiar to man. In part this may be due to the fact that ancient Eastern people expressed themselves more visually and less abstractly than modern Western man does, so that a unity of form and essence is experienced to a greater extent. On the other hand it must also spring from the fact that God is indeed recognized and experienced in human representations. These naïve and realistic ways of thinking and feeling were partly caused by the immediate relationship with God, ... Thus we may take it that both these categories of anthropomorphisms in the Old Testament bear witness to a recognition of the personal nature of Israel's God.[25]

[24]K. Miskotte, *When the Gods are Silent*, p. 128.
[25]T. C. Vriezen, *An Outline of Old Testament Theology*, pp. 320-321. It is interesting to note that Vriezen has changed his emphasis in the second revised edition (1970) from a 'psychological approach to things' as the clue to the interpretation of the anthropomorphisms, to the conception of God as personal in

The problem of appealing to the familiar (but perhaps over-simplified) distinction between the Oriental and Western way of perceiving things actually conceals as much as it reveals. What this explanation conceals is the fact that there is a *theological* perspective and way of thinking which may or may not have some affinities with a particular cultural world-view. Israel's testimony to the reality of God is *not* typical of Oriental religious notions, despite the obvious use of a common thought form. While it may be true that the Oriental, less abstract, way of seeing reality offers less hindrance to the reality of act and being perceived as a unity, there is a theological, not a cultural, factor involved at this crucial point.[26]

For another thing, a naïve way of representing reality is not merely a way of expressing a spiritual belief, but actually may be a way of comprehending, and expressing, concrete realities which are hidden from a more reflective approach. When the anthropomorphisms and theophanies of the Old Testament are 'demythologized' into an 'immediate' experience of comprehending God, the bond between the absolute and the concrete has been severed—and this is an irretrievable loss.[27] The

character (cf. *An Outline of Old Testament Theology*, Basil Blackwell, Oxford, 1958, pp. 172-173). In his revised edition (1970), Vriezen seems to stress the idea of 'immediate communion', rather than psychological perception: 'But wherever there is immediate communion with God, all reserves imposed by reason are abandoned, consciously or unconsciously, and human feelings and a human shape are attributed to God without any hesitation.' (p. 321). Vriezen does, however, caution against attributing this immediacy of relation with God uniformly to the authors of the Old Testament: 'In some of the writings a certain measure of shyness is to be observed concerning the immediacy of God's presence, in others we find the absolute conviction of the reality of these experiences.' (p. 186). The problem remains, nonetheless, of just what Vriezen means by an 'immediate experience'. One could suspect that the change of emphasis from a psychological experience of God to a personal relation is an attempt to give the anthropomorphisms more content than a projection of human experience. The problem, as we shall see, is not of how one defines 'immediate experience', but of whether or not the anthropomorphism has concreteness as far as God's act of self-revelation is concerned.

[26]Vriezen himself, despite the importance which he gives to the conceptions and presuppositions which connect the religion of Israel with those of the ancient Eastern world, states: '... in the course of its history Israel has received from God experiences that are exclusively her own and that from the outset its particular moral and spiritual elements have left their mark upon this religion.' *Ibid.*, p. 24. But Miskotte has a clearer vision of this radical difference between a religion based on Oriental thought-forms and Israel's faith: 'In the Old Testament, Creation is opposed to eternal becoming, history is opposed to the cycle of existence, Providence to fate, the virtues of God to the dark ways of the gods. Election is opposed to the whim of fortune, obedience to tragic heroism, the future of the Lord to the world's collapse ... the Speech of God to natural or supernatural Being.' *When the Gods are Silent*, p. 135.

[27]Miskotte suggests that the emergence of allegorizing as an exegetical method followed from the embarrassment which the humanness of the Scripture, the

fact that there are non-formalizable, or non-specifiable truths intrinsic
to the nature of reality, suggests that trans-conceptual modes of expression are involved in the communication or understanding of these
truths. The cognitive functions of formalizing or specifying reality have
the same limits as the thinking subject has in determining an object
through thought. Love is not entirely a specifiable reality, in that the
reality of being loved may defy conceptual categories. A trans-conceptual reality, therefore, is not irrational, but a different level of rationality,
with rationality being considered as the capacity to behave objectively
in terms of the object.

For example, there is a dimension of trans-conceptual communication
in the arts, where the 'logos', or meaning inherent in that which the
work of art signifies, 'breaks out of' our forms of conceptual thought
to impose its own form of reality upon us. In somewhat the same way,
the anthropomorphisms can be considered to be trans-conceptual, rather
than merely as primitive projections of religious experience. That is,
they can be understood as representations of the non-formalizable relation of divine Logos to created logos, and as such, reveal the
humanity of God.[28]

But now we are at the fundamental problem which Vriezen does
not seem to have grasped. The Hebrew narrator, and Israel's testimony to the deeds and days of Jahweh around which their own history
was formed, seem to require us to take the theophanies and the anthropomorphisms as the concrete reality of Jahweh himself, giving himself
in self-communication in his Name and action *within* the horizon of
human action as well as human perception. To separate the anthropomorphism from a human-like action and give it only the content of
an immediate experience of God is to violate, and, as far as a theological
document is concerned, destroy the integrity of the narrative itself.[29]
How closely this is related to the inner logic of the Incarnation is seen
by Miskotte who says:

... in pursuing this path on which anthropomorphism, which is pre-

anthropomorphisms, caused: '... with their conception of "truth", they could
not come to terms with a concrete given of ultimate validity. History gave them
trouble because they were obsessed with the idea of the eternal.' *Ibid.*, p. 149.
For a helpful and profound discussion of the importance of genuine naïvety
as a necessary way of grasping concrete reality, see H. Gollwitzer, *The Existence
of God*, pp. 164ff.
[28]Cf. T. F. Torrance, *God and Rationality*, pp. 169-170.
[29]'We are free to speak of symbols, primary and secondary symbols, and also
of saga and legend, and even of myth. But if these are understood as projections
of human experience and not as the concrete form of the Name, not as the
precipitate of the meeting with YHWH which is initiated, established by Him,
then the qualifications of this event as a history of God with men again goes to
ruin.' K. Miskotte, *When the Gods are Silent*, p. 129.

cisely the way in which this God demonstrates his divinity, is allowed to evaporate, the whole manifestation of Christ becomes merely an illustration of a truth which we already knew from somewhere else, and 'God's blood'(!) (Acts 20:28) becomes only a seal of our own natural, innate religion.[30]

In the combination of the Name and the deed, Israel produced in its testimony to Jahweh a unique anthropomorphism in which God actually speaks (demanding a hearing), appears (demanding a recognition), and acts (creating a history). And yet, Jahweh 'has' no hands, nor an image, and 'is' not an entity among others. This is established by the second commandment (Exodus 20:4). Jahweh is not everything that happens, but a definite, particular and concrete event which occurs pre-eminently as *his* act. When God speaks and acts he is *there* in the anthropomorphic event—though this is not reversible. That is, an anthropomorphic event does not of itself mean that God is there. It is his Word of self-communication concretizing itself which constitutes the reality of the theophany. Thus the question 'who?' is the proper one, not 'how?' This is strikingly revealed in the narrative contained in Exodus 32-33, where the golden calf constructed as a result of the people's desire to 'see' Jahweh was no less anthropomorphic than the tables of stone on which the law was written by God. The difference is, the former was one answer to the question 'how shall we proceed without a god?' while the latter caused the question to be asked, 'who has redeemed us out of Egypt and bound himself to us?' The one was a projection of human religious need in anthropomorphic terms, the other a self-communication of God in an anthropomorphic event.

If we allow our minds to be conformed to the inescapable *fact* of the humanity of God in his self-communication, a fact which presses upon us the inner coherence of Word and deed, we can begin to understand that God's being-with and being-one-with human life is not something alien to the nature of God. 'It is inherent in his nature to be allied with man, to be intelligible to man, to have communion with man, indeed, to be a man among men.', says Miskotte.[31] This is echoed by Karl Barth:

> God's deity is thus no prison in which he can exist only in and for Himself. It is rather His freedom to be in and for Himself but also with and for us, to assert but also to sacrifice Himself, to be wholly exalted but also completely humble, not only almighty but almighty mercy, not only Lord but also servant, not only judge but also Himself the judged, not only man's eternal king but also his brother in time. And all that without in the slightest forfeiting his deity! All that,

[30]*Ibid.*, p. 130. Miskotte's parentheses.
[31]*When the Gods are Silent*, p. 131.

rather, in the highest proof and proclamation of His deity! ... In this divinely free volition and election, in this sovereign decision (the ancients said, in His decree), God is *human*. His free affirmation of man, His free concern for him, His free substitution for him— this is God's humanity.[32]

It is precisely here that we must concede what Israel was led to confess: God's self-communication is a unity of act and being. There is no Logos of God apart from the Logos of the flesh—this is not made explicit prior to the Incarnation, but the inner logic is there in God's self-communication to Israel, in his humanity. It is from God's *deeds* that we know of his virtues. This, of course, is also true in the Old Testament with regard to men: experiences, feelings and attitudes cannot be separated from conduct, performance and action. 'Hearing' can also mean 'doing'; not-doing can be not-hearing (cf. Genesis 22:16-18; 39:10; Exodus 18:24; 24:7). Likewise, God *performs* mercy (Exodus 20:6; Deuteronomy 5:10) and *chesed* bursts forth of itself as soon as he proceeds to act.[33] It is this unity between the inward and the outward, or one could say, between the concrete and the absolute, which is the fundamental logic of the self-communication of God to man. The men through whom God acts are not merely 'letter carriers', says Franz Rosenzweig, 'who bring news of something that happened the day before yesterday and may perhaps already have been rendered obsolete by events; rather God is acting and speaking directly through them in this moment of *their* lives.'[34]

But we have spoken of the days as well as of the deeds of God, and self-communication becomes self-revelation at its point of con-cretion. The humanity of God implies the temporality of God, and in this case an act of God has an inner logic of time as well as of space.

The Temporality of God in His Self-Revelation

God's particular presence in the historical community of Israel shattered the pagan concept of a natural, sacral relationship with the godhead. It was Israel's covenant relationship with Jahweh which de-termined its place among the nations as the concretized place of

[32]*The Humanity of God*, pp. 46, 48. The point where I would wish to differ from Barth is in his association of the humanity of God with his immanence instead of his transcendence: 'He is the Word spoken from the loftiest, most luminous transcendence and likewise the Word heard in the deepest, darkest immanence.' *Ibid.*, p. 43. I will show later on how God's transcendence must be seen *as* his humanity, not merely *in* his humanity.
[33]Cf. K. Miskotte, *When the Gods are Silent*, p. 194.
[34]'Die Schrift und das Wort', p. 136; cited by K. Miskotte, *When the Gods are Silent*, p. 205.

the revelation of God through his mighty acts. This was directly opposed to the concept of Israel's contemporaries, where the divinity was conceived as a deity of nature, reinforced by myths of salvation.[35] This unique status of Israel could be described as the effect of God's election, whereby Israel became a people chosen by God to reveal and execute his purpose through history. But Karl Barth has reminded us that before Israel was elected to be God's people, God elected himself to be Israel's God.[36] It is this election of God to Israel which constitutes the inner logic of what I would like to call the temporality of God in his self-revelation.

There are two things which appear to emerge out of this: first, God's election of himself to Israel firmly placed Israel in a truly temporal and historical relation to creation. When Jahweh disclosed himself to Israel, the mythical cord which bound history to the immanent godhead of nature was snapped, and a new concept of temporality, and history, became possible through a doctrine of creation and a Creator. It was the absolute otherness of Jahweh from the immanent godhead of natural religion which freed the world to have its own reality as a created world distinct from the Creator. But at the same time, it was the unconditional bond which Jahweh established with Israel that had the

[35]Cf. T. C. Vriezen, *An Outline of Old Testament Theology*: 'When the Old Testament regards the relationship between God and the people as a covenant-relationship, this means that the relationship is not looked upon as natural but as placed in history by Yahweh. The importance of this doctrine becomes evident only when we see it against the background of the other ancient oriental religions. Often the latter represent the relation between the chief deity and his people as a natural unity: deity, country and people bear the same name (Assur).' p. 167.

[36]*Church Dogmatics*, IV/1: ' "I am Yahweh thy God" (Exodus 20:2) is the indicative on which the imperatives rest, both great and small, both legal and cultic. When, or even before Yahweh elected Israel to be His people, He elected Himself—we are already confronted by the phenomenon of the humility of God—to be the God of Israel.... It is not primarily because Israel belongs to Him but because He belongs to Israel and has covenanted with it that He is such a jealous God, the God who is so interested in every detail of its life, who demands of it so scrupulous an obedience.' p. 424. It must be added that the concept of God 'electing himself' to Israel raises some problems, not the least of which is the implication that God chose himself out of some 'galaxy of gods' to be the God of Israel. This, of course, does not enter Barth's mind in his use of the expression. Barth has made it clear that he is thinking of the 'humility' of God, not his supremacy over 'other gods'. What is important here, and for this reason I intend to preserve Barth's way of putting it despite its difficulties, is the fact of God being 'for man' in his relation to Israel. I shall show later on how the concept of God 'electing himself' to Israel gives us the clue to the structure of God's relation to the world both as Creator and Redeemer. The fact that God 'belongs' to his world is therefore not to be deduced out of a necessary relation which the Creator has with creation, but God has 'chosen' to belong in both creating and redeeming. This is what I believe Barth means to say by his expression, God 'elected Himself to be the God of Israel'.

effect of temporalizing Israel with respect to its relation to the secular world and the realm of history. This is clearly revealed in the biblical account of Israel's primeval history, which is rooted in an act of creation and which excludes any notion of a mythological primacy assigned to her beginnings. The fact that this primeval history culminates with the table of nations (Genesis 10) serves to place Israel in a sphere of universal secular history, as well as to place the other nations, whatever their own concepts of origin might have been, into a true temporal secularity.[37]

Thus we can see that the means by which God elected himself to Israel was at the same time a desacralization of the world.[38] Israel, as the particularization of God's revelation in an actualized sense, becomes at the same time, the universalization of the covenant in a proleptic sense, as T. F. Torrance has aptly pointed out:

...for the Word of God spoken to man did not operate in a vacuum but penetrated human existence in the particular life and history of one people elected as the instrument for the actualization of God's revelation in humanity and separated as a holy nation in whose midst God dwelt in an intimate way through the presence of His Word.... The Covenant relationship between God and Israel which this set up was a particularization of the one covenant of grace which embraced the whole of creation and constituted its inner bond and ground, and therefore carried in it the promise of a final universalization of God's revelation in which His Word would bring light and salvation to all the peoples of mankind and indeed a new heaven and a new earth.[39]

[37]Cf. G. von Rad, *Old Testament Theology*, Vol. II: 'The Biblical primeval history, which has as its climax the world of the nations, gives Israel the same creaturely status as the nations, and excludes any mythological primacy assigned to her in primeval times. Her future experience of God will be in the realm of secular history and, indeed, according to Genesis 10, in the realm of universal secular history.... The way in which these disclose the out-and-out secularity of an age and, in particular, reveal men in their full secular human nature, represents a *ne plus ultra* of insight beyond which even the Christian faith does not go.' p. 342.

[38]Cf. G. von Rad, *Old Testament Theology*, Vol. II: '... this completely new way of picturing Jahweh's action in history, which led, as we have seen, to a new technique in narrative, certainly did not arise by chance; it was merely an expression of a more profound spiritual transformation. For an era which no longer experienced Jahweh's working mainly in the sacral form of miracles or miracle-like episodes, and which could therefore no longer satisfactorily express its faith in a sacral narrative-form, for such an era its whole relationship to the reality—we should say Nature and History—became secularized, and was, as it were, overnight released from the sacral orders sheltering it.... It did not mean however, any abandonment of belief in Jahweh, nor was it a veering to an attenuated relationalized piety. Jahweh too had taken this road; out in this desacralized, secular world as well he allowed men to find him,...' pp. 52-53.

[39]*God and Rationality*, pp. 146-147.

The call of Abraham, to leave the religious culture of Ur of the Chaldeans and step out into the world—which we have already termed the first in the series of historical acts of God with Israel which together form the 'spine' of the narrative—this call, was 'groundless' in the sense of any mythological or even ontological connection with an immanent divinity. The narrator simply says: 'So Abram went, as Jahweh told him;' (Genesis 12:4). It was the election of God to Abraham through his Word which 'broke the spell' of whatever magical or mythical connection the world had with the godhead, as the poet so well puts it:

> This is the first act. Come night and the journey unexpectedly begins anew, heaven knows where. Even heaven does not know since *the spell broke like an egg*. Resting is gone for good, the eggshells scattered among the nations; and Abraham steps out into the light, like one *separate word* from a poem.[40]

The language of the poet is helpful here in suggesting that the 'one separate word' is both the Word of creation and the Word of the Covenant. The 'separate' word has its own intrinsic meaning and reality; both creation and covenant are thus non-mythical in the sense that myth means to be derived from an immanent divinity.[41] To this extent, creation and covenant are the coordinate aspects of the Word which God 'separated' from himself. Barth puts it this way:

> As creation, according to Genesis I, is the outward basis of this covenant, and this covenant the inward basis of creation, there begins at once in and with creation the history of this covenant, and therefore the proper work of God to which all His other works are subordinate.[42]

The bond between the covenant and creation has as its inner logic the 'separated' Word which is utterly contracted to the reality of space and time, and yet, which is not derived from or inferred out of the world. It is a separated word *from a poem*, as the poet puts it; therefore, the space-time track itself is opened up to the 'transcendent reality' which preserves its creatureliness, as the theologian puts it.[43]

---

[40] From a poem by Guillaume van der Graft, 'Aangaande Abraham', in *Vogels en Vissen* (1953). Cited by Miskotte, *When the Gods are Silent*, p. 186. Emphasis is Miskotte's.

[41] Cf. W. A. Whitehouse, 'Christ and Creation,' *Essays in Christology*, T. H. L. Parker (ed.), Lutterworth Press, London, 1956, pp. 122-123.

[42] *Church Dogmatics*, IV/2, p. 588.

[43] Cf. T. F. Torrance: 'This gives us, in the language of the physicists, "an organized structure of space-time", but one that is made and kept *open* for a transcendent rationality that preserves its creatureliness and gives it meaning.

It is the 'groundlessness' of this Word 'in the midst of things' which Miskotte sees as the true 'temporalizing' of time:

> The terms 'groundless' and 'here, in the midst of things' are correlative.... one can look back to the beginning only from the midst of things in order to call it 'creation', and only from that vantage point can one look forward to the time of the end in order to call it the 'kingdom'. The beginning of Genesis is not the beginning of revelation, but rather, a retrospective application of faith in the Name, which has entered into the present. The silence of the gods is broken by the Voice; the Word can never be inferred and derived from the world. That which resounds in the midst of things puts its stamp upon extended time, it accompanies and fills it.[44]

The important distinction which Miskotte calls to our attention, between the temporality of the self-revelation of God and its 'groundlessness' in the casual connections of the world, makes it clear that we are talking about God's transcendence when we are talking about his temporality. However, there is a danger, to which Miskotte inclines, of making this distinction into a dialectical relationship between 'God's time' and our time.[45] This concept of 'theological time' tends to evaporate the true temporality of God's self-revelation, so that an 'act of God' vanishes into sheer contingency, or shrinks to a mathematical point. It is true that the Old Testament speaks of God dwelling in heaven as well as dwelling on earth, and the King who said, 'I have built thee an exalted house, a place for thee to dwell in for ever', said in the next breath, 'Behold, heaven and the highest heaven cannot contain thee; how much less this house which I have built!' (I Kings 8). But this does not speak of a dialectic as much as it does of a problematic. And so, rather than stressing the groundlessness of God's temporality, it seems better to say that God's temporality, his self-

This does not import the slightest rejection of this-worldly realities or the reduction of history to vanishing points in timeless and spaceless events, but rather the affirming and confirming of creaturely and historical existence in all its spatio-temporal reality by binding it to an eternal reality beyond the meaninglessness and futility to which it would be reduced if it were abandoned by God to itself.' *Space, Time & Incarnation*, Oxford University Press, London, 1969, p. 73.

[44] *When the Gods are Silent*, pp. 183-184.

[45] 'As in the case of other difficulties with which ordinary orthodox teaching has troubled us, the so-called "dialectical" theology has also brought us a good bit farther on the way to understanding this knotty problem of time.... The insights which are of most importance for the preaching of the Old Testament and which are of immediate relevance in connection with our task today are concerned with the doctrine of "theological time" (Noordmans).' *When the Gods are Silent*, pp. 110-111. I will suggest that the concept of a problematic rather than a dialectic, preserves the theological dimension to time without a chasm between an 'act of God' and history.

revelation, is his transcendence. I am returning here, of course, to the
theme established earlier, that God's transcendence is his act of concretizing himself as Spirit with and in human existence. The problematical aspect of self-revelation is that it is the free act of God as
Spirit, and thus is not a derivative of creation, and cannot be inferred
out of the relation between God and creation by the creature; and yet,
within the reality of historical existence, God is concretely *there* in
his self-revelation. I would rather say that it is creation which is
'groundless' apart from the transcendence of God, which interacts with
it in a thoroughly temporal way. It is this logic of interaction which a
dialectical relation between God and history destroys.

But is it now apparent that we have pushed beyond the limits of
the first implication drawn out of the assertion that God's election is
of himself to Israel: namely, that this places Israel in a truly temporal
and historical relation to creation; and we are well into the second:
that God's election of himself to Israel reveals the temporality of God
through his interaction with the created world in time.

The fundamental offence to the mind of man, of the Incarnation as
the act of God through Jesus Christ, has been primarily in the sphere
of cosmological concepts of space and time. Whether space and time
is absolutized and bracketed with God, after the manner of Newton,
or whether it is conceived as a receptacle, either of a finite nature
(Aristotelian and Stoic thought) or of an infinite nature (the Atomists
and Pythagoreans), the result was inevitably a fatal division between
two kinds of history and a dualism between God and the world. This
has been exhaustively demonstrated by T. F. Torrance in his book,
Space, Time and Incarnation, and needs no further development here.[46]

At the outset it should be noted that the Word does not cast off
the cultural elements of the period in which it is concretized. Rather,
the Word enters into the social and cultural matrix of Israel's life and
history and *overcomes* these limitations and imperfections by expressing
the reality of God through them.[47] So then, it is not a matter of
substituting a new cosmology for an older, less 'correct' one, and still

[46]See especially pp. 52ff.

[47]'As the Word of God invaded the social matrix of Israel's life, culture,
religion and history, and clothed itself with Israel's language, it had to struggle
with the communal meaning already embedded in it in order to assimilate it
to God's revelation of Himself. For new understanding to take root within Israel,
it had to take shape within Israel's language, and therefore, it had to remould
the inner structure of the society within which that language had its home and
had to determine the whole history of Israel in its physical existence.... And
so throughout Israel's tradition the Word of God kept pressing for articulation
within the corporate medium of covenant reciprocity and progressively took
verbal and even written form through the shared understanding and shared
response that developed in this people.' T. F. Torrance, *God and Rationality*,
pp. 147-148.

less of demythologizing the narrative to find the existential meaning, but rather it is a matter of discerning the inner structure of the *factual* (concrete) relationship of God to the created world.[48] It is only slightly incidental to this discussion to note at this point that the structures which inhere in the relationship of God to the world are the same intrinsic structures which determine a scientific understanding of the cosmos. Which is only to say that theological science and natural science are pursuing a common task in the search for truth, but from different perspectives.

Proceeding along the lines of the basic axiom that there is an organic relation between God's action through Jesus Christ and his action with and in his people Israel, the uncovering of the dynamics of God's inter-action with Israel in the time process should provide some clues as to the inner logic of the Incarnation itself.[49]

In considering some of the more familiar events in the narrative of God's dealing with Israel, one thing becomes quite clear. The interaction of God with man is considered by Israel to be constitutive of her worldly history, though not totally congruent with the natural process itself. It is this non-congruent dimension of Israel's history which points to the presence of the Word. For example, the calling of Abraham to leave his native land and culture could be construed, on the one hand, to be a rather typical migration of a basically nomadic people. Yet, the event itself in its origin and destiny is clearly not meant to be understood as a typical movement of people in that historical continuum. The narrative makes it emphatically clear that history is being determined here, not

---

[48]Cf. K. Miskotte: 'Every culture sees a correspondence between the order of the cosmos and that of human society.... God chose the least brilliant, the least cohesive, the poor and despised culture, in order to transmit to us something which, for example, cannot be conveyed through our Western conceptions; even the Ptolemaic cosmology (which, of course, is not "correct") serves to say something which cannot be said with the Copernican cosmology. When one respects this functional unity of the testimony and these human conceptions, one may, of course, try to translate; but if one really wants to translate this, it is impossible to "substitute" the new cosmology for the old.' *When the Gods are Silent*, p. 157. While I would take issue with Miskotte's assertion that the 'Ptolemaic cosmology serves to say something which cannot be said with the Copernican cosmology' as misleading and even confusing, I think he has made the right point in stressing the fact that the functional unity of the testimony should not be disturbed for the sake of a more modern cosmology. What Miskotte does not suggest, is that within this functional unity there may well be an inner structure, or a coherence of relation between God and the world which has cosmological significance.

[49]Cf. G. von Rad, *Old Testament Theology*, Vol. II: 'Thus one intrinsic like-ness between the message of the New and Old Testaments is that both speak of man and his potentialities, of the "flesh", and of the world and the realm of secular history, as the sphere in which God reveals himself. These ideas as they are expressed in the New Testament are no different in principle from ideas which were current in ancient Israel.' p. 350.

from within its own possibilities or out of its own causal connections, but through Jahweh's interaction.[50] There is no question in the narrator's mind as to *how* Abraham could have verified this determinative Word and interaction of God without being able to appeal to a historical or rational precedent—the reality of Jahweh's determinative Word and act is taken to be self-evidencing and utterly historical, despite its non-typical historical character. The interaction of God points forward in a completely natural way, while at the same time overcoming natural limitations. There is to be a land, even though there is no natural right to any land. There is to be a son, even though there is no natural possibility of a child. There is a rationale—'I will bless you ... and by you all the families of the earth shall bless themselves (Genesis 12:3)—and yet the venture cannot be rationalized.

This is brought into even sharper relief with the command given to Abraham to offer his son Isaac as a sacrifice (Genesis 22). Abraham's faith, which was to serve as a paradigm for all of the faithful, was no less rational for its lack of ethical rationalization, but was, in a sense, lifted to the heights of rationality in being conformed to the Word of Jahweh. It is this 'non-formalizable' reality in the relation between God and Abraham which can be seen when one looks *into* the event rather than at the external, or so-called miraculous aspect of it. It never occurs to Abraham, or Israel, to conclude that either history or ethics has been drained of its reality structure by the participation of God. This is not construed as irrational ethics, nor licence to do magic with history. Indeed, when it comes to magic, 'Jahweh is the great magician',[51] as the Egyptians discovered in their conflict with Moses, but the inner logic of the exodus was the rationale of the Name embedded in the *history* of God—'I am the God of your father, the God of Abraham, the God of Isaac, and the God of Jacob' (Exodus 3:6).

God's election of himself to Israel meant the temporalizing of God

---

[50]Cf. Genesis 12:1-3; 15:1-22.

[51]Cf. K. Miskotte, *When the Gods are Silent*, p. 177. The way in which Jahweh participated in history through personal will rather than through the impersonal and arbitrary power of magic is well stated by G. von Rad: 'In this sense the early Israelite cult altogether carries the impress of an understanding of the world that was still largely magical—perhaps it might better be called "dynamistic". Here then the issue is not as yet joined. But it is valid to speak about Jahwism's unyielding inflexibility against magic from the moment that magic reveals itself as a well-tried technique for influencing the deity, or when man, with its aid, takes into his own control, to further his own needs, events or powers that belong to the deity. We are certainly not wrong to explain as deriving from the peculiar nature of Jahwism the limit here set to magic and its competency, unique in the history of religion. Jahweh's invasive power, revealing himself on all sides as personal will, was absolutely incompatible with the impersonal automatic action of the operation of the forces of magic.' *Old Testament Theology*, Vol. I, pp. 34-35.

in his self-revelation through participation in history. The non-congruent aspect of God's temporality is not the miracle—these all had their imitations—but in the rationale for Israel's history which was confessed to be the self-expression of God himself, that is, Logos. This is of vital importance when it comes to discerning the inner logic of the Incarnation. For the act of God by which he becomes temporal is not primarily the 'supernatural' act by which he 'stands out' in history in a mythological sense, but the natural act by which he participates in history in a real sense. When G. von Rad says, 'From first to last Israel manifestly takes as her starting-point the absolute priority in theology of event over *"logos"*.'[52], he sets up an unnecessary dichotomy between the two, even though he qualifies 'logos' as the Greek urge towards a universal understanding of the world. Israel's history with God was as much a 'logos-history' as an 'event-history', even though it is true that the two were inseparable. For the saving acts did not simply 'happen' to Israel, but were constitutive events which had their meaning in the election of Jahweh to be their God. In this participation and interaction of God, history is shown to be open to the reality of God in such a way that both space and time are relativized to a dynamic rather than a static Creator-Logos. Because there is no dualism in this structure, there is no need of a mythological 'bridge' to correlate the reality of God with the reality of the world, and no need for the fatal division of history into two spheres of sacred and profane. This is made clear in the inner structure of the historical events of the Old Testament despite the fact that, as Miskotte says, 'a large part of the testimony concerning him [YHWH] comes to us in a garment of language which was originally cut to fit the gods and the godhead'.[53]

It is this understanding of the temporality of God in his self-revelation which cuts through the impasse created by the attempt to conceive of an 'act of God' as a timeless act taking place within time, or as a non-historical or supernatural event occurring within the closed continuum of history and nature.[54] The two interacting realities of God and the

[52]*Old Testament Theology*, Vol. I, p. 116.
[53]*When the Gods are Silent*, p. 116.
[54]A survey of the problems inherent in the concept of an act of God would be an excursion far beyond the scope of this book. For a recent discussion of this problem one should see Gordon D. Kaufman, 'On the Meaning of "Act of God"', *Harvard Theological Review*, 1968, pp. 176-201. Kaufman rejects the traditional concepts of an act of God as a finite event which does not have a finite antecedent as inconceivable, and goes on to suggest his own solution based on the personalist analogy of God as personal agent. Along with this, Kaufman ingeniously divides up an act into 'simple' or 'sub-acts', which are always derivatory and secondary, and the 'master act'. He then sees God's act as the 'master act' which takes in the entire course of history, from which the sub-acts derive their significance as they advance the master act. This, in effect, reverses the biblical emphasis on the particular and the concrete as the primary dimension of God's self-revelation

world have an absolute distinction—hence the non-congruency of Word and history in the event—and yet the *movement* of Word and history becomes one reality, whose name is Israel. It is this unity of interaction which we saw to be the inner logic of the humanity of God in his self-communication. The cosmological dimensions of space and time are likewise incorporated into this free interaction of the Creator with creation so that God's election of himself to Israel exposes the temporality of God in his self-revelation. The self-revelation of God, thus, is never purely contingent to history, despite its non-congruence, but is ontically present in history. That is, God is *there* in what actually *is* the case through the act of his Spirit and Word. I will only call attention, at this point, to the way in which this helps us to understand Bonhoeffer's warning that to retreat along the ontological path (finding God in being) is to abandon the ontic and is not admissible by revelation; further, that basic ontic relationships are normative for the experiencing of that revelation.[55]

What we have not discussed yet, is the implicit corollary of the humanity and the temporality of God—that is, his self-condescension. It can now be seen just why this is at the very heart of the inner logic of the Incarnation.

The Hiddenness of God in His Self-Condescension

In what becomes remarkable only when we ignore it, and allow it to spring upon us almost full grown in the last voices of the Old Testament, that is, the hiddenness of God, we can trace the descent of the Logos of God from the very beginning until it disappears altogether in the figure of Jesus Christ. It is there in the giving of the Name—Jahweh is the 'nameless Name'. It is, as Karl Barth says, the revelation of a name which is, in fact, a refusal to be named among the gods.[56] Jahweh reveals himself without really disclosing himself, and the patriarchal history knows full well that to see God face to face means death.[57]

The experience of Israel, especially through the bitter times of d'stress,

and has the effect of reducing the transcendence of God to an immanent teleology. Cf. K. Miskotte, who says just the contrary: '... his universal love is perceived only in a very special election, his omnipotence in a very special redemptive power, his nature in the Name and his Name in the Messiah, his divinity in his humanity and his divine act in his human act. He who hears the special and particular encounters the centre and core.' *When the Gods are Silent*, p. 129.

[55]See above, p. 80.
[56]*Church Dogmatics* I/1: 'That the revelation of the name (Exodus 3:13f.) is in fact, in content, a refusal of any name—"I am that I am" can scarcely mean anything else than just, I am He whose name proper no one can repeat—is significant enough; for the revealed name itself by its wording is to recall also and precisely the hiddenness of the revealed God.' p. 365.
[57]Cf. Genesis 16:13; 32:30; Exodus 33:20; Judges 6:22; 13:22.

sickness and punishment, brought upon them the theological knowledge of this hiddeness of God: 'Truly, thou art a God who hidest thyself, O God of Israel, the Saviour.' (Isaiah 45:15). G. von Rad points to a particular pattern in this hiddenness when he says:

> Ancient Israel also had to bear the mystery of God's withdrawal, and often spoke of the experiences and trials which this entailed. The whole history of the covenant is simply the history of God's continuous retreat. His message that Israel was the one in whom he was to be glorified, and that his salvation and judgment were henceforth to be determined by the attitude adopted towards his historical saving work in Israel ('I will bless those who bless you, and him who curses you I will curse,' Genesis 13:2), is the message of a God who was hiding himself from the world.[58]

What are we to make of this? Von Rad's statement that 'the whole history of the covenant is simply the history of God's continuous retreat' is not too strong when the narrative of Israel's relationship to God is seen in its entirety. But in what sense can we understand the suggestion that God progressively 'withdraws' himself from Israel? Or even from the world? There is a kind of 'logic of suffering' to be discerned in the Old Testament, in which the faith that comes through suffering and seeking is a sign, not that God is far from his own, but that he is near to them.[59] But we should hesitate a bit before we make the hiddenness of God into a dialectic of faith, and listen to the words of Martin Buber:

> In these days the question is to be asked over and over again: After Auschwitz how is a Jewish life possible? I would like to frame this question more correctly: How in a time in which Auschwitz existed is any life with God possible? The strangeness has become too cruel, the hiddenness too deep. One can still 'believe' in the God who permitted to happen what did happen, but can one still speak to him? Can one still call upon him? Do we dare to recommend the Job of the gas-chambers to the survivors of Auschwitz: 'Call upon him, for he is good and his mercy endureth forever?'[60]

Perhaps we should back up and take a new start. The Name, which is unutterable, is the giving of himself to Israel on the part of God. We have said that it is the giving away of himself in the sense that the election of himself to Israel involved both humanity and temporality.

---

[58]*Old Testament Theology*, Vol. II, p. 374.
[59]Cf. Job; Ecclesiastes; Psalm 49; 73; Jeremiah 5:23-28; 15:10; 20:14-18; Lamentations 3:1-32.
[60]Martin Buber, *An der Wende* (1952), pp. 105ff.; cited by K. Miskotte, *When the Gods are Silent*, p. 249.

This is the free act of condescension by which the Creator takes on the existence-form of the creature. Body is the existence-form of Spirit, as Bonhoeffer has suggested.[61] The act of God as Spirit, then, involves 'enfleshment'—*assumptio carnis*. As God moves progressively from the eternal to the temporal order, as his dwelling place on earth becomes more and more identified with Israel as a people, he literally becomes the nomadic, forsaken God in the world, which is Israel. The holy places, Shechem, Hebron, Beersheba, Bethel, and Penuel, which originally were located as permanent dwelling places of God became places of temporary (temporal) manifestations. The Lord 'desired Zion for his habitation' in order to dwell on earth. And so the temporal, nomadic, existence-form of the people of Israel became his dwelling place.

The withdrawal of God, then, if this is the word to be used, is a withdrawal *into* flesh, not away from it.[62] The hiddenness is a progressively intensified unity and identity with Israel, which is his 'son'.[63] It would not be too strong a word to say that this hiddenness is already a *kenosis*, a condescension which has no form of beauty (Isaiah 53:2), but which is itself recognized as an act of transcendence.[64] This 'nomadic' God is himself the God who is repeatedly reviled, despised and constantly misunderstood. He is a forsaken God; his 'presence' appears to be no match for the powers of paganism; the ark—the place of his 'presence'— is captured by the Philistines (I Samuel 4:11). He is like a farmer who learns that his own cattle do not know how to find their way to the master's crib (Isaiah 1:3). He is like the husband betrayed by his wife and despite everything remains with her, but all in vain (Hosea 3:1).

If we are to understand what is meant by the 'Word becoming flesh',

[61]*Creation and Fall*, p. 46. See also above, p. 79.
[62]Withdrawal into flesh is but another way of speaking of a closer identification on the part of God with the historical existence of Israel. To say that God becomes 'hidden in flesh' is to use language that properly belongs to the Incarnation, but is used here to show that the movement of God was towards greater union with the sufferings and destiny of Israel, rather than the concept of hiddenness pointing to God's withdrawal from Israel.
[63]Cf. K. Barth, *Church Dogmatics*, IV/1, p. 169.
[64]Cf. G. von Rad, *Old Testament Theology*, Vol. I: 'But Israel's most characteristic feature lies in the fact that she accompanied Jahweh's condescension to her, which went even to the point of a divine *kenosis*, with statements about beauty. Beauty was in the revelation of his will (Psalm 119 *passim*), and beauty also belonged to Zion.... But it would not be wise to set this emphatic expression in absolute contrast to the other, the Servant of God who has no form or beauty (Isaiah 53:2), for with the latter as well there is a splendour (otherwise he would not be pictured in poetic prose), only it is much more hidden. This bold accompaniment of the movement of the hidden God, in which Israel was still able to perceive splendour even in the deepest *kenosis* of God's action, is certainly the most noteworthy characteristic in the Old Testament's utterances about beauty.' p. 367.

we only need to see here how the Old Testament testifies pitilessly to
what is meant by flesh:

> Without anything to excuse or cover it, without any appearance of
> the accidental or merely external, the being and nature of man are
> radically and fundamentally revealed in the human people of Israel
> as chosen and loved by God, in the history of that people, in Jewish
> flesh. From the negative standpoint that is the mystery of the Jews
> and their representative existence.[65]

It is this hiddenness of God in the sufferings of Israel which begins
to set forth the inner structure of the Incarnation itself. The Logos of
God, which was active in creation, speaking to Israel in her primeval
history, given to her in the unutterable Name, accompanying her in the
cloud and the fire through wilderness journeys, now descends even more
deeply into Israel herself.

Israel is becoming the Logos of God. It was this 'Logos' which the
prophets interpreted to the people in their darkest hours and which
brought forth the concept of the Suffering Servant.[66] The Suffering Servant
was the activity of God himself, binding up the cords of the covenant,
pursuing man into reconciliation. It is in this representative capacity
that Israel can be seen to be the end of the world, or the judgment of
the world.[67] If Israel may be said to be judged, condemned and killed,
it is so that she may be brought back to life again.[68]

The more the Word became one with Israel, the more it became 'one
Israelite' in the figure of the Messiah—the more all humanity became
involved.[69] It was in just this narrowing down, and this particularizing
of the covenant, that the depth of the hiddenness reached the *assumptio
carnis* in a complete and final form—the one Israelite, Jesus Christ.

> God will really be the hidden God and be manifest in this very
> hiddenness, where God Himself has hidden Himself, in the way He
> was hidden here for Israel and for all these men of Israel, i.e., in the

[65]K. Barth, *Church Dogmatics*, IV/1, p. 171.
[66]Cf. Isaiah 41:8; 42:19; 44:1; 45:4; 48:20; 52:13-53:12.
[67]Cf. K. Barth, *Church Dogmatics*, I/2, p. 89.
[68]Cf. G. von Rad, *Old Testament Theology*, Vol. II: '... to say that Israel's
faith was always faith in Jahweh is not enough. Who was this Jahweh? How,
and where, was he present for men? Let us remember what was said above
about the disconcerting lack of continuity in Jahweh's relationship to his chosen
people. The Old Testament tells of sacral institutions set up and then destroyed,
of calls solemnly given and rejections which immediately followed them; possibilities of cultic communion with God were opened up and then shattered.
There is the Jahweh who commands sacrifice and then abruptly rejects it, and
the Jahweh who, as time goes on, hides himself ever more deeply from his people,
who kills Israel in order to bring her to life again.' p. 381.
[69]Cf. Isaiah 11:1-5; Jeremiah 23:5-6; Micah 5:2-4; Zachariah 9:9-10.

way of 'My God, my God, why hast thou forsaken me?' But we obviously have to repeat our assertion, that Jacob, Jeremiah and Job, the whole obscure happening in and to Israel, points towards this real hiddenness of God and so towards His real revelation, that the whole figure of 'the servant' in Isaiah 53—and Isaiah 53 is only a recapitulation of what is to be found in almost every chapter of the Old Testament—typifies the suffering and crucified Christ.[70]

Even as a suffering and crucified Christ cannot be understood apart from the logic of God's relation to Israel, so the suffering of Israel remains incoherent apart from the Incarnation towards which it points.

The organic connection between Christ and Israel becomes quite clear at this point. And the inner logic of that connection is the hiddenness of God which takes the form, not of a metaphysical or mystical, or even gnostic hiddenness, but it is the condescension of covenant love which takes on flesh in order to reconcile flesh to Spirit. The estranged, rebellious flesh of Israel is the flesh of humanity which becomes the particular existence-form of God. The Logos becomes more and more hidden in Israel through the power of God's Spirit by which he actually enters into humanity and temporality. We call this act of Spirit by which Logos becomes enfleshed, the 'hiddenness' of God. It is actually the transcendence of God when it is considered from God's standpoint. God moves freely 'outside' of himself to enter into the existence-form of his creatures. He elects himself to Israel in an act of utter condescension—this is his humanity and his temporality.

But what of the 'elected man' Israel? If he suffers *for* God through the reaction of the pagan world and its gods, he also suffers *from* God through his own self-estrangement and forgetfulness of God. As Barth says: 'Israel's sin is, so to speak, the human side of God's hiddenness.'[71] It is from the perspective of this 'human side' of God's hiddenness, or his transcendence, as I would prefer to call it, that we must explore a further dimension to the inner logic of incarnation. In stressing the election of God to Israel, we have only alluded to the election of Israel to God and what that entails. Implicit in the narrative of God's dealings with Israel is the human side of the covenant. And not only in its negative form of estrangement, but in its positive responsibility of response.

The question which we must now pursue, is: to what extent the transcendence of God, that is, his humanity and temporality, entered into the covenant response which is an action from man to God.

[70]K. Barth, *Church Dogmatics*, I/2, p. 89.
[71]*Church Dogmatics*, I/2, p. 90.

2 'The Problematic of Covenant Response'

'Let it be good'—
He breathed, as he kneaded
The swirling dust into every hope and hue
   of his own image.
And then, stepping back a bit
From his still-new creation,
   separating its fresh consecration
   from his older glory,
He whispered again, to no one in particular,
      'It is good!'

But even then, as the green world groaned
   and stirred to life—
   making minor miracles seem common enough,
The image lost its footing
And set the whole plan ajar—
   the simplicity of good splintered
   into a thousand possibilities
Of greed
      of lust
         violence
   and worst of all, unawareness.

And yet, there was a sliver of hope
Prestressed into the likelihood of ungood,
A scalpel-edge of faith slicing through
   the senseless flesh to the bone
   of consecrated spirit.
The creature, still bearing resemblance
   to the Creator,
Embraces every hope and hue with remembrance
In the prayer of consecration—
      'Let it be good.'[72]

Man has always had the disadvantage of having to look back to his beginnings through the broken glass of poetry. For, however the muse turns his words, that simple prose spirit which lies behind all poetry is never more than partially resurrected. Though we must be grateful for

---

[72]R. S. Anderson, an unpublished poem.

the poet, who reminds us that the door is never completely closed.[73] And if there is the touch of a poet in the narrative of man's beginning with God, it is only to cause the Word to sing out again of how it was, and how it is, between men and God.

> Then God said, 'Let us make man in our image, after our likeness; ...' So God created man in his own image, in the image of God he created him; male and female he created them.

> —then the Lord God formed man of dust from the ground, and breathed into his nostrils the breath of life; and man became a living being. And the Lord planted a garden in Eden, in the east; and there he put the man whom he had formed.

> And the Lord God commanded the man, saying, 'You may freely eat of every tree of the garden; but of the tree of the knowledge of good and evil you shall not eat, for in the day that you eat of it you shall die.'[74]

This is how it was, and how it is. We are *told* this, and we are to hear it, and in hearing it we are to hear again the simple prose spirit of the Word which lies behind the rhythm of the narrative. The narrator himself is looking back through the broken glass, but he sees more than the refracted image of his own situation. He knows *Jahweh*, and when he says that the 'Lord God said', he is using the Name which has been given to him. The narrator is the 'covenant man', who first heard the Lord God say,

> I am the God of your father, the God of Abraham, the God of Isaac, and the God of Jacob.

> ... I AM WHO I AM ...; and I promise that I will bring you up out of the affliction of Egypt, to the land of the Canaanites,

> If you obey my voice and keep my covenant, you shall be my own possession among all peoples.[75]

The narrative of the beginning of man with God is the furthest horizon of the covenant, the *berith*, which is the term used to describe the

---

[73]'Before and beyond it [poetry] there was prose, and it was nonpoetry; it was nonrhythmical, unbound but not disengaged speech, unmeasured but not extravagantly fulsome (*masslos übermässiges*) word. All poetry which has since come into being within the circle of its light is inspired by its prose spirit. *Since that time* in the dark silence that surrounded the beginning of mankind the door which separates each from the other and all from the Outside and the Beyond *has been broken* and never again will it be altogether closed: the door of the Word.' Franz Rosenzweig, 'Die Schrift und das Wort', *Kleinere Schriften* (1937), pp. 134ff. Cited by K. Miskotte, *When the Gods are Silent*, p. 204.

[74]Genesis 1:26, 27; 2:7-8, 16-17.

[75]Exodus 3:6, 15, 17; 19:5.

fundamental relationship between God and Israel.[76] But because one can never speak 'merely' of Israel, but must always speak too of the larger circle within which Israel has its existence—universal man—the covenant is the basic relation between God and all men.[77] It is, as Barth says

the fellowship which originally existed between God and man, which was then disturbed and jeopardized, the purpose of which is now fulfilled in Jesus Christ and in the work of reconciliation.[78]

It is because of the fact that the covenant is the basic and original relation between God and man, that, though one may refer to several covenants (e.g., the Noachic, Abrahamic, and Mosaic, among others), none of them are *the* covenant. The one covenant between God and man, which has its bond with creation, seems to lie outside any of these forms of the covenant, while at the same time, it is expressed in these forms to some degree or other.[79] These forms never completely fulfil its expectations, or gather in the full significance of its intention.

This, then, is the rationale for beginning a discussion of the problematic of covenant response with a closer look at the inner structure of the original relation between God and man, rather than with a detailed analysis of the idea of the covenant in the biblical literature. There are certain fundamental aspects of the covenant which God effected with man through Israel which will be essential for our consideration, but this will come along in its proper place.

Certainly, one of the most significant things about the narrative of man's original relationship with God is that the relationship is founded in the 'speech' of God. Not only is God 'speaking' before the creation of man, but he speaks *to* man in the context of the creation itself. The fact that man comes into existence, not through a generative act, but through a speech-act, has as its corollary, the fact that in speaking of the relationship of man to God, Israelite theology usually avoids the Father-child

[76]The technical term '*berith*', of course, is not to be found in the Genesis account of creation. However, the ingredients of the covenant relation which exists between God and Man as explicated in the history of Israel, can surely be found there. God, as the creator, places man in a relationship of mutuality in such a way that God is the total source of the relationship, and yet, man has responsibility because of the relation. Creation is the story of God 'being for man' in such a way that man can be 'for God'. K. Barth says: 'The history of creation is a great cosmic prelude and example of that history of Israel which is the proper theme of the Old Testament. Creation is the outward basis of the Covenant (Genesis 1) and the covenant the inward basis of creation (Genesis 2).' *Church Dogmatics*, IV/1, p. 27.
[77]Cf. K. Barth, *Church Dogmatics*, IV/3, p. 688.
[78]*Church Dogmatics*, IV/1, p. 22.
[79]Cf. K. Barth, *Church Dogmatics*, I/2, p. 82.

image.[80] The *imago Dei* is rooted in the creative act of speech, which itself implies both an absolute distinction and a fundamental communion. The original relationship between God and man is, therefore, a dia-logic relation in which both a speaking and an answering are implied. However, this does not mean, as some have asserted, that man is in a true 'dialogue-situation' with God, in which man can speak his own word independently and of his own free will.[81] There is a freedom given to man for his own speech, but it cannot be a response to God without the Logos of God. Thus, as T. F. Torrance suggests, there is room for our 'transcendence' over against God, but the reciprocity follows from the divine initiative:

> By meeting us and entering into dialogue with us through His Word the transcendent God creates space for our 'transcendence' over against Him and at the same time creates between us and Himself the rational continuity in which reciprocity and communion can take place.[82]

Now it is this tension between freedom and response which constitutes the problematic in the original relation between God and man. It is problematic in the same sense as I have earlier used the term. That is, the correspondence between God and man, which has its constitutive structure in the *imago Dei*, is one of communion with a reciprocity of

---

[80]Cf. T. C. Vriezen, *An Outline of Old Testament Theology*, pp. 172ff. This assertion of Vriezen's, however, needs qualification. For the Father-child image is specifically used in Hosea 11 : 1 where Israel is called 'my son', and Deuteronomy 14 : 1; also in Deuteronomy 32 : 6 (to cite just one example), God is spoken of as the 'Father' of Israel. But Vriezen's point is well taken in that the Old Testament authors do generally avoid the implication that man is constituted by a 'generative' relation to God as the Father of all mankind.

[81]Cf. T. C. Vriezen: 'It must remain an established fact that communion between the Holy One and man is the essential root-idea of the Old Testament message, but equally, that the knowledge concerning this relation is only the effect of God's work of revelation and the relation itself was only ordained by God in His grace (Deut. vii; ix)! In this communion man may, on the one hand, realize that he does indeed stand in a personal relationship to God and may speak to God as God speaks to him; on the other hand this should never make him think that his relation to God is a true "dialogue-situation".... The discussion between God and man is never a dialogue pure and simple; the man who speaks must always realize and experience that he is addressing himself to the *Holy One*, and his word or answer spoken to God can fundamentally be a prayer only.

'The last word, therefore, never rests with man; even in Gen. xviii. 33 God terminates the discussion with Abraham more or less abruptly; and even Israel's prayers of penitence are not always answered by Yahweh (Jer. xv; Hos. vi). It is for Him to take the *decision* whether or not to accept man's words. Therefore Buber just oversteps the mark when he says that in the dialogue between God and His creature man is a real partner in his own right who can speak his own word independently and of his own free will. This view smacks too much of modern individualism and humanism.' *Ibid.*, p. 160.

[82]*God and Rationality*, p. 157.

speech. However, man's response, which is an integral part of the relation, and thus a responsibility, cannot be a response over which he has autonomous control. It is the image of God which constitutes the possibility and the actuality of human response to God. As such, it is authentic human speech—man has his own created logos—but the rationality of that speech, or response, to God, is valid only within the limits of God's Logos.[83] If man should step beyond these limits, and speak 'in his own right' he has lost the rationality of response—which is the rationality of communion—and slips into a 'senseless' relation with God and his brother. And yet, possessing full power of speech!

This problematic of response in the original relationship between God and man was portrayed in a way that was far less abstract than this:

> And the Lord God commanded the man, saying, 'You may freely eat of every tree of the garden; but of the tree of the knowledge of good and evil you shall not eat, for in the day that you eat of it you shall die.'[84]

> But the serpent said to the woman, 'You will not die. For God knows that when you eat of it your eyes will be opened, and you will be like God, knowing good and evil.' So ..., she took of its fruit and ate; and she also gave some to her husband, and he ate. Then the eyes of both were opened,... And they heard the sound of the Lord God walking in the garden in the cool of the day, and the man and his wife hid themselves from the presence of the Lord God among the trees of the garden. But the Lord God called to the man, and said to him, 'Where are you?'[85]

The freedom of the first man was given to him as a creative Word of grace *within* which was set a limiting response. That which has been ordinarily called the prohibition should actually be understood in a more positive sense as the responsive act of the *imago Dei* made possible by the limiting grace of God. The tree of the knowledge of good and evil is precisely this limit which makes response possible. The fundamental Word which God gives to the relation is not 'no', but *live*! And the response which is then made possible is an affirmation of 'yes'

---

[83]Cf. Karl Rahner, *The Trinity*, Burns and Oates/Herder and Herder, London, 1971, who says: 'Insofar as the self-communication must be understood as *absolutely* willed by God it must carry its acceptance with it. If we are not to downgrade this communication to the level of a human *a priori* and thus do away with it, the acceptance must be brought about by the self-communicating God himself. The freedom of the acceptance as a power *and* also as an act must be conceived as posited by God's creative power, without in any way impairing the nature of freedom. Insofar as the divine self-communication implies the will of its acceptance, it constitutes transcendence.' p. 97.

[84]Genesis 2:16, 17.

[85]Genesis 3:4-7, 8-9.

to this life—to God. The tree of life which is in the 'midst of the garden' places the centre of man's life in the provision of God. But the implication of the narrative is that the tree of the knowledge of good and evil also stands in the midst of the garden. That is, the limitation is also at the centre and issues from the same gracious source. God is at once both the limit and the centre of man's existence. And Adam knows that, and in affirming both the limit and the centre of his existence he is enabled to have a boundless freedom of response.

It does not seem totally irrelevant, nor anachronistic, that the creation of woman is placed just at this point in the narrative, and that it is introduced with the divine pronouncement, as if it were a sudden discovery: 'It is not good that the man should be alone.' (Genesis 2:18). There is a mystery here—Adam must sleep and be awakened to an 'other', one who is part of him and yet totally distinct from him. The greatest possibility of their belonging to each other is in the fact that they are different from each other. Bonhoeffer offers the provocative suggestion at this point, that the woman is to be the 'helper' for the man in 'carrying the limit imposed upon him'. It is in the knowledge of the other person who stands next to him, limiting him, that both the centre and the limit of his life which stands in the garden becomes flesh. It is now possible for man to love his limit as he loves his own flesh.[86]

Here we can see the outlines of the transcendence of God cast in the concrete forms of the original relationship of God and man. God's transcendence is his limiting grace which comes up against man to give him the boundless freedom of being an 'other' to God. But here is also the problematic in that relation. For the other—the limit—is what makes response possible, makes it possible to give the necessary affirmation to both life and limit as the grace of God. But the limit is not something which man possesses and has at his disposal. The limit is transcendence, and it is God's transcendence. The original relation between God and man has the characteristics of a covenant, because it is effected by the free act of God who binds himself to fellowship with man through his own image. While at the same time, covenant response is also given to the relationship through the establishment of the limit. What has become clear in this discussion, is the fact that the problematic of covenant response is intrinsic to the nature of the original relation

---

[86]'In what way is Eve a "helper" to Adam? In the context of the whole it can only be that woman becomes man's helper in the carrying of the limit imposed upon him.... He knew he was limited, but only in the positive sense that to him it was unthinkable to pass the limit. In this limitation he had his life, it is true, but he could still not really love this life in its limitation.... In his unfathomable mercy the Creator knew that this creaturely, free life can only be borne in limitation if it is loved, and out of this mercy he created a companion for man who must be at once the embodiment of Adam's limit and the object of his love.' D. Bonhoeffer, *Creation and Fall*, p. 60.

between God and man, and is not induced by the fact or consequence of a transgression. This now makes it possible to understand the place of redemption in the covenant relation and reveals an inner structure to the logic of Incarnation which is not simply a derivative of a soteriological act.

The fact is, Adam did transgress this limit by seeking to possess it. His transgression was not a defiant *no*, but a tragic *mine*! That is, he became, or attempted to become, his own limit. But without that divinely provided limit, no response is possible, no matter how desperately man seeks it, even through love.

> ...and God's power is love without limit. But when a man dares reach for that... he is only reaching for the power. Whoever goes to save another person with the lie of limitless love throws a shadow on the face of God. And God is what happened, God is what is; and whoever stands between another person and her truth is not a lover, he is... Maggie, we... used one another! [Maggie] Not me, not me! Yes you. And I. 'To live' we cried, and 'Now' we cried. And loved each other's innocence, as though to love enough what was not there would cover up what was. But there is an angel, and night and day he brings back to us exactly what we want to lose. So you must love him because he keeps truth in the world.[87]

And so the limit which had been given Adam in the flesh to help him carry and love the limit became strange to him. 'Then the eyes of both were opened', and they knew fear, and hate, and lust, and yes—death too. The mechanism of response is still there, and the hunger for it. But the movements now give pain as well as pleasure. The flesh brings coldness as well as comfort, love can hurt as well as heal.

The problematic of covenant response, which hitherto had been invisible in the possibility of a boundless freedom for God, now surfaces as an impossibility—'I was afraid, because I was naked; and I hid myself.' (Genesis 3:10). And it is at this point, when man was most alone, cold and comfortless, that the first movements of what will become Incarnation take place. And it is the movement of covenant response. Into man's limitless life, a limit begins to be inserted, from the creaturely side, an involuntary movement at first—a dumb creature yields up its inarticulate life to shape the first word in man's response: 'And the Lord God made for Adam and for his wife garments of skins, and clothed them.' (Genesis 3:21).

From this moment there is sacrifice, later an altar, which can be seen as the limiting response placed within man's temporal and physical existence. The altar enters into human experience as the limiting place, the Torah as the limiting commandment. These constitute possibilities

[87]Arthur Miller, *After the Fall*, p. 113.

again, not mere prohibitions. In setting out the limits, man was being enabled to make his covenant response in the flesh, though now the flesh is filled with dark pools of mystery, silence and dread:

As the sun was going down, a deep sleep fell on Abram; and lo, a dread and great darkness fell upon him. . . . and it was dark, and behold, a smoking fire pot and flaming torch passed between these pieces.[88]

Then Jacob awoke from his sleep and said, 'Surely the Lord is in this place; and I did not know it.' And he was afraid, and said, 'How awesome is this place! This is none other than the house of God, and this is the gate of heaven,'[89]

When the Lord saw that he turned aside to see, God called to him out of the bush, 'Moses, Moses!' And he said, 'Here am I.' Then he said, 'Do not come near; put off your shoes from your feet, for the place on which you are standing is holy ground.'[90]

And the Lord spoke to Aaron, saying, 'Drink no wine nor strong drink, you nor your sons with you, when you go into the tent of meeting, lest you die, it shall be a statue for ever throughout your generations. You are to distinguish between the holy and the common, and between the unclean and the clean.'[91]

For the life of the flesh is in the blood; and I have given it for you upon the altar to make atonement for your souls; for it is the blood that makes atonement, by reason of the life.[92]

The forms and rituals which centre around the sacrifice, structure that part of the life of Israel commonly referred to as the cult. This is the particular aspect of the covenant which came to Israel through its experience of redemption from Egypt.[93] While the ancient world of Israel's time was familiar with the concept of covenant, the uniqueness of the covenant as concluded with Israel, together with its cultic structure, was its unilateral divine nature. That is, rather than being a contract with mutually contracting partners, the covenant which God made with Israel at Sinai was consistent with the nature of *the* covenant relation which was intrinsic to man's original relation with God— it was a covenant of grace and was initiated totally by God. This means that the legal and cultic requirements of the covenant were not at the centre, as man's part in the establishment of the covenant, but were in the form of a covenant response. It is a serious misunderstanding to say, as some do, that the covenant given to Israel during this period

[88]Genesis 15:12, 17.
[89]Genesis 28:16-17.
[90]Exodus 3:4-5.
[91]Leviticus 9:8-10.
[92]Leviticus 17:11.
[93]See Exodus 19 through Numbers 36.

introduced a new dimension of law to the relationship of God to man.[94] This misunderstanding arises out of a failure to see that the cultic requirements of the redemptive form of the covenant are to be seen as a more elaborate representation of the covenant response conceived in terms of the limiting grace of man's original relation to God. The cult can only be understood in accordance with the hidden significance in the words: 'For all things come from thee, and of thy own have we given thee.' (I Chronicles 29:14). Far from being a legal provision by which man must provide his own response to God in order to attain and maintain covenant relationship, the cult is itself both a limit and a covenant response provided by God. The conditional aspects of the Sinaitic covenant, therefore, did not basically alter the terms of the God-man relation, but now emphasize the responsibility of appropriating the divinely-provided way of covenant response.

> In his covenant with Israel God not only promised to be their God and required of them to walk before Him and be perfect, but gratuitously provided for Israel in the sacred cult the appointed way of response in fulfilment of His divine requirement. The prophets, some of whom came from the priesthood, insisted that this vicarious response had to be enacted by way of obedience into the life and existence of Israel in order to be efficacious reality, and pointed ahead to the Servant of the Lord as the chosen instrument for its actualization.[95]

There are two important things brought to our attention in what T. F. Torrance is telling us here. The first is the reiteration of what

[94]This is the conclusion reached by G. Ernest Wright in his essay, 'The Histories of Israel', *The Book of the Acts of God*, G. Ernest Wright and Reginald Fuller, Penguin Books, Middlesex, England, 1965. He says: 'We note that in this case [i.e. Exodus 19:5-6] the promise begins with a condition; there is now a covenant which must be kept. Before this we have noticed the concentration upon the grace of God, upon his undeserved acts of goodness. The good news of God's marvellous and saving activity has been related with joy, but here now we encounter the divine requirement. Law is added to grace,...' p. 95. For an argument exactly contrary to this, one should see Karl Barth, *Church Dogmatics*, IV/1, pp. 22ff. Also, see K. Miskotte, *When the Gods are Silent*, pp. 156ff. For an extended treatment of the biblical concept of covenant, particularly as to the relevance of the political suzerainty covenants common to that period which were unilateral covenants on the part of a superior ruler with a vassal, see the article by G. E. Mendenhall on 'Covenant', *The Interpreter's Dictionary of the Bible*, Vol. I, pp. 714-723.

[95]T. F. Torrance, *God and Rationality*, p. 158. Cf. also, K. Barth: 'God's covenant with man, the covenant which God made with Abraham, with Moses and David, finds its reality solely, but completely and finally, in the fact that God was made man, in order that as man He might do what man as such never does, what even Israel never did, appropriate God's grace and fulfil God's law'. *Church Dogmatics*, I/2, p. 104.

has already been suggested, that the proper way to understand the commandments and the cult is to take them as a divinely provided way of covenant response, a movement from the human side of the covenant made possible by the transcendence of God which enters into human existence in the form of a limiting grace. Thus we are taken back beyond the first transgression to the inner structure of the original covenant itself, where covenant response was also problematic in that it was only humanly possible through the divine initiative.

The second thing we are to notice, is that the renewing of covenant response as a possibility for man following his estrangement due to transgression of the limit, is to be seen as a divinely provided covenant response which progressively works its way into the life of Israel. When the cultic life of Israel becomes a 'thing in itself', the prophets urge the people to go beyond the external and formal aspects of the cult and to make covenant response a matter of an internal and personal response to God.[96] But even this is to be made possible by divine provision: 'A new heart I will give you', cries Jahweh, 'and a new spirit I will put within you; and I will take out of your flesh the heart of stone and give you a heart of flesh. And I will put my spirit within you, and cause you to walk in my statutes.' (Ezekiel 36:26-27). The new covenant (Jeremiah 31:31-34) moves the divinely provided covenant response closer to the flesh of Israel by centring it in their actions which issue from the heart rather than in the actions which are merely formal and 'heartless'. It is just not correct to say that the new covenant is a 'spiritualized' form of the old covenant and therefore a movement away from the flesh to the inner life. The 'enfleshment' of the covenant response advances another step forward the promise of the new covenant which will be a response from the humanity of Israel made possible by the limiting grace of the *Spirit* of God given to them.[97]

[96]Cf. T. C. Vriezen, *An Outline of Old Testament Theology*, who says: 'When Israel thinks it possesses in its sacrificial cult the divine means of grace, the prophets must reject this means of grace and remind the people that God's mercy applies only to those who obey God. From the cult the people is thrown back on the mercy of the living God.' p. 88.

[97]One form of this tendency to spiritualize the new covenant rather than to see it as a deepening of the empirical nature of the covenant in the flesh of Israel is the concept of Rudolf Bultmann, in which he holds that the new covenant is meant to be eschatological. He feels that Jeremiah and Ezekiel were caught in the delusion of a possible realization of God's demands within this world, and that the New Testament drew the right conclusion in viewing the new covenant eschatologically, that is, not as a structure of history within this world. See Rudolf Bultmann, 'Prophecy and Fulfilment', *Essays Philosophical and Theological*, trans. James C. G. Greig, Macmillan, New York, 1955, pp. 205ff. Also see his *Glaube und Verstehen*, Vol. II (1952), pp. 162ff. Cited by K. Miskotte, *When the Gods are Silent*, p. 166.

It is the flesh of Israel which forms the 'womb' out of which covenant response is born, as T. F. Torrance tells us:

> The whole fact of Israel entrusted with the oracles of God was itself a mighty response evoked by the Word of God out of the midst of history, but within Israel the Word of God was mediated in such a way that a divinely prepared form of obedient response was included within it. That is what we find in the prophetic message about the servant of the Lord through whose passion a new covenant would be inaugurated bringing redemption to Israel and a light to lighten the Gentiles, and that is what we find fulfilled at last in the birth of Jesus. God had adapted Israel to His purpose in such a way as to form within it a womb for the incarnation of the Word and matrix of appropriate forms of human thought and speech for the reception of the incarnational revelation. And so Jesus was born of Mary, out of the organic correlation of Word and response in the existence of Israel, to be the Word of God made flesh in the life and language of man.[98]

We are very near to the heart of the Incarnation at this point, and it now becomes possible to see that the inner logic of the Incarnation is linked with the progressive enfleshment of covenant response through the action of the Spirit of God. When we look back and consider thoughtfully Bonhoeffer's suggestion that the creation of woman was the human 'thou' meant to help man carry the limit, that is, to make it possible for him to love his limit and in so doing to be enabled to make covenant response, we cannot help but be struck with the significance of the progressive enfleshment of covenant response through Israel as God pressed his Spirit into her. And then, of course, we cannot help but look forward and see that when the 'Word became flesh', it was an act of the Spirit of God, creating in human flesh the one who would make covenant response—not through the inarticulate flesh of some dumb creature—but through the flesh, and blood, of the Logos himself.

One cannot but also express the thought here, and then leave it to be picked up again if it is warranted, that there seems to be something 'unfinished' in the original created response of man to his transcending limit. If God did indeed mean for the limit to be personal, and 'in the flesh', does not the Incarnation point us to that possibility, rather than being merely a 'patch of an old garment?' What is implied here, is the question of how far the Spirit of God is to be taken as continuing the 'enfleshment' of God's transcendence through what the New Testament calls the Body of Christ. And how this relates to a more

---

[98]*God and Rationality*, p. 149.

dynamic understanding of the *imago Dei*, and, indeed, the creative act itself.

It is in the problematic of covenant response, as it originally was constituted in the reciprocity of the *imago Dei*, that we find the rationale for understanding a truly human life which is at the same time an act of the transcendence of God. For in Christ, as it only became perceptible in Israel through promise, both the limit and the response become one.

> It is into this created rationality (or *logos*) that the Word (or *Logos*) of God enters, assimilating it to Himself in the incarnation, in order to become Word to man through the medium of human word and in order to provide from the side of man for an appropriate response in truth and goodness towards God.[99]

What we begin to see in Israel is completed in Christ. The Spirit of God penetrates flesh through the *imago Dei* and frees the created logos to receive the divine, uncreated Logos. The purpose of this totally unique 'incarnation' is to address man in his capacity for freedom (response), not at the level of his needs or wants. That is to say, Christ is not the incarnate Son of God merely to meet human needs, as though the need itself was the vacuum which drew the response from God. The inner logic of the Incarnation moves in just the opposite direction even though the course of the movement is in God. It is a movement from man towards God in covenant response issuing out of the *original*, and thus, ultimate, intention. But that movement, as originally and ultimately conceived, was only possible because God transcended himself in becoming concrete and actual limit for man.

It is the problematic of covenant response which reveals the transcendence of God to be the concrete limiting factor which makes human freedom authentic in man's affirmation of that limit. It is the transcendence of God which makes it possible for man to love that limit, for the transcendence of God becomes the limit in the form of absolute compassion, true humanity, and utter obedience. We are speaking, of course, of that which the New Testament calls the 'self emptying' (*kenosis*), or the 'humbling' of the Son of God in becoming man.

But there are two inseparable strands united in this inner logic of Incarnation, and these serve as the recapitulation of that which has emerged through the discussion in this chapter.

The first strand in this inner logic is the transcendence of God in the form of a limiting reality for authentic human existence. This is the concrete, and ultimately, human and temporal existence of God himself over and against man. What was earlier called the hiddenness of God in his self-condescension must now be called the transcendence of God.

To say that God is hidden in his temporal and human relation to man is to assume that we know a reality of God beyond the reality of God which confronts us in his revelation. It is to assume that the reality of God is somehow 'behind' or beyond the form of his revelation in some inaccessible way.[100] But this makes the 'limit' by which man knows that he is defined by the reality of God, and therefore *really* placed in his own created freedom, ambiguous and highly subjective. The result of this concept of hiddenness, is that the 'limit' becomes a conception, or an idea of God which man posits. So that man 'places' God in reality in attempting to define his limit. This is precisely the temptation and the transgression which overcame the first man.

We observed how the transcendence of God progressively penetrated the 'flesh' of Israel, until finally Israel became the 'logos of God'—the suffering servant of Jahweh. This is to be understood as the working of the limit by which God transcends the world into an utterly human form so that man is confronted with the reality of God without the need of 'interposing an anthropology' before the reality of God; without the kind of subjectivizing of God which says, 'God gives himself to us according to our attitude towards him.'[101] It is this strand of the inner logic of the Incarnation which prepares us to understand the transcendence of God in the humanity of Christ without coming to grief over the metaphysical problems of the relation of divine nature to human nature.

The second strand of the inner logic which has emerged in this chapter is found in the affirmation which man is enabled to give to his life precisely because of this limiting transcendence of God. One could say that it is the transcendence of God in the form of the concrete limit which makes possible the transcendence of man in the form of the

---

[100]Karl Rahner makes it clear that anything other than the unity of transcendence and its objective presence in history is the only alternative to the substitution of either transcendence or the concrete form for God himself: 'Transcendence and its whereunto have their history in the object itself. And it is the unity of these two elements, as it brings about distinction, which refers to God. Neither of the two moments alone should be made God's substitute. We maintain, against any kind of 'imageless' mysticism of an experience of transcendence in the mere anonymity of the mystery, that transcendence is seen and found in the object itself.' *The Trinity*, p. 92.

[101]As an example of the kind of subjectivizing which interposes an anthropology before the act of God, K. Miskotte quotes Heinz Zahrnt who says: 'The being of things depends upon our attitude toward them; things give themselves to us in the way in which we comport ourselves towards them. This also applies with respect to God. God gives himself to us according to our attitude toward him. The way in which we believe we know him is the way in which he is toward us, the way in which we too have him.' To this, Miskotte responds: 'No! Fortunately, honestly, in conformity with the narrative of his deeds, this is simply ruled out by the Word. And better things are provided for us.' *When the Gods are Silent*, pp. 201-202.

concrete response. The rational continuity and the coherence of this relation has its source in the divine Logos which gives to the created logos in man the intelligibility, and thus, the actuality of response. This covenant response from 'the human side' is problematical to man in that he cannot possess the rationality of response in any autonomous act which transgresses the transcendence of God in the form of the limit.

We observed how the covenant response from the human side was progressively worked into the humanity of Israel with the promise of a new heart and a new Spirit. In Israel, the transcending limit and the covenant response were brought closer and closer, so that the particularization of both limit and response could be prepared to break out in a true universality, so the 'one man' Israel, in becoming the 'one man' Jesus Christ, could unite both transcendence and response in a total and final way.

It is this union of both the transcendent limit, which is the reality of God for man, and the covenant response, which is the reality of man's perfect love for that limit, in the one man Jesus Christ which comprises the inner structure of the Incarnation. This is the centre which Israel lacked to give coherence to her own existence. It is the way in which the inner logic of Israel's relation to God points towards this centre, and the way in which the centre can only be understood in terms of God's dealing with Israel which constitutes the organic unity between Israel and Christ. It is this reality which permits the primitive Christian community to use the language of the Old Testament without tension or doubt.[102] And it is this inner logic, which provides the structure of thought as well as the content, for our explication of the Incarnation.

There is no Logos of God apart from the Logos of flesh. So then *kenosis* is not empty of meaning, and in this *logos* we are not far from the transcendence and the reality of God.

---

[102]Cf. G. von Rad, *Old Testament Theology*, Vol. II: 'Now, it is simple fact that the primitive Christian community was able to continue to use the language of the Old Testament, to link on to it, and to avail itself of this linguistic tool. This is a theological phenomenon of great significance. The New Testament contains no evidence of tension or doubt in connexion with Old Testament sayings ... Instead, what surprises the reader is the unbroken continuity, the lack of break at the transition; for, in the beginning at least, it was possible to express the new event effortlessly in the language of the old.' p. 353.

Chapter V

Kenosis and the Reality of God

1 'The God Who is for Man'

Yet the issue of attaching the unfamiliar vision to the familiar
description remains; the attachment of the strange to the usual, of the
final to the relative.[1]

Only those who have faced the agony of an unwritten page, and that
particular terror of the first one, will understand the surprise and the
delight of the man who wrote what no man had ever thought before:
'In the beginning was the Word ...., and God was the Word .... and
the Word became flesh!'[2] No poet has ever grasped with greater delicacy
the fragile beauty of an incredible theme; the words flirt wantonly
with the common language of mythology, on one side; and on the other,
lean drunkenly over the precipice of utter meaninglessness. But with a
certainty born of innocence, they lead whoever will follow directly to
a certain man—Jesus of Nazareth—and leave them there before him,
fully clothed and in their right minds. One can ask no more of words
than this.

And so we are brought to this: not to consider Incarnation as a theme,
but the Incarnate One. The one whose deeds and words were inseparably
bound up in a life which testified both to the reality of God among men
and the authenticity of man before God. While it is true that we have
already spoken of Incarnation and even of the logic of Incarnation, we
now speak neither about, nor of, but *from* a knowledge of the Logos
of God who 'became' flesh. That this is an event which comes under
the category of 'Incarnation' is secondary to and derivative from the
reality of the event itself. The Incarnate One is not a species among
the genus Incarnation. He who was in the beginning with God, through
whom all things were made ($\dot{\epsilon}\gamma\dot{\epsilon}\nu\epsilon\tau o$), himself became ($\dot{\epsilon}\gamma\dot{\epsilon}\nu\epsilon\tau o$) flesh.[3]
There is no 'category' of thought by which this phenomenon can be
classified. The 'becoming' which was ascribed to the creatures as distinct
from their Creator-Logos is now assumed by the Logos himself who

[1] D. M. MacKinnon, *Borderlands of Theology*, p. 214.
[2] John 1:1, 14. My translation.
[3] John 1:3, 14.

becomes the subject of a 'becoming'. In addition, it is said of the witness
John, who was 'not that light', and who was clearly distinguished from
the one whose 'life was the light of men', that he entered into historical
existence by a 'becoming' (ἐγένετο).[4] Again, in John 1:12ff., we read of
those who will believe and bear his name, to whom he gave power to
'become' (γενέσθαι) children of God. It is this larger context of the phrase
'the Word became flesh' which interprets to us the sheer incredibility
of this event—he who is himself the subject of the 'becoming' of his
creatures, of his witness, and of those who are called and chosen, 'becomes' as they are. The eternal Subject, as it were, loses himself among
those who are at the same time the objects of his action.[5]

   The dimensions of what I have earlier called 'historical transcendence'
are now sharpened up in the greatest possible way. By transcendence is
meant the Word (ὁ λόγος), the eternal Subject through whom all things
were made (ἐγένετο). By transcendence is meant the Eternal One who
is free to be the Subject of all becoming, and in that sense is 'totally
other' than that which becomes.[6] The Word does not owe his existence
to any 'becoming'—he *was* in the beginning with God, and *is* God—
but is, instead, the source of all 'becoming'. It is clearly indicated here
that transcendence is not that which is *predicated* about the reality of
God from the standpoint of the creatures as subject, but is rather that

---

[4]John 1:4, 6-7.
[5]Cf. K. Barth, *Church Dogmatics*, I/2, pp. 159ff. The necessity of 'thinking
together' the eternal Subject and his historical existence is well stated by Barth:
'He the eternal subject now exists—a stumbling-block to all Jewish ears and
foolishness to all Greek ears—just as anything else or as anyone else exists.
That is the meaning of ὁ λόγος ἐγένετο, if the words are taken in the sense
they bear in the context, that is, if no reduction is made which softens or weakens
either the ὁ λόγος or the ἐγένετο .... It is in respect of this Subject and only this
Subject that we arrive at the statement ὁ λόγος ἐγένετο. This Subject and only
this Subject is indicated by the statement. This at once implies that we are not
challenged to combine the two concepts in a third higher concept and so abolish
their object. In this case there can be no higher object in which the opposition
between the two concepts would disappear. In place of this higher concept stands
the name of Jesus Christ. In this case, therefore, to 'think together' can mean
only the responsibility which we owe to this name, so long as we keep to what
is already given us in Scripture. It can mean only to think both the ὁ λόγος and
the ἐγένετο with the strict simultaneity with which they are given us in Scripture.'
Ibid., pp. 159-160.
[6]The sense in which the Word is not simply a synonym for 'deity as such', but
is the Son, who as such, is the fullness of deity, is made clear by Barth: 'ὁ λόγος,
the "Word" spoken of in John 1:14, is the divine, creative, reconciling, redeeming
Word which participates without restriction in the divine nature and existence,
the eternal Son of God.... It is not deity in itself and as such that was made
flesh. For deity does not exist at all in itself and as such, but only in the modes
of existence of the Father, the Son and the Holy Spirit. It is the Son or Word of
God that was made flesh. But He was made flesh in the entire fullness of deity,
which is also that of the Father, and of the Holy Spirit.' *Ibid.*, pp. 132-133.

which God as subject, as the Word, predicates about the reality of the creature. Hence, any diminution or depotentiation of the Word as subject with respect to that which 'becomes' will constitute a loss of transcendence, and as a consequence, a loss of the reality of God.

It can also now be made clear what is meant by historical. We have already noted in John 1:6 that John, the witness to Jesus, entered into his historical existence in the form of a 'becoming'—ἐγένετο ἄνθρωποζ. It is this 'becoming' which carries the force of an historical existence. ἐγένετο is the predicate which belongs to creaturehood, and as such, refers not merely to a static condition, nor even less to a blind and empty process of time, but to a definite existence of creaturehood which exists as the predicate of a Creator.[7] It is in this sense that 'becoming' points to the dimension of that which is historical. It is not simply that the Word has become conditioned in some manner by flesh, as though the flesh were an external and temporary concealment of the eternal Word —that has been recognized from the beginning by the Church as the docetic error. But, the Word, the Eternal Subject, has become (ἐγένετο) flesh, has entered into the experience and existence of creaturehood. The transcendence of God has become historical in a real sense of the Word. The Creator takes up himself the existence-form of the creature.

Here again we are put up against the fundamental question for this book: can the transcendence of God be understood in an utterly historical form? This is the question of the reality of God in an historical sense, and as such, it is a christological question. Is the deepest penetration of human existence—the Word becoming flesh—the transcendence, and thus, the reality of God? And if this is so, how can the Eternal Subject 'lose himself' among those who are his own creatures, as Barth puts it?[8] This 'losing himself', or what Paul calls the 'self-emptying' or *kenosis* of Christ, takes us to the very heart of the problem of historical transcendence:

Have this mind among yourselves, which you have in Christ Jesus, who, though he was in the form of God, did not count equality with God a thing to be grasped, but emptied himself, taking the form of a servant, being born in the likeness of men. And being found in human form he humbled himself and became obedient unto death, even death on a cross.[9]

The so-called 'kenotic' question which is raised in this text, is in actuality

[7]Cf. K. Barth: 'Becoming is therefore ascribed to His creatures, as distinct from Him, the Creator. If they all became by Him, there is nothing we expect less than to hear that He, too, is Himself the subject of an ἐγένετο or becoming, that He can exist Himself in the same way as the things created by Him.' *Ibid.*, p. 159.
[8]*Ibid.*, p. 159.
[9]Philippians 2:5-8.

the question of historical transcendence. It is the problem of 'thinking together' ὁ λόγος and ἐγένετο—the *Word* and the *becoming*. It is the problem of sustaining both the real transcendence of God as the Eternal Subject acting through the Logos and the genuine historicality, and thus, the authentic humanity of Jesus Christ.

It must be said at the outset, that the methodology which controls the development of this chapter takes us on a different course than the one which captured the attention of those who have sought to work out a 'kenotic' Christology. That is, a concept of the person of Christ which involves some alteration or modification in the eternal Logos in order to accommodate it to a human personality. One must be cognizant of these efforts, and even appreciate them to the extent that they help us to take seriously the fundamental depth of the problematic involved, but this chapter cannot take on the form of a critique of, or an argument for, a kenotic Christology.[10] Instead, the *kenosis* of Christ will be taken

[10]Kenotic Christology is a relatively modern development in the history of theology, marked by two distinct periods of doctrinal controversy, first in the 16th and 17th centuries between the Tübingen and Giessen schools of Lutheran theology, and second, a quite distinct, though not unrelated, kenotic controversy in the latter half of the 19th century extending into the 20th century, first on the continent, and then in Britain. The dominant idea of a specifically kenotic Christology is a doctrine of the Incarnation which asserts some real modification, of an absolute or a relative nature, on the part of the pre-existent and divine Logos as the necessary condition for the assumption of a true and complete humanity. While Lutheran Christology stubbornly clung to the dogma: 'The Word not outside the flesh, nor the flesh outside the Word.' (A. B. Bruce, *The Humiliation of Christ*, T. & T. Clark, Edinburgh, 1881, p. 141), the voice from Geneva was equally adamant: 'Another absurdity which they obtrude upon us—viz. that if the Word of God became incarnate, it must have been enclosed in the narrow tenement of an earthly body, is sheer petulance. For although the boundless essence of the Word was united with human nature into one person, we have no idea of any enclosing.' (John Calvin, *Institutes of the Christian Religion*, trs. Henry Beveredge, T. & T. Clark, Edinburgh, 1879, Vol. I, Book II, 13/4, p. 414). The issue at stake, that of the permanent subject of the manhood of Christ, was blurred by an intra-Lutheran controversy centring on the implications of the *communicatio idiomatum*, so essential to Luther, only to be picked up again by Gottfried Thomasius in the 19th century. With the emerging concept of the human personality, centring in 19th century thought with its emphasis on the psychology of personhood in terms of self-consciousness, these questions concerning the person of Christ were raised to a highly speculative level. Thomasius, making subtle distinctions between Ego and person, sought to maintain the unity of the divine Ego with human self-consciousness through a doctrine of *kenosis*, or self-emptying, of the divine Logos of those attributes which were relative to the world, i.e., omnipotence, omnipresence, omniscience. W. F. Gess took a more extreme position than Thomasius, asserting that in the *kenosis* the Son of God allowed his eternal self-consciousness to be extinguished in order to regain it as man. The Danish theologian Martensen posited two life-centres of the Logos, retaining the essential deity of the person of Christ. This was the position basically assumed by Bishop Charles Gore, who ignited the kenotic controversy within Anglican theology by asserting that the subject of the manhood of Christ was the

as a 'way into' the inner logic of the Incarnation, particularly with respect to the problematic of historical transcendence.

If, instead of assuming, as has so often been done, that the transcendence of God is somehow inimical to his condescending to exist in a creaturely (historical) form—with the result that transcendence is set over against immanence[11]—if one does not begin with this assumption,

divine Logos who had limited himself so that we must think of Christ as holding the views of his own contemporaries and as being actually ignorant of those things not accessible to human reason. For literature pertaining to the kenotic Christologies, see: A. B. Bruce, *The Humiliation of Christ*; F. J. Hall, *The Kenotic Theory*, Longmans Green and Co., London, 1898; Frank Weston, *The One Christ*, Longmans Green and Co., London, 1914; C. Welch (ed.), *God and Incarnation in Mid-nineteenth Century German Theology*, Oxford University Press, New York, 1965; Charles Gore, *The Incarnation of the Son of God*, John Murray, London, 1909, second edition; *Dissertations on Subjects Connected with the Incarnation*, Charles Scribner's Sons, New York, 1895. For some modern commentary on the kenotic theme see: Karl Barth, *Church Dogmatics*, I/2, pp. 166ff., IV/1, pp. 180ff.; Donald Dawes, 'A Fresh Look at the Kenotic Christologies', *Scottish Journal of Theology*, 15 (1962), pp. 337-349; Thomas A. Thomas, 'The Kenosis Question', *Evangelical Quarterly*, Vol. 42, 1970, pp. 142-151; John Macquarrie, 'The Pre-existence of Jesus Christ', *The Expository Times*, 77, 1965-66, pp. 199-202.

[11]While it cannot be said that Karl Barth holds that the transcendence of God is inimical to his condescension, to his humanity; nevertheless, he does place transcendence in a dialectical relation to immanence, so that the transcendence of God is protected from a *kenosis* in the historical sense: 'He is absolute, infinite, exalted, active, impassible, transcendent, but in all this He is the One who loves in freedom, the One who is free in His love, and therefore not His own prisoner. He is all this as the Lord, and in such a way that He embraces the opposites of these concepts even while He is superior to them. He is all this as the Creator, who has created the world as the reality distinct from Himself but willed and affirmed by Him and therefore as His world, as the world which belongs to Him, in relation to which He can be God and act as God in an absolute way and also a relative, in an infinite and also a finite, in an exalted and also a lowly, in an active and also a passive, in a transcendent and also an immanent, and finally in a divine and also a human—indeed, in relation to which He himself can become worldly, making His own both its form, the *forma servi*, and also its cause; and all without giving up His own form, the *forma Dei*, and His own glory, but adopting the form and cause of man into the most perfect communion with His own, accepting solidarity with the world. God can do this.' *Church Dogmatics*, IV/1, p. 187. While Barth triumphantly concludes with 'God can do this', we are not sure just what it is that God can do, except balance himself on the dialectical edge, and Janus-like, turn one face towards the world and keep one face turned away. The specific point at which I would take issue with Barth, and it certainly is a very modest challenge, albeit crucial to my argument, is that the coordinate terms transcendence and immanence, with their primarily philosophical orientation, do not answer to the reality of God's relation to the world as revealed through the inner logic of the Incarnation. I will attempt to show that when transcendence is understood as the act of God by which he moves outside of, or beyond his own 'immanent freedom' to interact with the world, either as Creator or redeemer, there is no need of a dialectic to preserve God's transcendence in his interaction, even in his Incarnation.

but rather with the assumption that transcendence is the reality of God in his action *whatever* the form it takes, then the way seems to be opened up for a new understanding of *kenosis*. The warrant for this assumption could quite easily be found in the inner logic of Incarnation as revealed in God's relation to Israel. As we saw in the last chapter, this can be expressed in the form that the condescension of God in becoming more and more identified with Israel as his 'son' is not a withdrawal, nor an act of hiddenness on God's part, but the act of his Spirit, and thus, his transcendence. We saw that there were two strands to this inner logic of historical transcendence: first of all, the transcendence of God is God's *placing* of himself into concrete, historical relation to man as the limiting reality of man's authentic existence. As the Logos becomes increasingly identified with Israel, the transcendence of God becomes increasingly personal and material, rather than formal and cultic. When man comes up against this limit of transcendence, his existence is qualified by the 'God who is for man'. Secondly, the transcendence of God acts as the 'covenant response' which is made possible by the transcendent limit itself. Because this covenant response is intrinsic to the creation-covenant, it is man's original affirmation of his own authentic humanity in terms of response in freedom towards God. Thus, from the human side, God's transcendence works out the covenant response through the humanity of Israel, pointing towards the 'Man who is for God'.[12] This logic of Incarnation converges upon the person of Jesus Christ and seeks its concrete fulfilment. He is the 'God who is for man', and at the same time, the 'Man who is for God'. The question which this chapter asks is: can the *kenosis*, or self-emptying of Christ, be understood as the transcendence of God in both of these ways?

Professor Roger Mehl, in a thoughtful essay entitled, 'Die Krise der Transzendenz', shows the way forward, I believe, to just such an understanding of *kenosis*.[13] Mehl's central thesis is that it has become impossible to think of transcendence as an 'other world' (*Jenseits*) which exists over and against this world.[14] This 'crisis of transcendence' occurs at each level of human experience, depending upon how one views the reality of the world. The three views of the world which Mehl sketches, with their corresponding concepts of transcendence, are: (1) the sensible or material (*sinnliche*) world which was common to Greek antiquity, with a corresponding level of the supersensible (*Übersinnlichen*) which is only accessible to the human subject when he succeeds in reaching beyond the sensible world in order to become mere *Nous*.[15] (2) The world of

[12]See above, pp. 143ff.
[13]*Neue Zeitschrift für Systematische Theologie und Religions-philosophie*, Vol. II, 1969, pp. 329-346.
[14]*Ibid.*, p. 330.
[15]*Ibid.*, p. 330.

Christian thought which has its origin in the creative act of God with a transcendent Creator who appears as the world's first cause, although the world is essentially different from him.[16] And (3) the world view of modern intellectual thought which takes the form of history (*Geschichte*) and for which the concept of the eternal as the fullness of presence is seen as the transcendent.[17] Concerning the concept of transcendence as the supersensible (*Übersinnliche*) world, Mehl asks:

> If the supersensible must produce in us the insight and the understanding for the sensible world, and our location in it, why must then this supersensible (as a key for the understanding) be a separated (absolute in the etymological sense) reality? This question, already raised by Aristotle, produces to a certain extent, the prelude for the crisis of transcendence. But this crisis only becomes evident with the development of modern science.[18]

What Mehl refers to here is the fact that the explanations for the phenomenon of the cosmos are no longer sought in either causes or forms which impress reality upon the sensible world, while remaining transcendental to it, but rather, the cosmos contains an intrinsic intelligibility within its structures. While Descartes may well have been the last scholar to defend the opinion that physics has a metaphysical basis, says Mehl, and that the unchangeableness of God constituted the explanation for the unchangeableness of the quantitative movements in the world, Kant was certainly the first who broke the connection which bound rational knowledge to the theological knowledge and thus opened the door to theological agnosticism.[19]

[16]*Ibid.*, pp. 330-331.

[17]*Ibid.*, p. 331.

[18]*Ibid.*, p. 331. My translation here, and in all subsequent citations. Mehl's reference to the question 'already raised by Aristotle' more than likely points to Aristotle's argument against the Platonists' theory that the Forms are patterns, not only of sensible things, but of things in themselves. What Aristotle actually says concerning this is: 'Again it must be held to be impossible that the substance and that of which it is the substance should exist apart; how therefore, can the Ideas, being the substance of things, exist apart?' *Metaphysics*, p. 991b.

[19]"The philosophy of Kant has become, according to our opinion, a decisive, and perhaps even a triggering factor for the crisis of transcendence. In his demonstration, that knowledge, precisely on the basis of its structure, can reach to the absolute, neither through inference nor through intuition, Kant has shattered the connection which bound rational knowing to theological knowing; since that time, it became impossible to include God in a system of knowledge and to make out of transcendence the pillar that carries the weight of the system. But this connection had guaranteed transcendence for centuries. In order to proceed from knowledge of the world to knowledge of transcendence, one had in the future to take a leap, which Kant defined as the leap of faith. It was certainly not Kant's intention to disavow transcendence. Faith remained admissible from the standpoint of reason, and Kant thought he was able to write a genuine theological essay.

This hiatus between that which is conceivable, but which has become no longer comprehensible and can no longer be subsumed under the concept of knowledge, is precisely the intellectual beginning for the crisis of transcendence.[20]

When one can no longer hold fast to the objective foreignness (*Andersartigkeit*) of transcendence across this epistemological hiatus, the world loses its sense of createdness even as it loses touch with a transcendent Creator. So that transcendence, conceived as a moral law, can exist for Kant without the lawgiver.[21]

The third and more existential crisis of transcendence thus occurs for modern man when his own sense of history loses its transcendental roots for the life of the spirit. The sociological and political forces take over the role of controlling and determining human destiny. Thus, the freedom, which man once could conceive of as the life of the spirit, now takes the form of engagement with history. The genuinely human act is not merely a material existence, for the dimension of the body, without the dualism of a spirit-transcendence, becomes the personal and mutual interaction where spiritual life discloses itself.[22] Given this kind of a world view then,

... transcendence can be nothing more than an alibi for other worldly (*diejenigen*) men, who become deserters in the battle of history and who resign from the creation of values. Only an immature and powerless humanity could project the battle of the gods into heaven; since man has become conscious of his historical possibilities, history is the place for the battle of the gods, and in history for values to arise and disappear.[23]

What Mehl concludes from this survey of the crisis of transcendence, is that the twin-concept, transcendence-immanence, has lost all significance, not only for the secular man who seeks his destiny and his freedom within history, but for theological man as well, who wishes to speak of the reality of God.[24] Mehl goes further to suggest that the theology of the Reformation, in failing to explicate transcendence as the reality of the Incarnation, produced this very irrelevance, if not impossibility, of transcendence.[25] It was not that transcendence was excluded from

Transcendence is even an ethical demand. But it is—and this is the significant point—no longer comprehensible even if it is still conceivable.' R. Mehl, 'Die Krise der Transzendenz', p. 334.
[20]*Ibid.*, p. 334.
[21]*Ibid.*, p. 335.
[22]*Ibid.*, pp. 335-336.
[23]*Ibid.*, pp. 336-337.
[24]*Ibid.*, p. 337.
[25]*Ibid.*, p. 338.

the doctrine of the Incarnation, but that it is not accessible in itself. And, says Mehl, 'When a possibility becomes unexaminable, then it runs the risk of soon becoming forgotten.'[26]

We live in a world without an 'other side' (*Jenseits*), says Mehl, where there is no longer a distinction made between astronomy and physics, and where the cosmos is no longer a dimensional order of values, but rather a uniformity, with its intelligibility to be found within its own structures. The tendency then is to give transcendence the role of placing the value or meaning (*Sinn*) upon history in such a way that it directs history to its highest possibilities. But here Mehl warns that as we approximate the transcendence of God to the meaning of comprehensive history, we bring into danger the concept of God as Subject, who is not only the meaning in history, but also its Lord.[27]

The importance of this preliminary consideration of Mehl's argument can now be seen. The crisis of transcendence is actually a crisis of Christology. And the crisis of Christology is a crisis of the doctrine of God. When the theology of the Reformation refused to seek an auxiliary position through an ontology, that is, speculation over the being of God, it grounded the doctrine of God in the declaration that God is in himself just as he gave himself in the historical revelation of Jesus Christ.[28] Mehl can even cite Feuerbach in support of his argument that Protestant theology is virtually Christology: 'Protestantism no longer occupies itself with what God is in himself, but what he is for man,... it is only Christology.'[29] Now Mehl is not about to take issue with the basic premise that our knowledge of God is essentially Christological, for he will later assert that a doctrine of the transcendence of God must take as its point of departure the act of God in Christ.[30] But what Mehl protests against is the process by which the doctrine of the transcendence of God is resolved into Christology, and then if Christology is made the inaccessible hiding place of that transcendence, contact with God as subject is made impossible. Therefore, Mehl's basic thesis is that transcendence must be put in connection with a subject who is not inaccessible at the historical level. Otherwise, a doctrine of the transcendence of God evaporates into the meaninglessness of the 'other side' (*Jenseits*) which stands contrary to every comprehensible experience.[31]

[26]*Ibid.*, p. 340.

[27]*Ibid.*, p. 341.

[28]*Ibid.*, pp. 337-338.

[29]'Der Protestantismus beschäftigt sich jetzt nicht mehr mit dem, was Gott in sich selbst, sondern was er für den Menschen ist.... Er ist nur Christologie.' *Ibid.*, p. 338.

[30]*Ibid.*, p. 342.

[31]'From the philosophical point of view, one must put transcendence in connection with a subject, for unless one does this it inevitably becomes a beyond which stands over against and contrary to every comprehensible experience. God

The loss of transcendence as a 'foregone conclusion' (*Selbstverständlichkeit*) of an intellectual nature,[32] has served to expose the crisis of transcendence in Christology. This crisis involves the reality of God as the Subject of the Incarnate life of Jesus Christ in his concrete historical existence. What is at stake is the reality of God as the God who is there for man, who is there in a 'limiting' sense. We are at the point where it becomes quite clear why this thesis concerning historical transcendence involves a Christological critique. A Christology which makes the transcendence of God inaccessible at the concrete level of Jesus' historical existence, either through a concealment (κρύψις χρήσεως)or a *kenosis* (κένωσις χρήσεως) of that transcendence, interposes an anthropology between God as revealing-Subject and man as responding-subject. This removes the reality of God as a limiting reality at the *centre* of man's historical existence. It is this particular problem which eluded the grasp of the modern kenoticists.[33] It remains to be seen just how this problem can be approached through a deeper probing into the interconnections between the act of transcendence and the act of self-emptying, which is ordinarily referred to as the humiliation of Christ.

We are now ready to pick up the thought of Mehl again, as he explores the significance of the transcendence of a subject. 'The transcendence of the subject exhibits itself in that distance which makes its appearance between me and my I, in that dialogical structure in his relation to himself and his environment.'[34] When a subject acts to declare itself, according to Mehl, it stands apart for the purpose of that self-expression from its physical, bio-psychological and sociological restrictions. That is, when the subject comes to a self-realization in his real historicality, not only to engage in history, but to make history, it becomes an experience of 'growing beyond oneself' (*Hinauswachsens über sich selbst*).[35] Mehl thus makes transcendence the personal act by which a subject moves

becomes a totally Other, over which I can utter nothing and whom I can also compare, as some mystics have done, completely and totally with a Nothing. Because modern philosophy since Kant in essence is a philosophy of the subject, we must today of necessity think of transcendence in this perspective. Moreover, we are encouraged to do it: for in the experience of every subject that declares itself as such, one can find an analogy of transcendence.' *Ibid.*, pp. 342-343.

[32]'Die Transzendenz erschien lange Zeit als eine Art unvermeidlicher intellektueller Selbstverständlichkeit, als die Garantie jedes Denkens überhaupt.' *Ibid.*, p. 329.

[33]This was particularly true of the Lutheran kenotic controversy of the 16th century, but was not entirely absent from the 19th century kenotic Christologies with their attempts to manipulate the divine attributes so as to protect the humanity of Christ without abandoning the deity of the Logos.

[34]'Die Transzendenz des Subjekts zeigt sich in jener Distanz, die zwischen mir und meinem Ich in Erscheinung tritt, in jener dialogalen Struktur in seiner Beziehung zu sich selbst und seiner Umgebung.' R. Mehl, 'Die Krise der Transzendenz', p. 343.

[35]*Ibid.*, p. 343.

out of or beyond his individuality to interact with and effect change in
his total structure of reality—that is, the subject enters and makes history
through this transcendence of himself.

But, according to Mehl, there is also a boundary to this 'growing
beyond oneself' which works in two ways: first, the progressive renunciation which accompanies the growing beyond the self never extends to a
complete disavowal of the subject himself. However much transcendence
occurs in the form of moving 'outside' of oneself to interact with others,
the subject can never absolutely renounce his own subjectivity.[36] Second,
there is a boundary which prevents this renunciation of the self as an
act of transcendence from becoming completely identified with the Other,
so that, other than in a figurative sense, one cannot really 'sit in the place
of the other'. At this point, Mehl suggests that this experience of 'growing beyond oneself' could only open up the way for a discovery of
transcendence if these two conditions could be realized. That is, if self-
renunciation could take place to the extent that a subject could actually
become the other subject. Here Mehl drops the development of
transcendence in terms of renunciation as psychologically and even
mentally inconceivable,[37] and proceeds directly to apply this analogy
to the *kenosis* of Christ:

> Nothing is comprehensible of the person and work of Christ, nothing
> of his death and his resurrection, if one looks away from his humilia-
> tion. This kenosis of Christ consisted in the act of not grasping to
> himself his own divinitity, gaining distance from (*Abstand zu
> gewinnen*) his divinity and renouncing (*das zu verzichten*) what in
> being and actions, his divinity had made possible for him. In him,
> the boundary, which we have recognized for all growing beyond our-
> selves, is crossed; here appears that unconditional self-renunciation
> which is the necessary condition for a genuine representation over
> against the other.[38]

Mehl is venturing into some very deep water here. He is immediately
aware of this himself, and says that in his renunciation of that which
divinity makes possible 'in being and actions', Christ has not *lost*
his divinity, for 'what remains on the other side (*Jenseits*) of the
renunciation, is precisely that act of absolute transcendence, or freedom
by which Christ renounces all privileges of divinity. Transcendence

---

[36]'Das Subjekt muß zumindest im Blick auf das transzendentale Subjekt
weiterexistieren; denn dies ist ja die Vorbedingung für jedes Hinauswachsen
über sich selbst.' *Ibid.*, p. 343.
[37]'Die Erfahrung des Hinauswachsens über sich könnte nur den Weg für eine
Entdeckung der Transzendenz eröffnen, wenn diese beiden Bedingungen verwirk-
licht wären. Sie erscheinen uns psychologisch wie auch geistig undenkbar.' *Ibid.*,
p. 343.
[38]*Ibid.*, pp. 343-344.

belongs to a subject who brings a freedom to speech, by which it says no to itself.'[39] By avoiding the concept of divine or human substance (nature) and approaching the *kenosis* through the analogy of a subject who can transcend himself, Mehl seeks to locate the transcendence, as well as the *kenosis*, in the same act. It is both an act of repudiation in a total sense, so that Christ actually does become 'other' to his divinity —that is, really man; and it is an act of freedom by which the renunciation itself is only possible as an act of transcendence—that is, he is really God.

It is strange to hear Mehl speak of an 'other side' (*Jenseits*) to the renunciation, for he has earlier said that all talk of an 'other side' (*Jenseits*) in which transcendence is rooted is now incomprehensible.[40] It is difficult to hold back the suspicion that Mehl has, after all, lost touch with the eternal Subject in the Incarnation, especially when he says: 'He could make man his own in his complete fulness, because he had renounced divinity in such a way that he could *receive* the same and more all over again (resurrection, ascension).'[41] While Mehl would protest that it is only God who would act as a subject to cross the boundary of absolute self-renunciation without at the same time abandoning or annihilating himself as subject, and thus the humiliation is itself an utter act of transcendence, nevertheless, Mehl has given us no answer to the question of what becomes of the Incarnation when the renunciation (humiliation) is no longer necessary and the divinity is 'received all over again' in the resurrection and exaltation. What happens to the atonement when the Incarnation comes to this sudden end, is a question which Mehl does not take into consideration.[42] But this

[39]*Ibid.*, p. 344.
[40]*Ibid.*, p. 331. Cf. also what Mehl says about the concept of 'this-worldly' transcendence as held by Gregor Smith: 'Must one in defining this transcendence, speak, with R. G. Smith, of a "this worldly transcendence"? (*diesseitigen*). This expression does not seem to us to be an especially happy one, because it calls forth the thought of a sort of possibility beyond, to an other transcendence, while we are able to seek it only on the side of the act, which establishes the new history; into this history we become integrated through faith.' *Ibid.*, p. 346.
[41]"Er konnte das Menschsein in seiner ganzer Fülle sich zu eigen machen, weil er auf die Göttlichkeit in einer Weise verzichtet hatte, da β er dieselbe nur mehr wider aufs neue *empfangen* konnte (Auferstehung, Himmelfahrt).' *Ibid.*, p. 344.
[42]What is at stake here is what has been called the 'permanent manhood' of Christ hypostatically united with the divine nature of the Logos in such a way that created humanity becomes ontologically one with the intra-trinitarian life of the Son of God. This is the point which Professor E. L. Mascall makes when he cites the Athanasian Creed (the *Quincunque vult*) which makes the assertion that Christ is one 'not by the conversion of godhead into flesh but by taking up of manhood into God.' (*Christ, the Christian and the Church*, Longmans, Green and Co., London, 1946, p. 54). The difficulties involved with this concept of the *assumptio carnis* considered in a substantialistic form of nature,

is not the problem which we are concerned about at the moment.

The question is, can Mehl really sustain his thesis that 'if we want to grasp the biblical transcendence in its peculiarity, then we must seek its trace in that act of humiliation and humility, which appears at first as the opposite of a sovereign and lordly transcendence.'?[43] This is what he feels Bonhoeffer was on to in his concept of the powerlessness and weakness of God. It is also what Mehl feels gives an objective foundation to the freedom which the Christian has in positing a transcendence *within* history, through a 'standing apart' of being to itself in Christ's humiliation. While Mehl is somewhat obscure at this point, he seems to mean that the transcendence of God exhibited in Christ through weakness and humility, has opened up history to this kind of transcendent faith which is utterly historical because it does not destroy the fabric of historical, conditioned existence, but at the same time, is a 'new beginning' and thus a new history.[44]

There is no question but that Mehl seriously attempts to see *kenosis* as an act of transcendence rather than the concealing or the abandonment of it. This is what gave such hope at the beginning of this critique of his essay. Unfortunately, his attempt seems to have run aground in the shallow waters of his anthropology, while he himself has safely made it to the familiar shore of existentialism. The 'new beginning' and the 'new history' sounds interesting (although we have heard this before), but we were talking about the transcendence of God, not the possibilities of faith.

Mehl's valuable insight into the nature of transcendence as the act in which a subject goes beyond his own self-existence to inter-act in a real way with the reality of that which is 'other', is an important step forward in opening up Christology to the full range of theology—that

or of Godhead and manhood, should not be allowed to obscure the important truth of the continuing reality of the Incarnation, and thus, the ontological ground of the covenant response made by Jesus Christ. Because, as I will show, the *egeneto* was an intra-divine act in which an intrinsic '*kenosis*' between Son and Father became extrinsic in a completely historical and human way, the *assumptio* can be given its full value without diminution of the real humanity of Christ.

[43]R. Mehl, 'Die Krise der Transzendenz', pp. 144-145.

[44]"If one wants to find transcendence again, in the last analysis, it is a question therefore not of departing from the line of thought which bears the impress of the Reformation, that thought in which Christology is privileged and thereby constitutes the only way of entrance to theology. It is, therefore, not a question of the restoration of an ontology through which it would become possible for Christology to arrive at transcendence. This has already been given to us in Christology itself, with the presupposition that the dogma of the two natures is not interpreted in a substantialistic way, and accordingly the humiliation shows us a transcendence which is not bound up with a co-presence of two natures, but with an act, through which a new history has become possible.' *Ibid.*, p. 146.

is, to a doctrine of God. The two conditions which limit this 'standing apart' from one's own subjectivity—namely, one can never absolutely renounce himself as subject and one can never totally become the 'other'—these two conditions are anthropological, and therefore, as Mehl has suggested, cannot be crossed over without venturing into that which is incomprehensible. But this is precisely what Mehl does in maintaining that Christ, in his humiliation, has crossed the boundaries of renunciation:

In him, the boundary, which we have recognized for all growing beyond ourselves, is crossed; here appears that unconditional self-renunciation which is the necessary condition for a genuine representation over against the other.[45]

Because Mehl has taken as his starting point the anthropological concept of what constitutes a subject, he is forced to go beyond these limits in attempting to explain how transcendence works when God is the subject, and consequently has to create a dialectic out of transcendence and renunciation which defeats his initial purpose. For just at the point where one wants to say 'there God is in Christ', Mehl is forced to reply that this is really God 'standing apart' from his own being.[46] The boundary which limits our own transcendence so that we can never absolutely renounce our own subjectivity, is said to be crossed by God in becoming man in Christ. Otherwise, says Mehl, God could not make a 'genuine representation over against the other'. This seems to mean that for Christ to be really man in the face of God as 'other to him', he had to renounce his own divinity. It does not help to make this an existential renunciation on Christ's part, as Mehl does. For this destroys the ontic character of the Incarnation, and leaves Christian faith with no ontology at all.

What has led Mehl into his unresolvable difficulties is his methodology.[47] If he had taken Christ as his starting point for the actual subject

[45]"In ihm ist die Grenze, die wir für jedes Hinauswachsen über uns selbst erkannt haben, überschritten; hier tritt jene vorbehaltlose Selbstverleugnung in Erscheinung, die die Vorbedingung für eine wirkliche Stellvertretung gegenüber dem Anderen ist.' *Ibid.*, p. 344.
[46]"Das Christusereignis bringt in die Geschichte ein absolutes Neuwerden herein und setzt in einen neuen Anfang und eine neue Spannung auf die Zukunft hin; dies geschieht deshalb, weil es diese Erniedrigung ist, die einen Abstand des Seins zu sich selbst voraussetzt.' *Ibid.*, p. 345.
[47]In his essay on 'A Fresh Look at the Kenotic Christologies', *Scottish Journal of Theology*, Vol. 15, 1962, pp. 337-349, Professor Donald Dawes suggests that: 'If such a new Christology is not to fall into the same kind of impasse as did the kenotic Christologies of the recent past there must be a basic change in methodology. The priority of questions asked about the kenosis must be changed. The starting-point for these questions is in the full actuality of revelation in Jesus Christ. The starting-point is not Church doctrine or philosophical doctrine

of the transcendence of God, he would have been immediately led into some consideration of the Trinity, which he does not once mention in his essay. At the depth of Jesus' humiliation, at the utter end of his weakness, in the grip of his greatest helplessness, he was the Logos who had become flesh—he was the Son to the Father and also the God who was there for man.[48] The further implications of the *kenosis* as a particularly trinitarian 'way of *kenosis*' intrinsic to the nature of God will be explored in the last part of this chapter when we consider *kenosis* as the 'Man who is for God'. But it seems that the point which Mehl has missed is that the 'God who is for Man' must be considered as an *intra*-trinitarian kenotic act rather than an *extra*-trinitarian act. If we consider the kenotic problem from the standpoint of Jesus as the Son of God who *became* flesh, and who in the depth of his humanity did not cease to be the Son to the Father, we cannot posit an ontic and inward cleft in God himself.[49] Instead—and here we can

within which the possibility of revelation is to be described, although the constructive role of both of these will be recognized. The starting-point is in the actuality of revelation. The question of kenosis is no longer: How is kenosis possible in light of God's nature? The question is rather: What is God's nature in light of the kenosis? The question of the God-Manhood of the Christ is modified. Traditionally the question was: How is God-Manhood possible in light of the nature of God and Man? The more fruitful question is: What does the reality of Christ's God-Manhood tell us about the nature of God and Man?' p. 348. Dawes goes on to suggest the beginning of such a fruitful questioning, and in what he suggests, we can see already a way out of the difficulty encountered by Mehl's methodology: 'Kenosis says that God is of such a nature that the acceptance of the limitations of a human life does not make him unlike himself. Kenosis is a way of saying that ... He is free to be our God without ceasing to be God the Lord.... In Christ we perceive that self-emptying does not mean a loss of divinity; ... He is God equally in the hiddenness of the servant form as in His transcendent glory.' p. 348. I would go further than Dawe to say that he is God equally in the transcendence of the servant form as in his immanent glory.

[48]I am thinking particularly here of the situations in which Jesus' relationship to the Father as the Son brought a new dimension of reality to bear in the context of human life with respect to God the Father 'being there for Man' through the Son. See, for instance, the parable of the prodigal son, Luke 15:11-32; the association of Jesus' redemptive work as 'my Father's work', John 5:15-17 (the healing of the blind man); and then also Jesus' prayers, which invoked mercy, healing, and life as the direct gift of the Father through the Son: Matthew 11:25-30, 15:36; Luke 11:1ff, 23:34; John 11:41-42; John 17. See also Mark 1:11, where Jesus is asserted to be the Son of God from the beginning of his public ministry.

[49]A helpful commentary on this point is given by K. Barth: 'We begin with the insight that God is "not a God of confusion, but of peace" (I Corinthians 14:33). In Him there is no paradox, no antimony, no division, no inconsistency, not even the possibility of it.... What he is and does He is and does in full unity with Himself. It is in full unity with Himself that He is also—and especially and above all—in Christ, that He becomes a creature, man, flesh, that He enters into our being in contradiction, that He takes upon Himself its con-

follow Mehl's suggestion profitably—if we consider that transcendence has to do with a subject, God as the eternal Subject acts to transcend himself as Father, Son and Holy Spirit. Transcendence is thus not associated with a 'mode of being' as such, but with the subject who acts as such in a particular mode of being. It is doubtful, then, whether one can talk as Mehl does of God 'crossing the boundary' of absolute renunciation of his own being in becoming man, without placing the Word—the Son—outside of the trinitarian relationship altogether. And in that case, whatever or whoever Jesus is, he cannot be the 'God who is there for man'. What is also doubtful, is whether one can speak of renunciation at all in terms of a *kenosis* if the Word as the eternal Subject is himself the man Jesus Christ. Certainly there is an inconceivable condescension on the part of God who, as the eternal Word and the subject of all becoming, also takes on that creaturely mode of being. *Kenosis* may not be too strong a word to express such a 'transcendent' act, but the particular nuance of meaning which we give to the word 'kenosis' will be determined by the subject of the *kenosis,* the one who 'empties himself'; the one who, 'though he was in the form of God, did not count equality with God a thing to be grasped, but emptied himself, taking the form of a servant.'[50]

Without taking up the exegetical problems of this 'Christ Hymn' which Paul places in his letter to the Philippian Church, for these questions are better left to those who are more qualified to consider all of the implications involved,[51] the text can still be considered as

sequences. . . . It is this that we have to see and honour and worship as the deity of Christ—not an ontic and inward divine paradox, the postulate of which has its basis only in our own very real contradiction against God and the false ideas of God which correspond to it.' *Church Dogmatics,* IV/1, pp. 186, 188.

[50]Philippians 2:6-7. At this point, with certain qualifications which will become apparent, I am following the traditional exegesis of the passage in assuming that the subject of the phrase 'he emptied himself' is the divine Logos, and not merely the will of the already incarnate Logos, the man Jesus, who abandons himself to death. Cf. John Calvin, *The Epistles of Paul the Apostle to the Galatians, Ephesians, Philippians and Colossians,* trans. T. H. L. Parker, Oliver & Boyd, Edinburgh, 1965, pp. 246-247. But for the latter interpretation, see John Gibbs, 'The Relation Between Creation and Redemption According to Philippians 2:5-11', *Novum Testamentum,* Vol. 12, 1970, pp. 270-283, who also lists as those supporting an interpretation of the subject as the man Jesus: O. Cullman, C. H. Dodd, A. M. Hunter and J. A. T. Robinson. p. 278.

[51]The exegetical problems to which I refer deal (among others) with the matter of the paraenetic purpose of the passage with respect to the rest of the Epistle; the way in which 'in the form of God' (ἐν μορφῇ θεὸυ) is to be understood; whether 'grasp' (ἁρπαγμός) is to be taken in an active or a passive sense; who is the subject of the verb 'emptied himself' (ἑαυτὸν ἐκένωσεν); and more recently, the question of whether or not the hymn reflects a Hellenistic myth of an Original Man-Redeemer or whether the background is Jewish with a creation-redemption motif with Christ seen as the suffering Servant of Isaiah or as the Second Adam. In addition to the standard commentaries on

a pointer to the interior meaning of the Incarnation, particularly with respect to the act by which Christ takes up the form of a servant though he exists in the form of God. As Käsemann well puts it: 'Here again, an event is described, not a static situation, and as a result it is neither an object for inspection nor an example.'[52] Nor can the event be 'plotted on a curve' of descent and ascent, with humiliation being the lowest point in the curve and the 'self emptying' calculated to be the quantifying factor which turns pre-existence into existence. These words which Paul has chosen to include in his letter to the Philippians, whatever their literary or paraenetic relation to the larger context, have as their hermeneutical horizon the dynamic and personal reality of Jesus Christ. More important than what this text says about the person of Christ, is what the person of Christ says about this text. When we wish to know what it means to be 'in the form of God' and also 'in the form of a servant', we must look to the one who is the subject of *this kind* of an existence. There can be little doubt but that for Paul, the answer to the question: Who is the subject of this kind of existence? was self evident—it is Jesus Christ.

And if we, at this point, persist with the question 'Who?', rather than with the question 'How?', we shall avoid the speculative and fruitless metaphysical or psychological questions which were the bane of all modern kenotic Christologies. The question 'Who?', as Bonhoeffer says, is the question of transcendence; while the question 'How?' is the question of immanence.[53] Thus, if one wishes to speak of such a thing as *kenosis*, and there is no reason to avoid this way of speaking,

the Epistle to the Philippians, one should take special note of the essay by Ernst Käsemann, 'Kritische Analyse von Phil. 2,5-11', *Zeitschrift für Theologie und Kirche*, Vol. 47, 1950, pp. 313-360; English translation by Alice F. Carse, 'A Critical Analysis of Philippians 2:5-11', *Journal for Theology and the Church*, Vol. 5, 1968, pp. 45-88. Käsemann's position is that the passage has no paraenetic purpose in the epistle, and that its basic background is to be found in its association with the Hellenistic redeemer myth. For an interpretation which takes issue with Käseman in these two points, see John G. Gibbs, 'The Relation Between Creation and Redemption According to Philippians 2:5-11', pp. 270-283.

[52]'A Critical Analysis of Philippians 2:5-11', p. 72.

[53]'The question "Who?" is the question of transcendence. The question "How?" is the question of immanence. Because the one who is questioned here is the Son, the immanent question cannot grasp him. Not, "How are you possible?" —that is the godless question, the serpent's question—but "Who are you?" The question "Who?" expresses the strangeness and otherness of the encounter and at the same time reveals itself as the question of the very existence of the enquirer himself. He enquires about the being which is alien to his own being, about the boundaries of his own existence. Transcendence puts his own being in question. With the answer that his Logos has found its limit man comes up against the boundaries of his existence. So the question of transcendence is the question of existence and the question of existence is the question of transcendence.' *Christology*, pp. 30-31.

then it is a question of transcendence if we ask: Who is this one that, existing in the form of God, nevertheless, takes on the existence-form of a servant? But why do we say 'nevertheless'? Is this not already a confession that our mind has gone 'snap' with the expression—'form of God'—and a logical trap has been sprung whose jaws can only be forced open again with great intellectual effort? And would not some even say, with a great intellectual sacrifice?

But what do we really know of the 'form of God' other than the one *Who* exists for man? True, there are ideas of God which are as old as the history of human thought, and these ideas may not be entirely unrelated to the God who is for man; that is, these ideas may even reflect to some extent a genuine theology. But this theo-logic can only be a language of signification which authenticates itself in the reality of that which is signified. Thus, when it is said that there was one who existed 'in the form of God', and who 'emptied himself, taking the form of a servant', we have words whose meaning can only be explicated by referring to the subject himself, to that *One*.

It is for this reason, that the typical exegesis of this passage which concentrates on finding literary or etymological antecedents for the Greek word 'form' ($\mu o \rho \phi \acute{\eta}$), and so attempts to give content to the phrase 'form of God', fails in spite of its valuable contribution to the science of biblical interpretation. More relevant to the real task of interpreting this passage, though hardly more successful, are the more recent attempts to find antecedents for the language of Philippians 2:5-9 in Old Testament motifs of the Suffering Servant from the relevant passages in Isaiah, and also in the Creation-Redemption motifs centring in the first and second Adam.[54] While these latter attempts

[54]Among modern commentators on the Epistle to the Philippians, E. Lohmeyer, *Die Briefe an die Philipper, und die Kolasser und an Philemon*, Göttingen, 1930, was one of the first to attribute this Christological Hymn to the oldest Palestinian tradition and to see in it a Servant figure of the Deutero-Isaiah type as well as the Son of Man figure of Daniel. Professor O. Cullman, *The Christology of the New Testament*, trans. S. C. Guthrie and C. A. M. Hall, SCM Press, London, 1959, pp. 174ff, following J. Hering, holds that the word 'image' as used in Genesis 1:26 is the antecedent thought behind the use of 'form' ($\mu o \rho \phi \acute{\eta}$) in the *kenosis* passage of Philippians 2:6; he thus seeks to establish a link between the creation account of Adam and the Incarnation of the Son of Man. Others who find this theory attractive are R. P. Martin, '$\mu o \rho \phi \acute{\eta}$ in Philippians 2:6', *The Expository Times*, Vol. 70, 1958-59, pp. 183-184; A. J. Bandstra, "Adam" and "The Servant"', *Calvin Theological Journal*, Vol. I, 2, 1966, pp. 213-216; John Gibbs, 'The Relation Between Creation and Redemption According to Philippians 2:5-11.' An interesting variation of this school of thought can be found in the concept of Joachim Jeremias, 'Zu Phil. 2,7: ἑαυτὸν ἐκένωσεν', *Novum Testamentum*, Vol. 6, 1963, pp. 182-188, who suggests that the phrase 'he emptied himself' is a precise rendering of the Hebrew phrase 'he poured out his soul unto death' in Isaiah 53:12. Thus, he concludes that the self-emptying refers more to the crucifixion than to the Incarnation.

do seek to find a basic 'theological grammar' in the Old Testament motifs, the fundamental point is missed concerning the logic of the *subject* of this kind of self-emptying existence. The moment this passage is approached from the perspective of transcendence, the proper question is 'Who?', and we are now confronted with an entirely different perspective; however, it is a perspective that we have already encountered in 'the Word became flesh', and before that, in God's election of himself to Israel.

If the point which I am making seems to have been belaboured a bit, it is only because it was necessary to show that there has been no serious attempt to interpret the kenotic passage in Philippians 2 : 5-9 from the standpoint of the inner logic of the Incarnation as it is first of all revealed in the relation between God and Israel. This inner logic, as has already been shown, is a logic of the transcendence of God moving progressively towards enfleshment through the relation of Word and Spirit to Israel. That which has been called the hiddenness of God with respect to his relation to Israel, can be called his transcendence. That is, God becomes more and more identified with Israel and the Logos becomes more and more 'pressed into' the life and flesh of Israel, but not 'without remainder', as it were.

The failure of the traditional, as well as of the modern attempts, to give a proper explanation of the *kenosis* passage in Philippians, has been, in my estimation, a failure to understand the nature of the transcendence of God. And particularly, a failure to work out this transcendence through the inner logic of God's relation to Israel. When the transcendence of God has been assumed to be either his eternal aseity or his divine attributes, the act of self-emptying, or *kenosis*, could never be understood as something that God could do without modifying, or at least concealing, his transcendent nature. One only needs to consider the history of the kenotic Christologies to observe both the dilemmas and the highly speculative solutions which followed from this fundamental misunderstanding of transcendence.

But this has been more than a kenotic problem; it has become a serious crisis for Christology itself. A crisis which has become all the more clearly exposed through the crisis of transcendence in the intellectual and spiritual spheres of human existence, as Professor Mehl has helpfully pointed out. To a certain degree, Christology has sometimes worked as a crippling constriction to the doctrine of God through a

However, against these interpretations one should see E. Käsemann, 'A Critical Analysis of Philippians 2 : 5-11', who argues for a strictly Hellenistic frame of reference. Following Käsemann in this hypothesis is F. W. Beare, *A Commentary on the Epistle to the Philippians*, Adam and Charles Black, London, 1959, pp. 76ff. For an argument against the association of 'form' (μορφή) with 'image' ἐικών), and thus against an Old Testament antecedent for the word, see D. Wallace, 'A Note on μορφή', *Theologische Zeitschrift*, Vol. 22, 1966, pp. 19-25.

failure to grasp the nature of God's transcendence. The Council of Chalcedon, with its language concerning the two natures hypostatically united in one person sought to put an end to the question 'How?' by stating the relationship between the two natures in such a way that no explanation could be given, and one was forced to return to the question, Who is this One?[55] Unfortunately, the Greek concepts of transcendence dominated Western Christology from that time, up to and beyond the Reformation itself, so that, as a result, the Hebrew concept of transcendence in terms of a God who acted within and through history was obscured. Consequently, the concept of God's transcendence was worked out in terms of the two natures, and thus Christology itself restricted and concealed the very thing which the Incarnation revealed.[56] If there is to be a way of liberating Christology from this constriction, without opening the doors to speculation which Chalcedon closed, it must be through a new understanding of the transcendence of God. For the question of transcendence is the question 'Who?', and in this sense, represents the primary concern of the Christology of Chalcedon. In this question, we are brought back to the *subject* who places our predications, even our very existence, into question.

We can now give the first part of the answer to the question of this chapter: can the *kenosis* be understood as the transcendence of God?[57] Yes, it can. Jesus is the God who is for man. He embodies the transcendent limit of the reality of God. In fact, it is in the unpretentious and even powerless way in which the being (*ousia*) of Jesus confronted men that the Kingdom of God impinged most directly, and even most dramatically and violently, upon his contemporaries. It was the authority (*exousia*) of Jesus' person that roused the forces of evil against him, drove out unclean spirits, healed the sick, confounded the wise and liberated the sinner.[58] His birth, lowly as it was, brought a

[55]The key phrases of the Chalcedon definition of the person of Christ were: 'One and the same Christ, in two natures, without confusion and without change, without division and without separation.' As Bonhoeffer says, 'It stated the *a priori* impossibility and impermissibility of taking the divinity and humanity in Jesus Christ side by side or together as a relationship of objectifiable entities. Simple negation remains. no positive pattern of thought is left to explain what happens in the God-man Jesus Christ.... After the decision of Chalcedon it is no longer permissible to objectify the divinity and the manhood in Christ and to distinguish them from each other as entities.' *Christology*, p. 91.

[56]Cf. Bonhoeffer, *Christology*, pp. 91ff.

[57]See above, p. 151.

[58]*Exousia*, translated as either authority or power in the New Testament, is attributed to the words and teaching of Jesus (Luke 4:32), to his supremacy over evil spirits (Luke 4:36), to his right to forgive sins (Luke 5:24), and was communicated by him to those who were his followers (Mark 6:7).

sword, not peace.[59] He renounced all worldly power, rejected the power
(*exousia*) of Satan,[60] and exposed the thoughts and motives of men's
hearts, forcing a division between those who 'believed' and those who
did not.[61]

The 'terrible' thing about Jesus was that there was no sanctuary from
the exposing power of his presence, which people could flee. There was
no way of avoiding that ultimate and final 'being' (*ousia*) which was
most openly and clearly exposed in his utter humanity. It was the
sheer freedom, sovereignty and lordship of his grace that acknowledged
no sanctions or authorities, religious or secular, natural or supernatural,
which pierced the hearts of men. The axe was laid to the whole tree
of humanity, at its very root.[62] The sword which pierced the hearts
of men, causing them to betray their 'being' for or against God, cut
through the life of his own community and even his own home, creating
misunderstanding and attempts to twist his words and life into conformity with their own assumptions.[63] It was not just the religious
institution and tradition of Judaism which Jesus challenged; the confrontation was at a much more profound level. For it was a confrontation
of the truth of being with being in untruth. As such, it was a confrontation
of human being with the transcendence of divine being. It was not just
his humanness, but his truth of grace and love which compelled the
confession 'Truly you are the Son of God.'[64] Within the reality of his
human presence and compassion, there was a depth of divine grace
and power which drew to him the poor, the sick and the spiritually
impoverished. It was as if his very transparency of human life revealed
the reality of his inner being. His simplicity of being shattered the
complexity and rigidity of human limits supported by traditions wrapped
in religious restraints. By taking human being beyond these limits he
revealed the inhumanity which all but the proud and the self-righteous
recognize to be a deep injustice to the spirit of man.

But what is all the more remarkable when it is seen in the light of
transcendence, is the fact that the greater was Jesus' meekness and
humility, the more violent and murderous was the opposition raised
against him. He was the embodiment of the 'still small voice'—the
Logos made flesh—penetrating and exposing the inner being of man.[65]

[59]Luke 2:34-35.
[60]Luke 4:6.
[61]Cf. Luke 5:17-26, where the healing of the paralytic produced a division
among the people, some believed, others violently accused him of blasphemy.
Cf. also, John 7:43; 9:16; 10:19.
[62]Cf. Luke 3:9.
[63]Cf. Luke 2:49-50; 4:28-30; John 7:5; Mark 3:21; Matthew 13:53-58.
[64]Matthew 14:33.
[65]The reference to the still small voice, of course, is from I Kings 19:11-13,
where Elijah does not find God in the earthquake or the mighty wind, but in the

The more the 'truthful love' of Jesus entered into the sphere of man's social relations, the more violent became the inner contradiction of man's 'untruthful being'. That which demons recognized and confessed with terror, men refused to acknowledge and accept with love—the transcendence of God, the divine Logos in human flesh. In a desperate attempt to avoid the reality and finality of their own inner contradiction to that divine Logos, they said of him, 'He has an unclean Spirit.'[66]

Here we see that the 'Logos which became flesh' actually appears to some men as the 'anti-Logos'—a Logos which refuses to be classified and which annihilates the power of the human logos to maintain its autonomy in the face of God. The human logos in untruthful being keeps itself in power by limiting itself; by setting the limits, even to God, it maintains its own authority and seeks to assimilate the 'anti-Logos' into its own system.

But what if the Anti-Logos raises his claim in a completely new form? If he is no longer an idea, but a Word, which challenges the supremacy of the Logos? If he appears at some time and in some place in history as a person? If he declares himself to be a judgment on the human Logos and points to himself; I am the Way, the Truth and the Life; ... Transcendence puts his own being in question. With the answer that his Logos has found its limit man comes up against the boundaries of his existence. So the question of transcendence is the question of existence and the question of existence is the question of transcendence. In theological terms: man only knows who he is in the light of God.[67]

It is precisely here that we are forced to see that the enfleshment of the divine Logos is neither a renunciation of the divinity nor a concealing of it, but a particularly total revealing of it which could only occur as the Son of God, existing as the form of God, also takes on the form of servant. This *kenosis* is the act of God as Subject who transcends his own immanent existence and *becomes* man, thereby placing himself transcendently in relation to man at the most intimate and most absolute level. The form of the servant is thus, first of all, the God who is for man. When one comes up against the form of the servant in Christ, one is up against God himself. There is no

small voice which speaks out of the calm. One should compare also the reference by Jesus to John the Baptist as one who is the 'Elijah which is to come', and the reference in this context to the fact that the Kingdom of God has suffered violence and the violent take it by force. Matthew 11:11-15. The particular kind of violence which Jesus refers to here can only mean the kind of power which comes through the transcendence of God which comes as a 'still small voice.'

[66]Mark 3:30. Cf. also, Matthew 18:26.
[67]D. Bonhoeffer, *Christology*, pp. 30, 31.

Logos of God apart from the Logos of flesh. It is the transcendence of God which makes it possible to say this. It is God, who places himself into transcendent relation with us, and who thus becomes the limit at the centre of our existence; it is this God who has taken the form of a servant, who has become our brother, who makes it possible for us to love our limit and to affirm the core of reality at the centre of our life in affirming him.

But this is only the first part of the answer to the question about transcendence. And we wait numbly for the second part. We have seen the God who is for man; but we have seen his blood too—the blood of God—and our complicity mutes the rising cheer. We want to be, but we are not, the Man who is for God.

2 'The Man Who is for God'

from its very conception this gift was doomed
to sprinkle the earth—
    was it water or blood?
too great a need and too much love
conjugate the new verb—a sacrifice presumed
to be a senseless act devouring alike
    the giver and the gift.
    a crucifixion of logic
upon the tree of knowledge of good
    and evil. therein lies a god entombed
    too holy to be allowed to live.
earth drinks in its thanksgiving feast—
    is it water or blood?

the finest gifts are not always consumed
upon the parched altars of ravenous thirst.
renunciation is itself a sacrament exhumed
from eternal immutability: god the dispersed
gathered up again in those who have communed.
out of all our eucharists, this is the first.[68]

The simplicity of the Incarnation as an idea of God is shattered upon the cross. We had grown accustomed to thinking of ourselves as not more than an 'arm's length' from God, and whatever that entailed for us in terms of either fear or comfort; and then we heard his cry: 'My God, my God, why hast thou forsaken me?'[69] There is now, it appears, more depth

---

[68]'An Elegy For God—Based on II Samuel 23:15-17', R. S. Anderson, an unpublished poem.
[69]Matthew 27:46.

and more distance involved in the 'Word becoming flesh' than was first conceived. The problem is, it is not a matter of taking the Word deeper into the flesh, for that is simply (simply!) to reveal the transcendence of God in a still more profound humanity. What we are confronted with here is the question of how we can continue to speak of the transcendence of God at all in the face of this cry of dereliction. We now see that *kenosis* is not too strong a word to speak of the one who, though existing in the form of God, took the form of a servant, and humbling himself, 'became obedient unto death'.[70] And we can now understand the dilemma which drove the kenoticists to the desperate expedient of suggesting that what was involved in this humbling unto death was, at least in part, a renunciation of divine transcendence altogether.[71] Has transcendence been driven back beyond the veil of the humanity, and has our attempt to show that the transcendence of God is historical, been driven off course, or even turned back in an utterly hopeless way?

It would, of course, be premature to conclude that this is the case. The argument has been constructed too slowly and carefully to be abandoned at the first real encounter with that which we suspected would have to be faced sooner or later. What remains to be seen, is whether or not the inner logic of the Incarnation in its two levels of understanding can now be integrated in a meaningful way; and specifically whether or not the transcendence of God can be found in such human helplessness.

It should be made clear at the outset that what is involved is not merely the resolution of an apparent antinomy between humiliation and glory, as, for example, E. Käsemann attempts in taking an eschatological view of the unbroken unity between Jesus and the Father.[72] Nor are we to seek the solution in the concept of a 'paradoxical identity' to which R. Bultmann resorts, in order to hold together the divinity and the humanity of Jesus by reducing the historical dimension to a *kerygmatic* word.[73] The 'scandal' of the cross is not made more existential, and thus more powerful in its effect, by making the death of the incarnate Logos into a crucifixion of logic. That is ultimately to cast faith back on its own resources, and destroys the ontic character of salvation. It is the question of transcendence which keeps us on track because it raises again the question

[70]Philippians 2:6-8.
[71]It was W. F. Gess who argued that for there to be a unity of self-consciousness in Christ, the Son of God had to lay aside his consciousness of relation within the Trinity in becoming the human soul of Christ. Gess held that in becoming flesh by an act of self-divesting, the Son of God allowed his eternal self-consciousness to be extinguished in order to regain it as man. See, *God and Incarnation in Mid-nineteenth Century German Theology*, C. Welch (ed.), p. 305; also, cf. F. Weston, *The One Christ*, p. 119.
[72]*The Testament of Jesus*, SCM Press, London, 1968, pp. 11ff.
[73]*Theology of the New Testament*, Vol. II, Charles Scribner's Sons, New York, 1955, pp. 47ff.

of the subject. When we ask: *Who* is the man who died, the man who cried out in his abandonment by God?—we can only answer: the same one who was the Word, the eternal Subject. And so it comes down to a matter of the transcendence of God. Can the 'God who is for man' be at the same time, the 'Man who is for God?'

The question will be taken up in the following manner. First, we will examine the problematic of covenant response with respect to the way in which Jesus worked out this response in both his life and death. Then we will consider what this reveals to us about the nature of God, particularly in regard to his transcendence through both Son and Holy Spirit; and finally, saying something about the implications of this understanding of transcendence for man himself.

In the earlier discussion of the problematic of covenant response,[74] it was shown that intrinsic to the covenant of creation, was the possibility of man's freedom to affirm the transcending limit of his existence through his created logos. Thus, the creation of man in the image of God is itself an act of transcendence on the part of the Creator by which man is given the possibility and the freedom to respond. This response is both an affirmation on man's part of the reality of his own created nature and an affirmation on God's part of the transcendent act which makes it possible. The inner logic of Incarnation was then shown to include this basic structure as its fundamental rationality. The importance of this for our discussion can now be shown in greater detail.

When it is said that there is such a thing as genuine, or authentic humanity, the validity and the rationality of this statement rests upon the transcendent reality of God which gives to the created logos its own freedom, and thus its own reality. While man is, therefore, 'Other' than God, because he is related to him as creature to Creator, this 'Otherness' is constituted by the transcendence of God himself, so that God would not have to renounce, or restrict his transcendence in order to himself become that 'Other'—that is, to become man.[75] Because the relation is problematic to the creature does not mean that it is also problematic for the Creator. The eternal Logos can act as a created logos, even though this possibility is not reversible.

There are two things that are important to distinguish here: *first*, the subject of covenant response is constituted human, not in virtue of its freedom from God, but in virtue of its freedom for God. What it is to be man, therefore, cannot be abstracted from what it is to be God. The image

---

[74]See above, p. 135f.

[75]'Other', as distinguished from 'other' (lower case), refers to the Other as a personal subject, as another *Agent*, and not to another *thing*. In this context, there is no implied reference to the Other being a divine subject as distinguished from a human subject through the capitalization. The Other can be either the divine or human Subject acting as a personal agent.

binds the two together.[76] However, because the image is grounded in transcendence, the response remains problematical to man in the sense that he does not possess it in an autonomous way. The covenant response is therefore a human response, not merely because the subject is a creature, but because it is an affirmation of the transcendence of God as the limit, and, therefore, the centre of creaturely existence. *Second*, the subject of covenant response can therefore be immediately as well as mediately human. That is, the response from the side of the creature (a human response) can be made as well by the eternal Logos as the created logos, or, one could say, as well by God as by the image of God. It is the transcendence of God which is active in constituting the image of God in its reality. The point which I wish to make here is that the eternal Logos can take humanity to himself, and in and through that humanity make a real covenant response towards the Father because the Logos is also the eternal Son. This would appear to avoid the Apollinarian tendency towards monothelitism by constituting the covenant response in a creaturely will towards the Creator, while at the same time stopping short of Nestorianism which tends to restrict a human response to a merely human subject. When humanity is not defined in static, substantialistic terms, but in a dynamic, relational sense, a truly human act is thus constituted by that creative power and love which transcends it by limiting it.[77] This would also seem to offer us a way through the question which tormented the kenotic Christologists—namely, the question of the proper subject of the manhood of Christ. The more important question as to how both human covenant response and the divine transcending limit which constitutes that response can be understood as one act of God will be taken up shortly.

The covenant response which man did not make in Adam, remained to be worked out through the humanity of Israel. This, which we have shown to be the second part of the logic of the Incarnation, has as its

[76]Another way of stating the distinctive quality of 'being human' in terms of the image of God is to ground humanity in *ek-static* personhood. See below, p. 240, n. 29.

[77]My argument for this rests upon the doctrine of the image of God as explicated by the person of Jesus Christ. In this case I am making certain anthropological assertions based on Christological conclusions. As this is consistent with my general methodology, I see no reason why these assertions are not valid for the purpose of my exposition. While not accepting all his conclusions concerning the need for the divine Logos to restrict his deity in becoming the subject of the manhood of Christ, I think Bishop Weston has stated the case well when he says: 'I think the fundamental error of all who seek a human or divine-human subject of manhood lies in the false belief that the ego of manhood must, in some sense, be necessarily a man.... If man be God's image, may not the Son of God be presumed to possess, at least, all those characteristics that are essential to man's ego?' *The One Christ*, Longmans, Green, and Co., London, 1914, pp. 107-108.

pre-history the 'one Israelite', the man who is for God.[78] When the 'Word became flesh', not only was the limiting transcendence brought into human, historical existence in an absolute sense, but the covenant response was at the same time being worked out through this Man who was for God. This constitutes a preliminary statement of that which we could expect to be the case based on the inner logic of Israel's relation to God. It remains to demonstrate how this was the case in the person of Christ.

Perhaps a comment is in order at this point concerning the slogan which has been wrested from Bonhoeffer's later writings: Jesus—the man for others.[79] There is no lack of truth in the statement that Jesus had an ultimate concern for others. But this does not reach the fundamental truth of the fact that first and foremost, Jesus was the man who was for God; or rather, one should say, that first and foremost he was the God who was for man, and as this, he also was the man who was for God.[80] The language of ultimate concern expressed in terms of co-humanity simply does not grasp the profound truth of the Incarnation, nor does it expose its inner logic. If Jesus is only a man for others in an ultimate sense, the cross becomes a monstrosity where Jesus crucifies his own manhood in an ultimacy that only carries the whisper of an ethical ideal. The transcendence of co-humanity cannot be computed to a 'higher power' and so become the transcendence of God. Our first parents learned this to their sorrow, and *nonetheless*, were not left without a way of making a response through the cultus which God himself provided. It is this response on the part of man to God, rather than merely response of man to man, that marks both the style and the content of the life of Jesus Christ.

The 'community of reciprocity' which was portrayed in the life of

---

[78]See above, p. 144.

[79]What Bonhoeffer actually says is: 'Encounter with Jesus Christ. The experience that a transformation of all human life is given in the fact that "Jesus is there only for others". His "being there for others", is the experience of transcendence.' 'Outline for a Book', *Letters and Papers From Prison*, p. 381. Paul van Buren is one among several others who interprets Bonhoeffer here to mean that one can see in this kind of a Jesus an alternative to the 'God hypothesis': 'To experience God, he wrote [i.e. Bonhoeffer], means to meet Jesus Christ. To be in a relationship to God means to live for others, sharing in that form of life which was Jesus Christ's. . . . For to live with God, *"vor und mitt Gott"*, is, as we have said already, to meet Jesus Christ, to live a new life of "being-for-others". Again, the frame of reference is the same: the biblical story of "the man-for-others".' *Theological Explorations*, p. 114.

[80]'It is upon this humanity of the Word in Jesus that we must reflect deeply if we are to penetrate into the inner relation between the Word of God and man's response, but we must not forget that He is word of man in answer to God only in that He is first and foremost Word of God become man.' T. F. Torrance, *God and Rationality*, p. 139.

Israel, that is, a covenant with God with its appropriate form of covenant response, can be seen as the rationale of the Incarnation. Jesus, as the 'one Israelite', unites humanity with the will and Word of God. From the beginning to the end, he is one person, his actions are not different from his innermost heart. He *is* the truth, even as he *does* the truth.[81] That which was true *of* him became truth *in* him. The unity of the Word with flesh was grasped by him as the single truth of his life. His early years of growth were years of growth into this knowledge and into this responsibility. A growth, not merely into 'adulthood', but growth of the covenant response itself in two dimensions. *First,* an increasing solidarity with human 'flesh', so that by the end he was identified with the lowliest and with the lost. In this growth of his own identity with humanity, he increasingly began to bear the sicknesses, the injuries, the weakness and the condemnation of the god-less. His saying: 'Come to me, all who labour and are heavy laden, and I will give you rest,'[82] was not merely an offer of an easier way, but was a self-conscious 'yoking' of himself to their lives. 'Take my yoke upon you, and learn from me,'[83] continued Jesus, and here we see the *second* dimension of his growth: a deepening passion for the union of flesh with God through the supreme word-act of love. 'I have a baptism to be baptized with; and how I am constrained until it is accomplished!'[84] That which we tend to think of as an 'act of reconciliation' and centred in the death upon the cross, was not a 'transaction' which took place above and distinct from his own person. This 'reconciling' work is already at work through the growing covenant response which Jesus is working out through the unity of Word and flesh. The concept of growth here must not be confused with a growth of self-consciousness either in terms of his deity or his mission, that is, a growth in what we would

[81]Cf. John 14:6: 'I am the way, and the truth, and the life.'
[82]Matthew 11:38.
[83]Matthew 11:39.
[84]Luke 12:50. As an example of the way in which this progressive deepening of Jesus' own passion for the unity of the Father's will with humanity as the single purpose of his own life proceeds, one should take note of the structure used by Luke to portray this process. There are at least four phases in this progression, each introduced by the literary landmark 'on the way to Jerusalem'. The first is at Luke 9:51: 'When the days drew near for him to be received up, he set his face to go to Jerusalem.' This is followed by 13:22: 'He went on his way through towns and villages, teaching, and journeying towards Jerusalem.'; 17:11: 'On the way to Jerusalem he was passing along between Samaria and Galilee.'; and 19:28: 'And when he had said this, he went on ahead, going up to Jerusalem.' Within each of these sections, a progressive intensification of tension between Jesus and the authorities takes place, while at the same time, his own life and ministry is narrowed down to a determination to die at Jerusalem, if need be, to complete the 'baptism' by which the Spirit has united Word to flesh and so bring man to the truth of God. See Luke 9:57-62; 13:31-35; 17:33.

call 'personality'. Rather, the growth is a life of perfect and active obedience to the will of the Father—a progressive 'working into' the estranged flesh of humanity and also a progressive 'working out' of that same humanity, a will that perfectly conforms to the will of the Father.[85]

That which takes place on the cross is no different in kind from that which has been taking place throughout his life incarnationally. The steadfastness of his obedience to God and his dependence upon his Father's will was perfectly manifested from the beginning. But with his increasing solidarity with estranged humanity, the dimensions of that obedience and that dependence deepened and widened. So that, by the end, his obedience was from the 'other side' of that gulf brought about by man's wilful estrangement. The steadfastness and obedience in his Baptism was a 'younger' response than his steadfastness and obedience in Gethsemane, though perfect in its unity with the Father. The very truth of that response on the part of man to God had not yet been driven by untruth into the wilderness to be tempted, into the temple to be scorned, onto the dusty roads and into the cold nights to be wearied, and last of all, into the hands of his enemies to be betrayed, spat upon, and nailed to the cross, there to be himself estranged and banished from the face of God.

[85]The theme of growth is a predominate emphasis in the thought of Irenaeus, both with respect to the true nature of man: that is, creation is growth into the image of God; and with respect to the person of Christ: that is, the Incarnation is the completion of creation through the growth of the man Jesus into that which he actually is—the second Adam. 'For thou, O man, are not uncreated being, nor didst thou always co-exist with God, as did His own Word; but now, through His pre-eminent goodness, receiving the beginning of thy creation, thou dost gradually learn from the Word the dispensations of God who made thee ... this Being alone is truly God and Father, who formed this world, fashioned man, and bestowed the faculty of increase on His own creation.' *Irenaeus Against Heresies*, Ante-Nicene Christian Library, T. & T. Clark, Edinburgh, 1868, Vol. I, pp. 214, 219 (II/25/3; II/28/1). The motif of growth for Irenaeus follows the scheme of child-son-man. Adam awakens to his existence much the same way as a child comes to discover his own existence. Thus, instead of Adam being created as 'completed' man, he is to 'become man' through his human growth which will culminate only with the final realization of his destiny, which is actually to be in the 'likeness and image of God'. Cf. G. Wingren, *Man and the Incarnation*, Oliver and Boyd, Edinburgh/London, 1959, p. 26. Between the child (Adam) and the man (perfected humanity) stands the Son, Jesus, as the Son of God, in bearing Adam's flesh brought the humanity of Adam (all men) into a state of health (possibility of growth) and removed the 'injury' which occurred through the fall. The relation of Jesus' 'growth' to the creation of man is completed in the resurrection: 'The Father accomplishes His first decree for Creation in the life which Jesus lived. Uncorrupted human life ends in *resurrection*—lordship over death—by the same inner necessity which brought Adam's perverted life to end in death—the destruction of the power of life. The conflict which Jesus had to undergo for His life to be fully human and the reverse of Adam's embraced the Resurrection also, and not merely the period up to his death.' *Ibid.*, p. 127.

The cry from the cross, 'My God, my God, why hast thou forsaken me?', is the full measure of the distance from which the covenant response had to come, even as it was also the full measure of the dimensions to which the Incarnation had to reach. But the cry of astonishment and horror must not be abstracted from the logic of the Incarnation and made into a kenotic Christology on its own terms. It must be understood within the dynamic of covenant response, where the solidarity of the Word with the heart of the Father was as deep and irrevocable as the solidarity with the estranged flesh of humanity. It is the 'Man who is for God' who utters the God-forsaken cry, and because of this, and only because of this, this cry becomes the covenant response. And with it, the created image is restored, and the way of authentic human freedom opened up. Through a life of sonship which even the death of an estranged man could not shatter, he brought freedom to a humanity in bondage.

This gift of freedom and covenant—which in cultic language is called atonement—is intrinsically bound up with the Incarnation from beginning to end, and comes to man, not merely through a legal imputation, as though a transaction takes place 'over the head' of Jesus, but is given in the humanity of Christ himself. As the second Adam, he is also the last Adam. The covenant response has been worked out to the end (the eschaton), and thus is both historical and eschatological; it is both the first and the final covenant response. As the Man who is for God, the covenant of creation finds its fulfilment in his person which is also his act. He received the Spirit upon humanity by taking estranged humanity back into the 'Father's house'.[86] The gift of the Spirit is thus the gift of completed covenant response, it is the gift of freedom which has its ontic structure in the person of Jesus Christ where the transcending limit meets the covenant response in a completed and living unity.[87]

[86]Along with the concept of growth in the thought of Irenaeus, there is the concept of the Word and the Spirit as the 'two hands of God' which 'formed' the first man in the image and likeness of God, and also work to 'prepare' man in the Incarnation to attain that image and likeness. Cf. *Irenaeus Against Heresies*, Vol. I, p. 377, (IV/pref. 4); p. 442 (IV/22/5); and Vol. II, p. 58 (V/1/3). The relation of the Holy Spirit to the humanity of Christ is pictured by Irenaeus as having a 'preparatory' function in the Spirit's dwelling in the human race: 'For God promised, that in the last times He would pour Him [the Spirit] upon His servants and handmaids, that they might prophesy; wherefore He did also descend upon the Son of God, made the Son of man, becoming accustomed in fellowship with Him to dwell in the human race, to rest with human beings, and to dwell in the workmanship of God, working the will of the Father in them, and renewing them from their old habits into the newness of Christ.' *Ibid.*, Vol. I, p. 334 (III/17/1). Cf. also, p. 442 (IV/20/5), and Vol. II, p. 44 (IV/38/3).

[87]Cf. here the gift of the Holy Spirit after the resurrection (John 20:22). When the ontic structure of the gift of freedom by the Spirit is said to be constituted by the 'living unity' of transcendence and response in Jesus, the matter of the resurrection is brought into view. It is beyond the scope of this book to take up

The question which we asked at the outset was, to what extent we could still speak of transcendence in the face of the cry of dereliction from the cross. This now seems possible to answer in two ways. *First*, the covenant response which Jesus worked out through his life of obedience was totally human in an immediate sense. That is, it was a life directed towards the limiting transcendence of the Father by the divine Logos in utter solidarity with estranged human flesh. From this, I would argue that the covenant response worked out by Jesus was an act of the transcendence of God through the divine Logos. I have already shown how this can be understood in such a way that the humanity of the covenant response is no less real, even though the divine Logos be the subject of that human response.[88] Second, the gulf between estranged flesh and God revealed through the experience of Jesus on the cross does not obliterate the covenant response of Jesus worked out in the flesh, but exposes the real dimension of estrangement from which that covenant response had to be made. In this sense, the 'God-forsaken' experience is integral to the covenant response as the lesser is included in the greater.

To be God-forsaken is a lesser dimension of reality than to be God-created. If this were not true, the transcendence of God would itself have a limiting reality other than God himself. The Incarnation then is the greater love which includes within it the lesser evil of estrangement. It is the greater act of belief which includes within it the lesser act of unbelief. What I am saying is that Incarnation as an act of God is the act of his transcendence, and, as such, from the 'far side' of man's estrangement towards the centre, the limit which gives freedom and life. Jesus

the problems of the resurrection from the standpoint of both textual and historical criticism, but it is not irrelevant to my argument to say that the resurrection of Jesus is presupposed to be a reality of an ontic nature which preceded the testimony of the gospel accounts. The Incarnation, therefore, continues to be the ontic structure for the gift of the Spirit through the living person of Jesus Christ. It will be shown in the final chapter (Chapter IX) how the resurrection of Christ is the eschaton of all humanity.

[88]The assertion made earlier (see above, pp. 157, n. 42, 170f.) that the eternal Logos can make an immediate human covenant response from the side of the creature without falling into the error of Nestorianism involves a merging of both a creaturely will and a divine will in a dynamic and personal life of obedience. Rather than starting with two 'wills', one human and one divine, and then proceeding to think of them as one act, I would rather begin with the one person Jesus Christ whose personhood is constituted as eternal Sonship acting towards the Father from and as creaturely being. What this involves, though it is not yet made clear, is an intra-divine transcendence with an intrinsic cosmic structure concretized as the image of God in man through the dynamic power (*exousia*) of Logos and Spirit. What I have called 'historical transcendence' might then be said to be the extrinsic reality of an intrinsic structure which is the nature of God himself. Thus, instead of positing two distinct realities which create a dualism between God and the cosmos, we would be led to think of one reality (God) who expresses himself intrinsically (eternally) and extrinsically (creatively).

Christ, then, is both the 'far side', indeed, the furthest side of God's transcendence, as well as the centre of God's transcendence. We must remember that in the creation covenant, the distance between Creator and creature was set at its absolute limit. In other words, the space between God and man was set as the space of God's transcendence. The estrangement of man through a failure to make covenant response and taking over the limit for himself, cannot *increase* that distance and so pass beyond God's transcendence.[89] Therefore, it is still possible for a human covenant response to be made, even when the estrangement is absolute, *as long as* transcendence is in view. For it is transcendence as the limit which gives covenant response both its possibility and its actuality.[90] In Christ, when the 'Word became flesh', transcendence did 'come into view', so that what was humanly impossible for the created logos was now humanly possible for the uncreated Logos. It is in this way that the *kenosis*, the self-emptying, of Christ can be understood as the transcendence of God.

What remains inexplicable, at least to the extent that we have considered transcendence, is how transcendence can be conceived of as being active on 'both sides' of the gulf of absolute estrangement. Or, how Christ can be both the limit and the response to that limit. What is forced upon us, is the implication that if the transcendence of God is the greater love within which the lesser evil of estrangement is included, the cry of God-forsakenness from the cross took place *within* the relation of Father and Son. To be precise, within that eternal relation. If there were no other hints in the history of revelation, the *kenosis* itself would seem to demand a doctrine of the Trinity. The inner logic of historical transcendence appears to have its roots in the intra-divine structure of God's own being. Some tentative explorations in this direction should at least be made.

The doctrine of the Trinity has already been brought into consideration

---

[89]The suggestion that a doctrine of universalism is implied if 'nothing can pass beyond God's transcendence', is probably indefensible, although not thereby established. To consider the alternative, that something could pass beyond God's transcendence, involves an equally serious problem, and in my mind, a totally unacceptable conclusion—that God does not transcend total reality or total possibility. It would be an interesting exercise to explore the language of the Apostle's Creed concerning the 'descent into hell', and see if this is not, in fact, a way of speaking of the transcendence of God through the *kenosis*, and so a way of considering hell itself to be the lesser evil within the greater love of the Incarnation. I do not think that what I am setting forth here is in any way a 'minimizing' of the reality of what it is to be 'God-forsaken', but rather, is a way of 'maximizing' what it is to be 'God-created'.

[90]Whether there is an 'eclipse of God' possible of such a nature that transcendence 'never comes into view', and thus an eternal estrangement takes place, I am not prepared to say, and furthermore, do not consider it relevant to the argument I am making.

by the earlier suggestion that the *kenosis* could not have represented an ontic cleft within the Godhead, and that the penetration of the Word into flesh must, therefore, be considered to be an *intra-* rather than an *extra-*trinitarian movement of divine transcendence.[91] As Barth so well puts it, the Son who goes into the far country in order that man may return home, does not do this without the Father, for he and the Father are one.[92] One of the most fruitful insights into this relationship between Father and Son, even at the furthest extremity of self-emptying on the part of the Son, is the life of prayer which Jesus experienced. The prayers of Jesus exhibit two things: first, the intimate communion which he possessed with the Father in virtue of his sonship. That is, prayer was for him an intimacy of communion brought into the flesh, not merely a necessity of communication occasioned by the flesh.

> I thank thee, Father, Lord of heaven and earth, that thou hast hidden these things from the wise and understanding and revealed them to babes; yea, Father, for such was thy gracious will. All things have been delivered to me by my Father; and no one knows the Son except the Father, and no one knows the Father except the Son and any one to whom the Son chooses to reveal him.[93]

The second thing which the prayers of Jesus reveal is that prayer is possible from the 'far side' of estrangement, as well as from the 'near side' of intimacy. Though Jesus prays 'in the flesh' and subject to all the limitations and even contradictions of the flesh, not least of which is the disinclination of estranged flesh towards God, he not only *can* pray through a nature which is common to ours, but he *does* pray. And there is no force, demonic or delusive which can break that communion. His prayers unfolded the life of the eternal Son with the Father out into the world and brought the tattered and tormented edges of all creation into that life. At least two of the words from the cross were prayers—'Father, forgive them'; and, 'Father, into thy hands I commit my spirit'—and there is no reason to think that the cry of dereliction was not also a prayer: 'My God, my God, why hast thou forsaken me?' If in that moment, the estranged flesh was brought into that space between the Son of God and the Father, so that the face of the Father was eclipsed from the face of the Son, we are given a new and terrible glimpse of the depths of divine transcendence.

Whatever the depth of the humility, or humiliation, which the Incarnation demanded of the eternal Son, we are not to conclude that there was any 'way of humility' here which was not intrinsic to the eternal

[91]See above, p. 240.
[92]*Church Dogmatics*, IV/2, p. 43.
[93]Matthew 11:25-27.

life of the Son with the Father.[94] When we see God for us, we see him *as he is*.[95] This 'way of *kenosis*' which we see as the movement of the Son towards the Father in the Spirit, is not a *kenosis*, or a self-emptying in the form of a renunciation of the nature of God himself, but is a self-emptying precisely because self-renunciation is the very nature of God himself. Here, self-renunciation must be understood in a positive, and not a negative sense. It is the renunciation of a negative self-existence, in the form of a 'separate' kind of existence, which constitutes the eternal relation of Father, Son and Spirit. Thus, the Incarnation of the Son of God is the same Spirit of positive self-renunciation which is the very nature of divine existence. It is actually the dynamic dimension of love as activity.

Therefore, this movement of God 'outside of himself' to become flesh, and so bring estranged humanity into eternal and perfect unity with himself, demands that we now understand the nature of God in such a way that 'outside of' is also 'within'. At this point, our language, with its 'opticizing' tendencies, becomes too rigid for the dynamic and fluid inner logic of the transcendence of God, which is an *intra*-active personal reality of love and not just an *inter*-active force. When the eternal Subject prays to the eternal Subject, as a son talks with a father, we can hear what we cannot see—the intra-action of divine communion with one of the voices speaking out of history.[96]

[94]It should be noted here, that if one makes a distinction between the Incarnation and the humiliation, as Bonhoeffer does (*Christology*, p. 111), then the humiliation is related to the bearing of sinful flesh while the Incarnation is related to created manhood. Thus, humiliation becomes an act of the Incarnate one and is restricted to the period prior to the exaltation. With this distinction, and in this case Bonhoeffer is following the traditional Lutheran Christology, one is left with a humiliation which is not intrinsic to the Son's eternal relationship with the Father, unless the Incarnation itself is presumed to include the humiliation, in which case, the distinction would seem to be irrelevant.

[95]Cf. K. Barth, *Church Dogmatics*, IV/2, who says: 'We can only say that in its great inconceivability—always new and surprising when we try to conceive it —this reason is holy and righteous and worthy of God because it corresponds to the humility of the eternal Son as it takes place in supreme reality in the intra-trinitarian life of God Himself; and although it cannot be deduced from this, in the light of it can be recognised as a reason which is in itself both clear and well-founded.' p. 43.

[96]For the assertion implied at this point, that the structure of the Trinity which is disclosed to us through the redemptive activity of Christ and the Spirit through the Incarnation is also the inner structure of the eternal Trinity, cf. Karl Rahner, *The Trinity*, who has as the basic thesis of this book: 'The "economic" Trinity is the "immanent" Trinity and the "immanent" Trinity is the "economic" Trinity.' p. 22. Rahner argues that the true and authentic concept of grace interprets grace as a *self*-communication of God in Christ and in his Spirit. Therefore, what we know of God as grace *is* the nature of God, and not merely a created 'mode of being' which would not actually reflect his own nature. What Rahner calls the 'immanent' Trinity is what I have called the eternal relation of the Son and Spirit

When that voice which speaks out of history is heard to be the voice of the eternal Son of God, then the subject of that manhood is the transcendence of God fully and actively revealed within history.[97] But the inner logic of historical transcendence is not simply the inter-action of history and transcendence, but the intra-action of divine transcendence, with history and humanity now given speaking parts! History is not devaluated, nor humanity violated by its active participation in this divine transcendence. For the covenant of creation was established out of the transcendence of God and destined to this end.[98] What I am suggesting here is that the *kenosis* seems to expose to us a relation between the Son and the Father in which each 'transcends' the other. This is what I have called an intra-divine transcendence. While this way of putting it is not a very happy choice of expression to state the inner relations of the triune God, as it would appear to divide the unity of God into a plurality of persons, I would like to hold to the use of transcendence as a word which expresses activity rather than simply 'nature', or 'being'. This

to the Father. What he calls the 'economic' Trinity I would now call the transcendent Trinity. That is, the immanent Trinity is historically revealed as an intratrinitarian communion which transcends itself to inter-act with man. This follows from my basic thesis that when God acts, he transcends himself to act in and with history. Where I would like to question Rahner further is what he means by the Incarnation of the Son as an act which takes place 'outside' the intra-divine life of the Trinity (*ibid.*, p. 23). If he only means that the Son becomes the Incarnate Word while the Spirit and the Father do not, then I could agree. But if he means that the humiliation of the Son involved an act on the part of one person in the Godhead to the exclusion of that intra-divine action which is constitutive of the nature of God, I could not agree. And I do not think that this is what Rahner would want to say. And this is borne out by what Rahner later says: '... the immanent and the economic Logos, are strictly the same.' (*Ibid.*, p. 33.) This basically supports what I have already said concerning the fact that there is no 'way of humility' for the Son which is not already intrinsically part of his relationship with the Father.

[97]That controversy over the person of Christ which took place in the 16th century between the Reformed and Lutheran theologians had the truth on both sides. The Reformed Christology which stressed the eternal Logos who existed *totus intra et extra*, wished to maintain the transcendence of the Incarnation outside of the flesh, while the Lutheran Christology which stressed the eternal Logos *totus intra* wished to maintain the transcendence of the Incarnation within the flesh. The resulting kenotic controversy foundered hopelessly on a scholastic methodology which could not conceive of divine transcendence in dynamic and trinitarian terms. It was the *kenosis* itself which could have permitted them to come to a new understanding of the doctrine of God, if their concepts of the nature of God had not already been so rigidly formed. T. F. Torrance holds that the thought patterns which prevented them from grasping the dynamic of transcendence was a 'container' concept of space. *Space, Time and Incarnation*, pp. 28ff.

[98]Cf. here, Ephesians 1:3-10, especially verse 4: '... even as he chose us in him before the foundation of the world, that we should be holy and blameless before him.' Paul appears here to have grasped this fundamental relation of transcendence to the covenant of creation, and sees its fulfilment in the new covenant which Jesus effects in a final, or eschatological sense.

activity of communion *within* the unity of the Godhead becomes absolutely distinct through the Incarnation, as the Son, Father and Spirit act in particular ways which presuppose the activity of each other. It is this *activity* of the Son with respect to the Father, an activity which I have pointed to in the prayers of Jesus, which I choose to call the *intra*-divine transcendence of God.

We can say then, that the first result of our tentative exploration into the inner logic of the trinitarian structure of historical transcendence has been the discovery that divine transcendence is, first of all, an intra-active personal reality which can have an historical as well as an eternal dimension. The exploration can now be carried one small step forward by suggesting that in the Incarnation there is also an *inter*-active personal reality of divine transcendence through which a community is established between the eternal Logos and humanity. The *inter*-action as distinguished from the *intra*-action of divine transcendence suggests that, while there is a real 'otherness' between God and man constituted by God's transcendence of man as limit, there is also a structure of real inter-relatedness between God and man. The *inter*-action between God and man which has its ground in the created image, is a reality of relation constituted by the transcendence of God, but it is not the *intra*-action of divine transcendence itself. That is to say, the community of relation between the Creator and creature is 'other' than the community of relation which exists between the Father, Son and Holy Spirit. Although it must also be said, that the former is the image of the latter. Consequently, I would say that the transcendence of *inter*-action is the image of the transcendence of *intra*-action.

Now what does this mean? It means that just as the Son could make the covenant response through his own humanity, taking humanity into the intra-divine movement of Son to Father, so he could make that response in and for our humanity through a community of relation —or inter-action—with humanity itself. For there exists intrinsic to humanity itself the real image of a community of relation. This image, which is grounded in the intra-divine transcendence, provides the basis for solidarity, or a community, between the humanity of Christ and the humanity of every other person.

This community of inter-action can be clearly seen as an integral part of the Incarnation itself. From the very beginning of Jesus' ministry, he gathered around himself a little flock of 'learners', the twelve, who would not only share his teaching, but share his life and inevitably share his sufferings. Not only were they summoned to share his life, but he entered into *their* existence as well. Baptized by John, Jesus placed himself into a solidarity of community with the 'sinners'.[99] While one could

---

[99]Matthew 3:13-17.

see obvious significance in the twelve as the re-constitution of a new Israel, there appeared a more profound basis for their existence after the 'point of no return' at Caesarea Philippi. 'From that time Jesus began to show his disciples that he must go to Jerusalem and suffer many things from the elders and chief priests and scribes, and be killed, and on the third day be raised.'[100] Not only would he be dissuaded from this by a loyal but misunderstanding Peter, he made no attempt to break the bond which he had established between them and himself, but instead, drew it all the tighter by sharing with them his own kenotic way: 'Then Jesus told his disciples,"If any man would come after me, let him deny himself and take up his cross and follow me".'[101] Here was a concept of community which cut deeper than any form of social or fraternal bond. This was more than co-humanity. Their own humanity was being prepared for a gift which they could not possibly have understood, though he gave them intimations: 'I will pray the Father, and he will give you another Counsellor, to be with you for ever, even the Spirit of truth.'[102]

But now it is Gethsemane and Calvary. And the little flock draw back in horror and fear. An unbridgeable chasm seems to be opening up between them and him, made all the more impossible by his words: 'Take, eat; this is my body.... Drink of it, all of you; for this is my blood of the covenant, ...'[103] He was giving them himself, and yet he was giving himself up to death. He was going where they could not follow, and yet he was not going to leave them desolate, but would come to them.[104]

When the *kenosis* is followed as it makes its way deeper into the humanity of Jesus' flesh, there is also to be discerned a progressive development of a kenotic community which cannot be understood purely in terms of the Incarnate Word. By that I mean that the transcendence of God which we have seen to be operative in covenant response exposes the intra-divine transcendence of the eternal Son in relationship to the Father. But now, with the growth of this little community around Jesus, there emerges a dimension to the *kenosis* which calls for a third dimension of intra-divine transcendence. The Son is leaving, but his little flock will not be alone. They are to receive the 'one he will send to them', and then not only will he be with them, but the Father as well.[105] 'Here we are forced to see that the *inter*-action between Jesus and his little flock has its place in the *kenosis* as the *place* where Spirit forms the true community between God and man. But this community is formed by transcendence, for it is brought into the intra-divine transcendence so that

[100]Matthew 16:21.
[101]Matthew 16:24.
[102]John 14:16.

[103]Matthew 26:26, 27.
[104]Cf. John 13:33; 14:18-19.
[105]John 14:18-19.

it is also the *place* where Father and Son make their 'home'.[106] When it was earlier suggested that the 'existence-form of Spirit is flesh', we can now see how this is realized in the community of lived transcendence. For Spirit needs *place* in which to work out the intra-divine transcendence which belongs to the historical reality of the Incarnate Logos.[107]

What we see happening in the life of Jesus, along with his covenant response, is the self-conscious way in which he takes man 'into community' with him. The way of humility, is not just the way of the Son, but it is the way of sonship. It is the 'place' where the intra-divine transcendence is concretized as an inter-acting community between God and man. The self-emptying is not just a vicarious act on the part of one for the many, but is itself essentially an act of community. It is first of all an act of intra-divine community in which the Son moves towards the Father in the Spirit. But this is at the same time divine transcendence which *inter*-acts with humanity and binds men into community by binding them to God himself. This 'law of *kenosis*' then, which is intrinsic to the intra-divine community, and which is the 'mind of Christ', forms the ontic structure of the community to which men

---

[106]John 14:23. Cf. T. F. Torrance: '... the Spirit is the presence of the Transcendent Being of God.' *God and Rationality*, p. 175.

[107]For a more penetrating analysis of the concept of 'place' as a two-dimensional 'house of being', one should see the essay by William Kluback and Jean T. Wilde included as the Introduction to Martin Heidegger's book, *The Question of Being*, Vision Press, London, 1959. Kluback and Wilde argue that Heidegger can be faulted for disregarding the importance of the practical, or horizontal dimension of man's existence, and that his concern with ontological existence (spirit) is at the expense of the historical level (the state, or political existence). 'Place' is not merely a conjunction of time and space, but the structure of being where transcendence (spirit) has concrete reality: ' "Place" places man in that dimension which reveals the revealing meaning of being. Man is involved in "place" in two dimensions, horizontal and vertical. The horizontal dimension is determined by his political relationship. Vertically, being is a dimension hiding the uniqueness of Being, but at the same time it is the place of Being. "Place" places man in such a way that it reveals the external bounds of his existence and at the same time the depths of his freedom and reality.... The two dimensions appear in separation but are housed in unity and reveal each other to each other.' (p. 19). With this concept of 'place', the state is the 'house of man' in which he is lifted from his exclusive individuality into a higher totality, from which he receives meaning and to whose end he is inseparably united. With the substitution of community for state, one can find here an interesting paradigm for a way of understanding how 'community' is the 'place' where the intra-divine relationship of the triune God has its 'house' in man. And also, how man can live from this 'place' of transcendence, and yet not be drawn out of the historical reality of his 'place' in the world. One can also see in this an explanation for the fact that, while Judas had no 'place' with the little flock, despite his fellowship in the flesh, Peter did, despite his wavering in the flesh. With the giving of the Holy Spirit, that which had only been ambiguous and precarious now becomes concretely the Body of Christ—the 'place' where transcendence is placed into the world.

are called in Christ. This ontic structure is, in fact, the intra-divine transcendence of Father, Son and Holy Spirit concretized in history through the Incarnation. Thus, Paul appeals to the Christians at Philippi to 'have this mind among yourselves, which you have in Christ Jesus, who, though he was in the form of God, did not count equality with God a thing to be grasped, but emptied himself, ...'[108] When *kenosis* is seen as the form of intra-divine community, the appeal is not merely to an ethical type of individual self-renunciation, but the appeal is to this kenotic way of life, which is the way of community.[109]

We can no longer be in any doubt about this: it is not lowliness or suffering, or even humility, which is divine in itself and as such.[110] The tendency, which was even a temptation to Bonhoeffer, to make the divine way of kenosis reversible, is to distort the transcendence of God itself[111] There is no 'power in weakness' which, by itself, transcends the world and offers an ontological vision of Christ. Nor can one simply make the way of humility an ontic form of existence and thereby reach the transcendence of God. This is what it means to say that the divine way of *kenosis* is not reversible. The virtue of Christ was not a superior humility and a more ultimate and self-less suffering, but it was his Sonship which was his eternally, and which he worked out through his humanity. This is why I have said that the ontic structure of community is not in co-humanity, not even in a co-suffering-humanity, but rather, it is in the intra-divine transcendence concretely given in the Incarnation. While this may well have been implicit in Bonhoeffer's thought, his failure to explicate it in terms of 'this worldly' transcendence cut the top off his Christology and paved the way for a 'post-Bonhoefferian' concept of transcendence with its ontic structure located in co-humanity. While there is a dimension of co-humanity to Christ's Sonship, because his humanity was also ours, his Sonship became a way of suffering and humiliation in order to make good the covenant response. So that

---

[108]Philippians 2:5-7.

[109]For a fine commentary on the 'law of humbling' which is found throughout the New Testament, and which reflects the kenotic way of divine Sonship, see K. Barth, *Church Dogmatics*, IV/1, pp. 188ff.

[110]There is no lowliness which is divine in itself and as such. There is therefore no general principle of the cross in which we have to do with God (in principle). The cross in the New Testament is not a kind of symbol of an outlook which is negatively orientated, which speculates *à la baisse*. The limits of humanity are one thing, but God's visitation of us in the limits of humanity, in our creatureliness, in our humanness, in our sinfulness and mortality, in the incarnation of His Word and the crucifixion of His Son, that is quite another.' K. Barth, *Church Dogmatics*, IV/1, pp. 191-192.

[111]E. Bethge says of Bonhoeffer: 'The belief in the power of weakness was one of Bonhoeffer's most basic insights, and he was to hold to it throughout his theological life.... In the interpretation of the weak Word, we are close to the profoundest thought ever expressed by Bonhoeffer.' *Dietrich Bonhoeffer*, p. 374.

the particular way of humility for Christ was not what was left after stripping himself of divine transcendence, but what was there when divine transcendence in the form of eternal Sonship brought man into total and final obedience to the Father. The inner logic of historical transcendence is then, first of all, the intra-divine transcendence of Sonship worked out through the humanity and history of the Incarnation, which is the existence-form of the creature. This is the transcendence of the 'God who is for man'. In this way, the *kenosis* brings the limiting transcendence of God as a transcendence which is already community, into inescapable proximity to man.

But having said 'first of all', there obviously is a further truth implied in the logic of historical transcendence. This too is revealed through *kenosis* in the form of an *inter*-active transcendence by which community is created *between* God and man. The covenant response worked out through the estranged flesh which the eternal Son assumed, became a 'community of covenant response' through the inter-active transcendence of the Spirit. The kenotic way which is intrinsic to the nature of God, and thus is the way of intra-divine transcendence, is no special way which the Son of God took so that man could go 'another way'— the way which leads to individualism. But it is the way of unity with God, it is the way of freedom, it is the way of life, it is the way of the Spirit, and as such, it is the way of lived transcendence. This is the transcendence of the 'Man who is for God'.

And so there does appear to be a rationale for the transcendence of God. The basic 'grammar' of this transcendence is given to us in the inner structure of the Incarnation. Which, as we have seen, is the inner structure of the intra-divine communion of God himself. That is, from the depths of our humanity, the Son meets himself in the Father through the Spirit. The 'grammar' of the language of transcendence, thus, is decidedly trinitarian, and, therefore, ontologically derived from the intra-divine transcendence of God himself.

The reality of God comes to us as an activity of transcendence in which God acts as the divine personal agent whose own nature is to inter-act with his creation and his creature. The argument for the basic thesis that transcendence is the act of a personal agent, who is concretely embodied in the act and the inter-action, can now be brought to its conclusion. But the conclusion is not the end. For establishing a rationale for historical transcendence carries with it the imperative of a continuing action.

Where in the world is the 'place' of the Spirit? Where in the world is the limit which man can love, so as to find the centre again? And what does it mean that the reality of God is a 'lived transcendence?' These are the questions which will rise again after the rationale of historical transcendence is tidied up in its neat little package. And these

are the questions which carry more than a little concern, not only for
the 'little flock', but for the one who has already given thanks—

god the dispersed

gathered up again in those who have communed.
out of all our eucharists, this is the first.

Chapter VI

The Rationale for Historical Transcendence

'The Desire to be Disillusioned—a Way of Knowing'

Neighbours, believe it or not,
God is looking after my father's sheep.
But the simple truth is harder to tell than a lie.
The trouble I'll have, and the trouble they'll have to
    believe it! ...

Cuthman, your father is dead. We came to tell you.

You can't say that to me. I was speaking the
truth.

We were speaking the truth.

    You came to make me sorry,
But you're breaking the sun over your knees to say
My father's dead. My father is strong and well, ...

    Come
Down with us and see him.

    Let me alone.
No; if I come you'll take me to a place
Where truth will laugh and scatter like a magpie.
Up here, my father waits for me at home
And God sits with the sheep.[1]

Strange it is, that the truth can sometimes cause us to lose our grip on reality! For the truth ought to be a friend to the honest person, and a source of strength to the rational man. We do desire truth in other men, and pity the deluded as deeply as we hate the devious. The illusions that we can see in the lives of others are at best a tolerable weakness and at worst a dangerous instability. And it is not that we are totally unaware of our own illusions, but they seem *real* to us, and we would not know

---

[1]Christopher Fry, *The Boy With a Cart*, Frederick Muller Ltd., London, 2nd edition, 1945, pp. 4, 5.

what to think if they should suddenly be stripped away. For reality in the subjective sense is the way in which we *think* of ourselves as related to the world about us. The limit of reality in this case, is the limit imposed by our way of thinking. That which is 'unthinkable' is also unreal to us, and, if it impinges directly upon us so as to threaten our sense of reality, it is also unbearable to us.

It is precisely because illusion and reality can exist together within the self as a thinking subject, that the discovery of truth is such a difficult, and even painful process, involving a quite radical re-orientation of the self with respect to truth. There is an element of disillusionment involved in knowing the truth, as John Macmurray puts it:

> The discovery of truth must be from the subjective side a process of disillusionment.... We all confess to the desire to get at the truth, but in practice the desire for truth is the desire to be disillusioned.[2]

This desire to be disillusioned is a mark of maturity considered from a psychological perspective, but from the philosophical perspective, it is the capacity for knowledge itself. One could even say that it is the core of rationality, and thus, the distinctive element in the form of the personal. 'The capacity to love objectively', says Macmurray, 'is the capacity which makes us persons. It is the ultimate source of our capacity to behave in terms of the object. It is the core of rationality.'[3]

In seeking, therefore, a rationale for historical transcendence, the problem of reality is the crucial problem. And because historical transcendence is concerned with the transcendence of God, the problem is that of the reality of God. The 'desire to be disillusioned' must first of all be awakened before the truth of the reality of God can be discovered. What is involved particularly is the illusion that reality is that which the self as a thinking subject confers upon that which is experienced either intellectually or intuitively; in Kantian terms, one could say that which is discriminated through the categories of pure reason or that which is intuited from sense experience. In either case, the problem of the reality of God is first of all the problem of how the self as subject is constituted in reality. What is meant by a rationale, depends upon how this problem is considered.

The line which I have been following from the beginning has sought to avoid the dilemma which enters when the self is constituted as a thinking subject and all else as the object which the subject determines through thought. Therefore, a rationale for the historical transcendence, and thus, the reality of God, was first of all sought in the original relation of God as Creator with the world as his creation. There we saw that if one

[2]*Reason and Emotion*, p. 22.
[3]*Ibid.*, p. 32.

assumes a correspondence between the absolute Otherness of God and the utter profaneness of the world, both the world and God have a distinct reality while at the same time, a real relation. It was this rationale which we said logically precedes the Incarnation so that the Incarnation has its own inner rationality to be discovered—that is, it does not lie in the mind of the subject.[4]

However, it also became clear that this rationale was problematical in the sense that it could not be inferred out of the relation between God and man, but was a rationality given to the relation by the free act of God as Spirit.[5] It followed from this, that the rationale was necessarily theological; that is, the rationale of historical transcendence has its intrinsic reality located in the act of God which is also his person.[6] Attempts to resolve the problematic by first of all casting the relation of God to the world into the form of a paradox, and then asserting the paradox as a single reality of the thinking (or believing) subject, were shown to be inherently subjective, and, therefore, liable to illusion. It is the problematic in the rationale of historical transcendence which served the disillusioning function and enabled us to proceed with the exploration of the inner logic of the Incarnation.

It became increasingly clear that the transcendence of God was also a revealing of God through his inter-action with man at the historical level. This revelation took the form of an active participation in the history of man through the humanity, first of all in a preparatory way, of Israel, and then finally and completely, of Jesus Christ. It was here that we discovered that transcendence is to be connected with a subject, and that, when the Incarnation was seen as the 'God who was for Man', and at the same time, the 'Man who was for God', the transcendence of God was disclosed as the activity of God as personal subject. An activity which first of all is an intra-active reality of divine love, and then, an inter-active reality. What is especially important for the formulation of a rationale of historical transcendence, is the way in which the intra-active and the inter-active reality of God is concretized in the historical existence of man as *one* reality. That is, not only is the rationale of the transcendence of God trinitarian, but *because* it is trinitarian, it is also kenotic. This means that the particular form of the reality of God carries with it the form of its apprehension. So that, we could expect that an intelligible rationale for the transcendence of God can now be given.[7]

There are two ways in which I want to proceed in developing a rationale for historical transcendence. The theological way is, I would

---

[4]See above, pp. 61ff.
[5]See above, pp. 63, 67.
[6]See above, p. 74.
[7]This, as stated above, is the precise purpose of this book.

think, more vital to the particular problem of the reality of God, and at the same time, more helpful in leading us on to further considerations of historical transcendence. Therefore, I shall set this aside for the moment in order to take up a somewhat more philosophical question as to the *form* of the reality of God in terms of transcendence as the act of a personal agent.

From the beginning, I have taken a position which involves a re-thinking of the concept of transcendence as it has generally been understood in philosophical terms. The particular methodology which I adopted called into question the priority of the thinking subject as the point of reference for reality. Instead, I proceeded on the presupposition that there was an intrinsic reality with its own form of intelligibility in that which confronts the self as a knowing person. Instead of transcendence defined as that which lies beyond or at the furthest reach of finite reason, and thus a limit which man 'places' at the boundary of his existence, I chose to think of transcendence in terms of the act by which a personal agent moves beyond his own self-existence to confront and inter-act with an 'Other'; this immediately opened up new possibilities, and new problems for the understanding of the transcendence of God. What began as an attempt to consider transcendence from a standpoint other than the priority of the thinking subject, and thus make room for the possibility of a real transcendence in a form of reality totally 'Other' to man—that is, the transcendence of God—exposed a more fundamental issue involving the form of personal reality itself. By 'form of personal reality' I simply mean that form of reality which is constitutive of man as person. So that the rationale of historical transcendence now involves a radical questioning and restructuring of the rationale which properly belongs to the nature of man as person. This implicit problem in the rationale of historical transcendence must now be raised and dealt with explicitly, though little more can be done than to identify the problem and point to a solution which more adequately provides for an understanding of historical transcendence on its own terms.

Thankfully, the groundwork for this task has already been laid in the work of John Macmurray, whose Gifford Lectures for 1953 under the title, *The Form of the Personal*, have been published under two titles.[8] While his thought only incidentally touches upon the theological problem of transcendence, his critique of modern philosophy in terms of a concept of personal reality concerns the rationale which we have found to be the implicit problem in the rationale of historical transcendence.[9]

Macmurray offers a two-fold criticism of the modern philosophical

---

[8]*The Self as Agent* and *Persons in Relation*.

[9]This 'implicit problem' only can be seen as a problem if one is willing to be 'disillusioned'—or, to know the truth of the 'Other'.

tradition: first, that it is purely theoretical in its conception of the self as a thinking subject; and second, it is egocentric in its conception of the self as the determining subject which turns the Other into an object.[10] While Macmurray concedes that Kant is probably the most adequate of modern philosophers because he succeeds more than any others, including his successors, in holding together the various aspects of human experience, his uncritical acceptance of the Cartesian starting point of the 'I think' doomed his system to an inevitable dualism of subject and object.

This brings us to the supreme principle of knowledge, which Kant, echoing Descartes, calls the 'Cogito', the 'I think' which accompanies all my representations; or, in his technical terminology, the transcendental unity of apperception.... To think is to determine an object; so the fact that the manifold in intuition stands under the unity of thought transforms it into a world of objects, in systematic relation with one another in space and time.... So I perceive the world, and distinguish between the world and myself. I am the Subject; the world is the Object. My imaginings are subjective; but what I think is objective. This dichotomy of Subject and Object is the abstract form of all our knowledge. Subject and Object are correlatives, or polar opposites which depend upon one another, and the principle of their correlation is that the form of thought is the form of the object.[11]

While it is true that Kant exposed the uncritical idealism of the Romantic philosophers where both science and morality were subsumed under the artistic standpoint, and as a result, created a philosophy of organic development, nevertheless, Kant failed to overcome the incoherence in his own system. This incoherence, says Macmurray, centres in the doctrine of the 'thing-in-itself', which left him unable to relate the theoretical to the practical. For Kant, the real world was the noumenal, which is not subject to the determination which knowledge presupposes, and thus cannot be known as a 'thing-in-itself'. Hence, he sought to preserve both freedom and determination by restricting thought only to the phenomenal world, the determinate sphere which only has the appearance of reality.[12] But this will not do, concludes Macmurray,

for the justification of this conception lies in the claim that it enables us to think the unity of the same self in the theoretical and the practical fields. If it does not do this—as it does not—then there is no ground for retaining it. But if we reject the doctrine, we must be aware of the consequences.... If Kant's solution fails, then another

[10]*Persons in Relation*, pp. 16, 24.
[11]J. Macmurray, *The Self as Agent*, pp. 50-51.
[12]*Ibid.*, p. 64.

solution must be found if philosophical adequacy is to be achieved. For it is essential to philosophy that a means should be discovered of thinking coherently the unity of experience as a whole.[13]

We have now found the point at which Macmurray moves from a criticism of the Kantian viewpoint to a reconstruction of it. The incoherence in this concept is a *formal* one, resulting from the basic assumption that reason is primarily theoretical: as if the 'Cogito' were an adequate premise on which to proceed to the practical as the conclusion and verification of thought itself. But, says Macmurray, thought is essentially private, and one can never proceed from the theoretical to the practical in the field of inter-personal relations.[14] This formal incoherence in Kant's thought leads Macmurray to suggest that a new instrument for thought is necessary which takes into account the adequacy of the Critical philosophy in terms of both the theoretical and the practical, but one which conceives of the self as primarily constituted by the practical. It is this which Macmurray calls the 'form of the personal'.

The self cannot be conceived on the analogy of the form of the material (as Hume made clear), but neither can it be conceived on the analogy of the form of the organic (as Kierkegaard showed). The self is not an organic unity nor is it a substance whose essence is thinking. By substituting the person for the self, Macmurray made a formal shift in the emphasis between the theoretical and the practical, and so introduced, in effect, a different rationale for the reality of human existence.

> Reason is traditionally the *differentia* of the human. If the personal individual is essentially the thinker, then rationality must refer to the logical faculty, and to this faculty in contrast with the empirical capacities which belong to our practical nature.... The human *differentia* we have decided is not the capacity to think, but the capacity to act. If, then, we continue to use the term 'rationality' in the specialized theoretical reference we must surrender its use to denote the essential characteristic of the personal.... It will be clear from this discussion that the term 'person' fulfils the same function from the standpoint of the agent as the term 'self' does in traditional philosophy, which thinks from the standpoint of the subject.[15]

The two-fold criticism of traditional philosophy—namely, that it is

---

[13]*Ibid.*, p. 66.

[14]"We may then reformulate our criticism of the adequacy of the Critical philosophy by saying that it fails to do justice to, and even to allow for the possibility of our knowledge of one another; and this failure arises because its formal conception of knowledge excludes this possibility by postulating the "I think" as the primary presupposition of all experience.' *Ibid.*, p. 73.

[15]*Persons in Relation*, pp. 26-27.

theoretical and egocentric—can now be overcome by Macmurray in his form of the personal where the self is conceived of as an agent who acts and inter-acts with other agents. Thus, the starting point of thought is from the standpoint of action, and while this does not rule out theory in the strictest philosophical sense, it eliminates the dualism between the theoretical and the practical by making thought the necessary, but subordinate, constituent of action.

Pure thought is derived from the concept of action by abstracting from action and so excluding from consideration the implications of the practical and the personal. Thus, thought falls 'within' action as the negative and subordinate activity of the person. Action is primary and concrete while thought is secondary, abstract and derivative.[16] The self, then, is not primarily the thinker, but the doer, says Macmurray. In its positive sense, the self is an agent, while in the negative sense, it is the subject which reflects.[17]

Action is constituted by a unity of movement and knowledge. It is knowledge which makes the movement an action and not merely a blind activity.

'By 'movement' is not meant an observed displacement in space; nor by 'knowledge' an ascertained truth. The two terms represent, on the contrary, a theoretical analysis of the 'I do' into 'I move' and 'I know'. 'Movement' here refers to our experience of moving ourselves; 'knowledge' to the awareness of the Other which 'informs' this moving.[18]

Without going into the complex factors of time and space, which Macmurray relates to action and reflection respectively,[19] we can define the act of a personal agent as that which determines or brings into existence a possibility by actualizing it in time and space. To determine, in this sense, is to make actual what is merely possible apart from the action. As such, it may be said to be a determining of the future.[20] On the other hand, reflection can only be an activity directed towards that which is already determined, that is, to that which is past. Reflection cannot actualize possibilities, but can only 'know' the actual, the existent.

When we insist on the primacy of the practical, and adopt the standpoint of the Agent, rather than of Subject, the antinomy between freedom and determinism vanishes. Knowledge is necessarily of the actual, or the existent. The merely possible, the non-existent, cannot be known. We have seen that the actual or the existent is the

[16]*The Self as Agent*, p. 89.
[17]*Ibid.*, p. 90.
[18]*Ibid.*, p. 128.
[19]*Ibid.*, p. 132.
[20]*Ibid.*, p. 134.

past. It is that which is determinate because it has been already determined. To act is to determine the future: the past is already determinate. Knowledge, then, in its primary form, is the theoretical determination of the past in action.[21]

Reflection, then, has both a primary and a secondary function, according to Macmurray. Its primary function is to inform the action through intention by taking into account a right and wrong possibility among the alternative directions for action to proceed.[22] Here again, it is the action which actually determines a right or wrong movement; the reflective activity has determined nothing apart from the act, and so, is subordinate and negative. In a secondary sense, reflection is an activity restricted to the spacial form, proceeding along the lines of inferences based on that which is already determinate, i.e., past.[23]

When the self is considered as person, with action as the primary mode of being and thought included within it as the secondary and subordinate, the correlative of the person cannot be the material world, nor the organic world. For neither provide the necessary possibility for action which constitutes the person. In other words, the self as agent cannot exist in a personal sense in isolation; action will be impossible in the complete sense because apart from the Other, who is also an agent, there will be no 'resistance' to the self of the kind necessary to produce a personal act.[24] Without resistance, which Macmurray defines as the core of tactual perception, the self as agent cannot experience itself, because there will be no 'other' than self to constitute a limiting factor to the movement of self.[25] This opposition, which comes in the form of that which is Other than the self, constitutes the unity of the experience of the self as Agent. 'The distinction of Self and Other is the awareness of both; and the *existence* of both is the fact that their opposition is a practical, and not a theoretical opposition.[26]

It now becomes clear just how Macmurray overcomes the dualism which he charged was implicit in the Cartesian dichotomy between Subject and Object. When the unity of the self *includes* the Other, it

---

[21]*Ibid.*, pp. 134-135.

[22]*Ibid.*, p. 136. The distinction between right and wrong here has no specifically moral connotation: 'The distinction between right and wrong is inherent in the nature of action. Knowingly to actualize one of a number of possibles, and in doing so to negate the others, is to characterize the act that is so performed as right and the others as wrong. Again, it is the doing of the action which so distinguishes between right and wrong, not a theoretical judgment which may or may not precede, accompany or follow the doing. Consequently, if we may say that a proposition is that which can be true or false, we may also say that an action is what can be right or wrong.' *Ibid.*, p. 140.

[23]*Ibid.*, p. 135.   [25]*Ibid.*, pp. 108, 109.

[24]*Ibid.*, pp. 144, 145.   [26]*Ibid.*, p. 109.

cannot be simply the object of the discrimination of the self as thought; that is, a purely logical distinction. Rather, the distinction is made first of all at the practical level through the act of the self, and it is through this act, which is also a distinction between self and Other, that the reality of the self is constituted.

This is what I meant when I implied that there was a rationale of personal existence in the thought of Macmurray which was implicit to the rationale of historical transcendence. And this is the reason that it will be impossible to *think* the rationale of historical transcendence if the rationale of personal existence is that of the Cartesian model, with primacy given to the self as a thinking subject. With this rationale (the Cartesian), transcendence never can be more than a logical distinction within the *self*, for a transcending reality which is totally other to the self would be unthinkable, and thereby, unknowable. However, if one chooses the rationale suggested by Macmurray, the distinction between the self and the Other is first of all experienced at the practical level in a unitary way.[27] Thus, the self as agent can really know the Other because the knowledge is grounded in the practical and not in the theoretical. Just how this rationale opens up the way for an understanding of transcendence will become clear as we follow Macmurray further in his development of the person in relation.

If we accept Macmurray's assertion that the self as agent is constituted by the experience of that which is Other, it becomes clear immediately that the Other must also be an agent if the self is to know itself in reality. Material resistance to the self at the practical level offers the possibility of indiscriminate movement, but not action in the personal sense. When I come up against a tree, or a wall, I encounter resistance to my intention to move, but there is no particular way implied in the resistance as to which movement is the right one. In other words, resistance at the purely material level does not 'inform' my intention to act in any particular way, other than to follow out a movement of 'blind' activity. But if we assume that the resistance to the self is offered

[27]Another way of seeing the concept of person in terms of the subjective and objective states of existence, is provided by Michael Polanyi, *Personal Knowledge*, Routledge and Kegan Paul, London, 1958, who says: '... I think we may distinguish between the personal in us, which actively enters into our commitment, and our subjective states, in which we merely endure our feelings. This distinction establishes the conception of the *personal*, which is neither subjective nor objective. In so far as the personal submits to requirements acknowledged by itself as independent of itself, it is not subjective; but in so far as it is an action guided by individual passion, it is not objective either. It transcends the disjunction between subjective and objective.' p. 300. The difference between Polanyi and Macmurray at this point, is that Macmurray would prefer to say that the personal *includes*, rather than transcends, the individual passions as well as the independent requirements which impinge upon the self, and that this inclusion constitutes a functional and necessary, but subordinate, reality of the person.

by an organism, then we make possible more than movement, we make possible behaviour. The organic environment will provide the type of resistance to the self at the practical level which offers stimuli to which it can respond but still there will be no grounds for discrimination. Macmurray's conclusion, then, is that only the resistance offered by the Other as a moving Agent constitutes the proper correlative to the self as Agent, and it is only in this 'field of action' that the self can exist in reality.[28]

We now have the complete outlines of the 'form of the personal', although there are many dimensions which Macmurray proceeds to work out in a more systematic way. I will only take up two or three of these as they relate to the rationale of historical transcendence. One important dimension of the 'form of the personal' is the concept of individuality. Obviously, the self as Agent must retain individuality in order to act as an agent, even though that act can only be constituted by the Other. The development of individuality within the form of the personal is considered by Macmurray to be the negative phase. This negative phase constitutes a withdrawal into Egocentricity, that is, to be concerned for oneself in relation to the Other.[29] The important thing for the rationale of the personal which Macmurray proposes is that the primary aspect of self existence is the relation with the Other, while the secondary aspect is the Egocentric dimension within that relation. It is called negative because any Egocentric attitude on the part of the self can only occur by abstracting from the relation to the Other. This subordinate dimension of the relation, constitutes the sphere of individuality, and can either be motivated out of love or out of fear. If it is motivated out of love, withdrawal into individuality will always be for the sake of the Other. The intention will be towards the Other, that is, towards relation, even when the self is concentrated on its individuality. But fear of the Other is fear for oneself, and concentrates the interest and activity of the self on defence rather than on relation.[30] When individuality assumes the primary role, the self will either assume a passive or an aggressive role in relation, but in either case, 'personal' relation is not

---

[28]*The Self as Agent*, pp. 144, 145. Following Macmurray's principle of correlation here, one could suggest as a further step, the 'form of the spiritual', where the correlative of the self as Agent demands not only a personal agent 'other' than the self, but a personal spiritual Agent who is Other. Macmurray virtually takes this step at the conclusion of *Persons in Relation*, p. 223, where he conceives of God as the 'infinite Agent' whose intentionality constitutes a personal universe. However, there are problems with this conception which I will subsequently point out. I only wish to make it clear at this point, that I feel the rationale of personal existence which Macmurray provides includes the possibility of a conception of spirit, even though Macmurray does not proceed in this direction.

[29]*Persons in Relation*, p. 94.   [30]*Ibid.*, pp. 94, 95.

possible. Here we have the distinction between what Macmurray calls society and community. Community is formed by the positive relation of individuality where the intention is to be concerned for the Other. Society is an indirect, and therefore, impersonal relation based on the negative (individualistic) aspect of the self. Society can either form itself around the passive instincts of individualism and assume a contemplative form of idealism, or around the aggressive instincts of individualism and assume a more pragmatic form based on power.[31] Community, therefore, includes the concept of society as the negative which constitutes its own positive intention, but society does not include the concept of community, though community may exist within it as a practical reality.

The important thing here for our consideration is the way in which individuality is seen to be the secondary and subordinate aspect of the reality of person, though nonetheless real in its own constituent part of the act which forms relation. The reality of a person is in his action with the Other, because this action includes his individuality. When the Other agent 'knows' me in my action, he knows the *real* me. In effect, I transcend myself, my individuality, in my action. My transcendence of the Other is not my withdrawal from him into the inaccessible realm of individuality, but my action with him by which he knows me as a person in relation. In the same way, the transcendence of the Other is his action and inter-action with me by which I can really know him. In this sense, one could *not* say that an agent was transcendent of another agent and yet immanent 'in him'. If immanence is to be used at all as the correlative of transcendence, it must be in terms of the agent himself. The immanence of a personal agent is constituted by his individuality which is the negative and subordinate dimension of the positive and primary, and, therefore, transcendent act.

It follows, then, that immanence is *not* the dimension of relation nor is transcendence the dimension of 'otherness', as is the case when one thinks from the standpoint of the primacy of the self as subject. In a certain sense, this way of speaking, and thinking, is still valid if one wishes to make a logical distinction in an objective way. For example, Macmurray would say that, while man is an organism and thus shares in the immanence of organic existence, he transcends the organic in the form of the personal.[32]

---

[31]*Ibid.*, pp. 137ff.

[32]'For there can be no action without an agent, and an agent, whether finite or infinite, though he is immanent in existence, necessarily transcends it. For the existent is what has been determined, and the agent is the determiner. What has been determined is the past; but the agent is concerned with the future and its determination. So in action he passes beyond his existence, transcending the past which constitutes his determinate being. His reality as agent lies in his continual self-transcendence.' *Ibid.*, p. 223.

However, one cannot say with respect to the other agents, that one is immanent in their existence and yet transcendent over them in this same way. For the transcendence of the person over the organism constitutes the inaccessibility of the person to the organism. While, in the form of the personal, the act of the agent is what makes the person accessible and knowable to the other agent. If one is going to speak of the transcendence of God as the infinite Agent, then it simply cannot be done by saying that God is transcendent over the world in the same way that person is transcendent over organism. For this makes God inaccessible in his transcendence, and introduces a dualism between God and the world.[33]

Admittedly, it is confusing to use the word 'transcendence' in these two different senses. What is actually involved is the more fundamental confusion of two different rationales, or two different ways of thinking. By deliberately retaining the word 'transcendence' for the reality of God, the way of thinking which views God from the standpoint of the theoretical can be tracked to its lair and flushed out into the open. For what is at stake is more than the use of a word—the issue is the reality of God as a reality which is truly 'other' to man, and yet, in relation. The form of the personal as an instrument of thought has a rationale which includes that which is Other to the self as Agent in a unity of experience without limiting the freedom of the Other. This rationale not only asserts the reality of that which is totally Other to the self as Agent, and this is what one wants to assert in the statement that God is transcendent of the world, but it also asserts the reality of the Other as a constituent dimension of the reality of self-existence. My argument is simply that to understand the transcendence of God as his act which constitutes the reality of that which is Other to him is a better way of stating the case for the reality of God, while at the same time, conceiving of the reality of God in his transcendence as accessible to man through the form of the personal.

A question which naturally arises out of this discussion of the way in which the Other agent can be 'known' in his transcendence, which is his action, is to what extent the Other thereby retains his freedom in his

---

[33]The fact that Macmurray does say that 'God, therefore, as the infinite Agent is immanent in the world which is his act, but transcendent of it', *ibid.*, p. 223, confuses the issue. Macmurray has obviously taken over the language of transcendence and immanence from the philosophical tradition which he has already criticized as being fundamentally dualistic and applied the concepts to his assertion that God is an Agent, and presumably is to be known within the structure of the personal which has already been given. From the standpoint of the practical, which is Macmurray's presupposition, the act of the Other agent *is* his self-transcendence. The agent can only transcend his previous action (which is now his past) by further action. He cannot be transcendent over his own action without acting, which is what Macmurray appears to suggest is the case with God.

action. If the Other agent becomes a constituent dimension of the unitary
reality of self-existence, can this 'transcendence' of the Other really be
preserved? Here we discover a second dimension to the form of the
personal as Macmurray develops it which further clarifies this point.
'The freedom of any particular agent', says Macmurray, 'depends upon
his knowledge of the Other, and this knowledge is problematic....
Again, his freedom of action will depend upon the adequacy of his
knowledge: ...'[34] 'This problematic,' Macmurray continues, 'is in terms
of the distinction between reality and illusion, between "real" and "unreal".'[35] While the 'I do' is the primary certainty of self-existence, because
it is the reality of existence constituted by the reality of the Other, and
not merely the reality of existence which is determined through thought,
what the Other is and *what* I am remain problematical.[36] When the
Other is discriminated through action, or in the sphere of the practical
rather than the theoretical, the knowledge of the Other as well as the
knowledge of oneself constituted in that action, can never be an infallible
judgment on the part of the agent as a thinking subject. That is, the
reality of existence at the practical level is problematical to the agent
in his individuality. The thought, as well as the act, of the agent may
be 'wrong', that is, not according to the reality of the Other. In which case,
upon further reflection (this is withdrawal for the sake of movement
towards the other in reality), the self as Agent carries out a modified
intention into action seeking to know the Other in truth.[37] One could say
that this is the 'desire to be disillusioned'. It is, as Macmurray has already
said, 'the core of rationality', for it is the capacity to love objectively in
terms of the Other.

It is the problematic in the form of the personal which preserves the
freedom of transcendence in the action, while at the same time, providing
for the possibility of real 'disillusionment' and, thus, a truthful self-
existence in terms of the Other. For, if self-existence were not problematical, but matter of fact, and as such, an already determined reality,
the self would be constituted by its individuality rather than by its community with the Other. It is doubtful whether community could then
be achieved, for there would be no possibility, or at least no need of,
change, and thus, no real modification of the self by the action of the
Other. In a certain sense, at least, the capacity to love is the capacity to
place the Other within the reality of self-existence in such a way that
real modification occurs for each.[38]

[34]*Ibid.*, p. 166. [36]*Ibid.*, pp. 209, 210.
[35]*Ibid.*, p. 170. [37]*Ibid.*, p. 113.
[38]'To act, then, as the essential unity of these two freedoms is to modify the
Other by intention. To this we add that since the agent is part of the Other, he
cannot modify the Other without modifying himself, or know the Other without
knowing himself. In determining the future for the Other he also determines his

Again, we can see that the place of the problematic in the rationale for a reality of personal existence makes a helpful contribution to an understanding of a rationale for historical transcendence. For, if the transcendence of God, and thus his reality, is fully given in his inter-action with man at the historical level, God has made himself accessible while at the same time preserving his freedom. The revelation of God never becomes a 'matter of fact' to the extent that there is no longer any problematic involved in knowing him as personal reality. It is the 'problematic of the personal' which serves, not so much to 'protect' God from being at the disposal of man, as to give man a future as well as a past. The problematic, then, is not an uncertainty built into the structure of reality, a metaphysical puzzle with no certain solution, but is, rather, the structure of reality itself which draws man as individual into the fullness of personal existence. It is the act of the Other which *reveals* to us our own reality as well as the reality of the Other, so that one could say that *revelation* is the inner rationality of the problematic of the personal.

If the question is asked: is the form of the personal problematical for God as well?—an answer can only be suggested in terms of revelation. Does the act of a human person constitute revelation for God? It would hardly seem that this would be the case. While our actions can be said to be our 'transcendence' of God,[39] and as such, a revealing of our in-tentions towards him, this may not be a revelation to God of something

own future.' *Ibid.*, p. 166. This raises the theological question as to what ex-tent, if any, God is modified by his act of loving and knowing man. If the form of the personal as Macmurray develops it is strictly followed as a model for our understanding of the nature of God, there would be little choice but to say that God is modified in his act of love for man. What modification means here is, of course, the crucial question. There seems to be sufficient grounds in the Incarnation to allow this to be said, as long as it is understood that the modification is not a matter of correcting any 'error' on the part of God's intention towards man, nor a matter of making up any deficiency on his part. The concept of the passibility of God cannot be made a subject of this book, and so the question must be left open.

[39]When transcendence is understood as the action of an agent, one could say that inter-personal relation is the transcendence of each person by the other. It is in this sense that man can be said to 'transcend' God in personal relation. T. F. Torrance explains this further when he says: '... in both [the world of things and the world of persons] we are engaged in the rationality of acting in accordance of what is not-ourselves and enlarging our knowledge of it. In the world of persons, however, it is particularly with inter-personal transcendence that we are concerned, in which we distinguish ourselves from each other and communicate with each other. ... By meeting us and entering into dialogue with us through His Word the transcendent God creates space for our "transcendence" over against Him and at the same time creates between us and Himself the rational continuity in which reciprocity and communion can take place.' *God and Rationality*, pp. 156-157.

which he could not himself know.[40] It seems sufficient to say that if there is a problematic for man in terms of personal knowledge of God, there is a problematic to the relationship which is intrinsic to the Creator-creature relation. It is not necessarily man's problematic, or God's, but simply the structure of the relation itself. The important point to be gained from this, is the fact that the problematic of historical transcendence, as already developed, can now be shown to be supported by the rationale of the 'form of the personal' itself.[41]

We have briefly discussed two dimensions of the 'form of the personal' to see how a rationale for personal existence can provide a support for a rationale of historical transcendence. The first was the concept of individuality as the subordinate aspect of the reality of the personal, with the action of the person considered the primary aspect, and thus, the way in which 'self-transcendence' moves towards the other in action rather than withdrawing towards individuality. The second dimension was that of the problematic in the 'form of the personal' which constitutes the transcendence of the Other, and the Self, in a relation of 'concrete freedom', so that, while the 'revelation' of the Other becomes historical (it has a past), it also has a future reality.

There is a third dimension which should at least be mentioned here, for it provides a way of taking a somewhat more critical look at Macmurray's thesis, while at the same time, creating a transition to a more theological perspective in our consideration of the rationale for historical transcendence. This is the concept that the 'form of the personal' is a reli-

---

[40]This particular capacity of knowing what men reveal about their intentions seems to be attributed to Jesus by the Gospel of John: 'But Jesus did not trust himself to them, because he knew all men and needed no one to bear witness of man; for he himself knew what was in man.' John 2:24-25.

[41]This rationale of the 'form of the personal' which includes the problematic of knowing the other through the practical, reveals the basic metaphysical structure of reality itself. It is this structure to which I referred when I defined metaphysics as 'The problematic of the concrete man's bond with the absolute.' (see above, pp. xviiiff.). This is a metaphysic which cannot be reduced to the theoretical; for to abstract from action is to reduce the problematic to the single pole of thought, and breaks the bond between the absolute and concrete existence. This is a metaphysic which grounds knowledge in the absolute, but which also grounds existence in the problematic of the personal. The 'form of the personal' is an instrument for thinking the reality of God as the Other, but only when thought is subordinated to the problematic of concrete existence. It is a metaphysic which provides the 'way of disillusionment' for *both* faith and knowledge through the primacy of the practical. But, because the practical is also problematic, the absolute retains its freedom, and can never become a mere 'object' of discrimination for thought. The relation between this metaphysic, or this rationale of the 'form of the personal' and what has been called a 'natural theology', will become clear later in this chapter when the same rationale is thought through from a theological standpoint.

gious community of I and Thou.[42] The basic criticism which Macmurray levels at Kant, and at all systems of thought based on a dualism between the self as subject and the world as object, is that the form of *religious* experience involves the distinction between the first and second persons—between the I and the Thou. The validity of religious belief, says Macmurray, depends upon the validity of this form, 'Consequently, a philosophy which does not formally recognize the distinction between "I" and "You" cannot even formulate the religious problem.'[43] For the purpose of his systematic development of the 'form of the personal', Macmurray identifies the communal aspect of personal reality with the religious mode of reflection, and asserts that the religious mode is the original and most complete mode of experience, with the other two

---

[42]Macmurray's construction of the form of the personal along the lines of an I-Thou relation, obviously parallels the work of Buber and raises the question of Macmurray's dependence upon Buber. Because I was unable to locate any reference to Buber in Macmurray's works, I put the question to him in a personal interview. He responded by saying that he worked out his own concepts of the personal before reading Buber, but that he feels that both concepts are proceeding along similar lines. Macmurray added that Buber seemed to have approached the concept of the personal along poetic lines, while he (Macmurray) thought his own approach was more strictly philosophical. The strongest point of similarity between Buber and Macmurray would seem to be the way in which both define man in terms of relation with the Other, rather than in terms of individualism or organism. In making a distinction between Buber and Macmurray, one could point to Buber's emphasis on the 'between' as the place and 'bearer of what happens between men' (*Between Man and Man*, p. 245). But Macmurray places the emphasis on the act of reciprocity which constitutes both the self and the Other in reality. Buber also places 'feelings' in the category of that which man 'has', while love is what man 'does', or what occurs when man dwells in love (*I and Thou*, trans. Walter Kaufmann, T. & T. Clark, Edinburgh, 1970, p. 66), while Macmurray holds that feelings are rational in that they move through intention into action (*The Self as Agent*, pp. 196-197). Perhaps the most vital distinction between the two men would be in the way in which each relate the cognitive element of relation to the act of relating itself. Buber carries his concept of 'two-foldness' (that is, the 'I' of the I-Thou is different from the 'I' of the I-It) into personal relation in such a way that a cognitive awareness of the Other immediately changes the Thou into It, and thus makes the relation impersonal (cf. *I and Thou*, pp. 53-54, 69, 143). Macmurray, on the other hand, as we have shown above, shows that cognitive awareness of the Other can form a positive role in the act of relation; indeed, apart from this cognitive knowledge, an act of relating becomes blind activity. Macmurray seems to be of more help in attempting to work out a rationale of historical transcendence because of his concept of the relationship of the absolute to the concrete, rather than the mysterious 'between' which preoccupies Buber. On the other hand, one should take into account what Ronald Gregor Smith says: 'In an important sense, Buber may be said to be battling here for a new view of transcendence—for the reality of spirit in an age which has no notion, or only the most primitive notions, of what this cardinal reality means for the life of man.' *Martin Buber*, 'Makers of Contemporary Theology', The Carey Kingsgate Press, London, 1966, p. 28.

[43]*The Self as Agent*, p. 72.

modes, art and science, derived from the religious mode by a process of exclusion of attention. That is, by a limitation of attention in the reflective activity to the narrower dimensions of human experience.[44] The formal aspect of this division is not the primary concern of this discussion. What is more pertinent is the equation of religion with community.

In an earlier work, Macmurray has said that religion is unlimited because it is personal. 'It is the whole unity of reality gathered into the life of a person and so gathering into its own unity all the subordinate aspects of himself, ... religion reaches up to the full reality of knowledge, to the knowledge of God, ... because God is the unity of the whole.'[45] The equation between religion and community thus seems to coincide with the superimposing of the knowledge of God over the 'whole unity of reality', which, for Macmurray, is the basic structure of 'persons in relation'. The basic religious question for Macmurray is the question of a distinction between the real and the unreal. In searching for reality in religion, Macmurray was led on a personal pilgrimage from a highly experiential, though unreal, religious life, to a more concrete, and thus more real concept of religion as the original and essential community of persons in relation.[46]

> Now when we go back to the beginnings of human existence, we find only one form of reflection, and that form is religion, the others are contained in it; and in the course of social history they are gradually separated out, becoming independent and autonomous. But in the beginning there is only religion, ... human life is always life in common.... In reflection they are aware that they belong together in a personal unity; that all their activities are parts of the unity, and they rejoice in the awareness of it. This reflection is their religion. It sanctifies the common life and gives it meaning and purpose.[47]

Therefore, Macmurray can say that 'Religion ... is the reflective activity

[44]*Ibid.*, p. 188.

[45]*Reason and Emotion*, p. 192.

[46]Cf. *Search For Reality in Religion*, George Allen and Unwin, London, 1965, where Macmurray, in an autobiographical sketch (pp. 5-28), traces his own search for reality in religion from his early experiences as a Bible student in a strongly evangelistic home; as a candidate for the mission field in China in pre-university days; as a leader of a boys' Bible class; as an assistant evangelist to a tent mission in Aberdeenshire; as an officer in the Medical Corps in the First World War; and following that, as a convinced Marxist-Christian committed to rediscovering a non-idealist Christianity. The conclusion of this pilgrimage led him to join the Society of Friends after his retirement from University teaching. A fitting enactment of his basic concept that 'All meaningful knowledge is for the sake of action, and all meaningful action is for the sake of friendship.' *The Self as Agent*, p. 15.

[47]*Search for Reality in Religion*, pp. 30-31.

which expresses the consciousness of community; or more tersely, religion is the celebration of communion.'[48]

When we seek the connection between religion thus understood, and the concept of God, Macmurray simply says that the idea of God as a personal Other who stands in the same mutual relation to every member of the community is necessary to represent the unity of a community of persons. Thus, the universal Other is represented as the infinite Agent who stands within the 'form of the personal' as its universalized and unifying principle. There is, says Macmurray, 'an inherent logical necessity' for this representation.[49]

There are two things which need to be said at this point. First, the logical move by which Macmurray proceeds from the many agents in relation to the One Agent in relation to all, is a 'logical fallacy' according to the principle of logic, as we saw earlier.[50] While one cannot logically deny the existence of such an infinite Agent, related to all finite agents, neither can one logically assert such an existent. In our previous discussion of this point, it was shown that the assertion of the existence of God on this basis could only have a regulative effect as the guarantee of existential values, and that even the necessity of this representation was doubtful.

What Macmurray seems to have failed to do, and this leads us to the second thing to be said, is to give his basic rationale for the 'form of the personal' freedom to operate in a theological dimension. The reality of personal being is that which is constituted by the action of person as agent, transcending self-existence and *revealing* himself to the Other through action. What is conspicuous by its absence in Macmurray's attempts to relate his religious dimension of the personal to the reality of God is the concept of revelation as an act of God. If God is a personal Agent, as Macmurray seems to claim, whose universal intention leads to a universal action,[51] there should at least be a concrete and practical dimension of revelation in this action. But the only action which Macmurray recognizes of a religious nature is the action of co-humanity. 'Our human Being *is* our relations to other human beings and our value lies in the quality of these relations. Our relation to God is itself real only as it shows itself in our relation to our neighbours.'[52] The fact is, that even when the world is conceived as the act of God, Macmurray says that God is transcendent over his action,[53]—but this is unreality.

Our final judgment must be that the rationale which Macmurray

[48]*Persons in Relation*, p. 162.
[49]*Ibid.*, p. 164.
[50]See above, pp. 22f.
[51]*Persons in Relation*, p. 164.
[52]*Search For Reality in Religion*, p. 72.
[53]*Persons in Relation*, p. 223.

offers us in the 'form of the personal' is an adequate one, but that he failed to use it properly when he came to speak of the reality of God. The discovery of reality, as with the discovery of truth, is indeed a process of disillusionment, as Macmurray has already told us. It could well be that the identification of community with religion was an illusion which Macmurray found difficult to surrender. After a long pilgrimage, he had found what seemed to him to be a tangible reality—the basic communal reality of human existence. To say that this exists, apart from whether or not it is called religion, is just the first part of the process of disillusionment. The other part is to allow the revelation of God himself in his act through the person of Jesus Christ to confront us, to inform us in such a way that our intention is to interact with God's Spirit; and, thus, to begin to discover that the 'form of the personal' is also the 'form of the Spirit'.

But if it is to be a search for reality, one has the feeling that Macmurray will not be left behind. For he does have the 'desire to be disillusioned', and he has called God his Friend.[54]

2 'The Will to Belong—a Way of Believing'

Our believing is conditioned at its source
by our belonging.[55]

If there can be said to be a particular discipline of thought called theology, it must have as its primary intentionality the will to community with God. For with all thought, theological thought not excluded, the validity of thinking must find its place in the action of belonging. This is simply the nature of the case with reality as such.[56] Theology has to do with community with God, therefore theology is believing, and believing is belonging.

A theological rationale is, therefore, no different in form from a philosophical rationale, although there may be significant difference in content. The form of the rationale common to both philosophy and theology is the 'form of the personal'. The form of the personal is

---

[54]My criticism of Professor Macmurray is not entirely fair because he would be the first to state that his competence is primarily as a philosopher and not as a theologian (cf. *The Self as Agent*, p. 17). He has himself told me in a personal conversation that he has never attempted to think through the problem of the reality of God from a theological standpoint, but that if he were to do this, it would be from the standpoint of God as his friend.

[55]M. Polanyi, *Personal Knowledge*, p. 322.

[56]This is the proper assertion to make given the rationale of personal existence as presented in the first part of this chapter. 'Reality as such' is now taken to be the unity of all reality in the community of the personal, and therefore, it includes the realities of both art and science which are derived from 'reality as such' by a limitation of attention.

community, and the reality of community is belonging. The belonging-in-community constitutes the objective reality of love which extends into the self-consciousness of the individual and asks for commitment to community. This commitment is faith, and its rationale is the will to belong.

The commitment which moves the individual into community, and therefore into truth, is conditioned at its source by the evidences of the individual's truth-in-belonging. Thus, the commitment is rational, for it is the will to belong in truth. Because truth-in-belonging is problematical, for such is the rationale of the 'form of the personal', the evidences necessary to elicit commitment are both past and future. That is, the evidence which can be discriminated by taking thought lies in the ambiguity of history, while the evidence which can be determined through the act of commitment lies in the belonging itself. The belonging is future because it is personal and is determined in action, not by reflection. This act of commitment is called faith, not because it is blind, or has no need of thought, but because the act of commitment is the movement of the whole person, upon the ground of sufficient evidence, into the truth of belonging.[57] It is not the *kind* of evidence, but the sufficiency that elicits commitment.

Because it is a movement of the whole person, and of the person into wholeness, commitment involves both reflection and action. Or, better expressed, it involves action which includes reflection as a necessary constituent in the action. Action which is not informed through the intellect is blind activity, even though it be a response to an external stimulus. The commitment must be on the basis of transcendent grounds, that is, evidences upon which the person moves towards the reality of the Other. The transcendence of the Other can be determined through the reflective aspect of action as the 'history of transcendence', or, one

[57]In a too-little known and too-little appreciated book (*Christian Commitment*, Macmillan, New York, 1957), Edward John Carnell works out a rationale for faith along similar lines using Kierkegaard's dictum that thought must yield to action for one to exist in the truth. It is from Carnell that I have taken the concept of commitment to express the act by which person moves into community, or becomes fully person in community. The univocal point between God and man, Carnell asserted, is love, not thought. This love is expressed as a law of life which binds the person into a community of truth by his very existence. It is the 'moral self-acceptance' of this community of truth which provides the individual with knowledge necessary to enter into fellowship with God through a commitment. This is the 'third method of knowing' which informs the will and demands commitment to God by a response of love (pp. 24ff). Faith he defined as 'a resting of the mind in the sufficiency of the evidences'. p. 76. In a later book (*The Case For Orthodox Theology*, The Westminster Press, Philadelphia, 1959), he was to say: 'When a person assents to truth, or when he believes in an object, he commits *part* of himself. This is general faith. But when he trusts another person, he commits the *whole* of himself. This is vital faith. Fellowship is a union of life with life. The essence of one person passes into that of another.' p. 30.

could say, historical transcendence. Therefore, the Other must have a history, a past, which satisfies the reflective dimension of action. One could say that the Other must have a transcendence which endures as well as acts, otherwise the transcendence of the Other would be sheer contingency, and inaccessible for reflection. However, while commitment as an act of belonging has possibility because the transcendence of the Other informs the act through a reflective determination of a *past*, or historical transcendence, it only becomes a real commitment when belonging is determined through action out of the *future*. Difficult as it is to conceive of transcendence bringing a dimension of future reality to bear upon the act of commitment, it must be made clear that an act of an agent, as Macmurray pointed out, is an act which determines the future, otherwise, it is not an act. But believing is conditioned at its source by belonging, which is only another way of saying that community has its own transcendence through the existence of the Other, the reality of belonging 'comes to meet us' in the act of belonging.[58] This also constitutes a form of 'evidence' which provides transcendent grounds for commitment. It seems that intrinsic to the 'form of the personal', there is a transcendence of what one might call 'spirit', the immediacy of the Other in the most personal sense. To call this 'future' is only a way of making a distinction between spirit and history, or, between the personal and the impersonal, within the metaphysic of the 'form of the personal'. I suggest that we leave it at this for the present while proceeding to show the two-fold function of transcendence in providing the grounds for commitment in terms of basic human relations.

When the person moves into the truth of community where other human beings are involved, some evidences which are of an historical nature are involved. The person, or persons, to whom one makes a commitment must have demonstrated or revealed their own intentions towards the one considering commitment. These evidences are ambiguous in and of themselves because they now lie in history and constitute the 'past'. What the other has done or said is now, in a sense, public evidence of an historical nature. However, it can inform the will to belong and provide transcendent grounds for the commitment, and as such, can serve to place the possibility of communion with the Other

---

[58]This language reminds us again of Heidegger, who liked to speak of encounter with Being itself as 'an encounter fleeing into unmasked presence'. *Essays in Metaphysics*, p. 57 (also, see above, p. 30). Unfortunately, Heidegger's anti-metaphysical ontology reduces this encounter to sheer contingency, and thus to the point of blind activity under the mask of poetry. It seems to me that the two dimensions of contingency (spirit) and enduring (history) are both dimensions of transcendence, so that the transcendence of spirit which 'comes to meet us' in the act or the encounter is rooted in the transcendence of the word which already has its existence in history. But this is by way of anticipation. The relation of Word to Spirit as transcendence lies ahead of us.

in perspective. These evidences of an historical nature, are the evidences
that an 'Other' exists, or has existed, and in this sense provide transcendent grounds. For they point to an agent who has acted, and thus to a
reality extrinsic to the self. But, without the future impinging upon the
will to commitment in the form of an immediate encounter of a personal
nature, no commitment is possible because the evidences which lie in
history have no future in and of themselves. A person can leave evidences
of being trustworthy scattered around, but must *be there* as a person for
a commitment to be consummated in belonging. In this case too, transcendent grounds must be there of a personal or future nature. For
example, if I discovered the letters of another person, and even voice
recordings which contained the evidences of love expressed towards me,
I could *intend* a response and so seek relationship. But, if I was also
subsequently informed that the other person was no longer alive, but, was
in fact dead, I could still *think* about the evidences of that person's love,
but could not experience a relationship. An act towards that person is
now impossible—there is no future. And while there are transcendent
grounds on which one can reflect, there are no transcendent grounds on
which to act.

This, then, is the form which the rationale for belonging-in-community
takes. The will to belong is conditioned by the evidences of belonging,
and if they are sufficient, acts through commitment, and this is believing.
When we speak of a theological rationale, therefore, we mean the same
by way of form, but know immediately that we are speaking of community in the reality of God. What is more difficult in this case, and
the difficulty is so extreme that many are tempted to seek a different
rationale, is that the reality of God seems to be so unlike the kind of
reality which is constituted by our space-time dimension of the personal.
But it is just at this point that we need to bring together the rationale of
historical transcendence as it has been exposed most clearly through
the Incarnation, particularly through a kenotic understanding of transcendence, and the rationale of the 'form of the personal', which we have
already asserted to be the same.[59]

---

[59]One could, I suppose, speak of a 'natural' theology at this point. For there
is a correspondence between the 'form of the personal' which is constitutive of
personal existence and historical transcendence. However, because there is a
problematic involved in both, whatever this means in terms of a 'natural' theology,
it does not mean that man can proceed from the form of the personal to fellowship
with God. It does mean, that the total of what we might call 'natural' reality
is constituted by the reality of God, and, therefore, an intrinsic rationale exists
between a created and an uncreated reality. It has been the making of this rationale
into a 'religious *a priori*' that raised such a storm of protest (e.g., Karl Barth)
against natural theology. When the rationale between created and uncreated
reality is accepted with its problematic, it does not seem that Barth's objections
have the same force.

Historical transcendence, as we have said, has as its basic rationale a double movement which is constituted by a third; that is, it is trinitarian in structure. The double movement is revealed through the Incarnation. First, there is the movement of the eternal Son in a relationship of reciprocity with the Father, with the Son utterly conditioned by history and by humanity. He is as the Son to the Father, not only truly man, but estranged man. This we called the *intra*-active transcendence of God, but it is now a transcendence which is historical *without* becoming an extra-trinitarian act. There is also a movement of *inter*-active transcendence by which the Spirit causes community with God to impinge immediately upon humanity and thus opens up man to his future with God in a way that makes belief possible. Here the historical transcendence of the Son is the history of the Spirit, and the immediacy of the Spirit brings the person of the Son to community with man. But the will to belong issues from the Father, and it is this 'belonging' which conditions our believing at its source.

Now it is significant at this point to see how the rationale of historical transcendence is similar in structure to the rationale of the 'form of the personal'. The structure of community as revealed through the Incarnation has both Word and Spirit which complete the Father's will to belong. The Word, as the eternal Son to the Father, revealed, in a completely historical life, not only the will of the Father to love, but the response of the Son as servant through human history. It was the nature of this kenotic act on the part of the Son to make the transcendence of God historical, that is, accessible to reflection as entity, and yet problematical. The 'evidence' of the Son, even to his contemporaries, was not itself sufficient for the will to believe.[60] It is the very nature of the case that transcendence is now historical, but also problematical and ambiguous in itself. Here we see the correspondence between the 'form of the personal', where the evidences at the historical level were necessary but insufficient, and the historical transcendence of the Son of God. A revelation that is 'dead' has no future, and a transcendence that is merely historical has no life.

But we can also see a correspondence in the transcendence of the Spirit which brought the future of God—a living Christ—directly impinging upon the humanity of the first disciples. And then they became believers. Their faith was the commitment of their individual persons into the truth-of-belonging. It was the living person of Christ revealed through the Spirit that made the historical transcendence of the Son the grounds for fellowship with God. The rationale for the belonging to the

[60]Cf. Matthew 16:17: 'And Jesus answered him, "Blessed are you, Simon Bar-Jona! For flesh and blood has not revealed this to you, but my Father who is in heaven".'

community of God is the same as the rationale for the belonging to the community of man. It is only through the historical transcendence of the Incarnation that we discover the trinitarian structure of this rationale. The community which God enjoys within his own reality of being is thus the image in which man is created in community.

The two strands of historical transcendence then can be said to produce revelation and community, constituted in Word and Spirit, and they come together in the act of believing worship by which the communion of God is celebrated. But this is to anticipate, and raises questions which can only be dealt with in the final part of this book.

A positive theology of the reality of God through the rationale of historical transcendence now seems possible. As a very minimum of such a theology, an account must be given of the revelation of God which 'places' man into the truth of belonging to God. And by revelation is simply meant the act of God by which his reality is known to be a community of belonging which produces, correspondingly on the part of man, faith. The rationale of historical transcendence has taught us that there is a double movement in the revelatory act of God which is constituted by a third. That is, the movement of the Word to become flesh and the Spirit to become community both constitute the one movement of God the Father. If the historical transcendence of God seems to be revealed through the life of the Son, we would expect a particular aspect of the revelation of God to be determined in this act. In the person of Jesus Christ, the eternal Word became an entity within the history of man, haveable and graspable by man. His words, once spoken, could not be taken back. His life became public—his person was united with his actions. The reality of God now becomes a transcendence which is *there* for man.

As distinct from the Spirit, the Word *became* historical, and thus has a past as well as a future. The eternal Word spoke 'words' and initiated actions which became public, and, therefore, determined by reflective activity. In the person of Jesus Christ, the Word and the 'words' were inseparable. That is to say, for his contemporaries, his words and actions were problematical in themselves, and therefore led directly to the living Word as person. As was said by the people of the Samaritan village, 'It is no longer because of your words that we believe, for we have heard for ourselves, and we know that this is indeed the Saviour of the world.'[61] In this case, the words and the actions of Jesus, even 'second hand', served as one 'pole of transcendence' to place them in the truth, but only as they reflected upon the testimony concerning him, and allowed this to inform their intention to seek him out for a direct encounter. The

[61]John 4:42.

other 'pole of transcendence' in this case, was the living presence of his person.[62] What we might call the public, or historical past of Jesus' life had an indispensable function in the encounter. The words of the woman who had directly witnessed the words of Jesus became part of the revelation of his person, and thus carried an authority which had an 'absolute extrinsicality', to use Bonhoeffer's phrase.[63] The authority which these words of witness to Christ conveyed was derivative of his own person, and conditioned by the ambiguity of all historical words and acts, but nonetheless, constituted a pole of transcendence, and as such, a revelation of the reality of Christ. Here we see at work the operative principle for the formation of a larger body of witness to Jesus which became the Scriptures of the New Testament.

The second 'pole of transcendence', represented by the living person of Christ, came to be transferred to the Spirit as the time for the death of Christ approached. A revelation that is 'dead', as I have said earlier, has no future, but it does have a past, even as it had when it had a living present. The Spirit who was to come, however, would not have his own history, his own past, but would bring the reality of Christ, and thus the reality of God, to the future. 'When the Spirit of truth comes, he will guide you into all the truth; for he will not speak on his own authority, but whatever he hears he will speak, and he will declare to you the things that are to come. He will glorify me, for he will take what is mine and declare it to you.'[64] It is important to see here that the transcendent grounds for the Spirit's relation to man was the historical life of the Son. The Spirit's witness to Christ was placed with that of the disciples: '... he will bear witness to me; and you also are witnesses because you have been with me from the beginning.'[65] Again, on the day of Pentecost, Peter's interpretation of the manifestation of the Spirit was grounded in the historical life of Jesus of Nazareth, 'a man attested to you by God with mighty works and wonders and signs which God did through him in your midst, as you yourselves know— ... this Jesus, ... you crucified and killed by the hands of lawless men.'[66] Again I wish to emphasize the fact that the transcendent grounds for the testimony of Spirit was the historical life of Jesus, and apart from these grounds, a

---

[62]It is Bonhoeffer who makes the helpful suggestion that one is 'placed' between 'transcendent poles' by the reality of Christ: 'In faith Christ is the creator of my personal being and at the same time the Lord "with reference to" which— ἐιζ αυτόν —the person is created; thus existence is determined both prospectively and retrospectively in relation to transcendence: it "is" between transcendent poles.' *Act and Being*, p. 141.

[63]*Ibid.*, p. 138.

[64]John 16:13-14.

[65]John 14:26-27.

[66]Acts 2:22, 23.

claim to be inspired by the Spirit was not considered by the early Christian community to be valid.[67]

There is what we might call a 'kenotic' aspect to the rationale of historical transcendence which grounds revelation in the pole of conditioned, finite, historical existence as well as in the pole of unconditioned, eternal, future existence. It is this rationale which sets forth what can be called an inner logic to a doctrine of Scripture as revelation. If we exclude, for the time being, in what way the reality of the Spirit may also be said to be a revelation of God, we can consider the way in which historical transcendence as the particular act of the Son constitutes revelation. It is here that the rationale for the transcendence of God through the historical person of Jesus Christ must come to terms with the rationale of Scripture as the revelation, and thus the historical transcendence of God. This will immediately raise the ghost of so-called 'propositional revelation' for some, where saving faith is defined as a rational assent to the words of Scripture instead of a personal commitment to the living Word. Those who reject propositional aspects of revelation, protest that the equation of the living Word with the written word reduces revelation to a purely subjective act of rational belief and destroys the power of the Word to encounter the one who reads or hears the word with the reality of God.[68] In its highest sense, propositional revelation

[67]This assertion, as a generalization, does not claim that every reference in the New Testament to a manifestation of the Spirit is directly grounded in the historical life of Christ, but that as a general principle, the Spirit is correlated with the historical life of the Son. For example, this is true of the greater share of the passages in the book of Acts in which proclamation takes place (cf. Acts 2:22-36; 3:11-26; 8:34-36; 10:34-48; 13:16-41). Also, one can see this in the correspondence between the manifestation of the Spirit and the 'name' of Christ (cf. Acts 4:30-31; 19:5-6); and it can also be found in Paul's identification of the Spirit as the Spirit of Christ (cf. Romans 8:8; II Corinthians 3:17; Philippians 1:19). A negative test for the reality of the Spirit is given in I John 4:2ff, where every spirit which does not confess that Jesus Christ has come in the flesh is not of God. On the other hand, the attempt to work the power of God by invoking the name of Christ without the Spirit is not only fruitless, but a little humorous, as the 'seven sons of Sceve' found out: 'But the evil spirit answered them, "Jesus I know, and Paul I know; but who are you?" ' (Acts 19:13-15).

[68]Gregor Smith, who was strongly influenced by Bultmann at this point, made a distinction between the Word of God and the words of the Bible taken as any form of propositional revelation: 'Consideration of the Bible as the Word of God enables us to focus more clearly upon the meaning of God's historical action in Christ. Christ as the Word is God in action. Neither the words of the Bible, taken in isolation from Christ, nor any theophany, can replace the historical action. This historical action is God's redemptive action in Christ. ... The historical Word is not just a piece of past history, nor an externalized observable series of dramatic acts, so called "redemptive history". But it makes a present demand upon you, ... This means that the Word is not the Word by itself, but only when it is heard by you in your situation.' 'Introduction to Theology—Outline to the Course', *Collected Papers*, p. 4.

simply means that the Scripture constitutes the Word of God in its power to communicate as well as command the truth of God to man.[69] What is at stake in giving up that which a concept of propositional revelation seeks to preserve is the pole of transcendence which we have said lies in history and thus can serve to inform the act of faith 'in the Spirit' of its transcendent grounds in the person of Christ. Historical transcendence itself is at stake here, because if the cognitive link with the *content* of God's transcendence as historical act is broken, the act of faith must supply its own content to the divine Word. This 'pole' of divine transcendence which lies in the historical person of Christ can only be revelatory as it informs faith of its transcendent grounds— thus Scripture has the quality of transcendence only in its cognitive link with the ontic reality of God's historical transcendence. In this case, the ontic and the noetic can relate to each other without a human anthropology being inserted between the two. However one re-defines propositional revelation to avoid the distorting element of 'rationalism' (which is itself the insertion of an anthropology), this is the concept which must be preserved. T. F. Torrance, while carefully avoiding the implications of propositional revelation, attempts to state the case for the place of Scripture in a double sense, both above the Church, and thus transcendent of the words of man, but also in history, and thus subject to the limitations of all human finitude:

> As such the Holy Scripture, like the Apostolate, stands with sinners and among sinners, and belongs to the sphere where salvation is bestowed. That gives us the peculiar problem of Holy Scripture and its peculiar place. Holy Scripture is assumed by Christ to be his instrument in conveying revelation and reconciliation, and yet Holy Scripture belongs to the sphere where redemption is necessary. The Bible stands

[69]An example of this concept of propositional revelation is articulated with his typical lucidity by Edward Carnell: 'Therefore, in the one act of reading Scripture, we meet Christ in two complementary ways. *First*, we confront Christ's person. "By this we know that we abide in him and he in us, because he has given us of his own Spirit." (I John 4:13). *Secondly*, we receive a propositional revelation of Christ's will. "In many and various ways God spoke of old to our fathers by the prophets; but in these last days he has spoken to us by a Son." (Hebrews 1:1-2). These two elements cannot be separated without offending the unity of revelation.' *The Case for Orthodox Theology*, p. 34. Carnell goes on to show how Orthodox theology is often tempted to misuse the concept of propositional revelation: 'Since orthodoxy defends the plenary inspiration of Scripture, it is always tempted to make propositional revelation an end in itself. Whenever it yields to this temptation, it offends its own presuppositions. Propositional revelation is an instrumental value; it is designed to bring us into fellowship with Jesus Christ.' *Ibid.*, p. 48. My own position is quite close to this, but I think that it can be stated with more compelling logic from the standpoint of historical transcendence, and with less danger of incorporating the temptation into the concept.

above the Church, speaking to the Church the very Word of God, but the Bible also belongs to history which comes under the judgment and the redemption of the Cross. That double place of Holy Scripture must always be fully acknowledged, else we confound the word of man with the Word of God, and substitute the Apostles in the place of Christ.[70]

One can appreciate the efforts of Professor Torrance to maintain both the authority and the humanity of Scripture; but I am not so sure that it can be done by giving the Scripture both a transcendent and an immanent relation to man, and thus separating its transcendence from its historicity. For the problem of how one determines when it is 'above the Church' and when it is merely 'under the judgment of the Cross' introduces a position which is on a higher level, but on the same scale as that of Gregor Smith: that is, it can only be determined by how one 'hears it in his situation'.[71] Through our exploration of the rationale of historical transcendence, it seemed inescapably clear that the transcendence of God was most completely revealed when the eternal Son was under the judgment of the Cross. In Jesus, the word of man was the Word of God. And if this rationale is allowed to expose the rationale of Scripture, we would find that Scripture has this same 'kenotic' function within the rationale of historical transcendence.

This would mean that Scripture does not have the 'double place' of being existential and historical, but is the one pole of transcendence which confronts us completely as a revelation within history, with all the limitations and conditions which history imposed upon the eternal Word himself. But this means that the transcendence of Scripture, if one is going to recognize it as such at all, does not lie in the existential pole of the hearer, even though the hearer be 'informed' by the Spirit, but lies in the human and historical word of Scripture itself. Is this then an assertion of propositional revelation in the most rational sense? Not at all. Although I would nevertheless like to maintain that the transcendence of Scripture as revelation must be recognized and, as such, constitutes an indispensable and genuine pole of transcendence within which the reality of God places the believer.

---

[70]*Theology in Reconstruction*, Eerdmans, Grand Rapids, 1965, p. 138.
[71]See above, p. 212, n. 68. Cf. also, the essay by Professor Thomas A. Langford 'T. F. Torrance's Theological Science: a Reaction', *Scottish Journal of Theology*, Vol. 25, No. 22, May, 1972, pp. 155-170. Professor Langford says: 'The formal verification of theological statements, he [Torrance] states, is found through their conformity with biblical revelation. This leads to a most important matter and one with which Torrance does not adequately deal, namely the exact nature of biblical revelation. He appears to remain susceptible to the problem Hermann Diem revealed in Barth's method and remains in need of developing his biblical hermeneutic.' p. 162.

In asserting the transcendence of Scripture at the historical level, one thing must be kept in mind: that which is historical is past and, as such, can only be determined by reflection; therefore, it constitutes the subordinate and negative part of the act of faith. Negative in the sense that, by abstracting from the act of belonging itself, the transcendence of Scripture considered as an entity upon which one reflects, does not constitute an act of faith in the personal sense. Again, some will not like the subordinate position which this appears to give to Scripture, despite the fact that Scripture is at the same time recognized to be revelation in the propositional sense, as I think one is forced to say. But it should be immediately remembered that the subordination is not to the reason, nor even to the will of man, but to the other pole of transcendence, which is the Spirit. That is, it is only negative when one abstracts from the reality of a living Word; as a constituent part of the act of belonging to Christ, it is positive, though subordinate, in the way that history is always subordinate to the future.[72]

This subordination of Scripture as transcendence is perfectly in

---

[72]'The essent [*Das Seiende*] is disclosed in the logos as gathering. This is first effected in language. Consequently the logos becomes the essential determinant of discourse. Language—what is uttered and said and can be said again—is the custodian of the disclosed essent. What has once been said can be repeated and passed on. The truth preserved in it spreads, and in the process the essent originally gathered and disclosed is not each time experienced for itself. In the transmission the truth detaches itself as it were from the essent. This can go so far that the repetition becomes a mere babbling by rote, a *glōssa*. Statement is always exposed to this danger.... Logos in the sense of discourse and utterance becomes the realm and the scene of decision concerning the truth, i.e. originally, the unconcealment of the essent and hence its being.' M. Heidegger, *An Introduction to Metaphysics*, pp. 185-186. Heidegger is showing us here how 'propositional' revelation in the form of the 'statement' of the logos as the gathering of 'unconcealment' (*aletheia*) runs the danger of being detached from the 'truth of being' and becoming a standard of 'correctness'. 'Truth that was originally unconcealingment, a happening of the dominant essent itself, governed by gathering, now becomes an attribute of the logos.' (*Ibid.*, p. 186). It is this 'shift' in the locus of truth in revelation which is the temptation in propositional revelation. For to say something 'correctly' about God is not thereby to know him. It is for this reason that I maintain that revelation becomes propositional as disclosure (for language is the 'custodian of the disclosed essent'), but that it is subordinate to the act of Spirit by which the 'logos' becomes being, that is, 'emerges-into-unconcealment' *through* the propositional statements. What Heidegger does not consider is the fact that correctness is a *functional* necessity in revelation, if not a logical one. The testimony of the Samaritan woman to Jesus had to have a certain intrinsic genuineness to it, otherwise her neighbours would only have been led astray and into confusion, and would not have 'heard for themselves' (John 4:42). One cannot, therefore, separate the credibility of Scripture (its intrinsic genuineness) from its power of disclosure in an existential sense. Here certainly lies the fundamental source for a doctrine of the 'inerrancy' of Scripture, although I should myself prefer to speak of its genuineness and, therefore, its trustworthiness as the pole of historical transcendence.

keeping with the intra-divine transcendence itself as revealed in the Incarnation. The eternal Son revealed through the *kenosis* a subordination, in the positive sense, of divine Sonship to all the conditions of history and humanity, a subordination which was at the same time constitutive of his eternal Sonship with the Father. To 'know' Jesus at the level of his human, historical existence, was to be confronted with the transcendence and the reality of God. In him, the two poles of of transcendence coincided, so that one could both 'know' and 'belong' in fellowship with him. But the limitations of this were fully accepted by Jesus, and ought to be obvious to us. 'It is to your advantage that I go away', Jesus told his disciples, 'for if I do not go away, the Counsellor will not come to you; but if I go, I will send him to you.'[73] It was for the sake of 'belonging' that Jesus accepted and fulfilled his incarnate life of love. The belonging is the future, because it is conditioned at its source by the reality of God. Through the Incarnation, the eternal Word has conditioned our belonging to God at the historical level. This is the 'once and for all' dimension of God's redemptive love, for it has brought transcendence under the terms of flesh and under the judgment of the Cross. Without this pole of transcendence, there would be no hope of belonging, because our humanity, and our history, would not be conditioned at its source by the transcendence of God. Therefore, it is the Scripture as the revelation of historical transcendence which 'places' us in the life of the Spirit, which is the other pole of transcendence.

Despite the obvious limitations of using such expressions as the two 'poles of transcendence', which, like all figures of speech, must be respected for their limitations as well as for their usefulness, I have chosen to follow Bonhoeffer here in seeking to ground transcendence in an historical reality which is extrinsic to my own existence. Where I take issue with Bonhoeffer is when he makes the sociological community, instead of Scripture, the embodiment of revelation, and thus, the pole of historical transcendence. Without reviewing the exposition of Bonhoeffer's thought which occupied us in Chapter III, we can nevertheless quickly grasp the situation with regard to Bonhoeffer's view of revelation. Bonhoeffer accepted the thesis of Karl Barth that man is placed into the truth by the sheer truth of revelation, and not through any capacity, potential, or effort on his own part. What Bonhoeffer could not accept in Barth, was his view that revelation was totally contingent to man as an act of God, and thus, had no ontological existence itself. Bonhoeffer suspected that this view of Barth's had traces of 'transcendentalism' in it, that is, God recedes constantly from the sphere of the historical (*geschichtlich*) into non-objectivity.[74] Bonhoeffer attempted to counter this with the

---

[73]John 16:7.
[74]*Act and Being*, pp. 81, 82.

argument that revelation could be both transcendent and historical if it was embodied in the sociological entity called the Church—that is, Christ existing as community.

The three basic assumptions of Bonhoeffer's thought tend to support this argument: (1) the intrinsic coherence of the reality of Creator and creation is concretized in community; (2) the normative character of basic ontic relationships; and (3), God is identical with himself in his revelation.[75] For Bonhoeffer, revelation as the reality of God's presence in the world has a Christian sociology of its own. Christ is the corporate subject of the community; this means that the 'being of revelation' in an ontological sense, has objectivity as well as transcendence. The other members of the community constitute the objectivity, or the historicity of revelation, while the person of Christ constitutes the transcendent subject who is identified with the community itself. What Bonhoeffer specifically rejects is the idea that revelation has a past:

> The being of revelation does not lie in a unique occurrence of the past, in an entity which in principle is at my disposal and has no direct connection with my old or my new existence, neither can the being of revelation be conceived solely as the ever-free, pure and non-objective act which at certain times impinges on the existence of individuals. No, the being of revelation 'is' the being of the community of persons, constituted and embraced by the person of Christ, wherein the individual finds himself to be already in his new existence.[76]

Because Bonhoeffer identifies 'being' with revelation, and because he asserts that 'being' always transcends entity, revelation transcends entity as such, and can only be discovered in the 'extrinsicality' of the personal 'thou' of community. An entity, that which is past, and therefore an object of reflection, can never be extrinsic to man; therefore, the Scripture is not revelation because it is entity—it is non-extrinsic and non-transcendent of existence.[77] The Bible belongs to the 'remembered happenings of the Christian community', and as such, is entity, and the object for reflection on the part of the community—this reflection is theology.[78]

What Bonhoeffer fears the most, is that revelation will be delivered into the power of the human subject, either through a static ontology which institutionalizes revelation and thus puts the authority of revelation under the authority of the 'I', or through a transcendentalism which dis-objectivizes revelation and, accordingly, places its authority

[75]See above, pp. 77ff.
[76]*Act and Being*, p. 123.
[77]*Ibid.*, pp. 132, 138, 139.
[78]*Ibid.*, pp. 143, 144.

also under the 'I'. In either case, revelation does not stand extrinsic to the human subject.[79] The alternative for Bonhoeffer was to equate the living Word, the person of Christ, with the believing community and out of this context create his 'two poles of transcendence'. However, the one pole of transcendence was constituted by the objective and sociological transcendence of one person over and against the other, while the second pole was constituted by the contingent act of Christ 'existing as community'.[80] This constitutes, for Bonhoeffer, historical transcendence; and while it is true that he came to abandon his earlier concept of the sociological structure of Christ existing as community, he simply moved this pole of transcendence out into the world.[81] The deeper into the world he could place this pole of transcendence, the more historical he could make the person of Christ.

That which Bonhoeffer failed to see, and this may have been hidden from him by his Lutheran Christology, was the fact that *both* poles of transcendence must be rooted in the person of Christ. What Bonhoeffer sought to make historical, had already become historical through the Incarnation. That is, the revelation of God was not a contingency of pure act united with humanity, but was the act and therefore the history of the eternal Word as the person Jesus Christ. What Bonhoeffer has done is to take a transcendence of pure contingency (Barth) and join it to a transcendence of co-humanity (Dilthey) using faith as the operative mode of being.[82] But the transcendence of co-humanity provides only a *form* into which the transcendence of God as pure act can be poured. We are left with an unresolved 'Kenotic' problem in Bonhoeffer's historical transcendence which cannot be solved on the terms which he established. Thus, in its own way, the debate on Bonhoeffer has tended to follow the lines of the earlier kenotic controversies.

Applying the rationale of historical transcendence as it has been worked out through an exploration of the *kenosis*, Bonhoeffer's placing of the historical pole of transcendence in co-humanity is shown to

[79]*Ibid.*, pp. 108ff.
[80]*Ibid.*, pp. 140, 141.
[81]See above, pp. 75-77, where I have shown how this shift occurred in Bonhoeffer's thought.
[82]Cf. *Act and Being*, p. 43. Also: 'The being of revelation, the Christ-communion, is only in faith. Faith knows that revelation is independent of it. These two propositions must combine to make a third: only in faith does man know that the being of revelation, his own being in the Church of Christ, is independent of faith. There is continuity of revelation, continuity of existence, only in faith, but there again in such a way that faith *qua* believing is suspended only in "faith *qua* being in the communion". If here faith were understood wholly as an act, the continuity of being would be disrupted by the discontinuity of acts. Since however faith as an act knows itself as the mode of being of its being in the Church, the continuity is indeed only 'in the believing' but thereby is really preserved as being in the Church.' *Ibid.*, p. 128.

be fundamentally wrong. For in the Incarnation a transcendence of God has been revealed that is itself historical, and as such, is extrinsic to co-humanity itself. What Bonhoeffer could not show, was an historical transcendence of God which was extrinsic to the historical community itself. If this is what he was seeking at the end in his concept of world-liness, and I am not all persuaded that this is the best interpretation of Bonhoeffer at this point,[83] then he was only enlarging the scope of the problem. One cannot create historical transcendence by 'historicizing' the person of Christ in community, or in the world. However historical this seems to make faith, it is not the transcendence of God with his own history. Only in Jesus Christ can one say that God has his own history with man apart from the history of any other human individual. The history of the person of Christ in community through the Spirit is, after all, a history of those who constitute the community.

The only possibility of a revelation of God as historical transcendence being extrinsic to man, even man in community, is that of Scripture as the Word of God. I therefore submit that Bonhoeffer's placing of revelation *exclusively* with community, and the stripping of Scripture of all revela-tory content, and thus, of transcendence, was a mistake. My reading of Bonhoeffer gives me the general impression that in practice, especially when he moved away from the sociological concept of the church, he *used* the Bible almost exclusively as the place of revelation. In this case I would say that his experience was more consistent with the rationale of historical transcendence than his theological (or perhaps one should say philosophical) presuppositions. Bonhoeffer seemed to look more and more away from community as the locus of revelation and towards the Bible.[84]

The principal argument for my assertion that the Scripture must be understood as the revelation of God in Christ, and thus as the transcen-dence of God which constitutes one pole for our believing and belong-ing, is that the evidence upon which faith moves, in both a past and

---

[83]See above, pp. 96ff.

[84]E. Bethge suggests that in the year 1936, Bohoeffer experienced a momentous inner revolution that could be likened to a conversion from being a theologian to being a Christian. During this period Bonhoeffer wrote a letter to his brother-in law Rüdiger Schleicher in which he said: 'Is it ... intelligible to you if I say I am not at any point willing to sacrifice the Bible as this strange word of God, that on the contrary, I ask with all my strength what God is trying to say to us through it? Everything outside the Bible has grown too uncertain to me. I am afraid of running only into a divine counterpart of myself. ... Also I want to say to you quite personally that since I have learnt to read the Bible in this way—and that does not date from such a very long time ago—it becomes more marvellous to me every day.... You will not believe how glad one is to find one's way back to these elementary things after wandering on a lot of theological side-tracks.' *Dietrich Bonhoeffer*, pp. 155-156.

future sense, must be the evidence which comes to us from the act of God himself. If there is to be an historical dimension to that evidence, and I would agree with Bonhoeffer that there must be, it must be evidence which is rooted in transcendence. That is, it must refer to that which is extrinsic to our own existence, even our existence in community. I would support that argument by appealing to the 'form of the personal', which places the reality of belonging in an act which *necessarily* includes a reflective activity directed towards and upon that act of the 'other' which is past, which is historical. Remembering that there is a problematic involved here, and that this 'revelation' of the Other does not constitute a real 'knowing' of the Other except as the Other gives himself to us in relation, one can assert the authority of Scripture as transcendent to human existence and as the one—and only—historical pole of divine transcendence. The only way that faith can be understood as an act of man as well as an act of God upon man, is that the reality of God be accessible to man in an historical reality. Far from Scripture then 'taking away' from man's act of faith by its transcendent authority, it alone makes possible a truly human act of faith. However, it must be immediately added that that which makes a human act of faith a reality in terms of faith in God, is the act of God in which man is brought into fellowship with divine love. This is what is meant when it is said that our believing is conditioned at its source by our belonging.

The question will of course arise, in what way can the theological writings of the Apostle Paul as an historical document be extrinsic to our existence in a way which the writings of Augustine or Karl Barth cannot? That is, what constitutes the uniqueness of the cannon of Scripture, which, admittedly, is a highly subjective and historically conditioned category? I think that it can be granted that the uniqueness of Scripture is not in the quality of its theological insight—not all would agree that Paul wrote 'better' theology than any modern theologian—but in whether or not historical transcendence is involved. If revelation is equated with God's transcendence of himself by concretely meeting man in history, and if the Incarnation is taken to be a complete act of transcendence, the revelation in terms of historical transcendence will have its locus in the Incarnation. As the eternal Word of God entered fully into human history, and into a specific human time and culture, it took shape within a context of interaction and response. That is, the Word acquired a history in which the verbal and written response became part of the transcendent act itself. This was in accordance with what had already been experienced in Israel's history and what we have called the inner logic of Incarnation.[85]

---

[85]Cf. here what T. F. Torrance says concerning what might be called a process of inscripturation in Israel's history with God: 'As the Word of God invaded

There would appear then, to be a centre of historical transcendence with a somewhat roughly defined boundary encompassing those events which were organic to the centre itself. The practical limit for the boundary of historical transcendence constituted in the Incarnation would then extend to the second or possibly third generation from the time of Jesus' life and death. At that point, the death of all living witnesses would mark the closing of the immediate context for the Incarnation itself. Those who would quickly point to the obvious ambiguity and uncertainty in delineating this boundary miss the point in their criticism. For the Incarnate One himself was subjected to constant misunderstanding and was no less ambiguous to his own contemporaries. The point is this: historical transcendence is just that— it is the transcendence, and thus, the reality of God, given within the limitations and ambiguities of historical existence. The question concerning the uniqueness of Scripture is the same question concerning the uniqueness of Christ—Who is the one who meets us in the history of Jesus of Nazareth? That question can only be finally answered, of course, through the commitment of faith which includes fellowship with this One. But the faith includes *both* 'poles of transcendence'—the historical as well as the personal.

Consider the alternative. Apart from Scripture, how can there be *any* pole of historical transcendence which is extrinsic to our human and co-human existence? This seems to account for the fact that, when Scripture is stripped of its revelatory content as historical transcendence, faith assumes grounds that are totally intrinsic to human experience. Even those grounds for faith which are placed in Spirit are intrinsic to experience and not extrinsic, for the Spirit has no history of his own. The transcendent ground for the Spirit is the revelation of the Word through the historical life of Jesus Christ. This means that in restricting revelation to the transcendence of God which becomes historical, the Scripture is uniquely revelatory because there was only one history to the historical transcendence of the Son of God. We may not be able to agree as to what that history is in its precise form as it comes to us in the Scripture, but we must agree that there is only

the social matrix of Israel's life, culture, religion and history, and clothed itself with Israel's language, it had to struggle with the communal meaning already embedded in it in order to assimilate it to God's revelation of Himself. For new understanding to take root with Israel, it had to take shape within Israel's language, and therefore it had to remould the inner structure of the society within which that language had its home and had to determine the whole history of Israel in its physical existence.... And so throughout Israel's tradition the Word of God kept pressing for articulation within the corporate medium of covenant reciprocity and progressively took verbal and even written form through the shared understanding and shared response that developed in this people.' *God and Rationality*, pp. 147-148.

one history because there was only one person named Jesus of Nazareth. In the Spirit, the same Jesus Christ is present to man today—but this is constituted by the other pole of transcendence. Here the future impinges directly upon us, and man's history now has new possibilities for living out of the transcendence of God. There is a history here too which includes transcendence, and also theological writings, but this is *not a new history of Christ*, but *a new history of man*. There can be no sense in which it is meaningful to say that God has a history through his act of Spirit with man in community, in the same sense as he had a history through the Son in the Incarnation. This is a fundamental point, and will become of further importance when we turn to consider transcendence through the life of the Spirit. Historical transcendence can only be that history of God which he has with man, not through man. Therefore, the distinction between Scripture and contemporary theological writing is not qualitative, but ontic.

This attempt to trace out the implications of historical transcendence for a doctrine of Scripture is, of course, elementary and tentative. Perhaps it shows the contribution which dogmatic theology can make towards the total field of biblical interpretation. Certainly, it indicates the rightful, if not the precise, place for dogmatic theology within the 'hermeneutical circle'.[86] The positive gains that come from a consideration of Scripture as the pole of historical transcendence in the total act of faith could be summarized as these:

(1) A genuine science of theology is made possible. The extrinsicality of God's revelation in Jesus Christ is assured through the pole of historical transcendence accessible in Scripture as the Word of God. Apart from this extrinsic transcendence at the historical level, theology inevitably leads to solipsism, that is, theological statements become expressions of one's own inner life. But because theology always has as its point of reference the transcendence of God, a true science of theology will also subordinate its reflection upon the historical grounds of God's transcendence (Scripture) to the living grounds—that is, to fellowship with God himself.

(2) A normative revelation is placed at the centre of the church, not above it. Historical transcendence stands at the centre of man's existence and thus limits and preserves that existence in truth. When the trans-

[86]For a discussion of the place of systematic theology in the 'hermeneutical circle', see the essay by Heinrich Ott, 'What is Systematic Theology?', *The Later Heidegger and Theology*, pp. 77-111. Ott, basing his position on the thought of the later Heidegger, seeks to ground hermeneutics in the transcendence of Being to *Dasein*, and thereby bring the existential hermeneutics of the Bultmann school closer to Barth. On the other hand, G. Ebeling seeks to ground hermeneutics in faith itself, and thus gives the Scripture a primarily Kergymatic function in awakening faith. See *The Nature of Faith*, The Fontana Library, Collins, London, 1967, pp. 31-43.

cendence of Christ as Lord of the church is not separated from the Bible as a human and historical document under the Cross, the church as an historical entity has the Word as an historical entity extrinsic to its own existence, while at the same time constitutive of it.

(3) The transcendent grounds for a 'lived transcendence' through the life of the Spirit are provided in the historical transcendence of the Word. The Scripture, as that pole of transcendence, grounds the life of the Spirit in that which is extrinsic to man's own histórical existence. While at the same time, a 'new man' is created whose own history is now opened up to the future of God. Between the poles of historical transcendence (Scripture as the Word of God) and personal transcendence (the indwelling Holy Spirit) there is 'lived transcendence'. This lived transcendence is expressed in the community which exists between man and God, and between man and man.

In bringing Part One to a conclusion, I suggested that historical transcendence was not punctiliar, but circular; and that there was a continued act of historical transcendence to be expected beyond the Incarnation. This I called 'closing the circle of transcendence'. This is the relationship which the 'secret discipline' has with the world.[87] There seems to be good reason now for making a slight modification in this concept in order to make a clear distinction between historical transcendence as the Incarnation, with its subsequent revelation in the Word of Scripture, and the life of the 'new man' in Christ who lives out the transcendence of the Spirit. It is well to understand that the believer in Christ and the Body of Christ to which he belongs does not constitute an extension of the Incarnation in any ontological sense, and that the historical transcendence of God in Christ, while constituting new life in Christ through the spirit, is not identical with that new life. That is, the Christian, though he stands in the world for Christ through the power of the Spirit, does not constitute the historical transcendence of God in the same way that Christ himself does. Therefore, I would now suggest that the term 'lived transcendence' more properly denotes that closing of the circle of transcendence by which the world is 'transcended' by the reality of God at the point of its utter worldliness.

There is, we have found, an overplus of value in the kenotic way of historical transcendence. For the kenotic way is not only the way of historical transcendence on the part of the eternal Word, it is also the way of lived transcendence on the part of the Holy Spirit. It is the closing of that circle which now concerns us.

Where in the world is the Spirit of the living God?

---

[87]See above, pp. 154ff.

Part Three

Lived Transcendence
and the Reality of God

Chapter VII

Living in the Spirit

1 'The Kenotic Community'

But how is the Presence known? How tested? And what is this life
with which man then is dowered? In the midst of a world constantly,
sullenly, wilfully, despairingly denying this life of persons as the one
historical reality, where is this community of which you speak? And
how, even if there is such a community, may it possibly continue in
life amid such hostile and perverse circumstances?[1]

'The wind blows where it wills', said Jesus, 'and you hear the sound
of it, but you do not know whence it comes or whither it goes; so it is
with every one who is born of the Spirit.'[2] The reality of the wind is in
the snap of the sail, the wing of the gull curved motionless between
earth and sky, in the pull of a kite string in the hand, and in the dance
of the leaves on an autumn day. The form of life *is* the reality, not as
aesthetics would have it—where the impression is captured in an image—
but as the sailor has it when the boat leaps forward, or as the child has
it when the kite string tugs in his hand like a living thing. Not every
form has the breath of wind in it—for a form can die, and can even
have a kind of beauty in death—but every wind of spirit finds its reality
in a form of life.

To speak then of Presence without also speaking of form is to lose
touch with reality. It is to take leave of one's senses, in the most sensible
use of the word. The style and shape of life in its most tangible form is
the reality of spirit which gives substance to faith. 'If a brother or sister
is ill-clad and in lack of daily food, and one of you says to them, "Go
in peace, be warmed and filled", without giving them the things needed
for the body, what does it profit?'[3] These 'works'—food and clothing—
constitute the reality of spirit according to James: 'For as the body
apart from the spirit is dead, so faith apart from works is dead.'[4]
Disembodied love is a state of mind, and thus does not exist at all. Dis-

[1]R. G. Smith, 'History is Personal', *Collected Papers*, p. 11.
[2]John 3:8.
[3]James 2:15-16.
[4]James 2:26.

embodied spirits have a particular terror for us—especially in the dark—
but there is really no certainty that they exist, except in our minds. If
there is such a thing as a disembodied act or presence of God as Spirit,
could one love it, or be comforted by it? What is the form of God in
the world—what is the life-form of Spirit?

This, of course, is Bonhoeffer's question: 'What is the form of Christ
in the world?'[5] It is the question of the reality of God for a world which
has 'come of age'. We have seen how Bonhoeffer attempted to answer
that question by grounding the reality of God in the pole of 'this-worldly
transcendence'—that is, in man's basic social relations—while at the
same time attempting to sustain the other role of transcendence in a
personal union with Christ centred in the secret discipline. As a result,
for Bonhoeffer, the experience of transcendence in terms of one person's
transcendence of another became the life-form of the historical transcendence of God. In effect, this makes man's historical existence the form
in which one seeks the historical transcendence of God as Spirit. Thus,
the Spirit of God (and so the person of Christ) *is* the reality of the form
of transcendence within history, and consequently, one can speak of
a religionless Christianity. Beginning with the problem, as was done at
the outset of this chapter, this appears to be a quite valid way of attempting a solution. However, in proceeding to expose the inner logic of God's
relation to the world, particularly through the Incarnation, we found
it necessary to assert that the transcendent ground for the life of the
Spirit in the world is the historical existence of Jesus Christ as the eternal
Logos. The Incarnate Word is the *form* for the reality of Spirit. The
historical transcendence of God has only one form—that of the Incarnate
Son. This was God's act in the world which, abstracted from all other
human acts, remains itself both human and historical, and yet, an act
of God. This is God's historical transcendence because it is the life of
God *with* man in history and not just through man. We were therefore
led to conclude that the Spirit has no history of his own, but has the
form of the Incarnate Son.[6] As a result, we must say that the work
and act of the Spirit is more like a re-formation of human existence in
the form of Christ.

This life-form of the Spirit in the world has its transcendent ground
in the life-form of the Incarnate Word—Jesus Christ—and its concrete
ground in the historical existence of the 'new man' who lives in the
Spirit.[7] Therefore, and on this point hangs the argument of this book,

[5]This is the phrase chosen by John A. Phillips for the title of his book on
Bonhoeffer's thought: *The Form of Christ in the World*. For the general idea
of this form of expression, cf. D. Bonhoeffer, *Letters and Papers From Prison*,
pp. 279-280.
[6]See above, pp. 218ff.
[7]Cf. Ephesians 2:14-22.

the transcendence of God is a reality of Spirit in which the historical existence of the man in whom the Spirit dwells is re-formed according to the form of Jesus Christ, the Incarnate Word, who is at once the image of the invisible God and the image in which man is created.[8] This reality of Spirit cannot be called the historical transcendence of God, for that belongs uniquely to the life of the Incarnate Word, but should rather be called a lived transcendence by which the reality of God impinges upon the world through the historical existence of the man who lives in the Spirit of God.

There are three implications of this which I wish to work out as a way of showing how historical transcendence is completed in lived transcendence, or, one could say, how Christology flows into Ecclesiology. These three implications constitute the theme for the three chapters of this final part: (1) lived transcendence is a community of life in the Spirit which takes the form of both a kenotic and ek-static existence; (2) lived transcendence is a reality of life in solidarity with the world which has both an incarnational and evangelical existence among men; and (3), lived transcendence is an eschatological life in God in which history and faith are bound up in the relation of the penultimate to the ultimate. While these three implications will each touch upon the nature and the mission of the church, the discussion will stay within the bounds of a critique.[9] That is, the overriding concern will not be with methodology, but with the imperative essence of the transcendence of God as it has been disclosed to us through the Incarnation. As such, these implications constitute more of a preparation for a doctrine of the church, or perhaps even a canon, according to which the church may work out and place into execution the doctrine of its own existence in the world.

Turning then to the first implication, namely, that lived transcendence is a community of life in the Spirit, it can be said that this life is a life of *kenotic* community. Here again, it must be made clear that we are not searching for a clever way of introducing yet another alternative way for the church to find a new form of expression in the world. A kenotic *way* of life simply does not grasp the fundamental content of the life of the Spirit, and thus fails to touch the imperative essence of that life itself. What is even more dangerous is that the assumption of a kenotic way of life on the part of the church in the world occludes the very truth which the *kenosis* discloses, and envelopes the ego of the church ever more securely in a posture of humility. A life which is devoted to self-emptying can be a life committed most powerfully to

---

[8]Colossians 1:15; 3:10.

[9]That is, a critique in the sense that Kant sought to clarify the nature and function of reason, rather than in developing an organon of reason. Cf. *Critique of Pure Reason*, pp. 58-59.

a manner of self-existence.[10] It is most understandable that the natural reaction to a power-full church is a radical call for a power-less church. But, while the way of poverty and powerlessness is indeed a more attractive virtue than a spirit of acquisitiveness and superiority, that way is a temptation because of its very attractiveness. When the right hand knows what the left hand is doing (Matthew 6:3), it is difficult, and probably impossible, to keep the 'subtraction' from becoming an addition.

When the kenotic life of the Spirit is equated with a kenotic principle of self-emptying, the church can be confronted with a challenge that it cannot possibly understand, much less put into practice. It is easy to sympathize with Bonhoeffer's impatience with the church, particularly when writing from a prison cell, but his final thoughts concerning the future of the church invoked a kenotic principle without coming to grips with the reality of kenotic community:

> The church is the church only when it exists for others. To make a start, it should give away all its property to those in need. The clergy must live solely on the free-will offerings of their congregations, or possibly engage in some secular calling. The church must share in the secular problems of ordinary human life, not dominating but helping and serving. . . . It must not under-estimate the importance of a human example (which has its origin in the humanity of Jesus and is so important in Paul's teaching); . . .[11]

My argument is not that what Bonhoeffer suggests may not need to take place; rather, I question the superficiality of what appears as a very radical proposal. If by the church, Bonhoeffer has in mind a specific group of people, and if they accepted his suggestion as the truly kenotic way of life and disposed of all their worldly endowments, what then? The example which this dramatic act would produce could not exist for long without some reinforcement. As an example, it may have some negative value in terms of the indictment which it pronounces against every form of misrepresentation of Christ through the seeking of power and privilege in the world, although the real value of this in terms of producing a positive result is questionable. But there is little here of an example of the kenotic community which lives in the Spirit. Many churches would only discover that without their endowments,

[10]I would want to distinguish here between a 'posture' of humility, which effects an attitude as a means to achieve an idealist form of *kenosis*, and a concrete life of humility which involves commitment and discipline. For example, I would consider Bonhoeffer's emphasis upon obedience and discipleship not merely a kenotic 'way of life', but kenotic living itself in the most concrete sense of the word. The humility of the kenotic life cannot be sought for and achieved, but comes more as humiliation arising out of obedience in the concrete situation.

[11]'Outline For a Book', *Letters and Papers From Prison*, pp. 382-383.

institutions and programmes, they would have very little in common as a fellowship of believers. This, of course, is not thereby to justify the existence of a church which depends upon such outward forms for its survival. I simply do not find such an approach very helpful in making clear the fundamental reality of lived transcendence in terms of kenotic community.[12]

The question is not, it seems to me, how the church can assume a kenotic way of life—for that assumes that there is such a thing as the church prior to and apart from a kenotic community—but, of where one locates the reality of the church itself. A life of kenotic community is not a way of life which will put new life into a dying institution if its primary virtue is a renunciation of privilege and power for its own sake. There may well be a genuine kenotic life which *appears* similar to this way of life, but its source and its (ultimate) power comes from another Spirit. In a word, the life of kenotic community is a life of *transcendence*.

When we probe the depths of *kenosis*, as we have done in an earlier chapter, we discover that what appears as a way of life through self-emptying on the part of the man Jesus, and thus looks to an observer

[12]More recent attempts to use the kenotic theme as a principle for renewing the church reveal a genuine concern for a more authentic christian community, but tend to use *kenosis* as a way to re-pristinate an original and more spiritual concept of christian faith. D. M. MacKinnon says: 'But the issue of *kenosis* and Establishment is in the end an issue of spirituality. To live as a Christian in the world today is necessarily to live an exposed life; it is to be stripped of the kind of security that tradition, whether ecclesiological or institutional, easily bestows.' *The Stripping of the Altars*, The Fontana Library, Collins, London, 1969, p. 34. MacKinnon has in mind the particular form of institutionalism represented by the Anglican Church, and he appeals to what he calls the 'law of *kenosis*' as the way to a more vital Christianity. He grounds this concept of *kenosis* in the 'initiating act of the whole incarnate life', and suggests that there is relevance in the concept for the 'articulation of an essential as distinct from an economic Trinity' (p. 17). This is a hopeful direction, and while MacKinnon does not elaborate upon this he does reaffirm the notion of *kenosis* as pointing to the 'deepest sense of the mystery of the incarnation' in a later writing (' "Substance" in Christology—a Cross-bench View', *Christ Faith and History*, S. W. Sykes and J. P. Clayton, eds., Cambridge University Press, 1972, p. 297). Robert Adolfs, from whom MacKinnon draws inspiration for the kenotic theme, has a good deal more to say about the way in which a 'law of *kenosis*' can be applied to the juridical and ecclesiastical power structure of the church, with specific reference to his own communion, which is Roman Catholic. Here again, the emphasis is upon practical modifications to the existing structure of the church (many of them highly appropriate to any type of modern church) without really showing how this can take place other than by imposing a concept in such a way that 'a change of heart' takes place: 'One final question still remains to be answered—how is this change of direction towards the kenotic Church to be accomplished? It will certainly not be brought about by any 'measures' or by reorganization. It will above all be the result of a *metanoia*, a change of heart or conversion, the development of a new mentality, a kenotic attitude.' *The Grave of God*, A Compass Book, Burns and Oates, London, 1967, p. 149.

like a God giving away his divinity, is actually a quality of life intrinsic to the relation of Father and Son which is exemplified by the Son's human obedience even unto death.[13] From the furthest side of human estrangement, the intra-divine transcendence exposed itself as a community of love which overcame the estrangement and reclaimed the estranged ones by inclusion in the divine life itself. The Holy Spirit, who was 'being accustomed' to dwelling in human flesh, as Irenaeus puts it,[14] through the intimate union of the Son with humanity, becomes one with the kenotic *form* as explicated by the Son in his humanity and thus creates a kenotic community which is itself an image or likeness of the intra-divine community. This became visible through the way in which Jesus brought his 'little flock' with him into the depths (and heights) of his own kenotic experience. They were partakers of his suffering, and thus bearers of his own glory.[15] There was then, along with the historical transcendence of God through the life of the Son, already a lived transcendence of kenotic community through the life of the Spirit. We have earlier observed how the transcendence of God in a living way became more and more identified with the Spirit during the final period of Jesus' life.[16] The form in which the Spirit would express the power (*exousia*) of the living God had already been determined through the life of the Son. It was not the ideal form (Platonic) of which the material and human form was only a shadow, but it was the kenotic form (Incarnational) in which the intra-divine transcendence of God exposed its own reality. To say then, that the transcendent form of the Spirit is the life of the Son is not to imply that there is any ideal form of a transcendental kind which determines the real life of the Spirit, but the form is a reality of historical transcendence. It is necessary to make this clear to avoid falling into the error of idealism whereby the kenotic life of the Spirit becomes a principle by which man determines his own existence, or a 'law of *kenosis*' by which the church achieves its own renewal. If one cuts loose from the historical transcendence of the man Jesus, the life of the Spirit tends to become idealized and confused with self-consciousness (Schleiermacher).

If we were to express the fundamental meaning of *kenosis*, then, it could be said to be the intrinsic character of divine love itself, and thus conceived as an activity rather than as essence. The intrinsic character of this love has its clearest explication in the life of the Incarnate Logos, but this also clarifies the nature of man as created in the image of God. The dogma of *kenosis* tells us that the transcendence of God is as real in the image of God as for God himself. *Kenosis* can be, therefore,

---

[13]See above, Chapter V, especially pp. 179ff.
[14]See above, p. 175, n. 86.
[15]John 17:10.
[16]See above, pp. 182, 211.

another way of understanding the image of God, or of stating the true nature of man. *Kenosis* means that man has his true nature completed when he participates in the intra-divine transcendence (love), and that this participation does not involve the repudiation or violation of that which is truly human.

The life of the Spirit, therefore, is the transcendence of God understood kenotically. That is, even as the Spirit was active in the Incarnate Logos, making possible a genuine human response and participation in the divine life, the Spirit continues to act in this *form* by re-forming man into the form of Christ. But this is also the *real* form (if not the actual) of man's intrinsic nature as the image of God. And by suggesting that the real form of man's nature as the image of God is not always realized in actuality, I do not mean to introduce a philosophical distinction between the real and the actual, but to point to an actual estrangement, which, because it is estrangement from the reality of community with God, is a real estrangement which man experiences from his own true nature. Man's estrangement is real, and not merely actual (in a phenomenological sense) because man is grounded by the nature of his own being in the transcendence of God. Therefore, one could say that man's real form of authentic existence is to be found in the person of Jesus Christ. In him the real and the actual were never split apart. This is what it means to speak of the 'sinlessness' of Jesus. He experienced the reality of fellowship with God with no actual deviation from that reality, even from the furthest side of man's estrangement. In its most positive sense, this is what kenotic community means.

It can now be said that the particular character of the kenotic way of life is not an ethical pattern of life modelled after the style of Jesus, nor is it a kind of suffering or self-renunciation which seeks to emulate Christ. And still less is it a programme for poverty, by which the church seeks to re-form itself in the shape of the destitute. I say that these do not constitute the particular character of kenotic community, as though one could use these methods as means to a higher end. In the kenotic community, life in the Spirit is the end, and not the means to an end. Because the kenotic community has first of all radicalized the presence of the Other in terms of my own existence, the Other in his concreteness becomes my end, and never my means to an end. The reality of the Spirit for me, thus, cannot take the form of my own historical existence and so confirm me in a state of perfectionism, with its corresponding intolerance of the Other, or reduce me to a state of hopelessness, unable to escape my actual limitations. But the Spirit can assume the historical existence of the Other in the kenotic community as the form of reality for me, so that now I can find my real existence in my actual relation to him. The Other then becomes the form of Christ for me as the Spirit assumes that particular historical existence in which Christ is re-formed. Because

I meet my own real existence when I act in love towards the Other, I see beyond his actual existence with its limitations and immaturities. I do not merely tolerate him, I see his reality as a person. We are touching again upon what was earlier alluded to as an 'unfinished' aspect to covenant response in creation. That is, if man's 'transcending limit' represented as the tree of knowledge of good and evil should be said to become 'enfleshed' through the creation of woman, so that man could then 'love his limit' as himself, this pointed towards the transcendence of Spirit in the form of an 'enfleshment' recognized in a community of relation. As the Spirit re-forms the Other in the form of Christ, I can love the Other as the transcending limit of my own existence in the flesh.[17]

This only explains the particular character of the kenotic community, and shows how the kenotic community can be re-formed in the likeness of Christ without denying or falsifying the actual life of persons. This explains how one can speak of the presence of Christ in the kenotic community—he is really there in the historical existence of the Other who gives concrete form to the Holy Spirit—without resorting to a mystical, and consequently, a subjectivizing way of thinking.[18] And finally, this shows, as Professor MacKinnon rightly points out, that the ultimate significance of Christian community is kenotic—that is, it is received, not imposed.[19] It is the gift of the Spirit which Christ himself promised, so that his followers should not be *alone*.[20]

There are quite clearly two things implied in the character of kenotic community as it has been explicated above. *First*, the kenotic community is formed of actual people who have their place in the community, not by virtue of their capacity to love or their maturity of spirit, but by virtue of their common humanity with Christ and the reality of the Holy Spirit which comes as a gift. When the Holy Spirit assumes the historical existence of the other man as the form of Christ for me, a cripple is no less real than a whole person. *Second*, and this follows from the first, the kenotic community offers to each person, to the extent that they are able to bear it, an actual growth into the reality of their own personhood, which is the capacity to live in love.

[17]See above, pp. 142-143.

[18]While I would not want to discount a genuine mystical dimension to theology, and to Christian experience, I am questioning here the kind of mysticism which operates out· of an antithesis between spirit and matter, and consequently, seeks to 'transcend' the world of sense-experience in order to know God in an immediate sense of oneness of spirit which has no cognitive or temporal structures. Cf. T. F. Torrance who says: '... an experience in which the mystic is said to take leave of his senses is to be discounted, that is, an experience in which cognition is not *rationally* mediated through the senses or which uses sense-experience merely as a spring-board to enter a realm that transcends it altogether. That is a form of *docetism*.' *Theological Science*, p. 189.

[19]*Stripping the Altars*, p. 40.

[20]John 14:15-17.

It is the transcendence of God which constitutes each person in the kenotic community; first of all, through the historical transcendence of the Son of God by which the appropriate human response is made from the furthest side of human estrangement, so that the weakest of human flesh *already* possesses a place of participation; and then through the Holy Spirit who takes each person's actual life into fellowship with Christ. This life in the Spirit has its ground in the historical life of Christ himself, but has concrete expression in the life of the community itself—such as it is.

Such as it is! And here we come to the heart of the matter. For the fundamental truth of the kenotic community is not revealed to the theologian at his desk, but to the pastor in the midst of his people. It is one thing to say that the kenotic community is formed of actual people, it is quite another thing to know how actually sick, how actually weak, how actually unable to love, and how actually unlovable actual people can be! But here is where the kenotic community establishes its real character, for it dares to include those who have the capacity (and often the compulsion) to destroy the community itself, and even more, it dares to offer love as a possibility of growth. The same Spirit who led Jesus to choose Judas as one of his intimate followers prior to the resurrection, baptized Ananias and Sapphira into the kenotic community of lived transcendence.[21] Here we see that the true kenotic community is marked, not by whom it is willing to renounce, but whom it is willing to receive. But there is more implied in this 'receiving' than a blind spot in the centre of one's vision. For the 'being received' is a participation in lived transcendence, for such is the nature of kenotic community.

The kenotic community thus touches man at his most vulnerable spot—his willingness to receive the Spirit of God and to enter into fellowship with Christ. Here again we can see just how the transcendence of God acts through a kenotic movement. The one who discovers that he is received into the community by virtue of his common humanity with Christ, and not by virtue of any 'qualifying' efforts of his own, does not stand in the circumference at some distance from the transcendence of God in the community, but is immediately placed in a relation of transcendence through the reality of Spirit who assumes the form of the Other's concrete existence. There are two marks of visibility for the transcendence of God at this point. One is the visibility of historical transcendence in the revelation concerning God's act in Jesus Christ as contained in the Scriptures. This is a form of visibility which assumes an audible form as the Word of God is 'heard', and yet, one is ultimately confronted by the historical existence of the Word as Jesus Christ. The other form of visibility is the presence of the Spirit in the concrete life of the other person in the community, or one could say, in the

[21]Acts 5:1-11.

concrete existence of the community itself.[22] These represent the 'two poles of transcendence' which come together in the kenotic community as two visible and concrete realities, each of which 'places' the person in a relation to God's transcendence.[23]

It is at this point, however, that the one who is 'received' in this kenotic way is touched at the crucial point of his own 'receptivity'. To receive the Spirit of God in this way, represents a radical and devastating confrontation with one's actual situation of spiritual autonomy, which we have already called estrangement from fellowship with God. To receive now means a reversal of the Ego and a 'turning towards' the transcendence of God with openness and a 'change of mind' (*metanoia*) which represents a conversion to God in the deepest sense of the word. It seems clear from the character of kenotic community as it has been exposed, that a conversion 'experience' cannot be demanded as the qualifying act on the part of a person for his belonging to the kenotic community. This has some very important implications which will be taken up in the next chapter. But it must also immediately be said that participation in the kenotic community does involve receiving as well as being received. And it may well be that only after 'being received' for a considerable length of love (one would naturally say 'time', but these 'lengths' have a duration which only love can measure!) can a person muster the strength and the will to receive. This is, of course, what is entailed in the second aspect of the character of the kenotic community: it offers to each person, to the extent that they are able to bear it, an *actual* growth into the reality of their own personhood, which is the capacity to live in love.[24]

There is, I think, something which can be said about the form, if not the structure, of the church at this point which arises directly out of the character of kenotic community. We have seen that the kenotic

[22]Lesslie Newbigin, in his book, *The Household of God*, SCM Press, London, 1953, lays great emphasis on the visibility of the church: 'The Christian community is precisely as visible as the Christian man.' p. 29. He suggests that Luther 'abandoned his deepest insight of justification by faith' when he substituted the unbiblical distinction between the visible and the invisible church (p. 127). I would think that Newbigin would agree that to speak of an invisible church is to retreat from the reality of the kenotic community. The more critical question, it seems to me, is the question of the distinction between the 'Christian man' and the non-Christian man in terms of the kenotic community. This will reappear as an area of concern in the next chapter.

[23]I only wish to note here that I see the two poles of transcendence as *both* concretely placed in history, contrary to Bonhoeffer (see above, p. 218). For Bonhoeffer, the historical transcendence of God was concrete and represented by the presence of the Other, while the personal transcendence of Christ through the Spirit was immediately related to this historical transcendence through faith. I would give a more cognitive dimension to faith by seeing revelation in terms of the content of Scripture as well as the immediate relation of Spirit.

[24]See above, p. 234.

community is the 'place' where both poles of God's transcendence come together in such a way that man is 'placed' in a living fellowship with God so that his *actual* existence is taken seriously in terms of his *real* personhood. The kenotic community can be said then to be the 'home of personhood' where man is both received as a person and then, at the same time, receives his personhood. The word which I am searching for in attempting to interpret this in terms of a form for the church could be best expressed as 'domestic'. The home, or domicile for man is community with God. There he receives his true personhood. In this sense of the word, domestic refers to the total context in which the Spirit of God works to create man's personhood. The Spirit can be known as the 'domesticating' Spirit of God, who creates the place where man *learns* to receive his personhood. It is not too difficult to interpret the creation story (as given in Genesis) domestically. The world is for man his domicile, his home with God, in which he is a participant with God in the creative process. All the while, man is learning to receive and growing towards his true personhood.[25]

I should think that it would be helpful for the church to see its true form as contiguous with that of the domestic shape of creation itself, and thus understand the redemptive dimension as integral to the creative, rather than as an end in itself. It would also seem that the immediate implication of the domestic motif of the kenotic community for the church in a practical sense would be the recognition of the need to help each person receive the Spirit of God and so live in the transcendence of a communicating and loving personhood. The question which would appear to have priority, and thus the determining question for the shape of the church's ministry, is the question: why is this person unable to receive? Assuming that the church is a genuine kenotic community where the transcendence of Word and Spirit are both concretely given and active, the church can creatively (in the true theological sense) take up the domestic functions of kenotic community by seeing actual persons as real persons, and providing the necessary (or perhaps overcoming the hindering) conditions for growth in true personhood. In Pauline language, the church thus is a 'household' of faith, gives itself to the 'edification' of the body, and identifies the particular domestic functions as 'gifts of the Spirit'.[26]

This 'domesticating' function of the kenotic community should then take into account the actual life of the person in the world. Rather than opposing a religious life to a secular life, or splitting a person's commitment between his life-work and his 'church-work', the domestic Spirit

[25]This recalls for us the central motif in the theology of Irenaeus, who sees Adam as the child who finds his completion in the man Jesus. This is brought out especially in G. Wingren's work on Irenaeus, *Man and the Incarnation*, pp. 49, 127.

[26]Galatians 6:10; I Corinthians 12:1-11; 14:12.

of kenotic community relates a man creatively to his place and function in a created world. It is not the least of the values of the kenotic community to suggest that it works to redeem the world, not by speaking with a posture of authority to issues, but by domesticating man himself to a life in the Spirit. But what the concept of kenotic community has to offer the church is a way of seeing that a true life in the Spirit is not alien to man's creative vocation in the world.

For the kenotic community, poverty is not that which it gives away, but that which it receives; powerlessness is not in the abandonment of a place in the world, but in refusing to let go of the weak for the sake of the strong; humility is not in taking less than the world, but in receiving more than the world can give. The kenotic community has no Presence other than its own existence, or rather, God's presence to himself in its existence. It has no sacristy to be profaned, no temple to be destroyed, no Prince to be exiled—or ignored; and it has no answer to the question put at the beginning of this chapter. For *such as it is*, it is the transcendence of God. The answer is in the wind.

2 'The Ek-static Community'

In a world of fugitives
One who moves in the opposite direction
Will appear to run away.[27]

Being something of an anarchist at heart (the Spirit blows where it wills), I have a notion that a domestic Spirit is not necessarily a housebound Spirit, nor is kenotic community necessarily an earth-bound fellowship. At this point, an important corrective needs to be applied, lest domesticity be misconstrued as slavery, and life in the Spirit be reduced to life with one another. Will a parable help?

Imagine that geese could talk, Kierkegaard once said, and that they had arranged things so that they too could have their church services and their worship.

Every Sunday they would assemble together and a gander would preach.
The essential content of the sermon was the exalted destiny of geese, the exalted goal for which the creator has destined geese (and every time his name was named all the geese curtsied and the ganders bowed their heads). With the help of their wings they could fly away to far countries, blessed countries, where they were really at home: for here they were just like exiles.
And so every Sunday. Then the gathering broke up, and every goose waddled home. Then the next Sunday off they went to the service

[27]R. G. Smith, 'J. G. Hamann and the Princess Gallitzin', *Philomathes*, Robert Palmer and Robert Hamerton-Kelly (eds.), Martinus Nijhoff, The Hague, p. 339.

again, then home again. That was all. They throve and grew fat, they became plump and tender. . . .

That was all. For while the sermon sounded so exalted on Sundays, on Mondays they would tell one another of the fate of the goose who wanted to take his high destiny seriously, with the help of the wings the creator had given it. And they spoke of the horrors it had to endure. But they prudently kept this knowledge among themselves. For of course to speak of it on Sundays was most unsuitable, for as they said, in that case it would be obvious that our service would be a mockery both of God and of ourselves.

There were also among the geese some that looked ill and thin. Of them the others said, 'You see, that's what comes of being serious about wanting to fly. It is because they are always thinking of flying that they get thin and do not thrive, and do not have God's grace as we do. That is why we get plump and fat and tender, for it is by God's grace that one gets plump and fat and tender.'[28]

So it is with Christians, adds Kierkegaard; they conclude that the domesticating grace of God is not meant to take seriously the wings of the spirit, for to do so emaciates one's well-being and destroys one's peace as an earth-bound creature. Whereas, in fact, the wings are meant to be used—man has spirit, and thus is destined to live a transcendent life.

For all of its visibility and concreteness, then, life in the Spirit is a lived *transcendence*. The kenotic community is earth-related, for it exists in the same flesh as that of Jesus of Nazareth, but it is not earth-bound, for it lives in the same Spirit as did Jesus. When we explored the kenotic life which Jesus lived, we saw that with the deepest penetration of humanity and from the furthest side of human estrangement, he lived in unbroken communion with the Father. His prayers were considered as evidences of this extra-human relation on the part of a genuinely human person. If his relation to humanity as the eternal Logos can be called a *hypo-static* relation, that is, as the particular man Jesus he was the bearer of human nature in its totality, one then could designate his movement towards the Father as an *ek-static* relation. These two aspects cannot be separated in such a way that Jesus could be considered a 'person' by virtue of either his hypo-static or his ek-static being, rather, as Dr. John Zizioulas says,

> *Ekstasis* and *Hypostasis* represent two basic aspects of Personhood, and it is not to be regarded as a mere accident that both of these words have been historically applied to the notion of Person. Thus the idea of Person affirms at once both that being cannot be 'contained' or 'divided', and that the mode of its existence, its *hypostasis*,

[28]*The Last Years*, 'Journals 1853-55', edited and translated by R. G. Smith, The Fontana Library, Collins, London, 1965, pp. 292-293.

is absolutely unique and unrepeatable. Without these two conditions
being falls into an a-personal reality, defined and described like a
mere 'substance', i.e. it becomes a thing.[29]

[29]'Human Capacity and Human Incapacity', an unpublished essay presented
at the Society For the Study of Theology, Oxford, April, 1972, p. 6. Dr. Zizioulas,
in developing an ontological concept of personhood, suggests that, rather than
man being a human person by virtue of what is contained in or possessed *qua*
individual, man's true humanity is expressed in his movement towards community in God. This 'ek-static' movement constitutes personhood, not merely
personality: 'Man's personhood should not be understood in terms of "personality", i.e., of a complex of psychological or moral qualities which are in some
sense "possessed" by or "contained" in the human *individuum*. On the contrary,
being a person is basically different from being an individual or "personality" in
that the person can not be conceived in itself as a static entity, but only as it *relates*
to. Thus personhood implies the "openness of being", and even more than that,
the *ek-stasis* of being, i.e., a movement towards communion.' *Ibid.*, p. 6. If one
follows Dr. Zizioulas here in thinking not of person as 'being' (*ousia*) but as
'presence' (*par-ousia*), the notion of being 'present to God' through direct communion underlines what I have termed 'covenant response'. Therefore, the question
of the divine Logos constituting a truly human response is not simply a question
of the 'being' of Christ and the 'being' of God (i.e., a question of an ontic cleft
within God), but a question of the movement (*ek-stasis*) towards community
in God from the standpoint of the creature in union with (*hypo-stasis*) the divine
Logos. The concept of *ek-stasis* as the distinctive dimension of personhood has its
roots more in the definition of person suggested by Richard of St. Victor than
that of Boethius. Richard held that a person is an incommunicable existence of
an intellectual nature (*person est intellectualis naturae incommunicabilis exsistentia*).
Dr. Heribert Mühlen shows how this concept of person was taken up by Johannes
Duns Scotus and developed ontologically as the *ex-sistentia* of a triune God
(*Sein und Person nach Johannes Duns Scotus*, Dietrich-Coelde-Verlag, Werl.,
Westf., 1954, pp. 4ff.). The two basic questions which Dr. Mühlen frames as the
outline of his study shows in what sense *ek-static* human personhood is ontologically derived from the *ek-sistence* of God himself: 'Is the essence of man
only a standing and a resting on one's own basis (*in sich ruhender Selbstand*) and
a having of oneself in one's own power, or does there not rather belong in addition to the essence of man, the "whence" and the "whither" (*das Woher und
Wohin*) of his existence? Is not the essential thing for man and the ek-static
(*ek-statische*) in the sense of Richard of St. Victor, the relation to the origin, to
the "whence" of his existence, a relation which "stands out" of itself (*aus sich
herausstehende Bezug*)?' p. 6. The retention of the hyphenated form of ek-stasis
is meant to retain in a visible way, the etymological construction of the word
and so reinforce the ontological derivation of the concept of person in the sense
of a dynamic 'standing out of' one's self towards the 'whence' of essential being.
In this way I hope to get behind the familiar connotation of 'ecstatic' as the
experience of being 'beside one's self' and reserve for the word 'ek-static' a more
restricted and technical connotation as the movement of being towards its
ultimate and original source. For this reason, the preposition is separated slightly
from the stem of the word to denote the 'whence' of personhood, a fundamental
fact, as Dr. Mühlen suggests, which must not be lost sight of: 'Person ist aber
nicht nur durch Sistenz, durch Selbstand, charakterisiert, sondern ebenso durch
den Bezug zum Ursprung. Dies drükt die Präposition "ex" aus: ... Personales
Dasein ist begründet durch das Woher des Wesens.' *Ibid.*, p. 5.

The idea of Personhood, then, which we are led to consider through this understanding of the person of Christ, includes the reality of Spirit as the ek-static reality of Word. When I have defined lived transcendence as kenotic community, these two aspects of Personhood must be included. That is, the kenotic community is constituted a community through both the hypo-static union of Word and flesh, which is the reality of the Incarnate Word, and the ek-static reality of Spirit. The kenotic community is not itself a hypo-static union of Word and flesh, that is, it is not the bearer of humanity in its totality in a unique and unrepeatable existence, it is not another Incarnation; but it is constituted in community with God through its humanity which it has in common with the humanity of the Incarnate Word. We have said that each person has his 'place' in the kenotic community by virtue of his humanity. The transcendent grounds for this 'being placed' in community is the hypo-static union of Logos with humanity in the person of Christ. Therefore, when the Spirit assumes the 'form' of the historical existence of the one who is Other to me in the community, that 'form' of the Other in his actuality becomes the real presence of Christ for me through the Spirit.

But now it must be made clear that this kenotic community is not thereby an 'introverted' community (fat geese) and earth-bound in the sense that the transcendence of co-humanity constitutes its limiting possibility. The domesticating work of the Spirit is not directed towards group dynamics and the adjustment of one person's life in terms of the other, but is directed towards the *receiving* of Spirit so that the ek-static reality of Spirit may issue from human hearts and hands and voices as one life expressed in relation with God.[30] My purpose in using a word such as ek-static is to point towards a reality which is the opposite of an introverted experience, where life is turned back upon itself. The introversion of love works as a fragmenting and destructive force within community. A spirit of introversion either serves to particularize community into a disruptive individualism, where the Ego of personhood is intensified in its opposition to other hypostatic entities, or it can produce quite another effect (and the two may well be related as cause and effect) in the form of a tyrannical collectivism where the Ego of personhood is hypostatized into one entity—the social or political unity which exists as the end towards which all personal life exists as means.[31]

[30]Cf. I Corinthians 12:4-13; Ephesians 4:4-6.
[31]One could also say that Capitalism and Marxism share a common anthropology which leads to two quite dissimilar political and economic systems. The one divides man up against himself, the other sacrifices man as individual to man as a social unit—both fall short of true personhood because they lack the ek-static dimension.

It is for this reason that I prefer the concept of ek-static community to that of charismatic community as a way of representing the transcendence of Spirit. The gifts of the Spirit (*charismata*) can tend either towards a hypo-static or an ek-static function. When they function primarily as an intensification of the hypo-static basis of community they produce disorder and confusion. In this case there is a tendency towards the individuation and division of personhood. The early church was not immune to this problem.[32] For this reason, Paul attempts to restore balance, not by seeking the suppression of the charismatic expression of Spirit, but by giving priority to the ek-static expression of Spirit. The ek-static community is a community united in one Spirit and thus participates in the life of God. The practical expression of this is love (I Corinthians 13), for 'God is love, and he who abides in love abides in God, and God abides in him'.[33]

Because love is not something which one person 'does to another', but is rather a dimension of reality in which God and man have communion, love can also be an extra-human reality and, thus, is the ek-static life of Spirit. The transcendence of Spirit means that God abides in every *work* of love. The food and clothing which are given in love become the life and reality of Spirit. But because the life of Spirit is ek-static, it also means that every work of love abides in God. The ek-static community is thus able to bring creation itself into relation with God. For the created world has no ek-static life of its own apart from Spirit. It is dumb and lifeless when it comes to an expression of love and response towards the Creator. Creation can only have 'presence' towards God as God 'meets himself' in his creation. Once again, we are touching upon that which I have alluded to earlier as the 'intrinsic cosmic structure' of historical transcendence.[34] That is, the intra-divine transcendence of God, which is but another way of expressing the trinitarian reality of God in dynamic terms, has an extrinsic *par-ousia* in the form of the presence of God as Creator in creation. Creation requires the Creator in order to exist in reality, but it does not possess the divine life as an immanent spirit in such a way that the relation is an extra-trinitarian reality. This would constitute creation as a reality 'outside' of the reality of God himself. In which case, creation plus God would constitute a greater reality than God himself. But, when the Creator-creature relation is understood as the extrinsic reality of the intrinsic transcendence of God in his triune nature, creation can be real in itself and at the same time, as Barth says, through the Holy Spirit creation is 'present' to God in the form of the relation of God to

[32]This would seem to be the precise nature of the problem in the church at Corinth. I Corinthians 12:1-14:40 becomes quite revealing when read in the light of the hypo-static/ek-static tendencies.
[33]I John 4:16.
[34]See above, p. 175, n. 87.

himself.[35] In the historical transcendence of God through the Incarnation, there lies exposed this intra-divine transcendence by which God meets himself from the side of creaturehood. All creation now has the possibility of its *ek-stasis* through the redemption of man from the introversion of the divine image. The ek-static community may thus be said to serve as the 'priest of creation', for only man, as he lives in the Word and Spirit of God has his personhood completed in a relation which passes 'beyond' creation to the Creator.[36] The ek-static community has a cosmic dimension—it is itself the 'horizon of revelation' for all of creation.[37]

The introverted community of man seeks distinctiveness in its autonomy over and against nature, and, as a result, either worships nature, or, as is more typical of our technological age, exploits it in the name of creativity. The emergence of a genuine ecological concern in the wake of such a despoiling of creation by man, has by and large exposed the Christian Church's own introversion. Here again, a charismatic community lacks both the desire and the theological tools to engage with

---

[35]*Church Dogmatics*, I/1, pp. 515ff. Barth says: 'The creature indeed requires the Creator in order to live. He thus requires relation to Him. But this relation he cannot create. God creates it through His own presence in the creature, i.e. in the form of the relation of Himself to Himself. The Spirit of God is God in His freedom to be present in the creature, and so to create this relation, and thereby to be the life of the creature.' *Ibid.*, p. 516. I think that Barth would see the relation of Spirit to creation as the immanence of God, a view which I have earlier criticized (see above, p. 150, n. 11). The difference may only be semantical, but I see no reason not to speak of God's 'meeting himself' in the creature as God's transcendence when it is understood as intra-divine transcendence such as is revealed in historical transcendence. This enables one to speak of solidarity with the world, while at the same time speak of the absolute difference, or of God's freedom. The gain in this conceptuality, it would appear, is that one can avoid dialectical language in speaking of God and man, and also can think in terms of a genuine natural theology without diminishing the transcendence (grace) of God. For if a natural theology is constituted in the transcendence, rather than in the immanence of God, it remains problematical in the sense that God remains free in being known by man in an intelligible way.

[36]Cf. John Zizioulas, 'Human Capacity and Human Incapacity', p. 12.

[37]This seems to be the meaning behind Paul's interpretation of the fall. When man turned his ek-static capacity back on creation itself (Romans 1:25) instead of the Creator, creation is subjected to a mute bondage to its own inarticulate nature and can only wait for man to once again liberate it through an ek-static life of the Spirit: 'For the creation waits with eager longing for the revealing of the sons of God; for the creation was subjected to futility, not of its own will but by the will of him who subjected it in hope; because the creation itself will be set free from its bondage to decay and obtain the glorious liberty of the children of God. We know that the whole creation has been groaning in travail together until now; and not only the creation, but we ourselves, who have the first fruits of the Spirit, groan inwardly as we wait for adoption as sons, the redemption of our bodies.' Romans 8:19-23.

ecological concerns creatively if it does not understand the ek-static relation of Spirit to creation. On the other hand, the ek-static community can come to the aid of ecological conservationism and supply the only possible transcendent grounds for such a concern. Lived transcendence then, as life in the Spirit, does not produce a division between man and creation, neither does it confuse the relation by identifying man with creation, but it turns creation back towards the Creator by giving creation its ultimate place in Being, that is, by giving creation an ek-static dimension through Spirit, so that God abides in the work and the work abides in God—through love.

The implications for the church are staggering and perhaps incomprehensible when considered in the light of traditional Western Christianity.[38] From the time of Augustine, the Western Church has been struggling with the doctrine of the 'Two Cities'. The City of God was basically set in opposition to the City of Man; what could be redeemed from the world was baptized into communion with God and the remainder left to destruction—or even worse, to be plundered by the redeemed citizens of the heavenly city who exercised a sort of

---

[38]The tradition of the Eastern Church as represented in the theology of Eastern Orthodoxy, in contrast to the Western Church with its Augustinian tradition, seems to provide a more congenial theological framework for the understanding of this concept of the ek-static community and its cosmic dimension of man's relation to God. For Eastern theology, both cosmology and anthropology are dynamic and inter-related. V. Lossky says that man is situated at the juncture of the intelligible and sensible spheres, and through him the created world can find its true destiny of 'deification' (*theosis*) as man unites created with uncreated being through relation with God. Lossky cites St. Maximus (580-662 A.D.) as saying that the human person was called 'to unite by love created with uncreated nature, showing the two in unity and identity through the acquisition of grace.' *The Mystical Theology of the Eastern Church*, James Clarke and Co., Cambridge and London, (1957) 1968, p. 126. A more comprehensive statement of the cosmological implications for Eastern theology is given by Timothy Ware (*The Orthodox Church*, Penguin Books, Middlesex, 1963) who shows how the Byzantium period was an attempt to accept and apply the full implications of the Incarnation to every facet of material and worldly life. The world was conceived as a living *icon* of the heavenly Jerusalem in that all created things were redeemed by the assumption of a creaturely humanity by Christ (pp. 43-50). Eastern theology tends to include creation in a sacramental and doxological movement towards God in a way that makes the eucharist not only the dynamic centre of all life, but incorporates all material life into this centre through the use of *icons* (pp. 269-302). The sanctuary of the Orthodox Church is divided from the rest of the interior by a solid screen called the *iconostasis*; this screen, covered with *icons*, serves as the meeting place between heaven and earth (pp. 266-267). The *icons* represent the first fruits of creation's redemption through the Incarnation, and thus point to the cosmic dimension of Eastern Orthodox's ecclesiology (pp. 239-240). One could almost say of the Eastern Church that it is more of an *icono-static* community than an *ek-static* one. However, I have only meant to show that, in contrast to the West, the East has a cosmic and dynamic concept of the redeemed community.

'eminent domain' over its resources. If the church is to link up again with creation, and ecology is only one aspect of this relation, the Spirit which has been so largely introverted in terms of both worship and ministry must become truly ek-static in the widest possible sense. The place where this can begin is with the kenotic community, for only here is both Word and Spirit united in a living transcendence of creative personhood.

In light of what has been said, one is led to question the way in which Bonhoeffer seemed to restrict the devotional and religious life of the community of Christ to the 'secret discipline' (*Arkandisziplin*). While Bonhoeffer only referred to the 'secret discipline' on two occasions in his letters from prison,[39] it was not as peripheral for him as this infrequent mention might appear. E. Bethge, who himself was a student of Bonhoeffer's at Finkenwalde, tells us that Bonhoeffer associated the concept of the 'secret discipline' with the early Christian practice of excluding the uninitiated, the unbaptized catechumens, from the second part of the liturgy in which the communion was celebrated and the Nicene Creed sung.[40] Later, when Bonhoeffer moves so deeply into the possibilities of 'religionless Christianity', he was concerned for what would happen to the worship of the Christian community. The events of worship, the sacraments, prayer and meditation, Bonhoeffer held, properly belong to the centre of the life of the Christian community, and, as such, are to be 'screened off' from the world. The 'creative events of the Holy Spirit' were centred in the inner life of the worshipping community, and Bonhoeffer wished to avoid 'cheapening' these events by exposing them promiscuously to the world.[41] However, his concern seemed to be that the world should be protected from religion as much as that the community of Christ be protected at its centre from the world. It was not that Bonhoeffer wished to erect spatial barriers between the church and the world, he had long since discarded that from his thinking,[42] rather, he felt that by making the cultic life private he could remove altogether the public barrier between the church and the world.

However, what Bonhoeffer has virtually done is to separate the ek-static life of the community from its kenotic life. What this does is restrict worship to a cultic event in which only the initiated participate. One lives in the world as if there is no God, and in the cultus as if there is no world! This dialectic between the 'secret discipline' and 'worldliness' cannot be sustained when one considers that the kenotic community is also the ek-static community—for Word and Spirit cannot be split apart.

[39]*Letters and Papers From Prison*, pp. 281, 286.
[40]*Dietrich Bonhoeffer*, p. 784.
[41]*Ibid.*, pp. 785, 786.
[42]*Ethics*, pp. 203, 205.

On the other hand, if we consider the alternative, that the kenotic community as the ek-static community includes a cosmic dimension, the worship of the church as well as its work gives creation its place in the life of the Creator. The redeemed community should not be considered as only a community with a cultus, for it is the community in which creation finds its ek-static fulfilment. It is the ones who do not receive the Spirit who are actually the 'cultic' community, for they are the ones who are 'screened off' from creation's true expression. Does this not also raise the question of a basis for a so-called 'religionless Christianity' when the 'events of the Spirit' are restricted to a discipline hidden from the world? While I would not be happy about the idea of considering the kenotic community as a religious community, if religion means a cultic posture as against a life of faith, on the other hand, I do not see how the kenotic community can even be Christian if the ek-static dimension is restricted to a hidden life. This appears to be an introversion of the Spirit of the worst kind. What a creative worship should actually be, remains for the church to discover in its own context. But I do not think this implication can be avoided if creation is to begin to find its ek-stasis in Christian community. There will be, it is true, a certain tension between the kenotic community in its ek-static form and the world which awaits its final redemption. This question of what it means to say that the kenotic community is not really 'earth-bound' will constitute the question for the final chapter of this book. There is an eschatological tension which Paul clearly speaks of (Romans 8:19-23), and which is true for the kenotic community as well as for all of creation. But if worship constitutes the ek-stasis of all creation through the kenotic community, especially in the form of the 'first fruits' of the Spirit, worship needs its windows open towards the world as well as towards God. It would seem that worship is most truly Christological when it ceases to be a private redemptive cult and begins to express the first fruits of redemption as the ek-stasis of creation through man in the Spirit. If kenotic community has its roots in the world, then the created world cannot be denied its place in the worship of the Creator.[43]

[43]I am well aware that I have raised the question of what constitutes true worship without intending to answer it in terms of specific forms. George F. Regas ('Explorations in New Liturgy for Man of the Future', *Theology, News and Notes*, Fuller Theological Seminary, March, 1972, pp. 16-18, 22) points to one dimension of contemporary worship which is attempting to take this seriously when he says: 'For centuries the sense of the reality of worship has been diminished in proportion to the way attention to man's sensory environment has been allowed to diminish. It is imperative that within the liturgical life of the Church we renew our appreciation of the body, the depths of emotion and the power of the visual arts. The Church must do more to bring the sensory world into our midst and celebrate it and discover the glory of being human and the intimate presence of God in creation.' (p. 18). But I am not sure that I follow him in his conclusion when he says: 'Corita Kent said it beautifully: "If we left

The consideration of the kenotic community as also the ek-static community enables us now to see that the distinction between 'community' and 'society' so common in recent theological as well as philosophical writings is not as helpful as it might be. In particular, the identification of the church as 'community' as opposed to other human social relations as merely 'society' does not stand up to the character of lived transcendence as we have seen it develop. Bonhoeffer, again, sought to make the distinction by thinking of community as 'will for meaning' and society as only constituted by a rational, or purposive will.[44] He further elaborated this distinction by holding that society is the concretion of metaphysical social relationships while community is the concretion of moral and social relationships.[45] The implications of Bonhoeffer's distinction was that society could never form communal type of relations apart from the moral dimension which is acquired when Christ becomes identified with society through a life of personal faith. All community for Bonhoeffer was community in Christ, and, therefore, the world could never have community, but only a common or rational purpose.

Emil Brunner is another theologian who sought to identify the form of the church in the world with a distinctive type of community. Although it must be said that his concern was not so much to make a distinction

---

it to the Spirit, there would be nothing left in Churches but Jesus and dancing." ' (p. 22). He is on solider ground when he refers to William Kuhn's book, *Environmental Man*, in which liturgy is related to man's total environment. This 'environmental interface' allows man to meet God in the 'facticity of an objective world, a world of colour and texture and form, a world of sensory impressions.' (p. 17). However, I am uneasy about liturgical renewal which adds to the triangular relationship of individual, community, God, a fourth dimension of environment. I am not sure that a rectangle is any more ek-static than a triangle. Closer to what I would want to say, although it does not suggest so much by way of form, is the essay by James B. Torrance, 'The Place of Jesus Christ in Worship', *Church Service Society Annual*, May, 1970, pp. 41-62, in which he says: 'God has made all creatures for His glory. The lilies of the field in their beauty glorify God with a glory greater than that of Solomon, but they do not know it. The sparrow on the housetop glorifies God in its dumbness, but it doesn't know it. The universe in its vastness and remoteness glorifies God but it doesn't know it. But God made man in His own image to be the Priest of creation, to express for all creatures the praises of God, so that through the lips of man the heavens might declare the glory of God, that we who know we are God's creatures might worship God and in our worship gather up the worship of all creation.' (p. 41). The central thesis of Torrance's essay on worship is that Christ is the one true worshipper who now by his Spirit leads us in our worship. 'The writer of the Epistle to the Hebrews describes our Lord as the *Leiturgos* (Hebrews 8:2)—"the leader of our worship", "the minister of the real sanctuary which the Lord pitched and not man",... The Worship of Christ is thus the worship which gathers up the worship of Israel and replaces it, and it is this Worship which is the substance of all Christian worship.' (pp. 43-44).

[44]*Sanctorum Communio*, pp. 56ff.
[45]*Ibid.*, p. 119.

between community and society as to make a distinction between the *Ekklesia* (community) and the Church as an institutional and legal entity.[46] Brunner, who was clearly influenced by the writings of Ferdinand Ebner and Martin Buber, found the I-Thou relation to be particularly expressive as a way in which man finds his authentic personhood. While this provides a basically anthropological basis for his concept of community, he would also say that apart from an 'encounter' with God which produces a corresponding 'answer' of faith, man is not in community apart from the proclamation of the *Kerygma*, and the reception of the Holy Spirit.[47] In effect, then, man is only capable of social relations and not true community apart from this encounter.

From a more philosophical perspective, John Macmurray holds that community is possible only when society moves beyond its common organic and functional unity and begins to relate out of motives which are 'intentional':

> A community, however, is a unity of persons as persons. It cannot be defined in functional terms, by relation to a common purpose. It is not organic in structure, and cannot be constituted or maintained by organization, but only by the motives which sustain the personal relations of its members.[48]

Macmurray, therefore, would maintain that true personhood is only possible when man is related intentionally to another person. Because the self is basically an agent who acts, personhood can only exist when there is a community of acting agents who intentionally relate out of love.

The common principle which unites these three concepts of community, despite their differing emphasis as to what community signifies, is the idea that true personhood, and thus true humanity, is primarily achieved through a relation of persons and not through any other level of social existence. In Brunner and Bonhoeffer there is a strong tendency to see in community the concretion of personhood in a particularly theological way. But because community is defined along relational terms, the distinctives of personhood are centred in the degree of inter-relatedness (love) which is now possible because of either faith or the presence of the Holy Spirit. Bonhoeffer would emphasize the ethical aspects of this inter-relatedness, while Brunner would see the distinguishing characteristic as fraternal. The tendency for all such emphasis on community as inter-relatedness in contrast to human society in its

[46]*The Misunderstanding of the Church*, Lutterworth Press, London, 1952, p. 107.
[47]*The Christian Doctrine of the Church, Faith, and the Consummation*, Dogmatics, Vol. III, Lutterworth Press, London, 1962, p. 41.
[48]*Persons in Relation*, pp. 157-158.

functional forms, is to maintain that human social relations cannot achieve this degree of personhood apart from faith in Christ, however it is understood. Unfortunately, this kind of qualitative distinction made at the level of inter-relatedness is difficult to sustain, if, indeed, it can even be made in the first place.

Certainly one would want to say that man is more truly personal and therefore more genuinely human when he exists in a community of relation than when he merely organizes himself into a society. But would one want to say that all community is Christian, or that only Christian faith produces community? The question again, is of how one understands the transcendence of God. If man is only truly man when he exists in a relation to the transcendence of God, does community itself as human inter-relatedness constitute that transcendence? I suspect that this was the case for both Bonhoeffer and Brunner, though Bonhoeffer moved towards the proposition that all true community was Christ, while Brunner approached it more kerygmatically, Christ produces community through faith.[49]

I have used the word 'community' as the basic form of lived transcendence in the Spirit because I believe it to be the fundamental character of man's true personhood. But if man's personhood is constituted by the transcendence of God, as we have already established, then true personhood is community which participates in the life of God. Therefore, an ontology of community can only be explicated on a trinitarian basis. That is, man's capacity for community becomes an incapacity when viewed from a strictly anthropological perspective. Man does move towards community, and I think one must say, does experience com-

[49]I have not included the concept of community as held by Karl Barth in this discussion because, though he taught that there was an 'inner circle' and an 'outer circle' constituted by the elect community (*Gemeinde*) living within the larger circle of 'world occurrence', his concept of the church was so strongly eschatological that one could not say that he saw community in strictly historical terms. (Cf. *Church Dogmatics*, II/2, p. 196; III/4, p. 490; I/1, p. 514). The 'time' of the community (the church) for Barth was the 'time between the times', that is, the time between the ascension and the final *par-ousia*. The community as the 'event' of the Kingdom points to the fulfilment, for Christ himself is already totally present, but on the other hand, it is provisional and weak. Because it is the life of Christ himself in the world, it has no form or power of its own, but rather exists to serve and to die. As 'event', the community *is* the Body of Christ, not merely a symbol or representation of that Body. But this is precisely why the church cannot have a history or be simply an 'event' in the daily life of the Christian. Because the 'event' of the community is the event of Christ himself in solidarity with the world, and yet, acting over and against the world, the event of the community is eschatological. Through the community, Christ continues to speak and act in a 'creaturely' way in history, but without having a history, that is, without being a predicate of history (cf. *Church Dogmatics*, I/1, p. 514). See also, Colm O'Grady, *The Church in the Theology of Karl Barth*, Geoffrey Chapman, London, 1968, especially pp. 91ff., 106ff., 190ff., 246ff.

munity, but he experiences community as merely a 'capacity'. However, the dimension of God's transcendence, as the constitutive element of community, can only be known as incapacity from the standpoint of man himself. Yet, this is a 'capacity' which expresses itself as a movement towards community, of which the interpersonal is evidence.[50] Through the Incarnation, the transcendence of God made human community both kenotic and ek-static. Through Word and Spirit, God entered human community to the depths of its incapacity, and from that depth raised a response to God which completed community through a union of man with God. In this sense, the ontological structure of community can be said to be trinitarian.

Because Word and Spirit can never be separated, the kenotic community is at the same time the ek-static community. Which is to say, the ek-static community reveals to the community of man its *incapacity* which it can only experience as a capacity for community. Therefore, the Spirit of God does not produce a qualitatively *better* human community, and enter with the claim that only in the Spirit is there community at all, but on the contrary, the Spirit speaks from the incapacity of community to complete itself, and speaks to God for community on the basis of the community of humanity with the Incarnate Word. Rather than making the distinction between community and society, and hoping thereby to distinguish between the church and the world, the distinction is solely one of the Spirit, and it is the distinction between the ek-static community, which experiences community as incapacity (thus as grace), and all other community, which experiences community as capacity. It would seem to follow from this that the kenotic community is not the point at which a distinction is to be made within the human community, but that it is rather the Spirit producing the ek-static dimension of community where the distinction arises. Having established the true distinctive of the kenotic community as its life in the Spirit, there will now emerge a new freedom to consider the implications of the relation of the transcendence of God to the world through a lived transcendence which seeks to close the circle of transcendence by living in the world.

---

[50]Inter-personal transcendence, therefore, cannot be a 'form' into which divine transcendence is poured, but is a capacity which reveals an incapacity for divine transcendence. I have drawn the concept of capacity/incapacity from the essay by Dr. John Zizioulas, 'Human Capacity and Human Incapacity': 'All that we have tried to say so far by looking at human capacity and human incapacity from the angle of Personhood shows that in being a Person man has his capacity *in incapacity*. This means that he is essentially dependent on communion and that ultimately, because of the idea of ontological presence implied in this communion, he can be fully in communion, only if he overcomes the tragic element of absence which is the inevitable form in which the presence of being is offered to him as a creature.' p. 10.

If it is true that the world is 'a world of fugitives', the Christian is a 'Christ' among fugitives, and the church, to some extent at least, must become the 'fugitive' church.

'As thou didst send me into the world, so I have sent them into the world.'[51]

[51]John 17:18.

Chapter VIII

Living in the World

1 'The Incarnational Christian'

Long ago there lived a Man who was crucified for being too loving and too lovable.

And strange to relate I met him thrice yesterday.

The first time He was asking a policeman not to take a prostitute to prison; the second time He was drinking wine with an outcast; and the third time He was having a fistfight with a promoter inside a church.[1]

If there are two sides to humanity, Christ will be found on the wrong side. This has never been acceptable to man, but it is the way of God. And it was the way of Christ. He was not a religious man in the way that men think of the religious 'side of life'. He did not have access into the privileged sanctuaries of the priests. In the midst of a religious culture that prized appearance and cultivated form, he appeared among men clothed simply in grace and truth. He refused to recognize as spiritual that which was artificial and affected. He valued the truth of being and doing over right-sounding words and beautiful prayers. He stated divine realities in terms of human experience. His life-style was that of a man who lived among men; where distinctions were made between the sacred and the profane which tended to be inhuman, he openly 'profaned' the sanctity of even the law to give dignity to man (Luke 6:6-11). He appeared in the world, as Bonhoeffer said, 'incognito as a beggar among beggars, as an outcast among the outcast, despairing among the despairing, dying among the dying'.[2] This incomprehensible solidarity with the destiny of all flesh, leading him to accept in obedience the death of a sinner—a refugee from God—caused his own disciple to protest, and brought forth a rebuke upon all human ways of thinking which seek to deny that solidarity: '. . . you are not on the side of God, but of men.'[3]

This solidarity of God with all humanity through the life of the Incarnate Logos, revealed the kenotic form of divine transcendence and

[1]K. Gibran, *Sand and Foam*, Alfred A. Knopf, New York, 1926, p. 40.
[2]*Christology*, p. 11.
[3]Matthew 16:23.

constitutes the kenotic community of lived transcendence in the Spirit. There now appear to be two distinct dimensions to this lived transcendence: the way of God coming to man, and the way of man coming to God. These two dimensions correspond to the kenotic community and the ek-static community of life in the Spirit. Instead, then, of three separate, but related implications of historical transcendence in terms of lived transcendence, it would now appear that there is but one implication: lived transcendence is a community of life in the Spirit which is both kenotic and ek-static. The two-foldness of this implication was explored in the last chapter. What will now be taken up in this chapter for further consideration is but one aspect of the kenotic community as it relates to the problem of how we should understand the relation of the kenotic community to the world. This was raised, and then left for further explication in this chapter, as the problem of how one can make a distinction between a member of the kenotic community and the world when the single 'qualifying' principle is to share the common humanity of Jesus Christ.[4] This will leave the second dimension of lived transcendence—the ek-static community—to be further explored in the final chapter.

There does exist a tension between Christ and the world expressed as an irreconcilable contradiction between good and evil, love and hate, and light as opposed to darkness (John 3:19-20); there is a corresponding tension, it appears, between the kenotic community and the world: 'I am praying for them; I am not praying for the world.... They are not of the world, even as I am not of the world ... the world has not known thee, but I have known thee; ...'[5] World history exists as an antithesis to God's thesis, that is, his creative purpose and will. When man seeks through religion a common denominator to these irreconcilable 'worlds', the essential solidarity between God and man is obscured in the religious movement which originates in man himself.[6] The conception of religion as a synthesis which resolves the antithesis (human contradiction) and the thesis (divine will) either dissolves the reality of God into the self-consciousness of the human subject, or volatilizes the reality of the human into a supra-human transcendence which takes the form of mysticism. In either case, the solidarity of God with man *in* his contradiction is lost. When the eternal Logos entered into the world and 'became flesh', a solidarity was established between God and man at the level of *actual* humanity, not idealized humanity. It is in this sense that one can say that Jesus is on the 'wrong side', if one makes any distinction at all within man as such, which, of course, is untenable in view of

---

[4]See above, p. 236.

[5]John 17:9, 16, 25.

[6]This is a theme established by Karl Barth. Cf. *Church Dogmatics*, IV/3, pp. 708-709.

the Incarnation itself. The particular tension between Jesus and the world was not between judge and lawbreaker, but it was a tension created by the 'yes' uttered through his life of obedience from the side of the law-breaker himself. 'I did not come to judge the world but to save the world', said Jesus.[7] As such he lived in the world as the 'new man', who was also at the same time 'one body' with estranged man.

It is in this sense, then, that the kenotic community exists in tension with the world. Not the tension of condemnation, making a distinction by separation from, but the tension which results from penetration of the world—the tension which is produced by the reconciling act itself. The Christian man also bears the irreconcilable contradiction in the 'one body'—the kenotic community. But not so as to dissolve the contradiction so that there is a religious synthesis. But the Christian is the 'new man' even as Christ was the 'new thing' of God's grace.[8] The conformity, then, of the Christian is to the Incarnate Son of God and not to the world,[9] but this conformity involves a solidarity with humanity—solidarity with the world—which can be expressed as the incarnational aspect of kenotic community.

> Solidarity with the world means full commitment to it, unreserved participation in its situation, in the promise given it by creation, in its responsibility for the arrogance, sloth and falsehood which reign within it, in its suffering under the resultant distress, but primarily and supremely in the free grace of God demonstrated and addressed to it in Jesus Christ, and therefore in its hope ... the community which knows the world is necessarily the community which is committed to it.[10]

The kenotic community does not merely penetrate the world as a privileged community which maintains its own distinctive boundaries and identity—a form of 'spiritual colonialism'—but the penetration can only be one which bears the 'incognito' of the Incarnation itself; not in a 'cunning masquerade', as Barth again reminds us, but

> in an unmasking in which it makes itself known to others as akin to them, rejoicing with them that do rejoice and weeping with them that weep, not confirming and strengthening them in evil nor betraying and surrendering them for its own good; ... by accepting the fact that it must be honestly and unreservedly among them and with them, on the same level and footing, in the same boat and with the same limits as any or all of them.[11]

[7]John 12:47.
[8]Ephesians 2:15.
[9]John 17:14-16; Romans 12:1-2.
[10]Karl Barth, *Church Dogmatics*, IV/3, p. 773.
[11]*Ibid.*, pp. 774-775.

Now if this is taken seriously, as it must be if the kenotic community follows out its own intrinsic character, the Christian dare not break the 'incognito' by setting the sacred over against the secular and the supernatural over against the natural. This would itself be a conforming to the world rather than conforming to the Incarnate Son of God. This was the distortion of the Pharisees in Jesus' own day—they represented God to the world in precisely the way in which the world expected it and in such a way that the world could securely embrace it without being confronted and shattered by it. The miracles of Jesus were far easier to live with than his own words. By his miracles he could be put in the category of a 'holy man' and allowed to remain within the society which had a place for the religious man. But his words—'if you have seen me you have seen the father'—had no form of accommodation because they were spoken 'man to man', out of the same secular, human context and existence in which his contemporaries lived. The transcendence of God in its kenotic form means precisely this. That the reality of God enters into an absolute relation with the world in its own forms. The transcendence of the eternal Logos was not demonstrated by the supernatural over against the natural, nor by the miraculous breaking into the historical, but through a solidarity of relation in which the total 'otherness' of God is actually there in confrontation. The attributing of miracles to Jesus, therefore, did not break this 'incognito' of kenotic transcendence, for the category of miracle belongs to the created world, not to God; but neither did the miracles attest to his transcendence in an unambiguous way, for the authority behind miracle was as often taken to be demonic.[12]

Now we have seen that the characteristic of kenotic community is solidarity, not separation. Conformity to the Incarnate Son of God entails solidarity with humanity, which shares a common nature with Jesus Christ. Therefore, we can conclude that the kenotic community does not exist as an entity in time and space distinct from the community of man as such.[13] This is the conclusion to which Bonhoeffer

[12]'The miracles are no breaching of the incognito. The ancient religious world is full of miracle workers and healers. Jesus is not alone in this. The realm of miracles is not identical with the realm of God. True, the miracles may exceed normal everyday happenings, but they are only on another level within the created world. The concept which goes with miracle is not that of God, but that of magic. Magic remains within the world. If Jesus does miracles, he preserves his incognito within the magical picture of the world. It is not miracle which accredits him as the Son of God in the New Testament. On the contrary, his authority is taken to be demonic.' D. Bonhoeffer, *Christology*, p. 115. It is this ambiguous quality of miracle which makes it unsuitable for an evidence of the transcendence of God in and of itself. A miracle has no ontic value in terms of divine transcendence while the humanity of Christ does.

[13]We are moving towards the point where 'kenotic community' will have a more specialized meaning. See below, p. 259.

was forced after making an attempt, first of all, to identify Christ with community and then to locate that community as entity within the world. We have already shown how, in Bonhoeffer's earlier works, the sociological aspect dominated his thinking in terms which gave shape and space to the community of Christ. This thinking can still be found in his Christology lectures of 1933 where he says: 'What does it mean that Christ as *Word* is also community? It means that the Logos of God has extension in space and time in and as the community.'[14] But even as this concept of the church was put at the disposal of the Confessing Church during the war in order to make an absolute distinction between the true community of Christ and the Nazi controlled State Church, Bonhoeffer was already creating a non-spatial concept of the community of Christ through an emphasis on Christ as the transcendent 'person' who was concretized, not by the spatial form of the community, but through a life of discipleship and obedience.[15] And so, by the time Bonhoeffer took up the writing of his lectures which were published posthumously as *Ethics*, he was to criticize the restriction of love to the 'closed circle of the devout', and suggested that we must leave behind the picture of 'two spheres', that of the church and the world, each with its own space.[16] And so he is led to make his strongest statement with regard to the relation of the church to the world:

> If we now follow the New Testament in applying to the Church the concept of the body of Christ, this is not by any means intended primarily as representing the separation of the Church from the world. On the contrary, it is implicit in the New Testament statement concerning the Incarnation of God in Christ that all men are taken up, enclosed and borne within the body of Christ and that this is just what the congregation of the faithful are to make known to the world by their words and by their lives. What is intended here is not separation from the world but the summoning of the world into the fellowship of this body of Christ, to which in truth it already belongs.[17]

What continued to plague Bonhoeffer, was the way in which the 'congregation of the faithful' could preserve its own identity if all men were assumed to belong to the body of Christ by virtue of their common humanity with the Incarnate Son of God. As we have seen, his concept of the 'secret discipline' was one such attempt to define the church in

[14]*Ibid.*, p. 60.

[15]Cf. John A. Phillips, *The Form of Christ in the World*, pp. 74-76. Out of this period came Bonhoeffer's two books: *Life Together*, SCM Press Ltd., London, 1970, first published under the title *Gemeinsames Leben*, Chr. Kaiser Verlag, Munich, 1949; and, *The Cost of Discipleship*, SCM Press Ltd., London, 1969, first published as *Nachfolge*, Chr. Kaiser Verlag, Munich, 1937.

[16]*Ethics*, pp. 129, 205.

[17]*Ibid.*, p. 206.

its dynamic life of the Spirit within the total body of Christ.

The matter with which we are concerned here, however, is the identification of the body of Christ with the total community of man. 'Everything would be ruined if one were to try to reserve Christ for the Church', says Bonhoeffer, 'and to allow the world only some kind of law, even if it were a Christian law. Christ died for the world, and it is only in the midst of the world that Christ is Christ.'[18] The language which Bonhoeffer uses here seems to state quite explicitly the situation as we have already done in terms of the kenotic community. In a kenotic sense, the body of Christ is co-extensive with all humanity, and this is the principle to which Bonhoeffer appeals as being intrinsic to the Incarnation. But is this in accordance with the New Testament's use of the expression 'body of Christ'?

The use of the figurative expression 'body of Christ', or its shortened form 'body', is restricted to those letters generally attributed to Paul.[19] It is obviously an expression and concept which is uniquely Pauline, and only a brief study is needed to see that he generally uses the expression as either an organic or a spatial metaphor to represent the redeemed fellowship of those who are baptized by the Spirit into Christ through faith. A passage which is typical of such an intended significance is found at the beginning of a long exposition on the nature of this fellowship:

> For just as the body is one and has many members, and all the members of the body, though many, are one body, so it is with Christ. For by one Spirit we were all baptized into one body—Jews or Greeks, slaves or free—and all were made to drink of one Spirit.[20]

In a passage with eucharistic overtones, where a strong ethical demand is considered to arise as an implicit condition of participation in the body of Christ, Paul draws the lines of fellowship around the body of Christ as it is defined by those who all 'partake of the one bread'.[21] Those who worship idols cannot participate in this fellowship because they are not of the *same body*. We are forced to the inescapable conclusion that Paul intended by the expression 'body of Christ' to include only those who have received the Spirit and thus constitute the fellowship of the redeemed, as distinct from the total community of man.

Now what do we say to this? First of all, it may be that it was unfortunate that Paul chose to use the very powerful and illuminating

---

[18]*Ibid.*, pp. 205-206.
[19]The relevant passages are: Romans 12:4-5; I Corinthians 10:16; 11:29; 12:12-27; Ephesians 1:23; 3:6; 4:4; 4:12; 4:16; 5:30; Colossians 1:18; 1:24; 3:15.
[20]I Corinthians 12:12-13.
[21]I Corinthians 10:17.

metaphor of the body to designate those who were participants in Christ
by receiving the Spirit as opposed to those who only share a common
humanity with Christ. I say unfortunate, because the phrase is thus
pre-empted from use in the kenotic sense of signifying that the Incarnation has incorporated humanity into a catholicity of covenant response.
It is this idea that Bonhoeffer has in mind when he says that it is
'implicit in the New Testament statement concerning the Incarnation
of God in Christ that all men are taken up, enclosed and borne within
the body of Christ'.[22] The expression 'body of Christ' has genuine
incarnational significance when referred to the fact that all men are
'brothers' of Christ through the flesh. The use of the expression by Paul
in a restrictive sense to those who are baptized into fellowship with
Christ through the Spirit tends to restrict Christ to the redeemed fellowship as defined in either ethical or spatial terms (and usually both).
This has the further effect of obscuring the kenotic community in its
relation to all men and has the danger of placing an obstacle between
the world and its solidarity with God—an obstacle which the Incarnation
itself removed once and for all.

I think that we also need to say that Paul certainly did not intend
to restrict the Incarnation in its effects to the body of Christ as he
defined it. 'God was in Christ', says Paul in another place, 'reconciling
the world to himself, not counting their trespasses against them, and
entrusting to us the message of reconciliation.'[23] While it is true that
Paul's correspondence was directed to the church, and thus his
Christology tended to be shaped by the ecclesiastical problems with
which he was dealing, he did at least recognize that those who were
on the fringes of the church, if not indeed outside the body of Christ,
were 'brothers for whom Christ died'.[24] In his personal ministry with
men in the world, Paul became 'all things to all men', including becoming a man 'outside the law', because he was 'under the law of Christ'.[25]
This would at least seem to be an implicit assertion that the ground
for all men's relation to Christ is the same, and that the 'law of Christ'
is in fact a governing principle which superseded distinctions made on
any other basis. But perhaps the strongest testimony to the incarnational
truth that those not considered as belonging to the church are nonetheless 'brothers of Christ' comes from Christ himself, who encouraged the
visiting of the sick and those in prison, the clothing of the naked and
the feeding of the hungry as equivalent to that which is either denied
or done to Christ (Matthew 15:31-46).

Because it is doubtful that one can follow Bonhoeffer in attempting

[22]*Ethics*, p. 206.
[23]II Corinthians 5:19.
[24]I Corinthians 8:11; Romans 5:6; 14:15.
[25]I Corinthians 9:19-23.

to re-interpret the expression 'body of Christ' and give it a more universal significance as representing the place which all men have in Christ by virtue of a common humanity, I would prefer to use the metaphor in the commonly accepted biblical sense, as long as it is clearly understood that it refers to but one aspect of Christ's relation to the world, and thus cannot be taken as a definitive distinction between the kenotic community and human society in general. Accordingly, I intend to signify by the expression 'kenotic community', that incarnational solidarity which the Christian has with all humanity, a solidarity which permits of no distinction made between the Christian and the world by limiting the Incarnation to a community of human fellowship within human society. Up to this point, kenotic community has been used in a general sense of solidarity with the world, with its general implication being that it includes all that is meant by the term 'church' as well. From this point on, the expression 'kenotic community' will take on a more specialized meaning, as it refers quite specifically to the solidarity which the church has with man in the world.

However, it must immediately be added that solidarity with the world does not constitute identity with the world. The solidarity with humanity which resulted from the 'Word becoming flesh', did not make Jesus 'identical' with the world, nor did it make him 'identical' with every other man in the sense that, as man, he had an existential existence independent of the divine Logos.[26] The distinction between Christ and man was absolute while at the same time there was a solidarity with man which is permanent. This is the implication of the *kenosis* when considered as the historical transcendence of God through the Incarnate Logos. The kenotic community, therefore, cannot be distinguished from the world by splitting the solidarity of all humanity in Christ, and thus cannot take the form of one entity within humanity set against another. That is, the distinction cannot be either an organic or a spatial one in terms of the church as entity. The kenotic community, considered incarnationally, is the foundation of all human community, and the church can never deny its common participation in this community without denying Christ himself. This, of course, does not yet say what 'church' is, but it says what 'church' cannot be—namely, an entity which distinguishes itself from the world by breaking solidarity with humanity. At the very least, this seems to be an imperative of the Incarnation which calls into question every implication that Christ can be contained within a specific organism which exists as an entity within the world.

[26]The question of how we are to understand Jesus as a 'real man', and yet not identical to all men, is explained with lucidity and keen insight into the historical problems by Lewis B. Smedes, *The Incarnation: Trends in Modern Anglican Thought*, J. H. Kok N.V. Kampen, 1953, pp. 147ff.

It calls into question the implication that absolute distinctions are to be made at the *boundaries* of the church which lie within humanity. But it also raises the question of how *any* distinction can be made within the solidarity of kenotic community.

Here again we must allow the implications of historical transcendence to be traced out patiently into the life of lived transcendence. We have seen that the solidarity of the divine Logos with humanity did not obliterate the distinction between God and man, but rather, clarified it in such a way that an intimate relation with God is now possible through the Incarnate Son of God. Historical transcendence taught us that Logos is not intrinsically alien to flesh, and that *kenosis* is not a renunciation of transcendence. The issue involved in the question of the divinity of Christ is that of the transcendence of God. Divine transcendence is not a quality of being which is defined by abstracting from a non-divine creation or nature. Transcendence is difference in solidarity, and as such, it is the extrinsic, rather than the intrinsic reality of Being. Or, one could say, it is *par-ousia* rather than *ousia*. Through the Incarnation we see exposed the *par-ousia* of God which is the 'presence' of God as three-in-one. But we also discover that the creation of God, and thus his creature, exists in the same form of 'presence' which is expressed as difference within solidarity. The image of God is rooted in the transcendence of God, which means that man is capable of experiencing absolute difference in solidarity. The kenotic community is the ground for the solidarity, within which the 'difference' can be experienced as transcendence without destroying the solidarity. The 'metaphysic' for grasping this lies in the very structure of the trinity itself as the 'presence' (*par-ousia*) of God given in the Incarnation.

When we speak, therefore, of the incarnational Christian, it is much more than a certain 'style of life' which is exemplified in the life of Jesus to be used as a model of kenotic living. The incarnational Christian bears witness to the 'presence' (*par-ousia*) of Christ within the solidarity of kenotic community. It is impossible for the body of Christ as an organism which exists as entity within the world to be this 'presence' without obliterating the very distinctives which give it the status of an entity. Why is this? Precisely because man is already entity by virtue of his solidarity with humanity. Each man bears the totality of humanity in himself and thus is the hypostasis of humanity. Two or three, or more men, cannot be 'hypostatized' into an entity distinct from other men and thereby have a particular ontological relation to the humanity of Christ which is different from that of each man's hypostasis of humanity. 'Where two or three are gathered in my name', said Christ, 'there am I in the midst of them.'[27] But what really is the

[27]Matthew 18:20.

difference between that 'gathering' and any other gathering on the part of any other two or three men as viewed from the perspective of the solidarity of man? There is none at all. The 'presence' of Christ in the two or three can only be known when the boundary between them and others is obliterated so that the difference can become 'presence' at the level of human solidarity. The moment the 'two or three' attempt to embody the 'difference' in any form or structure which separates them from other men, a boundary has been drawn which will place Christ either on one side or the other. It should be clear from the Gospel accounts of Jesus' life and ministry that he recognized no such boundaries. Therefore, I have asserted that it is impossible for the body of Christ to exist as an entity in the world in such a way that *its* distinctiveness represents the difference, or that its boundaries represent the transcendence of God as the 'presence' of Christ. This does not mean that the body of Christ as a fellowship of Christians does not have a significant life of its own within the kenotic community, but that is not the point under discussion here. The point is, the 'difference', or the transcendence of God, can only be expressed in solidarity with humanity. To this extent, when the church sets itself out to be 'different' from the world, it no longer makes a 'difference' to men in the world.

It remains, therefore, to state precisely how the difference or the transcendence of Christ within the kenotic community has its true expression. The subtitle of this chapter holds the clue. The 'incarnational Christian', not the incarnational church, is the point at which to begin. There is a sense in which the church too is incarnational, but only through the incarnational life of its members. Lived transcendence is an incarnational life which involves complete solidarity with an absolute difference. Only in 'man to man' relations can this occur. This is not simply a 'philosophy of personalism' where the I-Thou relation is seen as an ontological link with divine transcendence. I say 'man to man' only because I wish to emphasize that solidarity is involved with our being human 'entities' where one person's humanity is qualitatively the same as that of another. 'Man to man' does not mean 'individual to individual', but, person to person in the sense that there is a catholicity of humanity which locates the core of our personhood in the humanity which God has taken to himself. The capacity for I-Thou relations, of course, does mean that there is capacity for transcendence, that is, a difference within solidarity. But considered from the standpoint of divine transcendence, the human I-Thou relation fundamentally belongs to the kenotic community—it does not constitute the 'difference'.

Spirit and Word constitute the possibility of solidarity with a difference. It was through the Spirit that the Incarnate Word existed in

solidarity with man and yet brought 'difference' to bear in an absolute
sense—Jesus is God. The 'difference' was expressed 'man to man', that
is, at the level of Jesus' solidarity with man, his hypostasis of humanity
into the man that he was, yet, God's 'presence' was there in an
absolute sense. But it was the 'presence' (*par-ousia*) of God himself in
Christ by the Spirit which constituted the difference as well as the
unity. There was a 'oneness' with God which was particularly expressed
from a relation of solidarity with man. This is the truth captured by
the language of the prayer of Jesus: 'The glory which thou hast given
me I have given to them, that they may be one even as we are one,
I in them and thou in me, that they may become perfectly one, so
that the world may know that thou hast sent me and hast loved them
as thou hast loved me.'[28] The prayer that those who believe in Jesus
are 'to be one', is not simply a prayer for a communal type of life.
A communal group as 'entity' does not impress the world with the reality
of God, nor with the love of God, because the very boundary which
creates the entity of communal life breaks solidarity with the world.
No, the oneness must be incarnational. That is, it is first of all
the oneness which Jesus experienced with the Father which is to be
the same oneness which the Christian experiences with God in
Christ.

While Jesus made it perfectly clear that he was not the Father,
he did not hesitate to claim that he was standing 'as the Father'
among men. 'He who has seen me has seen the Father...'[29] Jesus did
not merely stand as the representative of the Father, pointing away
from himself as if to say: don't look to me, I am not the Father,
look away from me to the Father and then you will see God. But he
clearly said that the Father was *there* in him, and that to know him
was to know the Father. There was a transparency, as it were, not in
a docetic sense, where the humanity of Christ only seemed to be real,
but in the sense that truth is transparent and undivided. The distinction
between Father and Son did not involve a separation in terms of
'presence' (*par-ousia*). The 'presence' is, therefore, the 'oneness' in
the sense that 'presence' is the ek-stasis of divine being in communion.
When we say that God is 'there' in Christ, we do not mean present
to man as an entity among other entities, but God is 'present to
himself' in Christ. The humanity of Christ is the horizon of divine
existence which at the same time becomes the horizon of human personhood. This means that solidarity with humanity gives an ek-static
dimension to humanity through the oneness of Christ with the Father.
Christ, therefore, is not related in a 'one-to-one' relation with man as
individual, abetted by the Holy Spirit as another 'individual'; rather,

[28]John 17:22-23.
[29]John 14:9.

Christ is 'present' to humanity in its catholicity, which each person bears in its totality as one aspect of personhood. But this 'presence' of Christ is itself personhood as the ek-static movement of being into communion. Through the Holy Spirit, then, *each* person shares in the 'oneness' of personhood—'as we are one...that they may be one.' Therefore, the Holy Spirit cannot be said to 'individuate' Christ by relating him 'person by person', but as the Spirit brings man from his 'individuated' existence to completion of personhood in oneness with the life of God, this 'oneness' is oneness with 'presence', so that Christ is 'present' to the world through the horizon of his own humanity, which each person bears in its totality.

Now if we take this 'as we are one' to be the kind of thing signified by 'that they may be one', it becomes clear just what it means to express lived transcendence in terms of being an incarnational Christian. The Christian is enabled to express the same transparency within his solidarity with man and thus stand 'as Christ' in the world. Thus, instead of pointing away from himself, from his own humanity, to Christ, the Christian must say: to become involved with me is to come up against Jesus Christ who is 'present' to our humanity through the reality of the Holy Spirit who completes my life in the personhood of divine communion. While it is true that one cannot speak as another (or the same) Incarnation of Christ, one should live and speak incarnation*ally* so that Christ again has hands to reach out into the world to give, feet to walk the roads of life with men, and arms to embrace the lonely and hold close the estranged.[30] Here then is the closing of the circle of transcendence towards which we have been moving for a considerable time. The solidarity of the Christian with the world is not

---

[30]Karl Barth would not agree that the Christian 'stands as Christ' in the world, for his concept of being incarnationally related to the world is heavily weighted by an eschatological emphasis: 'In the community it takes place that Jesus Christ Himself, the living Word of God, is present and revealed to certain men together in world-occurrence as the One He is above in the height and hiddenness of God.... These men in their own time and place here find themselves commonly ruled and determined by the fact that in speech and action He always comes to their time and place.' *Church Dogmatics*, IV/3, pp. 756-757. What Barth wants to preserve is the hiddenness, the 'grace' of the church, in its world occurrence. It is only when Christ 'comes to their time and place' that the community of Christ becomes Christ. I feel that there is an important eschatological dimension to a life of lived transcendence, and I will deal with this in the final chapter, but to emphasize the eschatological at the expense of the incarnational aspect of the Christian's life is to introduce an unnecessary dialectic between eternity and time. I would like to feel that by understanding 'presence' as the presence of God to himself by the life of the Spirit in the solidarity of man with Christ, this 'presence' is *not* made the predicate of human existence (which is what Barth warns against), while at the same time, taking seriously the temporal and historical aspect of 'presence' as lived transcendence in the solidarity of kenotic community.

simply a fact of his existence in kenotic community with Christ in the humanity of all men, but it is the 'place' where God transcends the world in love. For God's transcendence is the *difference* which love makes in solidarity. Again, it is not that the world needs the Christian, and thus is incomplete without that love (though that is true), but it is that the Christian is incomplete without the world, without closing the circle of transcendence by loving the world that God loves (John 3:16). This is why I have shown that the kenotic community is not just the church assuming a posture of humility and poverty, nor is it just the world; it is Christ in solidarity with the world, but in such a way that there is tension also.

The kenotic community is also the ek-static community, but there no boundary can be drawn, though not all believe and receive the Spirit. But what the world receives, it receives by 'looking to' the Christian, who 'gives' the transcendence in which he himself lives. When Peter and John were confronted by the 'world' at the door of the temple, they interrupted their prayers and said to the man: 'Look at us....I give you what I have; in the name of Jesus Christ of Nazareth, walk.' (Acts 3:1-6). Through the Holy Spirit, God is present to himself in the Christian. This is the ek-static dimension of the kenotic community which has its primary focal point in the believer and only secondarily in the church as a functioning entity within the world. This does not mean that the Christian is an 'individual', who only has a subsequent relation to the community of Christ, for his believing, as we have asserted earlier, is conditioned at its source by his belonging.

The Spirit has no historical transcendence of his own, but has the historical life of Christ as transcendent grounds in history. Thus, when the Spirit of God assumes concrete form in the world, he re-forms man in the image of the Incarnate Son of God, which is the true image of God for man. We also said that the Spirit forms Christ in the concrete life of the *other* person in the kenotic community, not in one's own life. This makes it possible for one to have a real relation to Christ in the Spirit without denying one's actual existence. We can now see that this is rather an artificial way of stating the case. For, obviously, when I receive the Spirit of God as a gift, I am re-formed in the image of Christ *for* the other person, even as another is *for* me. In thinking now specifically of the way in which Christ is 'present' in the kenotic community in such a way that there is a 'difference' within the solidarity, one must assume that there is a 'difference' between the one who has received the Spirit of Christ as a gift of faith, and so belongs to the 'body of Christ', as Paul says, and the one who, though he is in the same kenotic community, has not rightly received the gift of faith and thus is not living a life of lived transcendence in the Spirit.

I wonder if one would want to go so far as Bonhoeffer and say that the one who has not professed faith in Christ is a Christian nonetheless, because he is in the kenotic community (the body of Christ for Bonhoeffer), and that the only difference is that the believer *knows* that he is a Christian while the unbeliever does not?[31] I think that I can understand why Bonhoeffer wants to say that, because he is anxious to avoid any implication that the church or Christian 'possesses' Christ in some way that the world does not, or even that Christ possesses the church in a way that he does not the world. And I would agree that one would want to eliminate the static 'spaces' and 'boundaries' which separate the church from the world by conferring distinctiveness upon the church as an entity within society.[32] But I think Bonhoeffer is closer to the truth when he speaks of the 'foreignness' and strangeness which enters in when the Christian testifies to the world's belonging to the kenotic community through Christ;[33] however, I would think that this 'foreignness' points to an *absolute* difference *within* the solidarity of the kenotic community which has its source in the transcendence of Spirit who re-forms particular entities of humanity into the image of Christ by making them one with the community of God's own life. And I would think that if the term 'Christian' is to have any significance at all it should have a transcendent significance, not a relative one. I would prefer, myself, to make a transcendent distinction between Christian and non-Christian, while at the same time preserving the solidarity.

But the transcendent significance cannot be determined by the boundaries of the body of Christ as entity, but only through the life of the Spirit where solidarity with humanity is ontologically united with the humanity of Christ. If we seem to have lost a great deal in relativizing the boundaries of the church, we have gained even more in now being able to absolutize the difference between belief and unbelief in terms of life in the Spirit, without splitting the solidarity of Christ with man. The 'difference', we can now say, is not institutional, or even sacramental, but evangelical. In fact, only an evangelical Christian can affirm the complete solidarity of humanity in Christ and at the same time testify to the absolute difference.

If one seeks to establish the transcendence of God (the difference) as sacramental or institutional, either the solidarity of Christ with humanity is ruptured in order to make the distinction, or what is basically implied in such a concept of transcendence leads (ultimately) to an explicit assertion—namely, that there is really no absolute distinction between the body of Christ and the world. In this case, the

[31]*Ethics*, p. 143.
[32]*Ibid.*, p. 201.
[33]*Ibid.*, p. 206.

Lived Transcendence and the Reality of God

kenotic community is taken to be identical with the church and the
boundaries are obliterated without retaining the centre. It would appear,
then, that one cannot be an incarnational Christian without also being
an evangelical Christian.[34] The boundaries can only be erased if there
is a centre. But what we must explore further is the question: How
does an evangelical Christian know where the centre is?

2 'The Evangelical Christian'

If therefore the divine style chooses the foolish, the shallow, the
ignoble, to put to shame the strength and ingenuity of all profane
writers, there certainly is need of the illuminated, enthused and eager
eyes of a friend, and intimate, a lover, in order to discern through
such a disguise the beams of heavenly glory. *Dei dialectus soloecismus*
...['God speaks bad grammar'].[35]

Not a few of J. G. Hamann's contemporaries (Immanuel Kant included),
were certain that he had taken leave of his senses after a conversion
experience in London upon reading the Bible through twice while
living alone in his small flat. What Hamann saw with 'the eager eyes
of a lover' was a language strange to the master of transcendental
empiricism.[36] For what Hamann had received was the gift of faith, and
in that gift, the reality of God's love and grace for him. Hamann's
faith was evangelical—he received Jesus Christ as his Lord and Saviour

[34] I think it would be fair to say that this is, in substance, the conclusion reached
by Lewis B. Smedes in his study of modern Anglican thought, and the way in
which the church is identified organically and incarnationally with the humanity
of Christ. A speculative view of the Incarnation, says Smedes, which seeks its
extension in the church and its completion in the Eucharist, separates the work
of Christ from the person. 'If Anglican theologians would, at the beginning of
their theological reflection, take their stance in the redemptive-historical situation
of the Bible, they would be led into more biblical thinking about Christ and the
believer's relationship to Him.' *The Incarnation*, p. 178. I am assuming that what
Smedes is referring to here is that which I would call an evangelical relationship to
Christ, that is, through the gift and in the power of the Spirit, one is united
to the whole person of Christ and thereby participates in his life of obedience
to the Father. I think that I am saying a bit more than Smedes, in suggesting
that the evangelical Christian also exists incarnationally in solidarity with the
kenotic community, and that if his Christianity leads him to deny this solidarity
he is in effect denying Christ. This, of course, is a much different concept of an
incarnational relation to Christ than that of the Anglican Church (as represented
by certain theologians) which Smedes is criticizing.
[35] J. G. Hamann, *J. G. Hamann—A Study in Christian Experience*, R. G.
Smith, Collins, London, 1960, p. 186. Smith's brackets.
[36] On one occasion, as Gregor Smith records it, Kant besought Hamann to
write 'in human language. Poor son of earth that I am, I am not organised to
understand the divine language of the intuitive reason.' *Ibid.*, p. 47.

through a direct response to the Word in the power of the Spirit.[37] It was also incarnational—for he lived a life of utter solidarity with man in his weakness and humanity.

> One must give oneself with just as much confidence to the stream of circumstances as to the stream of the passions when God is with us and our life is hidden in him ... If you see your friend on the list of tax-gatherers [a reference to the possible post at the excise office], do not be annoyed ... I will remain on the farthest shore, or begin to serve from below, as low as ever I can.[38]

In many ways, Hamann is a model of the man who can live an incarnational life because he has an evangelical faith. Because his life was totally centred in God, he needed no boundaries at which to reinforce his life in distinction from, or before, others. He prized neither success nor power, and avoided the semblance of even those religious postures which ordinarily accompanied the way of the Christian man in the world. His rule was to have none. He revealed Christ in the world, not by representing himself as a saint, but by driving the truth deep into the centre of his life and forcing his weakness and untruth to be exposed outwardly in such a way that he was transparent in his very concealment.

> A strict morality seems to me to be more contemptible and shallower than the most wilful scoffing and mockery. To drive the good deep inside, to drive the evil to the outside, to seem worse than one really is, to be really better than one seems: this I consider to be both a duty and an art.[39]

Thus avoiding the 'kaleidoscope of the inward life', he sought always to exist in relation to God and so needed no boundaries between himself and the world. Perhaps this is expressed most clearly in his 'marriage of conscience' to Anna Regina Schumacher. This relationship lasted for all of his life, and while some might interpret his unwillingness to go through the motions of a legal ceremony as an arbitrary and anti-social gesture, it is more likely that in his 'marriage' Hamann was 'expressing the immense weight which he gives to faith as the ground

[37]Hamann, in writing of his own conversion says: 'My son, give me thy heart!—Here it is, my God! Thou has demanded it, blind, hard, flinty, astray, unrepentant though it was. Purify it, make it new, and let it be the workshop of thy good Spirit. It has deceived me so often when it was in my hands that I no longer wish to acknowledge it as mine. It is a leviathan that thou alone canst tame— through thy indwelling it will enjoy rest and comfort and blessedness.' *Ibid.*, p. 155.

[38]J. G. Hamann, letter to J. G. Linder in Riga, *ibid.*, p. 62.

[39]J. G. Hamann, *Ibid.*, p. 109.

of his whole existence.'[40] Hamann himself spoke of the arrangement as being aimed at not 'lessening her happiness', and adds:

> This ongoing romance of my life, which has now been running for seventeen years... is for me a true sign and miracle of the ineffable and incomprehensible plan of a higher, invisible hand.[41]

The particular character of that which I have termed an evangelical faith is the reality of its centre resting totally on the act of God in Jesus Christ as the sole source of one's existence in the world. It was the reality of this centre to his life which marks both Hamann's remarkable consistency of faith as well as his unusual lack of concern for boundaries. Because the two are not usually found in what we have come to regard as evangelical Christianity, I want to explore this further in hopes of exposing the way in which a lived transcendence can be understood as solidarity with the world within which there exists an absolute difference.

C. H. Dodd makes the interesting suggestion that, while the centre of the new people of God is clear enough—Jesus Christ—the boundaries are not drawn at all.[42] One could show how this is true at several levels. For Christ, the boundary of the Logos was human flesh itself. Nothing marked him off from other men. He wore no halo, held no office, and recognized no boundary between his life and other men. His transcendent difference was totally contained in the centre of his human existence as the divine Logos. Again, while he became the centre of a group of followers and disciples, the boundaries were never clear. Judas the disciple proved to be a betrayer, while Nicodemus the Pharisee was revealed as a friend.

In contrast to the religious distinctives of Judaism, which was a 'boundary' religion, the 'new people of God' who received the Spirit and thus were recognized as 'belonging' to God, operated with no fixed boundaries. For example, in the days during which the early church was experiencing its own formative shape and style, Peter was prepared in a vision, which taught him that God makes no distinction between that which was formerly designated as clean and unclean from a religious and ceremonial standpoint, to proclaim the gospel of Jesus Christ to a gathering of Gentiles in Caesarea (Acts 10). When the Holy Spirit came upon the gathering, causing them to praise God, Peter responded by saying: 'Can any one forbid water for baptizing these people who have received the Holy Spirit just as we have?'[43]

[40]This is Gregor Smith's appraisal, *ibid.*, p. 61.
[41]*Ibid.*, p. 61.
[42]*The Founder of Christianity*, Collins, London, 1971, p. 92.
[43]Acts 10:47.

Clearly, a boundary was being erased between Jew and Gentile with no other boundary put in its place, with only the authority of the Spirit left at the centre. Nor was the boundary which was removed merely a racial distinctive, for in the writing of the gospel of Mark (was Peter one of the sources for Mark?), when Jesus' words concerning the defilement which comes, not from that which enters a man, but that which is expressed from his heart, were recorded, an editorial insertion immediately follows: 'Thus he declared all foods clean.'[44]

It would perhaps be an oversimplification to say that religion tends to reinforce its authenticity and power through the boundaries which are drawn between the sacred and the profane, while faith lives only before God in a world with no boundaries. For it must be admitted, that the religious life of Israel was circumscribed with boundaries which God himself had drawn rather severely between their life and that of the Gentiles, down to the calculation of the last hour of the Sabbath and the smallest plant of the garden. And yet, the operative principle of their life was faith—a life before God which exposed them to all the weaknesses and helplessness of a people *without* a powerful boundary. The character of their life was established in Abraham, the father of the faithful, says Paul, and not Moses, the giver of the Law.[45] Yet, it is unmistakably clear that with Jesus Christ the boundaries were totally removed in the form of religious distinctives and replaced by the boundary which is Christ himself: 'Now that faith has come', says Paul, 'we are no longer under a custodian; for in Jesus Christ you are all sons of God, through faith.'[46]

This is at the heart of what it means to speak of an evangelical Christian. It is not merely that man has been liberated from religious boundaries in order to take up residence as a citizen of a secular, desacralized world. Rather, the evangelical Christian lives in the reality of Christ as both the boundary and centre of his existence. But, henceforth, to say that Christ is the boundary of man's existence is not to be able to define that boundary in any way that draws a line between men which will serve to 'contain' Christ. Here the evangelical Christian has often failed to understand the true imperative of the Incarnation and the true significance of historical transcendence, for the boundary of Christ includes all humanity, both Jew and Gentile, both male and female;[47] the kenotic community of Christ places all men within the boundary of that community by virtue of a common humanity shared with Christ. This is the solidarity which belongs to historical transcendence which the church as the body of Christ must not violate

[44]Mark 7:19.
[45]Galatians 3:14-18.
[46]Galatians 3:25, 26.
[47]Galatians 3:28.

by the placing of boundaries between itself and the world. But here also is where we must learn from historical transcendence that solidarity of God with man is precisely the *place* where the absolute difference is experienced in the form of the 'presence' (*par-ousia*) of the oneness of God. Thus, while kenotic community is a way of expressing the solidarity of God with man in an incarnational way, it is also a way of pointing to the reality of transcendence, for it is the place where faith lives in utter dependence upon the life which God gives.

I have said that only the evangelical Christian can be an incarnational Christian. This is but another way of saying that lived transcendence is only possible because of historical transcendence. This life of faith is not simply the way in which man now comes to authentic self-understanding by taking a strictly eschatological view of his historical existence. Nor is it simply a life of the Spirit where Spirit assumes the form of one's own faith-existence, be it ethical, ideological or religious in form. The evangelical Christian can dare to be incarnational and affirm solidarity with the world without running into the error of spiritual solipsism at the centre or historical relativism at the boundary of his life. The reason for this is that *both* the boundary and the centre, both the solidarity and the difference, are rooted in the transcendence of God as historically given in the life of Jesus Christ.

It will now become clear why it was so important in Chapter VI to show how the historical transcendence of God comes to us as a revelation contained in Scripture. It also becomes clear why, if Scripture is severed from its transcendent authority as it refers to the historical reality of the person and life of Jesus Christ, the transcendent grounds for an incarnational life collapse in the ruins of either an existentialist or a rationalist theology. The distinguishing mark of the evangelical Christian is, therefore, the historical transcendence of the reality of God which serves as the noetic and normative impulse for a life of faith. Apart from Scripture, which admittedly can be rationalized into a dead letter without the movement of Spirit to quicken belief, one is cut off from the historical transcendence of God as it has been uniquely given to man in the life of Jesus Christ. But if this is true, then it also means that Scripture itself, despite (or even because of) its place in the ambiguity of all that is historical, has a transcendence of its own which stands over and against the epistemological and hermeneutical canons which (rightly) are brought to bear from the standpoint of man's contemporary place in history. It is this transcendence which the Evangelical discovers in Scripture which, rather than enslaving him to the supposed narrow boundaries of a deadly orthodoxy, actually frees him to take radically and seriously the Incarnation as an imperative which both draws the authentic boundary to the human situation and reveals its true centre.

The great temptation which lurks in the drawing of boundaries, is the power which it gives man to predicate the reality of his own existence. Because the motivation behind this quest for power arises out of man's basic insecurity and 'powerlessness' in the face of the threats to existence, the boundaries are usually drawn at the places where one's existence can be defined with the greatest precision. While most boundaries give the appearance of embodying the points at which man asserts his greatest strength, they are actually the points of greatest vulnerability. For this reason, they are defended with an almost irrational passion when someone challenges their existence. The boundaries which God placed around Israel, fencing her off from the rest of the world, were designed to show the radical difference which life entails when God is at the centre. When these boundaries became the points of Israel's strength, as predications of her own place of privilege and power in the world, rather than evidences of God's radical claim upon life, the boundaries become barriers behind which the ego entrenched itself in opposition to God himself. In this sense, all boundaries which separate man from man, and man from God, are 'semitical circles' which seek to contain and confirm man's identity within a particular horizon which he invests with something of an absolute quality.

There is a form of incarnationalism which is, strictly speaking, a 'semitical circle' of humanism. The Incarnation is abstracted into an ideological boundary within which the 'divinity' of man himself can be asserted. A transcendent God who invades this sphere and seeks to drain off all divinity for himself *has* to be denied the right of existence. Therefore, that which passes as a radical theology of incarnation is actually a radical ideological humanism, and, of course, it must assert the 'death of God'. For in this case, God's solidarity with man must not be allowed to destroy the boundary of absolute humanism, with its own intrinsic laws which govern the nature and destiny of existence.

So then, the boundaries which man asserts are inherently 'positivistic'; that is, the boundary actually does define the laws by which man interprets and orders his existence. There is, therefore, a common denominator running through the positivisms of the rational man, be they empirical, logical or historical; and of the psychical man, be they behavioural or Freudian and of the spiritual man, be they idealist, existentialist or fundamentalist. All of these boundaries can be termed 'semitical circles' because they are of the type which transpose a limitation of creaturehood, which is meant to signify man's dependence upon God as the centre of his existence, into a law by which man predicates the power of his own creaturely existence. When evangelical faith adopts a 'boundary mentality', it becomes fundamentalist, which is simply a variant form of the positivism which is inherent in all attempts to seek the laws of truth and reality within boundaries which man can control. When fundamentalism and liberalism attack each other in the name of the truth of God, the struggle is over *where* the boundaries are to be drawn. The true antithesis, on the other hand, is between the historical transcendence of God and *all* boundaries which seek to contain God or identify God through the laws of creaturehood, whether they are defined in religious, ethical or rational terms.

When the Incarnation is seen to provide, not only a solidarity of God with man, but a centre of transcendence within that solidarity, all of the laws of creaturehood, including all that is human, can be affirmed as real in that they point to the transcendence of the Creature-Redeemer. But here, as we have seen, it is not simply that the creature points to the Creator, the Creator meets himself in the creature in such a way that historical transcendence is *this* meeting of God with God, and not simply the creature's recognition of the Creator in historical clothing. This is the content and the core of evangelical faith, and this is why the Scriptures are a normative, and thus, transcendent source for this content. The *centre* which the evangelical Christian knows in faith within his solidarity with the world is neither the Word alone as a noetic source of revelation, nor the Spirit alone as an existential source of revelation, but both together. There is a danger of a 'positivism of Spirit' in the form of a charismatic experience, as we have seen, in which the kenotic community is introverted, and thus, ultimately divided and fragmented. But there is also a danger of a 'positivism of the Word' by which faith becomes a purely rational assent to the dead letter of Scripture. Here, too, there is introversion, and the boundaries drawn along the lines of a particular 'doctrine' of Scripture simply reproduce the 'semitical circle' of the orthodox Jews in Jesus' own day.

If then we are to follow this imperative of the Incarnation into some practical form for the church existing in the world as both the kenotic and ek-static community, what are the implications? Certainly, one would not want to confuse a boundary in the sense that it has been understood with the practical forms by which any organism functions in human society. By that I mean, institutional forms of a Christian community are not necessarily its boundaries. The so-called non-institutional forms of the church miss the point completely, it seems to me, and in attempting to direct their energies totally to the formation of an organism without any form or structure in the world, they may be judged to have failed. The failure may not be seen as any lack of a spiritual motivation, but in failing to be a truly kenotic community. The non-institutional church which attempts to function as an organism of personal relationship may even have more rigid boundaries than the institutional church itself. Nor is a compromise any better, where one makes a dichotomy between the church as an historical institution and the *Ekklesia* as a community of personal fellowship, while attempting to operate with both as valid and necessary.[48] The concept of kenotic community is not that of the formation of an organism as opposed to an institution, but that of solidarity with the world as one pole of the existence of the church. The kenotic community as an imperative which the Incarnation demands permits no distinction between the Christian and the non-Christian which resides intrinsically in the Christian (or the church) *as such*. When one 'defines' the church or the Christian, then, the distinctive must be solely in the 'difference' which has its source in the historical transcendence of God. The 'difference' is Christ, not that redemption is set over against creation, but so that the man is liberated to participate in Christ's ek-static fulfilment of all creaturehood through the life of the Spirit. The 'difference' is the centre (Christ) and not in distinctions drawn between men, or between the church and the world as entities. I do not see that the institutional forms of the church are intrinsically inimical to kenotic community, as long as the institutional form is governed by a faith which is both incarnational and evangelical.

There is a certain 'integrity' intrinsic to both the incarnational and evangelical aspect of the church. This integrity has its roots in the historical transcendence of God in Christ, and so too is without boundaries. Such an integrity can only take the form of fellowship which lives out of a centre. But in this case, the centre—Christ—demands that one live a life of solidarity with one's fellow-man in the world. To turn aside from one in the world, to show love only towards a fellow

---

[48]This was the attempt made by Emil Brunner, most clearly set forth in his book *The Misunderstanding of the Church*, where he sought to establish the fact that the *Ekklesia* was considered originally to be a brotherhood of called people, living in mutual love. Thus, it was essentially personal and not legal or institutional. It comes into existence as a result of the *Kerygma* and the reception of the Holy Spirit, and is structured by the gifts of grace (*charismata*) and ministries (*diakoniai*) rather than by legal or moral laws. Therefore, the *Ekklesia* can never become the church as an institution in society (pp. 107ff). See also, *The Christian Doctrine of the Church, Faith and the Consummation*, Dogmatics, Vol. III, pp. 32, 41, 45, 47. Because Brunner held that the *Ekklesia* as a personal organism was never intended to become an institutional entity within society, he did not set out to replace the church as an institution with *Ekklesia*, but saw it (the church) as the I-It dimension of man's experience within which the I-Thou relation took place through personal encounter. This, of course, reflects his reliance upon Buber for his basic categories for understanding faith. Not only does Brunner's *Ekklesia* slip dangerously close to becoming merely a 'brotherhood' of co-humanity, but he is unable to give it any real ontological relation to the historical transcendence of God in Christ. Brunner's 'event' language cannot adequately account for the existence of kenotic community as the incarnational dimension of *Ekklesia*.

believer, is a violation of the integrity of Christ himself.[49] It is a violation of kenotic community. The church which denies its solidarity with the world becomes an 'untruthful' church and no longer has the 'incarnational credibility' that is the mark of Christ himself.[50] But there is also the demand of evangelical integrity, in which the true distinctive of Word and Spirit as known in a life of union with Christ is to be preserved from untruth. Where evangelical integrity is violated through that which compromises the transcendence of Scripture in the sense that it is normative for the content of historical transcendence, the incarnational aspect of Christian faith is reduced to an ideal of ethical or social existence.

The outline which begins to emerge is that of a dynamic and evangelical faith which has its centre in historical transcendence and its circumference in kenotic community. The solidarity of kenotic community acts as a living context in which the Christian closes the circle of transcendence by living 'as Christ' in the world. The church, then, or body of Christ, as Paul likes to speak of it, does not have the centre in itself. As though, either as an organism or as an institution, it embodies the *ultimate* reality of Christ. The church exists, rather, as the penultimate along with the world, and cannot close the circle of transcendence, that is, cannot express the truth of Christ apart from its *ultimate* relation to the world. The removal of the boundaries from the church means at least, that it is de-ultimatized in terms of its own existence apart from the world, and in this way can find its oneness (in an ecumenical sense) if it has the mind of Christ.

[49]Cf. Galatians 2:11-12, where this is established in principle by Paul's rebuke to Peter. Cf. also the teaching of Jesus concerning loving those who are one's enemies, and those who cannot repay: Matthew 5:43-48; 25:31-46.

[50]'Is the church then credible?', asks Hans Küng, 'does she help men to be truthfully christian, to be truthfully human?' *Truthfulness: The Future of the Church*, Sheed and Ward, London, 1968, p. 126. A truthful church, for Küng, is a church that is *provisional*, that is, not an end in herself: *unassuming*, that is, to be constantly in need of grace rather than dispensing it: *ministering*, that is, to take the way of the cross rather than the way of triumphal procession: *conscious of guilt*, that is, to exist 'in grace' and not 'in righteousness': and finally, *obedient*, that is, to remain free from all claims except the radical will of God as revealed in Jesus Christ (pp. 51ff). Therefore, Küng suggests, it is not more 'truthful' to leave the church as an historical institution than to stay within it (p. 141). The evidences of truthfulness seem to be those which arise out of what I have called the kenotic community: 'Wherever, among individuals or groups, there is a truthful church, there occurs a necessary demythologising and de-demonising, a deepening and humanising of the world and of man; there dawns something of that complete justice, that eternal life, that cosmic peace, that true freedom and that final reconciliation of mankind with God, which one day God's consummated kingdom will bring.' p. 215. My difficulty with Küng comes with his starting point. He takes as the basic question: What did Jesus want? (p. 48). While it seems to me that the true starting point is in the question: Who was Jesus?

Again, in practical terms, as well as in the most profoundly theological sense, the form of such an incarnational, evangelical existence
in the world can best be expressed as *diakonia*, a transcendence of
service. Thus, more important than the *form* of the church in the world,
is the *mode* of the church's existence in the world. *Diakonia* refers
to function rather than status, and, as such, expresses first of all the
life of the Incarnate Logos as the mode of his freedom to be for
man in the expression of his life of divine Sonship with the Father
eternally. As T. F. Torrance so well expresses it:

> Thus through the Incarnation it is revealed to us that God in His
> own Being is not closed to us, for He has come to share with us
> the deepest movement of His divine heart, and so to participate in
> our human nature that the heart of God beats within it. We know
> that in the springs of His own eternal life God is ever open and ready
> and eager to share the weakness and sorrow and affliction of others
> and to spend Himself in going to their relief and in saving them.[51]

In *diakonia*, therefore, we are dealing with the essential character
of kenotic community itself. For the service which the Christian renders
is not the giving of something which he possesses to those who do
not possess it, nor is it the case of the rich or the advantaged sharing
with the poor and disadvantaged. It is Christ himself who has taken
our weaknesses upon himself, who has borne our sorrows and our
sins, who has absorbed our pain and tasted our death. He is the
diakonos, the servant who provided in his own person the ground and
the source of all such service. As members of the kenotic community,
we are made rich through his poverty (II Corinthians 8:9). Apart
from this transcendence of *diakonia* which creates the kenotic community out of all humanity through the suffering love and divine obedience of the Son of God in the flesh, the Christian's service to his fellow
man assumes the proportions of an offensive and self-ingratiating prosti-
tution of love. The church is not and cannot become the 'servant to the
world' and thus distinguish herself as incarnational. For the church
is also the kenotic community, and only *knows* that Christ's *diakonia*
takes all human weaknesses and needs upon himself. But the world
does not know this until the Christian closes the circle of transcendence
through *diakonia* in fellowship with Christ and gives material and
physical substance to the spiritual reality of this grace. The church is
the place where Christ, clothed with his gospel, meets the Christ clothed

[51]'Service in Jesus Christ', *Service in Christ*, Essays Presented to Karl Barth on
his 80th birthday, edited by James I. McCord and T. H. L. Parker, Epworth Press,
London, 1966, pp. 4, 5. Readers of this essay will note how indebted I am to
Professor Torrance for his exposition of the concept of *diakonia* with respect to
the Incarnation.

with the desperate needs and the human hopes of the world.[52]

The church, therefore, does not heal and help the physical and social needs of man as a kindly physician or a benevolent case worker, but struggles as the kenotic community to bind its own members into the body of Christ, sharing the battle against the forces of evil and exposing itself to the pain and anguish of emotional as well as physical suffering. This mark of service as the kenotic community is itself ek-static, for creaturehood finds itself lifted to fellowship in hope with the life of the Creator through the eternal Sonship of Christ, the Incarnate Word. The gospel is not simply clothed with physical and material dress to make it creditable to man, *diakonia* is the gospel, for it is lived transcendence. The evangelical and incarnational dimensions coincide in the same way as the Word has his mode of being in the flesh. The service of the Word brings to man a transcendent power of liberation from bondage and participation in the life of God. But this Word is itself the response, and thus the service of response has its ground in the historical transcendence of the divine Word made flesh.

How then can the church have its own 'space' in the world, or its own 'form'? How then could there exist boundaries around Christ which were smaller than the world itself? These are rhetorical questions, and meant only to confirm the truth of lived transcendence as a life of solidarity with man in which there is expressed an absolute difference. The difference is God. But with God the difference does not constitute division, or ultimately, separation. Lived transcendence, then, is not only a life in the world, but a life in God. For, while the kenotic community has its heart on earth, it has its head in heaven. If through historical transcendence we have discovered the 'lost lane-end into heaven', then we have found more than there is in this life.

---

[52]'The Church cannot be in Christ without being in Him as He is proclaimed to men in their need and without being in Him as He encounters us in and behind the existence of every man in his need. Nor can the Church be recognized as His except in that meeting of Christ with Himself in the depth of human misery, where Christ clothed with His gospel meets with Christ clothed with the desperate need and plight of men.' T. F. Torrance, *ibid.*, p. 9.

Chapter IX

Living in God

1 'Earth-Bound, Yet Boundless'

'I have eaten and drunk the earth, I have been lost and beaten, and I will go no more.'

'Fool,' said Ben, 'what do you want to find?'

'Myself, and an end to hunger, and the happy land,' he answered, 'For I believe in harbours at the end. O Ben, brother, and ghost, and stranger, you who could never speak, give me an answer now!' Then as he thought, Ben said: 'There is no happy land. There is no end to hunger.'

'And a stone, a leaf, a door? Ben? ... Where, Ben? where is the world?'

'Nowhere,' Ben said, '*You* are your world.'

... 'I shall save one land unvisited,' said Eugene. *Et ego in Arcadia*.[1]

It is the finite that is end-less. The creature can make a thousand beginnings, but not a single end. Both the agony and the ecstasy of human existence rise inconclusively out of man's earth-bound condition, unfinished symphonies of pain and pleasure. 'Lord let me know my end', says the Psalmist.[2] But is it not unreasonable, this seeking for the *eschaton*, the final movement which arrests all movement? Is it not a foolish game to expect to *know* the end from the beginning? Can wild geese ever have a home?

'Then the Lord God formed man from the dust from the ground, and breathed into his nostrils the breath of life,...'[3] It was not necessary that we should be told that we are earth-bound creatures. Our affinity with the dust flows out of every bleeding wound, the molecules of our flesh collapse with the measured cadence of the cosmic clock, we eat and are eaten by the organisms that comprise our own space ship. But who breathes the breath of life into our nostrils and makes us *more* than this, we could never have known. But it is this 'more than' that accounts for the great incapacity which is also a capacity. This incapacity

[1]Thomas Wolfe, *Look Homeward, Angel!*, p. 624.
[2]Psalm 39:4.
[3]Genesis 2:7.

to complete our own lives within the dimensions of an earth-bound existence can only be known by one who is 'more than' creature. But that this incapacity should also be a *capacity* to share the life of the Creator himself, that this 'absence' is also the form of the 'presence' of the one who is the true 'end' of our existence, that our creation is also our eschaton, this we only know through disclosure. From this it might be said that all revelation is also eschatology.

> We must understand that God is the measure of all reality and propriety, understand that eternity exists first and then time, and therefore the future first and then the present, as surely as the Creator exists first and then the creature. He who understands that need take no offence here.[4]

The tension, then, which exists between dust and spirit in man, and which gives rise to that problematic of the concrete man's bond with the absolute which we held at the outset to be the structure of metaphysics itself, is tension formed by the fact that the eschaton is intrinsically bound up with creation itself. It is the tension which we observed between the kenotic community and the ek-static community, wherein solidarity with the world is essentially an 'upward' movement in which creation has its ek-stasis towards the Creator in the meeting of God with himself through Word and Spirit.[5] Because the creature does not have its life by virtue of its own existence in the end-lessness of finitude, but rather by virtue of the life which the Creator gives to it (grace), creation has its true end in the Creator who does not merely give creation its eschaton, he *is* the eschaton.[6] We can also think of this in terms of the distinction made earlier between capacity and incapacity. The ek-static dimension of creaturehood is its capacity for participation in the life of God as its true eschaton. But this is an incapacity when considered from the standpoint of the creature itself. For the eschaton of creation is its future in the life of God, but only God can give this life. Neither the organic nor the inorganic part of creation has this capacity because it does not experience 'incapacity'. Only man experiences incapacity because he seeks the completion of his personhood in the 'boundless' sphere beyond either the organic or inorganic. Theologically speaking, this 'incapacity' is called the image of God, and as such, it is man's capacity for the 'eschaton' of participation in the life of God which man can only possess as God gives himself to man.

As an historical creature, then, man does not possess his true end in a teleological sense, that is, as a destiny tied up with a final purpose within the temporal process; rather he discovers his end (his real self-

[4]K. Barth, *Church Dogmatics*, I/1, p. 531.
[5]See above, p. 246.
[6]Cf. K. Barth, *Church Dogmatics*, IV/1, pp. 8ff.

hood) eschatologically. Hence the tension between the dust and the spirit and the eschaton and the world. This tension is not a dualism which must be mediated either mythologically or existentially, for creation has its perfection (its *telos*) given to it in the eschaton. There are, however, two levels of reality at work in the movement of creation which require a sort of 'dual control' in order to function. The eschaton of creation is the transcendence of God which is given to creation as its life and the source of its reality. God meets himself in his creation through the transcendence of Spirit, but in such a way that creation is given its own 'space' of transcendence over and against God in which to work out its perfection (*telos*). Hence, Barth can say that the future exists first and then the present, for the future is the eschaton which gives the present its own *telos*.

In our consideration of the inner logic of historical transcendence, we saw clearly how the transcendence of God could move in an ek-static sense from the side of the creature towards the eschaton. The solidarity of the eternal Logos with humanity brought the eschaton into the world in such a way that all creation can be said to have its completion in Jesus Christ.[7] Considered teleologically, the existence of Christ can be said to have its significance in his ultimate sacrifice of life upon the cross for man. But from the standpoint of eschatology, he *was* the eschaton, so that men were summoned to 'leave everything' and take up their cross and follow him.[8] Through the Incarnation the eschaton (the future) has come upon man, but in such a way that the tension remains, and historical existence continues as the context within which kenotic community prefigures the eschaton of creation through its ek-static life in the Spirit. It is thus that we come to the conclusion that lived transcendence is eschatological transcendence. But here we must thread our way cautiously between the Scylla of an apocalyptic eschatology where transcendence devaluates and even negates history, and the Charybdis of teleological universalism where history swallows up transcendence by opening its jaws a bit wider to include the divine purpose as a possibility. We can neither write a treatise on eschatology nor an essay on the philosophy of history at this point, but, nonetheless, the exploration of historical transcendence now brings us to the point where perhaps a modest contribution can be offered towards the framing of the problem. But to do this, we must now take a tight grip upon the essential argument of the book itself.

When the crisis of transcendence was radicalized, it was found to be a crisis of the reality of God. The old language of transcendence and immanence could no longer serve to express the correlation between a

[7]The miracle stories in the gospel accounts are surely meant to convey this truth. Cf. John 2:1-11; Mark 4:35-41. Also, cf. Colossians 1:15ff.
[8]Mark 1:17-18; 8:34-37.

God who is wholly 'other' and the world to which he is 'other'. Transcendence, therefore, was conceived as the act of Spirit by which the Other moves into concrete relation. But this means that transcendence, while it is perceived as the concrete action of the Other, is problematical in the sense that the reality of the Other can never become the possession of the one who perceives it or experiences it. This reality cannot be inferred out of the relation, but must be *given* to the relation by the act of the Other. Thus, while the reality of one totally 'other' to the world could never be affirmed as a logical certainty, through the act of the Other (transcending his own immanent existence) one comes up against the reality of the Other in concrete relation, for the concrete act is the transcendence.

Having reworked the language of transcendence into a form more congenial to the structure of metaphysics conceived as the problematic of the concrete man's bond with the absolute, we proceeded directly to the Incarnation as the most likely source for an understanding of the transcendence of God. The inner logic of the Incarnation as it was laid bare through an exploration of the relation of God to Israel pointed us, on the one hand, back to the covenant of creation with its covenant response grounded in the transcendence of God as Creator, and, on the other hand, forward to the Incarnation in which the eternal Logos completes the covenant response from the furthest side of human estrangement. This act could rightly be called the historical transcendence of God because it was an act of utter solidarity with the world through the assumption of a complete humanity, while at the same time it was the act of the Son of God towards the Father and the Father towards the Son within the perfect unity of divine love. What we call the *kenosis*, because it appears as an act of utter condescension and even humiliation, is actually revealed to be the depth of divine transcendence experienced as an intra-divine relation into which man is taken with his full humanity. Historical transcendence, then, is not simply a divine act playing on the stage of historical existence, such as would be commonly expressed in mythological language, but it is the God who is for man also acting as the man who is for God. Historical transcendence is God as the totally 'other', the Creator, meeting himself through solidarity with the creature in the reality of Spirit.

The crucial point in the development of historical transcendence was now reached. It no longer was possible to think in terms of historical transcendence as simply a concrete historical form present to all men by virtue of their existence as historical persons, into which the reality of God could be caught like the wind in a sail. The transcendence, and thus the reality of God, to be historical must originate from within historical existence, and yet must find its resting point in the Creator of that existence. The transcendence of God cannot become historical if it originates outside of historical existence—that is the source of a mythological way of thinking. For no matter what historical forms are given to such a concept of the reality of God, the historical and the transcendent remain only paradoxically united, and man is thrown back upon himself. But in the historical transcendence of God as we see it in the Incarnation, there is something utterly final and unrepeatable. For here we see the reality of God as it originates within the completely historical existence of the man Jesus Christ. And when I say 'originates', I mean thereby to say that the life of Jesus was the transcendence of God himself expressed as the Incarnate reality of the eternal Son with the eternal Father. Therefore, in the historical transcendence of God we have the act by which God as Spirit has his concretion in the Word as flesh. But it is in that flesh, and as that flesh, that the transcendence of God originates a movement from the far side of human estrangement which has its completion in the eternal love of the Creator-God.

When we now speak of the reality of God as life in the Spirit, we are called back to that solidarity of God with man which is constituted in the historical life of the Incarnate Word. This alone is the historical transcendence of God, and is the transcendent ground for the reality of Spirit. Therefore, when we speak of life in the Spirit we are called to the reality of kenotic community in which all men are placed by virtue of a common humanity with Christ. But this solidarity of God with humanity not only constitutes the historical transcendence of God, it binds man in his historical existence to the life of God. In the person of Jesus Christ, both the *telos* of historical existence and the *eschaton* of eternal existence were brought together. But they were brought together in such a way that the eschaton, which, as we have already said, is God himself, did not negate or destroy historical existence, but brought the whole purpose (*telos*) of that existence to its completion in the eternal life of God. The apocalyptic expectations which largely preoccupied the literature of the Jewish people under the oppressive domination of an alien nation, were not fulfilled in a final 'Day of the Lord' when history was to be interrupted in its course, and God was to restore his Kingdom. But on the other hand, neither did the forces of evil and the course of historical events swallow up the eschaton in the final irrelevance of death. The resurrection of Christ is the ek-stasis of the kenotic community, for it places man in the eternal life of God. Lived transcendence, therefore, is eschatological life because, through the Spirit, man is redeemed from historical existence *without* an eschaton, and given historical existence *with* an eschaton.

This is clearly portrayed in the figure of Baptism as Paul refers to it in his letter to the Romans:

Do you know that all of us who have been baptized into Christ Jesus were baptized into his death? We were buried therefore with him by baptism into death, so that as Christ was raised from the dead by the glory of the Father, we too might walk in newness of life.[9]

The transcendent ground for the life of the Spirit is the eschaton as it was revealed through the life, death and resurrection of Christ. But it is noteworthy that Paul, in this case, does not argue from the resurrection of Christ directly to our resurrection, but instead, to our 'newness of life' in the Spirit. The Christian then might be said to be the 'walking eschaton' of kenotic community. Through the life of the Spirit, the Christian has received the eschaton within his historical existence. When the Christian thus lives as the ek-static community, the eschaton is pre-figured for the kenotic community. For this reason, the Christian exists in a solidarity with the world through kenotic community but with a radical difference. And the difference is the eschaton. Just how this difference has its practical expression will be taken up in the last part of this chapter.[10]

What we have called the kenotic community and the ek-static community, is simply a slightly schematized way of carrying out the inner logic of the Incarnation in terms of what it means to be 'in Christ', to use the Pauline phrase. This helps us to see that creation, and particularly man as created in the image of God, has been placed by the transcendence of God into a relation of solidarity with divine life through the *assumptio carnis* on the part of the eternal Logos. That which we call the historical existence of man in a truly cosmic sense, has this solidarity

---

[9]Romans 6:2-4.

[10]The question which arises at this point is to what extent this understanding of the eschaton could be said to be a 'realized eschatology' (C. H. Dodd) which does not allow for any future aspect of the Kingdom of God. I would not want to deny that there are future implications to the eschatological relation of the Kingdom of God to history; the resurrection of the body is but one of these. However, as shall become clear, I wish to overcome the equation of an historical future with God's future, so that the eschatological significance of the resurrection of Christ is merely proleptic of the eschaton and is thus not the eschaton itself. Perhaps Joachim Jeremias's expression *'sich realisierende Eschatologie'* (eschatology in process of realization) comes closer to capturing this tension between a complete and yet to be consummated eschaton. *The Parables of Jesus*, SCM Press, London, 1958, p. 159, trans. S. H. Hooke from *Die Gleichnisse Jesu*, Zwingli Verlag, Zürich, 1954, 3rd edition. It should be noted, however, that Jeremias claims to have received this expression in a letter from Ernst Haenchen (*ibid.*, p. 159, n. 1). Also, Dodd has himself expressed dissatisfaction with his own label 'realized eschatology', and inclines towards Jeremias's way of putting it: '... the not altogether felicitous term "realized eschatology" may serve as a label. Emendations of it which have been suggested for the avoidance of misunderstandings are Professor George Florovsky's "inaugurated eschatology" and Professor Joachim Jeremias's *"sich realisierende Eschatologie"*, which I like, but cannot translate into English.' *The Fourth Gospel*, Cambridge, 1953, p. 47, n. 1.

as its eschaton. Therefore, even as one could only say that 'God was in Christ' from the standpoint of the resurrection, which is the eschaton of the humanity of Christ, so also, one can only say that the kenotic community is 'in Christ' from the standpoint of the ek-static community, for the Spirit is the eschaton. Apart from the Holy Spirit one cannot call Jesus Lord.[11] However, the kenotic community cannot be split apart from the ek-static community any more than one could split apart the human and divine in Christ. Therefore, to ask about the state of the kenotic community abstracted from the ek-static community is as meaningless a question as to question the state of the humanity of Christ abstracted from the divine Logos.

This also helps us to see that one cannot separate theology and history, or revelation and history, or faith and history, and talk about each as though they were separate entities. Nor can one confuse the two as though there were no difference. Our clue here must be the inner logic of the Incarnation where, as we have seen, there is complete solidarity and yet with a radical difference. But the difference is the eschaton. And in this case, the difference is that which completes in a final way without negating the reality of the difference. The resurrection of Christ, therefore, can be said to be the only 'difference' which the Incarnation has made to historical existence. For the resurrection is the eschaton of all historical existence.[12] But here then is a strange thing. The resurrection made *no* difference to historical existence considered from a strictly empirical, and, one is tempted to say, historical perspective. Setting aside for the moment the obvious difference which the historical movement of Christianity has made following the resurrection of Christ, I think that it can be said that in the resurrection of Christ, the eschaton was brought into an absolute relation to the world without any significant alteration in the terms of historical existence such as one would expect of such an 'eschatological' event. The apocalyptic events widely predicted in the Jewish literature preceding the time of Christ certainly did not occur in any cosmic form.[13] And even if one accepts the account of the empty tomb as an objective fact of the same quality as the body on the cross three days earlier, what real *difference* did this make to the order of how things occur? One can probably assume that since that time tombs continue to be filled with the corpses of dying humanity and that the tombs retain their contents with a high degree of regularity.

The point of this is that, while the resurrection of Christ is the eschaton

[11] I Corinthians 12:3.

[12] Romans 1:1-6; I Peter 1:3-9.

[13] I have in mind such passages as: Joel 2:30-3:3; Isaiah 13:6-22; 61:1-4. In regard to this last reference, it is interesting to note that in the reading of it by Jesus in the synagogue at Nazareth, he abruptly stopped in the middle of the sentence, omitting the references to an implied act of judgment upon history through divine intervention. Cf. Luke 4:17-19.

of historical existence, and as such is the only radical difference made by the Incarnation, the *kind* of difference made here is the same as that to be found in the historical life of the Incarnate Logos. For Jesus is the eschaton because he is God, and the resurrection is the eschaton of historical existence only because it was the same Jesus who was raised. When God is present to creation it is always as the eschaton of creation. When God is present to man in his historical existence it is always as the eschaton of that historical existence. The radical difference which the resurrection introduces into the historical existence of man is an eschatological life in the Spirit. For the Spirit is the eschaton, of Christ and of God. Theology, therefore, has to do with the eschaton of history. It is the radical difference which, existing in solidarity with history, is also the completion and fulfilment of history. The relation of theology to history is thus ek-static, not paradoxical (Bultmann) or universal (Pannenberg). Theology speaks from within history of the reality of the eschaton of history. In the same way, we can now say that faith is the ek-stasis of knowledge. For knowledge is not destroyed nor suppressed by faith, but faith speaks out of knowledge and affirms the eschaton of knowledge. The problematical dimension of both history and knowledge, then, is the eschaton; for that is given through the transcendence of Spirit. To this extent, the resurrection remains problematical to historical knowledge, for as the eschaton, it is given in the reality of Spirit.[14]

There remains, therefore, one final question which must be explored— namely, the question of how the resurrection of Christ as the eschaton of historical existence can serve as the univocal point for historical transcendence and lived transcendence. The question is one of locating the common 'hermeneutical horizon' for historical transcendence and eschatological transcendence. It is the resurrection of Christ which has raised the solidarity of man with God to its highest power. So that, the resurrection has a universal bearing upon historical existence. But is the universality itself the univocal point. This is the question which we must ask Wolfhart Pannenberg, who perhaps has made the most

---

[14]Again, speaking of the resurrection as problematical to historical knowledge does not imply that it is unhistorical, but that as the eschaton it is the transcendence of God, and as such, cannot be possessed as a matter of reflective knowledge. Is there also not significance in the fact that no account seems to have been given of any body of witnesses to the resurrected Christ who saw him and yet did *not* believe? I am not suggesting that the implication to be drawn from this is that faith is the presupposition necessary to have seen the risen Christ. From the accounts of the appearances of Christ after Easter, it seems clear that Easter faith was caused by the reality of the risen Christ. But, on the one hand, while there is every indication that the risen Christ could be seen (and touched) by a sceptical man, there is no reason to think that Jesus 'gave himself' to unbelieving man as an historical specimen of a resurrected person. It would seem that the eschaton is intrinsically a 'frustration' to the historical method, yet radically historical.

creative attempt to establish a univocal point between theology and history, and who, as Geoffrey Turner has said, 'is the only theologian in contemporary German theology who gives a cogent alternative to Bultmann'.[15] Pannenberg's central thesis is that God has given himself to man in the person of Jesus Christ, but that belief in Christ as the revelation of God is only possible within a context where reasons for such belief can be deduced from the stream of history, which is incorporated into what he calls the 'history of the transmission of tradition' (*Überlieferungsgeschichte*).[16]

The question which Pannenberg asks is: 'Is this significance of Jesus' history recognizable from within itself? ... Or is some supplementary explanation necessary, an explanation emerging out of faith in Jesus and not derivable from the bare facts of his story?'[17] The questions are purely rhetorical, for Pannenberg rejects the implication that a distinction should be made between the 'bare facts' of history and evaluation of them (that is, the distinction between *Historie* and *Geschichte*). What Pannenberg wants to do is to 'depositivize' history in the sense of 'brute facts' which conform to some intrinsic law of historical happenings; but at the same time, he wants to challenge the self-authenticating character of faith as a subjective, or existentialistic decision.[18] History, for Pannenberg, is 'reality as a whole', and while it is grounded in the historical existence of man, it is also open to the reality of God in such a way that God's revelation of himself *becomes* history and has a self-evident character to it accessible to any man.[19] He wishes to see theology *as* history, and thus to eliminate the distinction between faith and historical knowledge which tends to place the verification of revelation in the subjective act of faith. Revelation comes to us, says Pannenberg, not in a '*heilsgeschichtlichen* ghetto', but as history itself, and, therefore, can be cognitively understood and authenticated through the consistent application of the historical method.[20]

Because Pannenberg considers that the life and message of Jesus prior to Easter is without content for faith, and would only be a 'fanatical audacity',[21] he sees the resurrection of Christ as central to the revelation

[15]'Wolfhart Pannenberg and the Hermeneutical Problem', *The Irish Theological Quarterly*, Vol. 39, No. 2, April, 1972, pp. 107-129, esp. p. 127.
[16]*Theology as History*, 'New Frontiers in Theology', Vol. III, James M. Robinson and John B. Cobb Jr. (eds.), Harper and Row, New York, 1967, pp. ixff.
[17]'The Revelation of God in Jesus of Nazareth', *Theology as History*, p. 125.
[18]*Ibid*., pp. 126-127.
[19]W. Pannenberg, 'Response to the Discussion', *Theology as History*, p. 241.
[20]'Hermeneutics and Universal History', *History and Hermeneutics*, 'Journal For Theology and the Church', Vol. 4, J. C. B. Mohr (Paul Siebeck), Tübingen, Harper and Row, New York, 1967, pp. 122-152; p. 124.
[21]'The Revelation of God in Jesus of Nazareth', *Theology as History*, p. 116.

of God in Christ. It thus follows that Pannenberg must assert the resurrection 'as history'.

> Whether or not Jesus was raised from the dead is a historical question insofar as it is an inquiry into what did or did not happen at a certain time.... Now let us assume that the historical question concerning the resurrection of Jesus has been decided positively, then the meaning of this event as God's final revelation is not something that must be added to it; rather, this is the original meaning inherent in that event within its own context of history and tradition.[22]

Our concern here is not with the way in which Pannenberg appeals to the context of Israel's tradition of apocalyptic expectation as the historical rationale for the idea of resurrection in lieu of any historical analogue (thus indicating his leaning towards idealism as against positivism), but rather with the way in which he sees the resurrection as the eschaton in which all historical existence finds its end. If revelation *is* history, then the eschaton is historical. But in that case, the eschaton belongs to universal history and is self-evident to any one who uses the historical method in a non-positivistic way.[23] The inherent problems of this formulation have not gone unnoticed by Pannenberg's critics. Gerhard Sauter charges that the way in which Pannenberg locates the eschaton within historical reason destroys the apocalyptic correlation between 'complete' history and revelation; and as a result, 'the "simultaneity" of completeness and the end remains a teleological, but not an eschatological axiom'.[24] In this criticism (which is similar to that of Jürgen Moltmann), Sauter questions the way in which Pannenberg uses the concept of 'prolepsis' to account for the fact that, while the eschaton is part of the total reality of universal history, historical existence nonetheless continues without any real change. And it is in this context that we can discern the weakness of Pannenberg's argument, notwithstanding his helpful insights into the basic unity of theology and history:

> God's demonstration of himself through the ministry and the history of Jesus of Nazareth is that final revelation of God which is to be recognized by all peoples. It is that revelation, but for the time being

---

[22]*Ibid.*, p. 128.

[23]The universality of God's revelation as history, is made clear by Pannenberg in his third 'dogmatic thesis' on the doctrine of revelation: 'In distinction from special manifestations of the deity, the historical revelation is open to anyone who has eyes to see it. It has a universal character.' *Revelation as History*, Wolfhart Pannenberg (ed.), Sheed and Ward, London, 1969, p. 135.

[24]*Zukunft und Verheissung. Das Problem der Zukunft in der gegenwärtigen theologischen und philosophischen Diskussion*, Zwingli Verlag, Zürich/Stuttgart, 1965, p. 256, n. 12. Cited by James M. Robinson, 'Revelation as Word and History', *Theology as History*, p. 96.

it is only proleptically so, not yet as the general occurrence of the End for all men. One can understand the history of Jesus only if one understands the future salvation of mankind as having already appeared in and with him and as having been made accessible through him. In the history of Jesus a future was anticipated that has not yet appeared in its general bearing. Therefore those who penetrate into the meaning of Jesus' history will inevitably be led to God's not yet accomplished future, which nevertheless is held to have appeared already in and with Jesus when one speaks of his resurrection from the dead. Hence through knowledge of Jesus' history they are led to faith, to trust in God's future.[25]

In this important passage, several things emerge. First of all, the eschaton has been so submerged in history that faith must go beyond it to trust in 'God's future'. This, for all practical purposes, pushes faith into more of a teleological than an eschatological direction. And it would seem that Sauter's criticism is well taken. Second, the use of prolepsis here, while pointing to the obvious fact that historical existence (despite the eschaton) does not experience an apocalyptic intervention so as to significantly alter its conditions, nevertheless pulls the eschaton into the process of history in such a way that the 'idea' of universal history destroys the radical 'difference' which the eschaton gives to historical existence. And finally, the role of the Spirit in bringing man to the eschaton is virtually pre-empted by the universal-historical method so that faith is no longer 'given' by the transcendence of Spirit but is the logical expression of trust in the future which follows upon one's insight into revelation. There would seem to be good reason for accepting Martin J. Buss's criticism of Pannenberg as lacking a 'vision of the transcendent'.[26] Although I think I would mean by that something quite different from that which Buss has in mind.

While I would accept Pannenberg's insistence that the resurrection of Christ is pivotal to faith as the eschaton in which all historical existence has its completion, I wonder if he has escaped the net of subjectivism which he so hopefully swept away in grounding faith in historical knowledge? To make the certainty of faith subject to the exactitude of knowledge,[27] appears to give primacy to the cognitive dimension of knowing and thus places man at the centre of faith as the thinking subject. 'Flesh and blood has not revealed this to you', Jesus replied to Peter's assertion, 'but my Father who is in heaven.'[28] It is this problematic

---

[25]W. Pannenberg, 'The Revelation of God in Jesus of Nazareth', *Theology as History*, p. 130.

[26]'The Meaning of History', *Theology as History*, p. 154.

[27]'The Revelation of God in Jesus of Nazareth', *ibid.*, p. 129.

[28]Matthew 16:17.

dimension to a strictly cognitive grasp of the eschaton which one senses is lacking in Pannenberg. In his concern to depositivize the historical method, and thereby open it up to the possibilities of total reality, Pannenberg has perhaps shaved too closely with 'Occam's razor', and cut away the transcendent grounds of historical transcendence as it comes to us as God's Word in Scripture and lived transcendence as it is given to us through the indwelling power of the Holy Spirit.

So to come back to the question which we put to Pannenberg at the outset: is universal history eschatological simply because it is open to the resurrection of Christ on rational grounds?[29] The answer must be no. For at best, a universal history which is open to the idea of resurrection has not grasped the fundamental truth of the historical transcendence of God by which humanity is brought to its eschaton in the resurrection of Christ and thus speaks of a solidarity of act, not a universality of revelation. But if Pannenberg has not gained the solidarity with Christ which historical transcendence gives, neither has he left room for the 'difference' which the resurrection makes in historical existence through lived transcendence. It is still in hope of finding this univocal point that we pursue the Pannenberg discussion one step further, but through the eyes of a friendly critic.

Daniel P. Fuller, in his hermeneutical study of the resurrection, *Easter Faith and History*,[30] finds Pannenberg's thought to be the most adequate of contemporary attempts to relate the resurrection to history and faith, but still falling short of the biblical grounds for faith. Fuller shares the conviction that the resurrection is central to a theological understanding of historical existence, and deftly traces the attempts to relate an Easter faith to history from the Age of Enlightenment, through rationalism, romanticism, liberalism, dialectical theology, the New Quest theology, and finally, concluding with the most recent attempt by Pannenberg. All of this is done to show that the problem of understanding the resurrection within the horizon of the historical method can be reduced to three alternatives: an attempt to sustain knowledge of the resurrection apart from the historical method altogether (Karl Barth, Hans Grass, Hans F. von Campenhausen); an attempt to sustain knowledge of the resurrection partially through historical reasoning and partly through faith (Gerhard Koch, Richard B. Niebuhr); and an attempt to sustain knowledge of the resurrection wholly by historical reason (Wolfhart Pannenberg).[31] Fuller's sympathy lies primarily with Pannenberg, and he shares with Pannenberg the desire to locate the cause of faith in the revelation of the transcendent God in history.

[29]See above, pp. 284ff.

[30]Tyndale Press, London, 1968. First published in America by Wm. Eerdmans Publishing Co., Grand Rapids, 1965.

[31]*Ibid.*, pp. 145-187.

However, for Pannenberg this means that revelation becomes universal history, so that no particular historical act of God has revelatory content not accessible to the historical method, while Fuller insists that one can only account for the fact that some men believe and others do not by asserting that: 'God simply does not work supernaturally in the heart of everyone who hears the Gospel in order to overcome their prejudices so that they might own up to the truth of what is to be known in history.'[32]

The two specific charges, then, which Fuller lays to the account of Pannenberg, are first, that by equating revelation with universal history he cannot account for the reason why some men believe and others do not; for if transcendence causes faith to arise and transcendence is universally operative through history, then there is no 'rational' basis for not having faith. Secondly, Fuller says that by restricting faith to historical inquiry, those who are not trained historians will have an imperfect knowledge of revelation.[33] The basis on which Fuller judges Pannenberg's synthesis of theology and history to be inadequate, however, is the biblical account of how revelation actually becomes historical, and, therefore, how one can believe in the historical reality of the resurrection 'after the fact'.

In a closely-argued exegetical study of Luke-Acts, Fuller shows that it was Luke's intention to demonstrate to second generation Christians that faith in a risen Christ can be historically grounded in a past event. To do this, according to Fuller, Luke shows that under the leadership of Paul, who was himself radically changed through an encounter with the risen Christ, the growth and development of the Christian Church among Gentiles had its origin at Jerusalem. Luke's argument then is that the empirical fact of the Gentile Church under the leadership of an 'orthodox' Jewish scholar (Paul) could only be accounted for by the power of a risen Christ.

> The Gentile mission, therefore, was a fulfillment of the resurrection and ascension, which were the climax of the Christ event as set forth in Luke's Gospel; and because the Gentile mission, as led by Paul, could only be accounted for as stemming from the work of the risen Christ, it therefore functions as the means whereby one may know the certainty of the Christ event.[34]

Rather than restricting revelation to that which can be determined by the historical method in a non-positivistic sense, which Fuller sees as the basic weakness of Pannenberg's argument, Luke argues from

[32]*Ibid.*, p. 187.
[33]*Ibid.*, pp. 184-186.
[34]*Ibid.*, p. 220.

present, empirical historical grounds to a supernatural cause, and thus, according to Fuller, Luke sets forth a 'two-story' concept of history.

> Luke regarded reality as a two-story affair. There is the first story, in which events occur as effects of antecedent, immanental causes. There is also the second story, from which causes come and introduce effects on the first story that would never come to pass from first-story causes. But first-story effects are so tuned to act in accordance with antecedent causes and not in contempt of them that when a second-story cause comes downstairs, a commensurate effect is produced on the first story.[35]

Where Fuller departs from the typical 'redemptive history' (*Heilsgeschichte*) structure, is in his argument that Pannenberg's basic principle of allowing for the overly pronounced deviation' (a non-analogous historical event) while at the same time retaining the basic regularity of cause and effect, could as well operate with a supernaturally caused 'deviation' as with one which is naturally revealed in the form of a 'breaking out' (*Aufbruch*) of the resurrection in history.[36] Thus, Fuller argues that transcendent causes are not incompatible with historical effects, and that the historical method has no intrinsic 'contempt' for non-natural causes which produce real historical effects. Pannenberg's unwillingness to accept this argument reveals his deep distrust of the *Heilsgeschichte* approach altogether, but even more clearly, reveals his failure to overcome the Cartesian problem where rationality lies inherently in the thinking subject. Pannenberg can only 'think' the transcendence of God by bringing it totally within the realm of a universal 'idea' of history. While Pannenberg is a healthy check upon a kind of theological thinking which has not come to terms with the *historical* transcendence of God as it is exposed in the Incarnation, his philosophical debt to Idealism does not allow him to come to terms with the historical *transcendence* of the resurrection as the eschaton.

In light of this, one wonders if Fuller has made the best possible use of the fruits of his exegetical study in constructing an argument against Pannenberg? Pannenberg is not likely to be impressed with the 'second-story' argument which seeks its grounds in the 'overly pronounced deviation' of a gracious and loving Barnabas (Acts 11 : 24) or an ethically changed Paul. Fuller makes Luke lay the weight of the historical evidence of the resurrection upon the moral *person* of the Christian witness (Ritschl?), rather than upon the *Spirit*-ually convicting and convincing

[35]*Ibid.*, p. 252.
[36]*Ibid.*, pp. 186-187.

reality of the Word which comes in the message.[37] Fuller *does* want to
say that it is a Barnabas 'full of the Holy Spirit and faith' who provides
the historical grounds for divine transcendence,[38] but does not Luke
lay the grounds for the Spirit's historical appeal in 'Jesus of Nazareth,
a man attested to you by God'?[39]

This is not to deny that Luke makes his argument turn upon the
conversion of Paul and the mission to the Gentiles, nor is it to deny that
the power of the resurrection in terms of lived transcendence produces,
or ought to produce, moral and ethical qualities which are commensurate
with the life of God himself; however, to virtually equate the historical
transcendence of God in Christ with moral qualities of personal life—
'The Bible functions as a Barnabas because its message of God's grace
produces an atmosphere of love and hope'[40]—which are at best fallible
and often deceptive, is, I think, unfair to Luke and unconvincing to
Pannenberg.

I am not sure that Fuller has quite grasped the fundamental problem
with Pannenberg's concept of revelation as history. For Pannenberg
wants to be able to come to a faith in the resurrection on the basis of
strictly historical reasons and wants to then make the resurrection as
knowledge, a proleptic basis for faith in the future. 'He who understands
this meaning inherent in the history of Jesus is drawn, by knowing Jesus
as the prolepsis of the coming general salvation, into the movement
which is faith.'[41] The resurrection, in this scheme of thought, can be
'known', and as such, provides the necessary insight for faith to embrace
a future hope of salvation and resurrection. But how can the resurrection of Christ be 'known' apart from a personal relation with the living
Christ himself through the gift of the Holy Spirit? For there is no such
thing as a 'resurrection'; there is only a living Christ who is the eschaton
of all historical existence. Faith then is given within historical existence

---

[37]"Since men cannot by themselves be good and have faith and hope, the cause
for goodness, faith, and hope must lie apart from their capabilities and in the
living Christ whom such men proclaim as Saviour. Thus it is understandable how
Luke could have stressed that the faith of the apostles and of a Theophilus must
come through a reasoning based on infallible proofs, and yet declare that many
believed as Barnabas preached, for Barnabas was himself an infallible proof of
his message.... Barnabas has moral qualities men could not produce and which
must therefore result from the Christ whom Barnabas preached.... For every
man who is confronted with a Barnabas, for everyone who is rational is capable
of seeing the infallible proof represented by such a man. Such a system of thought
does keep Christianity as an historical religion.' *Ibid.*, p. 240.

[38]*Ibid.*, p. 259.

[39]Acts 2:22; cf. also, Acts chapter 9, where Paul's conversion is grounded in
the person of Christ and not in the ethical example of the martyr Stephen.

[40]*Ibid.*, p. 240, n. 45.

[41]W. Pannenberg, 'The Revelation of God in Jesus of Nazareth', *Theology as
History*, p. 130.

'eschatologically', and is grounded in the personal reality of the living God. Out of this faith proceeds an attitude of hope, because, if one is 'living in God', the future resurrection cannot be said to be only 'proleptically' indicated by the resurrection of Christ, but is already given to our historical existence. I suppose that one could say that lived transcendence as a reality of historical existence is proleptic of our future resurrection, but I do not see how one could say that the eschaton itself is only proleptic of its own historical reality.

But, because Fuller has not clearly seen this problem in Pannenberg, he slips into somewhat the same pattern of thought when he says that the Christian in living by faith is to

> live according to the things that are not seen, according to the resurrection from the dead, whose promise he knows in the resurrection of Christ but does not as yet see in the reality around him. By walking according to the *knowledge* of this promise and not by the world around him, he walks by faith and not by sight.[42]

Faith thus tends to be directed towards the future 'resurrection from the dead' based on the knowledge of the resurrection of Jesus which comes through the kind of historical reasoning which infers from an 'overly pronounced deviation' of love and hope on the part of a 'Barnabas' living in the first-story of history, an infallible, supernatural cause which originates in the second-story. This cause, in Fuller's way of thinking, can be nothing less than the resurrection of Christ, for apart from the dynamic power of a living Christ, no man could do what Paul, Barnabas, or any Christian has done in moving from an attitude of hopelessness and immorality to become the kind of good and hopeful person that marks the Christian. Fuller is thus confident that he has bridged Lessing's 'ugly ditch' by seeing a present historical reality (a Barnabas) as the effect produced by a past cause (the resurrection of Christ) which leads faith to affirm a living Christ.[43] In the final analysis, Fuller is left without a rationale for the transcendence of God, though he wishes to assert it as the second-story of history, since one does not believe on the basis of historical reasons after all, for 'God simply does not work supernaturally in the heart of everyone who hears the Gospel in order to overcome their prejudices so that they might own up to the truth of what is to be known in history'.[44] Pannenberg, on the other hand, does not want to assert the transcendence of God in any way that

[42]D. P. Fuller, *Easter Faith and History*, p. 254, my emphasis.
[43]'As Barnabas preaches the Gospel that Christ died for men's sins and rose again the third day, and as he testifies to the change that came about in his own life as he believed this message, the hearers, sensing the supernaturalness of Barnabas, are confronted with sufficient evidence to credit his message regarding the risen Christ.' *Ibid.*, p. 259.
[44]*Ibid.*, p. 187.

will break the unity of his rationale of universal history.

What both have failed to take into account, is that which has become the heart of this study on historical transcendence—namely, that as the eschaton of historical existence, God the Creator has acted from within creation to bring the *telos* of historical existence into the eschaton through Jesus Christ the Redeemer. The 'inner logic' of this relation is exposed to us in the Incarnation in such a way that the horizon of hermeneutics is given to us out of historical transcendence. As a result, the resurrection of Christ not only gives us a 'method' for uniting faith to history, but it constitutes that unity in the person of Jesus Christ. So that, through historical transcendence, we know that both the content and the form of faith are given to us in the transcendent life of obedience, death and resurrection of Christ. This constitutes the eschaton of historical existence, and faith, therefore, is the *gift* of the eschaton as worked into historical existence by the Incarnate Word, and as made real to us through the life of the Holy Spirit. The Scripture presents to us a cognitive basis for an understanding of historical transcendence, so that the gift of the Spirit can find verification, not in a subjective rationality (or irrationality), but in the transcendent rationality of the eschaton of history itself—Jesus Christ. The resurrection of Christ is not a 'past event' to be believed, any more than the life of Christ as a past event is to be 'believed'. The Scripture informs us of the content of faith as represented in the person and life of Christ (historical transcendence) and points us to the living Christ who engages us in a living relation to his own faithful life with the Father in the Spirit (lived transcendence). Therefore, we must say that it is not the resurrection, nor even a resurrected Christ who is the univocal point which unites historical transcendence and eschatological transcendence, but it is rather the life of the triune God. For the eschaton of human existence is the living God, and as such, he is the eschaton of all humanity in the resurrected Christ and the eschaton of all personal existence in the transcendence of the indwelling Holy Spirit.

The ek-static community, therefore, is not simply a proleptic community, waiting for the end, it *is* a community of participation in the life of God through the Spirit. And as such, it is eschatological and not simply teleological. The 'difference' which the Incarnation makes in solidarity with the world is therefore radical and absolute, because it relates historical existence directly to the eschaton through the reality of the Holy Spirit. There is no 'future' life in God which is not already given to man through the resurrection of Jesus Christ in the life of the Spirit.[45]

And does this make any difference? Can one speak of lived transcendence when there is 'no end to hunger' and 'no happy land'? Yes, there is a difference in being on the threshold of lived transcendence, even if that

[45]II Peter 1:3-4.

threshold is laid in solidarity with the world. For this is the difference which the last things make to the next to the last.

2 'Thresholds of Lived Transcendence'

Lord, though by mortal tyrannies beset,
Immortal freedom in my wild heart sings.
A pauper comes to pay a pauper's debt.
God, I shall not forget the four last things.[46]

And so it has come to this—the four last things. But at the end of the 'tedious magnitude known as Transcendence', as Barth once put it,[47] is there yet strength to bring forth the children who have come to birth, to paraphrase a more ancient man of God?[48] But, whereas confusion and diversity are a weariness to the spirit, to the one who bears in his toil, the finality of things, to that one, there is joy and strength, for finality is of God and not man. Here, in God's finality, in his transcendence, we discover that we are delivered from the burden of being gods.

God's transcendence is the 'end' of the world even as it is its beginning; the eschaton which made the difference between creation and chaos, now makes the difference between life and death. The resurrection of Christ, we have said, is the only difference which the transcendence of God makes to the historical existence of man, for it is the eschaton. But this difference is made within the total solidarity of God with man through the Incarnation, and as such, the eschaton of lived transcendence has its threshold firmly cast in the concrete situations of man's historical existence. From this 'threshold of solidarity' with the world, the Spirit of the living God binds man with the transcendence of God into the eschaton. This is the ek-static dimension of lived transcendence, and if it has its head in the heavens, it has its heart on earth, where the difference is made.

One could say, with Bonhoeffer, that the difference is that which the penultimate reveals as it gives space and expression to the ultimate. The ultimate, says Bonhoeffer, 'has become real in the cross, as the judgement upon all that is penultimate, yet also as mercy towards that penultimate which bows before the judgement of the ultimate.'[49] The penultimate, according to Bonhoeffer's view, is not simply historical existence as such, for apart from the ultimate, historical existence has

---

[46]'Ballade on Eschatology', Sister Mary Madeleva, *The Four Last Things*, 'Collected Poems', Macmillan, New York, 1959, pp. 174-175.
[47]*Church Dogmatics*, III/4, p. 479.
[48]Hezekiah, Isaiah 37:3.
[49]*Ethics*, p. 132.

no final meaning, and thus can never exist as the 'next to the last' moment.[50] I am not so sure that Bonhoeffer is as prepared as I think one must be to locate the threshold of the ultimate (the eschaton) within the concrete situation of man's historical existence. The penultimate, he insists, is a 'judgement which the ultimate passes upon that which has preceded it.'[51] As the eschaton, the ultimate does radicalize historical existence and thus gives it a true significance as the penultimate. What Bonhoeffer wishes to avoid, on the one hand, is the radicalism which would seek to negate the penultimate for the sake of the ultimate; and, on the other hand, a compromise with the ultimate in which it simply becomes the eternal justification for things as they are. What he suggests is that the Incarnation provides the way in which both the ultimate and penultimate can be given their true significance. The difference which the ultimate makes, as he sees it, is the distinction between the 'unnatural' and the 'natural' form of human existence. The 'unnatural' closes its doors against the coming of Christ, and the 'natural' becomes the penultimate as it is directed towards the ultimate.[52] This roughly corresponds to the distinction I have made between the kenotic and ek-static community, except that Bonhoeffer leaves no place for a 'threshold' of the ultimate within the concrete existence of 'unnatural' creaturehood. He therefore tends to see the 'difference' as an ethical one conceived in terms of a radical type of obedience to Christ.[53] I do not see that solidarity with the (unnatural) world can become the dialectical half of an ethical difference. We have discovered that the Incarnation issues us with an imperative in which the kenotic community forms the threshold upon which the ek-static community stands in the eschaton. It is of these thresholds that we now must speak in attempting to offer in a tentative, and yet quite practical way, the conclusions to

[50]*Ibid.*, p. 133.
[51]*Ibid.*, p. 133.
[52]*Ibid.*, pp. 144-145.
[53]"But the problem of ethics at once assumes a new aspect if it becomes apparent that these realities, myself and the world, themselves lie embedded in a quite different ultimate reality, namely, the reality of God, the Creator, Reconciler and Redeemer. What is of ultimate importance is now no longer that I should become good, or that the condition of the world should be made better by my action, but that the reality of God should show itself everywhere to be the ultimate reality.' *Ibid.*, p. 188. I don't think that Bonhoeffer would want to say that it is *not* of ultimate importance that the 'unnatural' become 'natural', for that surely was the final intention of Jesus' life, death and resurrection, but he is asserting that the ethical life does not consist in a motivation towards the penultimate, but towards the ultimate. However, what Bonhoeffer fails to point out here, is that the eschaton (and so the ultimate) exists in solidarity with the world (the penultimate) in such a way that one cannot make the 'ultimate' distinction by splitting the two apart. Therefore, as I shall attempt to do, the difference (which is the ethical dimension of lived transcendence) must be understood in such a way that it does 'make a difference' within the 'unnatural' world.

which this exploration of historical transcendence and the reality of
God has brought us. These thresholds point us to at least a few of the
concrete situations of historical existence which are radically qualified
by the transcendence of God. In each case, the formulation is expressed
in terms of the problematic of the concrete man's bond with the
absolute, with the historical transcendence of God (the Incarnation)
forming the bond with the concrete situation through which the reality
of God finds completion as the ek-stasis of lived transcendence (the
Holy Spirit).

(1) *The enemy that is also the friend.* Through the reality of the
kenotic community, estrangement and alienation are raised to a truly
tragic dimension. And it is in the recovery of the sense of the tragic
that lived transcendence finds its expression as ek-stasis. Enmity between
men has its roots in the loss of the eschaton on the part of man as
creature. The eschaton of creation was the transcendence of God
expressed as a limiting grace of God's lordship of man. With the denial
of this lordship on the part of Adam, historical existence lost its
ek-static dimension, human nature was fragmented into 'individual'
entities, each seeking to bear the totality of humanity in their own
hypostasis. When Cain turned against Abel as his enemy, the truly
tragic dimension of that encounter was not merely the death of Abel,
but the loss of true community in the life of God. As a result, the blood
itself became the ek-static voice crying out, not only against human
violence, but the 'murder' of God: 'What have you done? The voice
of your brother's blood is crying to me from the ground.'[54] It was only
when the reality of the eschaton of creaturehood is heard as the voice
of God that a human situation can be understood in its (often) tragic
dimension. And it is in this sense that the tragic is ek-static, for it brings
back to man with terrible reality, the fact that the enemy is also the
friend. No matter how alienated and deformed our common human
existence becomes, it can never destroy the common humanity that has
its source in the life of God. Thus, the tragic is the only ek-stasis left to
'unnatural' human existence.

It is because of this that we cannot simply pass off the brokenness
of humanity as 'tragic' and due to sin. As though inhumanity was
somehow more acceptable, even though more intractable, because it
could be attributed to a cause which lies within our historical existence.
No, creaturehood itself bears the intrinsic 'tragedy' of the possibility
of the loss of the transcendence of God as a living and real limitation
of grace. Therefore, the truly tragic dimension of human existence is
the ek-static voice of creaturehood itself, bearing the image of God
as 'incapacity'.[55] How often *after* a tragedy does not a community

[54]Genesis 4:10.
[55]Cf. J. Zizioulas, *Human Capacity and Human Incapacity,* p. 20.

rise up in moral indignation and demand that some law be passed, or some action taken to prevent the recurrence of this particular kind of violence or senseless loss of human life? The tragic points to the eschaton, and thus includes within it the transcendence of God.

But tragedies can have the opposite effect. Turning away from the eschatological implications of human existence, and faced with the stupefying horror of both atrocities and catastrophies, man seeks an immunity from the pain by taking refuge in what Miskotte called the 'imperialism of dumb facticity.'[56] Statistics no longer register, vivid images lose their power to shock. The spirit turns to recreation as an anodyne (instead of re-creation!) and the mind turns to technology with the hope of engineering human happiness. A modern journalist suggests that the major challenge for humanity may not be 'future shock' but *present shock*:

> People are thrown into mental or present shock much the same as are the victims of physical shock. They are battered by some forms of external reality; mental shock results in a reduced flow of emotions that the mind normally needs in order to respond humanly. The person in shock in the 20th century is one who is constantly learning of so much tragedy, horror, chaos and absurdity that he can no longer absorb it. He becomes numb.[57]

Because it has become impossible to care about everything of which we are incessantly and involuntarily informed, we end up caring about nothing. 'A sense of outrage is replaced by a sense of acceptance, a numbness of feeling, that no tragedy can touch.'[58]

But the kind of 'caring' which is necessary to meet this crisis is not to be found in a human 'capacity' to bear the sufferings of others, or even prevent them, but the 'care' is the transcendence of God's love which man possesses only as 'incapacity'. That is, this care is eschatological in the most concrete sense. It is 'down to earth' and not 'other-worldly', because the eschaton brings to the concrete situation the reality of man's existence in the life of God. Therefore, lived transcendence means, first of all, that there is a recovery of the sense of the tragic, which has its fullest expression in the exhortation of Jesus: 'Love your enemies and pray for those who persecute you.'[59] Just why this should be considered as an ek-static expression which has its basis in the tragic, can be understood if we consider, and accept, the reality of the Incarnation in terms of the solidarity of the eschaton with all

[56]*When the Gods are Silent,* p. 328.
[57]Colman McCarthy, ' "Present Shock": We Can Take Only so Much Reality', *Los Angeles Times,* April 2, 1972.
[58]*Ibid.*
[59]Matthew 5:44.

humanity. Thus, the kind of love which we are to have for one who has hostility towards us, or who may even have injured us or one that we love, is not a human 'feeling' which we can generate as a capacity to show affection, but it is the recognition that the enemy is also our friend, considered from the standpoint of the eschaton. In other words, the commandment of Jesus was eschatological in the most practical sense, for it will be tragic *not* to see that our enemy is also our friend, and to thereby seek reconciliation. But the concrete bond for such an assertion is contained in the historical transcendence of God himself. For Jesus teaches us that an action, or non-action, towards the criminal in prison, the sick, the poor, the starving, and the homeless is bound up with our relation with him. 'As you did it to one of the least of these my brethren, you did it to me.'[60]

The implications of this, of course, are complex and far-reaching. I only suggest that the starting point, and thus the threshold, for a practical life of lived transcendence must be found in the concrete situation in such a way that the solidarity of God with the human situation is expressed through our human (and therefore, Christian) action. I also suggest that in such situations as are intrinsically and hopelessly bound up with hostility, violence and alienation, and therefore are 'unnatural', Christian action may be necessarily tragic if the situation itself is to be 'transcended'. For the tragic may be the only ek-stasis which is possible for the kenotic community of Christ in solidarity with the world, in which case, we can rightly speak of transcendence as tears, blood and flesh.[61]

(2) *The flesh that is also the spirit.* If transcendence is conceived as a movement of spirit towards communion, then spirit will move towards flesh and not away from it. For if transcendence is not merely 'being' (*ousia*), but is 'presence' (*par-ousia*), the body is the appropriate form of being present within the reality of historical existence. The corollary of this is that the concrete level of human existence has its own real participation in the life of God. This is not only clear from the fact that the 'Word became flesh', and as such, brought the 'presence' of God to the concrete human situation, but it is expressly revealed through

---

[60]Matthew 25:40.

[61]One should not conclude from this that a doctrine of pacifism is necessarily implied by this concept of 'tragic action', although I would not want to exclude it. In Bonhoeffer's action of participating in a conspiracy to assassinate Hitler, his very complicity could be said to constitute the truly tragic dimension of the plot, and as such, his death could also be said to be the ek-stasis, and the transcendence, of what was intrinsically evil and inhuman. However, when resistance to evil, either of a passive or an active nature, lacks the element of the tragic it is merely solidarity without transcendence. And it makes no ultimate 'difference'.

the resurrection of Christ that the eschaton is of the body as well as of the spirit.

If, then, we follow through with the implication that lived transcendence is eschatological in the concrete situation of historical existence, the resurrection of the body has a direct bearing on our present relation to each other as persons. The 'koinonia of the Spirit', which may be taken as the community of life in which God participates, cannot be separated from the 'koinonia of the body'.[62] The body too has its ek-stasis in acts of love which acknowledge the reality and the presence of other *persons* through all of the physical senses. The element of true communion which the resurrected Christ had with his disciples was in 'the breaking of bread', and the physical embrace. While we read that only Thomas was offered the hands and side of Jesus to touch as an aid to his faith, could we really believe that John, the disciple who had lain on the breast of Jesus, had not already embraced the risen Christ with unrestrained joy and affection? But we are on more solid ground in considering the references to the *koinonia* of the early church, a common life which included the sharing of goods and property, the sharing together at common meals, and the sharing of physical affection.[63] True personhood as it has its ek-static fulfilment in the eschaton of the resurrection has its transcendent reality bound up with the concrete situation of human existence.

But we would fail to discern the true significance of this 'threshold' for lived transcendence, if we did not see it in terms of the solidarity which the kenotic community has with the world. For it is not in 'Christian' flesh that the Spirit transcends the world, but in human flesh. The transcendence of the resurrection as the reality of the eschaton for historical existence, has its threshold, not in the grave, but in the street, in the factory, and at the supper table. 'If a brother or sister is ill-clad and in lack of daily food', says James, 'and one of you says to them, "Go in peace, be warmed and filled," without giving them the things needed for the body, what does it profit?'[64] The particular kind of solidarity which exists between the body and the spirit permits no dichotomy between the spiritual and the physical. What James is saying, is that, for all practical purposes, eschatological faith is concerned with the present conditions in which the body of a living person exists. John reinforces this by an even stronger warning put in the form of a rhetorical question: 'But if anyone has the world's goods and sees his brother in need, yet closes his heart against him, how does God's love abide in him?'[65] And the implied answer is: it doesn't.

[62]Cf. Philippians 2:1; also, Romans 12:13, where the 'contributing' to the needs of the saints is expressed as the verbal form of *koinonia*.
[63]Acts 2:43-47; 4:34-37; 20:10-11, 37-38; Romans 16:16; I Peter 5:14.
[64]James 2:15-16.   [65]I John 3:17.

Here again we discover that lived transcendence is profoundly concerned with the reality of the earthly body precisely because it has its eschaton in the resurrection of Christ. In this sense, the custom of anointing the sick with oil (James 5:14) reflects an intuitive sense of an ek-static function of faith expressed in eschatological terms. So too, the respect shown for the corpse of one who has died represents the kenotic community in an ek-static function. For the body as well has its eschaton in the complete personhood of life in God.

But this then is the inescapable truth which comprises also the power and reality of lived transcendence .The threshold of transcendence is with the living and not the dead. And the flesh of the other is also the spirit of another. And so lived transcendence radicalizes the conditions under which humanity exists, and demands that we love others 'as we love our own bodies'.[66] Spirit comes in many colours, sizes and shapes. It can shiver with the cold, wilt with the heat, become weary with work, and needs to be fed, and caressed, with regularity. These are the ways in which the resurrection makes a 'difference' when it is considered as the eschaton of historical existence.

(3) *The sickness that is also the hope.* When we say that the eschaton is the 'end of history', and thus claim that the resurrection of Christ represents the eschaton of historical existence, we are also making the assertion that the eschaton is the hope of man. But here again, the hope must be the 'difference' which is expressed in man's concrete situation because of the eschaton. And when the word 'sickness' is used to identify the particular concrete situation of man's historical existence which becomes the threshold of lived transcendence, it is only meant to signify all that is *wrong* about the human situation. It refers us to the fact that human existence is often experienced as a negation of the normal, or the good. A physical disease is one form of this negation, emotional illness is another. In this sense, sickness is the word chosen to represent the threshold of solidarity between God and humanity by which the negation is included in the relation itself. This became visible in the ministry of Jesus to those who were oppressed with fever, malformity of body and torment of soul; and of this Matthew observes: 'This was to fulfill what was spoken by the prophet Isaiah, "He took our infirmities and bore our diseases." '[67]

But we are speaking of more than merely the treatment of sickness, for the condition of sickness represents a threshold for the eschaton to overcome the negation of the good. The difference' which the eschaton makes, therefore, is radical, and deals with the total 'sickness', not merely a form of its manifestation. Surely this accounts for the radical way in which Jesus brought healing, and even resuscitation of the dead

[66]Ephesians 5:28.
[67]Matthew 8:17; cf. Isaiah 53:4.

through the authority of the eschaton. There were no 'failures' of healing on the part of Jesus because his authority was the final authority of God himself in solidarity with man. But it is also made clear that this 'threshold' of sickness brought hope as an eschatological reality in more than physical, or even emotional healing. For the hope brought by a restored body was a limited hope; we can assume that even Lazarus had to face a second death and burial. The eschaton brings man into the reality of a total deliverance from that which negates man's true fulfilment in God, and this means forgiveness of sin. Salvation (*soteria*) is health and wholeness. Thus, when confronted with a man who was so paralyzed in body that he could only be brought to Jesus by the assistance of his friends, Jesus immediately said, 'My son, your sins are forgiven.'[68] Recognizing the radical nature of this authority, some questioned whether or not Jesus actually had the power to confer this eschatological gift, for 'Who can forgive sins but God alone?', they argued.[69] Granting the logic with which they had grasped the significance of this act, Jesus proceeded to accomplish the 'easier' act of healing the body, to demonstrate his eschatological authority.

There is a sense in which one could say with the American psychologist Dr. O. Hobart Mowrer, that 'sin is the lesser of two evils'; for, as against the alternative that man's torment is merely physical or even psychological, the concept of sin opens up the possibility of 'radical redemption', to use Dr. Mowrer's words.[70] The possibility of hope, then, is tied directly to the reality of the eschaton as the gift of God's own life to man. To minister only to the body or to the emotionally disturbed person, therefore, as to one who is suffering from a torment which needs to be alleviated, is to deny the eschatological reality of the situation and deprive the person of the radical 'difference' which the resurrection of Christ makes in solidarity with all that is wrong with human existence. Of course, it must be said immediately that the 'flesh is also the spirit', and that to speak of forgiveness without touching the flesh is as cruel as to speak of being warmed and filled without providing clothing and food. It would be simply incredible to suppose that Jesus could forgive a man's sins and walk away leaving

[68]Mark 2:5.
[69]Mark 2:7.
[70]*The Crisis in Psychiatry and Religion*, Van Nostrand, Princeton, 1961, pp. 83ff. Dr. Mowrer also suggests that guilt should be taken as a possibility of a *real* act of negation towards God, so that an emotionally 'sick' person can actually become a 'sinner', and thus find the possibility of forgiveness: 'I have repeatedly seen persons who have wallowed in neurotic illness for years recover with astonishing swiftness when they are given a little encouragement in admitting the reality of their guilt. The sociopath sins and does not have the decency to suffer. The neurotic and functional psychotic persons, while sinners, have to their credit the capacity for self-condemnation and self-punishment.' *The New Group Therapy*, Van Nostrand, Princeton, 1964, p. 94.

him a cripple in body. For the resurrection of Christ is the eschaton of the body as well. But here it must be made clear that the eschaton has closed with historical existence in such a way that historical existence is not destroyed. For this reason, lived transcendence is eschatologi*cal*. Sickness and even death are not destroyed as realities of historical existence even though the reality of the eschaton is already given in the resurrection of Christ. Therefore, *all* of the people whom Jesus heals die a mortal death. But this 'mortality' is also the hope, for it is the threshold from which the Spirit brings man to the eschaton.

What this means for the ek-static community in its solidarity with the kenotic community is that the common mortality is the threshold of a common hope. But this hope comes as the eschaton came into the mortal lives of those with whom Jesus lived. It came as the eschaton came into his own mortal flesh. There is a resistance to this eschaton which has its roots in a creaturely logos which has turned in upon itself. The forgiveness of sins, therefore, while it is the real hope of mortal existence, is shattering to the defences which have been built up to protect the Ego with its own will to survive in the only way it has known. Lived transcendence must struggle in solidarity with a humanity which does not know that it has been forgiven, and cannot bear to know it, that is, cannot bear to be mortal, cannot bear to die in order that the life which God gives might be received. If one should call this struggle of lived transcendence with mortality 'intercession', let it be understood that intercession is not a movement made from God's side, but from the side of man, and in solidarity with man. This eschatological life which the Spirit gives carries with it the audacity of a Moses who said, 'if you wilt forgive their sin—and if not, blot me, I pray thee, out of the book which thou hast written', as well as the compassion of Paul who cried out, 'I could wish that I myself were accursed and cut off from Christ for the sake of my brethren, my kinsmen by race.'[71] Here too is why there can exist no boundary between the church and the world—and yet the difference is radical because it is eschatological.

(4) *The place that is also the presence.* Tethered as we are to our 'place' in historical existence (and one must no longer think of this 'place' as limited to the planet earth), our presence to one very often means absence to another. We are always 'some place' or other. If we are alone, that is the place where we are at. If we are gathered with two or three, that is the place where we are present. It is true, that in a certain sense, others can be 'present' to us in a special sense just because they are absent. Our entire 'place' can then be filled with their presence, just because we know them as absent. But this has its limitations too, for one who has never been with me in my 'place' cannot be absent

[71]Exodus 32:30; Romans 9:3.

from this place, and, therefore, they can have no 'presence' (*par-ousia*) for me even in absence.

So that we could say that 'being in the same place' is fundamental to the reality of historical existence. This limitation, as well as possibility we share with all others in a common humanity. The solidarity, then, of God with man must be a solidarity of place if it is to be a reality of presence. To speak of the reality of God as 'presence' without also relating it to 'place' is the fundamental problem of mysticism, and of any concept of the transcendence of God which has no threshold as place within historical dimension. The reality of God as 'presence' is the ek-static dimension of 'place'; that is to say, in the solidarity of God with man established through historical transcendence (Incarnation), God became known to us in our own place and in our own time. His presence is the eschaton of place, for God is the reality of creaturehood. The reality of creation finds its fulfilment (its eschaton) in being ek-static towards (present to) the Creator. The resurrection of Christ becomes the true ek-stasis of creation, for in the living Christ man is present to God and God is present to man. This two-fold *par-ousia* is eschatological to historical existence in the form of historical transcendence and lived transcendence. In historical transcendence, the *par-ousia* of man to God is completed in the resurrection in such a way that Christ, being 'absent' from his 'place' with man, ensures that man is 'present' to God in the humanity of the risen Christ. 'I am the way, and the truth, and the life; no one comes to the Father, but by me', said Jesus, 'because I live, you will live also. In that day you will know that I am in my Father, and you in me....'[72]

But the 'presence' of Christ to the 'place' of man is possessed now as absence. 'I tell you the truth', said Jesus, 'it is to your advantage that I go away, for if I do not go away, the Counsellor will not come to you; but if I go, I will send him to you.'[73] Because the Holy Spirit is the Spirit of God as well as the Spirit of the living Christ, the eschaton becomes 'present' to man in his historical existence through the life of the Spirit. But this transcendence of God (the eschaton, the resurrection of Christ, the Holy Spirit) is only possessed in a concrete place— 'where two or three are gathered'—and it is possessed ek-statically, that is, it is possessed as 'absence'. It is the historical transcendence of God which binds the reality of God to the concrete human situation, so that the 'presence' of God through the eschatological life of the Spirit is a presence in the place which Jesus Christ has in solidarity with man. In this way, historical transcendence keeps the 'presence' of God from dissolving into sheer unhistorical mysticism. For ek-stasis is not simply man 'fleeing his place' into the transcendence of God, but ek-stasis

[72]John 14:6, 19b, 20.
[73]John 16:7.

is the completion of man's life by 'being present' to God through the historical transcendence of Jesus Christ. In this way, the absence of Christ ensures our 'place' with God eternally, but it also makes possible the 'presence' of Christ to our 'place' in historical existence.[74]

'Where two or three are gathered in my name', said Jesus, 'there am I in the midst of them.'[75] This is the place that is also the presence. So completely did Jesus identify himself with man in his concrete situation, that he could take the bread and wine of the common meal and say, 'Take, eat; this is by body.... Drink of it, all of you, for this is my blood of the covenant.'[76] And Paul added the words which he himself knew to be the Lord's: 'Do this in remembrance of me.'[77] In this way, presence is bound to place as surely as spirit is bound to body and body to bread. Every common table is the threshold of lived transcendence to which the presence of Christ comes as the ek-stasis of the Spirit.

But this presence (*par-ousia*) is also absence, and the ek-static community points the kenotic community towards the eschaton, which will be the 'presence' of Christ to the world in such a way that historical existence will be consummated in this *Parousia* of Christ as the Lord of creation. The ek-static community finds its 'place' in which to celebrate this *Parousia* in solidarity with the world. This celebration, whether it is in the form of the 'eschatological banquet' (the Lord's Supper) or in the polyphonic texture of worship, takes place on the threshold created by the solidarity of the kenotic community with the world.

So then, the church (the body of Christ), a refugee with the refugees, with no outer wall to separate saint from sinner, with no inner sanctuary to be guarded against profanation, is nonetheless the place which is also the presence of the living God. But here, too, the church is radicalized by the very fact that it has no place of its own, for its place is bound

---

[74]Readers of the essay by Dr. John Zizioulas, 'Human Capacity and Human Incapacity', will see how indebted I am to his concept of 'presence-in-absence' as the fundamental characteristic of creaturehood (cf. especially, pp. 7-8, 10-11). What Zizioulas has not done, at least to my satisfaction, is relate presence and absence to 'place', particularly when the concept is applied to the ek-static fulfilment of human personhood in the movement towards God borne out of a deep sense of God's 'absence' to man. Without a well developed concept of historical transcendence, the 'absence' of God tends to become more of a mystical longing for oneness with the divine life, rather than a specific absence of the Jesus who is now the risen Lord. Zizioulas's insistence that this is a proper ontology of relation to God, rather than mysticism, because mysticism does not know presence as *absence*, seems unconvincing to me, despite his Christology which enables him to say that God meets man 'from underneath', i.e., within space-time structures (p. 17).

[75]Matthew 18:20.
[76]Matthew 26:26-28.
[77]I Corinthians 11:24.

up with the humanity of Christ and is therefore the place of the kenotic community. Whatever structures the church erects will be no more than 'disposable containers', for disposability is the test of eschatological reality. Wherever 'two or three' gather in the name of Christ is the *place* where we will find the absence of Christ celebrated as his *Parousia*—his presence to God in which we have our life, and his presence to the world in which we have our hope. And so the church discovers within the kenotic community the shape of its own reality— a stone, a leaf, a door; and suddenly there is the place, the lost lane-end into heaven.

God the dispersed
gathered up again in those who have communed.
Out of all our eucharists, this is the first.

MARANATHA!

Bibliography of Works Cited

Adolfs, Robert, *The Grave of God*. A Compass Book: Burns and Oates, London, 1967. Trans. from *Het graf van God. Heeft de Kerk nog Toekomst?* Amboboeken, Utrecht, 1966, by N. D. Smith

Albrecktson, Bertil, *History and the Gods*. CWK Gleerup Lund, Sweden, 1967.

Altizer, Thomas, J. J., *The Gospel of Christian Atheism*. Collins, London, 1967.

—— *Mircea Eliade and the Dialectic of the Sacred*. Westminster Press, Philadelphia, 1963.

Aristotle, *Metaphysics*. (The Works of Aristotle Translated into English, vol. VIII.) The Clarendon Press, Oxford, 1908.

Athanasius, *De Incarnatione*. Trans. by Archibald Robertson. D. Nutt, London, 1891.

Bandstra, Andrew J., ' "Adam" and "the Servant" in Philippians 2:5ff' *Calvin Theological Journal*, vol. I, 2 (Nov. 1966), pp. 213-216.

Barr, James, *Old and New in Interpretation*. SCM Press, London, 1966.

Barth, Karl, *Church Dogmatics*. (Four volumes.) T. & T. Clark, Edinburgh, 1936-1962. Trans. from *Die Kirchliche Dogmatik* (I/1, Munich: Chr. Kaiser Verlag, 1932; I/2—IV/3, Zollikon/Zürich: Evang. Verlag, 1938-1959) by G. T. Thomson (I/1); G. T. Thomson, Harold Knight (I/2); T. H. Parker *et al* (II/1); G. W. Bromiley *et al* (II/2); J. W. Edwards *et al* (III/1); Harold Knight *et al* (III/4); G. W. Bromiley (IV/1); G. W. Bromiley (IV/2-3).

—— *The Humanity of God*. Fontana Library edition, 1967: first published by Collins, London, 1961. Trans. by John Newton Thomas and Thomas Wieser.

Beare, F. W., *A Commentary on the Epistle to the Philippians*. Adam and Charles Black, London, 1959.

Berger, P. L., *A Rumour of Angels*. Allen Lane, The Penguin Press, London, 1970.

—— *The Sacred Canopy—Elements of a Sociological Theory of Religion*. Doubleday, Garden City, New York, 1967.

Bethge, Eberhard, *Dietrich Bonhoeffer*. 'A Biography', Collins, London, 1970, first published by Chr. Kaiser Verlag, Munich, 1967. Trans. by Eric Mosbacher *et al*.

Blaikie, Robert J., *'Secular Christianity' and God Who Acts*. Hodder and Stoughton, London, 1970.

Bonhoeffer, Dietrich. *Act and Being*. Collins, London, 1962. Trans. from *Akt und Sein* pub. Chr. Kaiser Verlag, Munich, 1956.

—— *Christology.* The Fontana Library: Collins, London, 1971. First published in *Gesammelte Schriften*, vol. 3: Chr. Kaiser Verlag, Munich, 1960. Trans. by John Bowden.

—— *The Cost of Discipleship*. SCM Press, London, 1969. Trans. from *Nachfolge* by R. H. Fuller, pub. Chr. Keiser Verlag, Munich, 1937.

—— *Creation and Fall*. SCM Press, London, 1959. Trans. from *Schöpfung und Fall* pub. Chr. Kaiser Verlag, Munich, 1937.

—— *Ethics*. The Fontana Library. Collins, London, 1970. *Ethik*, pub. Chr. Kaiser Verlag, Munich, 1949, from the 6th edition (1963). Trans. by Neville Horton Smith.

—— *Letters and Papers* from Prison. The Macmillan Company, New York, The Enlarged Edition, 1972. Trans. from *Widerstand und Ergebung: Briefe und Aufzeichnungen aus der Haft* pub. Chr. Kaiser Verlag, 1970.

—— *Life Together*. SCM Press, London, 1970. Trans. from *Gemeinsames Leben* pub. Chr. Kaiser Verlag, Munich, 1949.

—— *No Rusty Swords*. The Fontana Library: Collins, London, 1970. Trans. from *Gesammelte Schriften* pub. Chr. Kaiser Verlag, Munich, 1958, by Edwin H. Robertson.

—— *Sanctorum Communio*. Collins, London, 1967. Trans. from 3rd edition pub. Chr. Kaiser Verlag, Munich, 1960, by R. G. Smith. First published in Berlin, 1930.

—— *The Way to Freedom*. Collins, London, 1966. Trans. from *Gesammelte Schriften* pub. Chr. Kaiser Verlag, Munich, 1958-1961, by. Edwin H. Robertson and John Bowden.

Bruce, A. B., *The Humiliation of Christ*. T. & T. Clark, Edinburgh, 2nd edition, 1881.

Brunner, Emil, *The Christian Doctrine of the Church, Faith and the Consummation* (Dogmatics, vol. III). Lutterworth Press, London, 1962. Trans. from *Die christliche Lehre von der Kirche, vom Glauben, und von der Vollendung* pub. Zwingli-Verlag, Zürich and Stuttgart, 1960, by David Cairns in collaboration with T. H. L. Parker.

—— *The Misunderstanding of the Church*. Lutterworth Press, London, 1952.

Buber, Martin, *Between Man and Man*. The Fontana Library: Collins, London, 1969. Trans. by R. G. Smith.

—— *Eclipse of God*. Harper Torch Books: The Cloister Library: Harper and Row, New York (1952)), 1957.

—— *I and Thou*. T. & T. Clark, Edinburgh, 1970. 1st British edition, 1937. Trans. by Walter Kaufmann from the German, *Ich und Du*.

Bultmann, Rudolf, *Essays Philosophical and Theological*. Macmillan, New York, 1955. Trans. by James C. G. Greig from *Glauben und Verstehen: Gesammelte Aufsätze II*.

—— *Jesus Christ and Mythology*. SCM Press, London (1958), 1966.

—— *Theology of the New Testament*. (Two volumes.) Charles Scribner's

Sons, New York, 1951, 1955. Trans. from *Theologie des Neuen Testaments* pub. J. C. B. Mohr (Paul Siebeck) Tübingen, 1948, 1953, by Kendrick Grobel.

Buren, Paul van, *The Secular Meaning of the Gospel.* Penguin Books, Middlesex, 1968.

—— *Theological Explorations.* SCM Press, London, 1968.

Buri, Fritz. 'How Can We Speak Responsibly of God?' *McCormick Quarterly*, vol. 21 (Jan. 1968), pp. 185-197.

Buss, Martin J., 'The Meaning of History.' *Theology as History* (New Frontiers in Theology, vol. III). James M. Robinson and John C. Cobb, eds. Harper and Row, New York, 1967.

Cairns, David, *God up There? 'A Study in Divine Transcendence'.* The Saint Andrew Press, Edinburgh, 1967.

Calvin, John, *The Epistles of Paul the Apostle to the Galatians, Ephesians, Philippians and Colossians.* Oliver and Boyd, Edinburgh/London, 1965. Trans. by T. H. L. Parker.

—— *Institutes of the Christian Religion*, vol. I. T. & T. Clark, Edinburgh. Trans. by Henry Beveridge from the 1559 Latin edition, *Christianae Religionis Institutio.*

Carnell, Edward John, *The Case for Orthodox Theology.* Westminster Press, Philadelphia, 1959.

—— *Christian Commitment.* Macmillan, New York, 1957.

Clarke, William N. *An Outline of Christian Theology.* T. & T. Clark, Edinburgh, 11th edition, 1902.

Cullman, Oscar, *The Christology of the New Testament.* SCM Press, London, 1959. Trans. by S. C. Guthrie and C. A. M. Hall from *Die Christologie des Neven Testaments*, J. C. B. Mohr (Paul Siebeck) Tübingen, 1957.

Dawes, Donald G., 'A Fresh Look at the Kenotic Christologies.' *Scottish Journal of Theology*, 15 (1962), pp. 337-349.

Dodd, C. H., *The Founder of Christianity.* Collins, London, 1972.

—— *The Fourth Gospel.* Cambridge, 1958.

Dorner, J. A., *The Person of Christ.* Clark's Foreign Theological Library, Third Series, vol. XV, division II. Volumes I and II: T. & T. Clark, Edinburgh, 1870. Third Series, vol. XIII, division II; vol. III: T. & T. Clark, Edinburgh, 1872.

Dumas, André, *Dietrich Bonhoeffer: Theologian of Reality.* SCM Press, London, 1971. Trans. from *Une théologie de la réalité: Dietrich Bonhoeffer* pub. Editions Labour et Fides, Geneva, 1968, by Robert McAfee Brown.

Ebeling, Gerhard, *The Nature of Faith.* The Fontana Library: Collins, London, 1967. Trans. from *Das Wesen des Christlichen Glaubens* pub. J. C. B. Mohr (Paul Siebeck), Tübingen, 1959, by R. G. Smith.

Fackre, G. J., 'The Issue of Transcendence in the New Theology, the New Morality, and the New Forms.' *The London Quarterly and Holborn Review*, vol. 192 (January, 1967), pp. 1-11.

Fairbairn, A. M., *The Place of Christ in Modern Theology.* Hodder and Stoughton, London, 12th edition, 1905.

Fairweather, Eugene, 'The "Kenotic" Christology.' *A Commentary on the*

Epistle to the Philippians. F. W. Beare. Adam and Charles Black, London, 1959, pp. 159-174.

Farley, Edward, *The Transcendence of God.* The Epworth Press, London, 1962.

Flew, A. and MacIntyre, A., editors. *New Essays in Philosophical Theology.* SCM Press, London, 1955.

Forsyth, P. T., *The Person and Place of Jesus Christ.* Independent Press, London, 1951.

Fry, Christopher, *The Boy With a Cart.* Frederick Muller, London, 2nd edition, 1945.

—— *A Sleep of Prisoners.* Oxford University Press, London, 1951.

Fuller, Daniel P., *Easter Faith and History.* Tyndale Press, London, 1968. First published by Wm. Eerdmans Publishing Co., Grand Rapids, 1965.

Gibbs, John G., 'The Relation Between Creation and Redemption According to Phil. 2:5-11.' *Novum Testamentum,* vol. 12 (1970), pp. 270-283.

Gibran, K., *Sand and Foam.* Alfred A. Knopf, New York, 1926.

Gogarten, Friedrich, *Verhängniss und Hoffnung der Neuzeit.* Siebenstern Taschenbuch Verlag, München und Hamburg (1958), 1966.

Gollwitzer, Helmut, *The Existence of God.* SCM Press, London, 1965. Trans. from *Die Existenz Gottes im Bekenntnis des Glaubens* pub. Chr. Kaiser Verlag, Munich, 1964.

Gore, Charles, *Dissertations on Subjects Connected with the Incarnation.* Charles Scribner's Sons, New York, 1895.

—— *The Incarnation of the Son of God.* Bampton Lectures for the year 1891. John Murray, London, 2nd edition, 1909.

—— *Lux Mundi.* Charles Gore ed. John Murray, London, 1891.

Hall, Francis J., *The Kenotic Theory.* Longmans Green and Co., London, New York, Bombay, 1898.

Hamilton, Kenneth, *Revolt Against Heaven.* Eerdmans, Grand Rapids, 1965.

Hamilton, William, 'The Letters are a Particular Thorn.' *World Come of Age,* R. G. Smith, ed. Collins, London, 1967.

Hartshorne, Charles, *The Divine Relativity.* Yale University Press, New Haven, 1969. First published in 1948.

Harvey, John, 'A New Look at the Christ Hymn in Philippians 2:6-11.' *The Expository Times,* 76 (1964-65), pp. 337-339.

Heidegger, Martin, *Being and Time.* SCM Press, London, 1962. Trans. from *Sein und Zeit* 7th ed. *Neomarius Verlag,* Tübingen, by John Macquarrie and E. Robinson.

—— *Essays in Metaphysics.* Philosophical Library Inc., New York, 1960.

—— *An Introduction to Metaphysics.* Yale University Press, New Haven, 1959. Trans. by Ralph Manheim from *Was ist Metaphysik?*

—— *On the Way to Language.* Harper and Row, New York, 1971. Trans. from *Unterwegs zur Sprache* pub. Verlag Günther Neske, Pfullingen, 1959, by Peter D. Hertz.

—— *The Question of Being.* Vision Press, London, 1959. Trans. and introduction by William Kluback and Jean T. Wilde from *Uber die Linie,* an article contributed to the publication issued in honour of Ernst Jünger (1955).

Henry, Carl F. H. 'The New Consciousness.' *Christianity Today* (Oct. 8, 1971), pp. 28-29.

Hepburn, Ronald W., *Christianity and Paradox*. Watts, London, 1958.

Holland, J. A. B., *The Development of the Trinitarian Theology of Athanasius, in His Conflict with Contemporary Heresies*. Unpublished Ph.D. thesis, University of Edinburgh, 1963.

Hudson, D. F., 'A Further Note on Philippians 2:6-11.' *The Expository Times*, 77 (1965-66), p. 29.

Irenaeus, *Against Heresies*. (Two volumes.) Ante-Nicene Christian Library. A. Roberts and J. Donaldson, eds. T. & T. Clark, Edinburgh, 1868.

Jenkins, David E., *The Glory of Man*. SCM Press, London, 1967.

—— *Living With Questions*, SCM Press, London, 1969.

Jeremias, Joachim, *The Parables of Jesus*. SCM Press, London, 1958. Trans. from 3rd edition of *Die Gleichnisse Jesu*, pub. Zwingli-Verlag, Zürich, 1954, by S. H. Hooke.

—— 'Zu Phil. 2, 7: ἑαυτὸν ἐκένωσεν.' *Novum Testamentum*, vol. 6 (1963), pp. 182-188.

Johnson, S. E., 'Kenosis.' *The Interpreter's Dictionary of the Bible*, vol. 3. Abingdon Press, New York, 1962, p. 7.

Kant, Immanuel, *Critique of Practical Reason*. Longmans Green and Co., London, 1909. Trans. by T. K. Abbott from *Kritik der Praktischen Vernunft*.

—— *Critique of Pure Reason*. Macmillan and Co., London, 1929. Trans. by Norman Kemp Smith from *Kritik der Reinen Vernunft*.

Käsemann, E., 'A Critical Analysis of Philippians 2:5-11.' *Journal for Theology and the Church*, vol. 5 (1968), pp. 45-88. Trans. from 'Kritische Analyse von Phil. 2,5-22.' *Zeitschrift für Theologie und Kirche*, vol. 47 (1950), pp. 313-360, by Alice F. Carse.

—— *The Testament of Jesus*. SCM Press, London, 1968. Trans. from *Jesu letzter Wille nach Johannes 17* pub. J. C. B. Mohr (Paul Siebeck) Tübingen, 1966, by Gerhard Krodel.

—— 'Zum Theme der urchristlichen Apokalyptik.' *Zeitschrift für Theologie und Kirche*, vol. 59 (1962), pp. 257-284.

Kaufman, Gordon, 'On the Meaning of "Act of God".' *Harvard Theological Review*, vol. 61 (1968), pp. 175-201.

—— 'Transcendence Without Mythology.' *Harvard Theological Review*, vol. 59 (1966), pp. 105-132.

Kee, Alistair, *The Way of Transcendence*. Penguin Books, Middlesex, England, 1971.

Kierkegaard, S., *The Concept of Dread*. Princeton University Press, Princeton, 1944.

—— *Either/Or*, Anchor Books, New York, 1959, vol. I.

—— *The Last Years*. 'Journals 1853-55.' The Fontana Library: Collins, London, 1968. Trans. and ed. by R. G. Smith from the Danish edition of Søren Kierkegaards Papirer, 1909-48, P. A. Heiberg, V. Kuhr (eds.), the Gyidendalske Boghan del Nordisk Forlag.

—— *The Sickness Unto Death*. Oxford University Press, London, 1941.

Trans. by W. Lowrie from *Sygdammen til Døden.*

Kierkegaard, S., *Works of Love.* Oxford University Press, London, 1946. Trans. from the Danish by Howard and Edna Hong.

King, R. H., 'Models of God's Transcendence.' *Theology Today,* vol. 23 (July, 1966), pp. 200-209.

Körner, Johannes, 'Die transzendente Wirklichkeit Gottes.' *Zeitschrift für Theologie und Kirche,* vol. 63 (1966), pp. 473-495.

Küng, Hans, *Truthfulness—The Future of the Church.* Sheed and Ward, London, 1968.

Langford, Thomas A., 'T. F. Torrance's Theological Science: A Reaction.' *Scottish Journal of Theology,* vol. 25 (May, 1972), pp. 155-170.

Leon, Arnold E, *Secularization—Science Without God?* SCM Press, London, 1967. Trans from *Säkularisation. Von der wahren Voraussetzung und angeblichen Gottlosigkeit der Wissenschaft,* pub. Chr. Kaiser Verlag, Munich, 1965.

Lohmeyer, E. *Die Briefe an die Philipper, und die Kolasser und an Philemon.* Göttingen, 1930.

Loomer, Bernard M., 'Christian Faith and Process Philosophy.' *The Journal of Religion,* vol. 29 (1949), pp. 181-203.

Lossky, Vladimir, *The Mystical Theology of the Eastern Church.* James Clark and Co., Cambridge/London (1957), 1968.

McCarthy, Colman, ' "Present Shock": We Can Take Only so Much Reality.' *The Los Angeles Times* (April 2, 1972).

McKinnon, Alastair. 'Believing the *Paradoks*: a Contradiction in Kierkegaard?' *Harvard Theological Review* (1968), pp. 633-636.

MacKinnon, Donald, *Borderlands of Theology.* Lutterworth Press, London, 1968.

—— *The Stripping of the Altars.* The Fontana Library: Collins, London, 1969.

—— ' "Substance" in Christology—a Cross-bench View', *Christ Faith and History,* S. W. Sykes and J. P. Clayton, eds., Cambridge University Press, 1972.

Mackintosh, H. R., *The Doctrine of the Person of Jesus Christ.* T. & T. Clark, Edinburgh, 3rd edition, 1914.

Macmurray, John, *Freedom in the Modern World.* Faber & Faber (1932), 1968.

—— *Persons in Relation.* Vol. 2 of the Gifford Lectures (University of Glasgow, 1954). Faber & Faber, London (1961), 1970.

—— *Reason and Emotion.* Faber & Faber, London, 1935.

—— *Search For Reality in Religion.* Swarthmore Lecture. George Allen and Unwin, London, 1965.

—— *The Self as Agent.* Vol. 1 of the Gifford Lectures (University of Glasgow, 1953). Faber & Faber, London, 1957.

Macquarrie, John, *God and Secularity* (New Directions in Theology Today, vol. 3). Lutterworth Press, London, 1968.

—— 'The Pre-existence of Jesus Christ.' *The Expository Times.* 77 (1965-66), pp. 199-202.

—— *Principles of Christian Theology.* SCM Press, London, 1967.

Madeleva, Sister Mary, C.S.C., 'The Four Last Things' Collected Poems, Macmillan, New York, 1959.

Martin, R. P., 'μορφή in Philippians 2:6.' *The Expository Times*, 70 (1958-59), pp. 183-184.

Mascall, E. L., *Christ, The Christian and The Church*. Longmans Green and Co., London, 1946.

Maxwell, Ronald [R. G. Smith], *Still Point*. Nisbet and Co., London, 1943.

Mehl, Roger, 'Die Krise der Transzendenz.' *Neue Zeitschrift für Theologie und Religionsphilosophie*, vol. II (1969), pp. 329-346.

Meilander, Gilbert Jr., 'The New Paganism.' *Christianity Today* (Sept. 24, 1971), pp. 4-6.

Mendenhall, G. E., 'Covenant' *The Interpreter's Dictionary of the Bible*, vol. I. Abingdon Press, New York, 1962, pp. 714-723.

Miller, Arthur, *After the Fall*. Penguin Books, Middlesex (1964), 1968.

Miskotte, Kornelis, *When the Gods Are Silent*. Collins, London, 1967. Trans. from *Wenn die Götter Schweigen* (1967) by John W. Doberstein. First published as *Als de Goden Zwijgen*. Uitgeversmaatschappij, Amsterdam, 1956.

Mowrer, O. Hobart, *The Crisis in Psychiatry and Religion*. Van Nostrand, Princeton, 1961.

—— *The New Group Therapy*. Van Nostrand, Princeton, 1964.

Mühlen, Heribert. *Sein und Person* 'nach Johannes Duns Scotus'. Dietrich-Coelde-Verlag, Werl, Westf., 1954.

Neville, R. C., 'Some Historical Problems About the Transcendence of God.' *The Journal of Religion*, vol. 47 (January, 1967), pp. 1-9.

Newbigin, Lesslie, *Household of God*. SCM Press, London, 1953.

Nielsen, J. T., *Adam and Christ in the Theology of Irenaeus*. Van Gorcum and Co., N.V., Assens, Netherlands, 1968.

Noro, Yoshio, 'Transcendence and Immanence in Contemporary Theology.' *The Northeast Asia Journal of Theology* (September, 1969), pp. 54-75.

Obayashi, Hiroshi, 'Implicit Kantianism in Bonhoeffer's Conception of Religionless Christianity.' *The Northeast Asia Journal of Theology*, (September, 1970—March, 1971), pp. 107-126.

Ogden, Schubert, *Christ Without Myth*. Harper and Brothers, New York, 1961.

—— *The Reality of God and Other Essays*. SCM Press, London, 1967.

—— 'Theology and Objectivity.' *The Journal of Religion*, vol. 45 (July, 1965), pp. 275-295.

O'Grady, Colm, *The Church in the Theology of Karl Barth*. Geoffrey Chapman, London, 1968.

Ott, Heinrich, 'The Problem of Non-Objectifying Thinking and Speaking in Theology.' *Journal for Theology and the Church*, vol. 3 (1967), pp. 112-135.

—— 'What is Systematic Theology?' *The Later Heidegger and Theology* (New Frontiers in Theology, vol. I). James M. Robinson and John B. Cobb, eds. Harper and Row, New York, 1963.

Otto, Rudolph, *The Idea of the Holy*. Oxford University Press, London (1923), 1936.

Pannenberg, Wolfhart, 'Dogmatic Theses on the Doctrine of Revelation.' *Revelation as History*. W. Pannenberg, ed. Sheed and Ward, London, 1969, pp. 125-158. Trans. from the third revised edition (1965) of *Offenbarung Als Geschichte*, pub. Vandenhoeck and Ruprecht, Göttingen, 1961, by David Granskou and Edward Quinn.

—— 'Hermeneutics and Universal History.' *History and Hermeneutics. Journal for Theology and the Church*, vol. 4 (1967), pp. 122-152.

—— 'The Revelation of God in Jesus of Nazareth.' *Theology as History*. (New Frontiers in Theology, vol. III). James M. Robinson and John B. Cobb, eds. Harper and Row, New York, 1967.

Parker, Thomas D., 'How Can We Think of God? Another Look at Transcendence.' *McCormick Quarterly* (January, 1967), pp. 79-96.

Paul, L. A., 'New Theology and the Idea of Transcendence.' *The Expository Times*, vol. 79 (December, 1967), pp. 72-76.

Peck, William J., 'The Significance of Bonhoeffer's Interest in India.' *Harvard Theological Review* (1968), pp. 431-450.

Pelz, Werner and Lotte, *God is No More*. Victor Gollancz, London, 1964.

Phillips, John A., *The Form of Christ in the World:* 'A Study of Bonhoeffer's Christology.' Collins, London, 1967.

Polanyi, Michael, *Personal Knowledge*. Routledge and Kegan Paul, London, 1958.

Porteous, Norman W., 'The Old Testament and Some Theological Thought Forms.' *Scottish Journal of Theology* (1954), pp. 153-169.

Prenter, Regin, 'Bonhoeffer and the Young Luther' (pp. 161-181), 'Dietrich Bonhoeffer and Karl Barth's Positivism of Revelation' (pp. 93-130). *World Come of Age*. R. G. Smith, ed. Collins, London, 1967.

Price, George, *The Narrow Pass*. 'A Study of Kierkegaard's Concept of Man.' Hutchinson and Co., London, 1963.

Rad, Gerhard von, *Old Testament Theology*, vol. I. Oliver and Boyd, Edinburgh, 1962. Vol. II, Oliver and Boyd, Edinburgh, 1965. Trans. from *Theologie des Alten Testaments*, vol. I, Munich, 1957; vol. II, Munich, 1960, by D. M. G. Stalker.

Rahner, Karl, *The Trinity*. Burns and Oates/Herder and Herder, London, 1969.

Ramsey, Ian T., *Religious Language*. SCM Press, London, 1957.

Regas, George F., 'Explorations in New Liturgy For Man of the Future.' *Theology, News and Notes*. Fuller Theological Seminary, Pasadena, California, March, 1972. pp. 16-18, 22.

Rex, H. H., *Did Jesus Rise From the Dead?* Blackwood and Janet Paul, 1967.

Robinson, James M. and Cobb, John B. Jr., eds., *The Later Heidegger and Theology*. ('New Frontiers in Theology' vol. I.) Harper and Row, New York, 1963.

—— *Theology as History*. (New Frontiers in Theology, vol. III.) Harper Row, New York, 1967.

Robinson, John A. T., *Honest to God*. SCM Press, London, 1963.

Sauter, Gerhard, *Zukunft und Verheissung. Das Problem der Zukunft in der gegenwärtigen theologischen und philosophischen Diskussion.* Zwingli-Verlag, Zürich/Stuttgart, 1965.

Schleiermacher, Friedrich D. E., *The Christian Faith.* T. & T. Clark, Edinburgh, 1928.

Schmid, Heinrich, *The Doctrinal Theology of the Evangelical Lutheran Church.* Lutheran Publication Society, Philadelphia, 2nd English edition, 1889.

Schmidt, Hans, 'The Cross of Reality?' *World Come of Age.* R. G. Smith, ed. Collins, London, 1967.

Shiner, Larry, 'The Concept of Secularization in Empirical Research.' *The Journal for the Scientific Study of Religion,* vol. VI, no. 2 (Fall, 1967), pp. 207-220.

―― 'Toward a Theology of Secularization.' *The Journal of Religion,* vol. 45 (Oct., 1965), pp. 279-295.

Smedes, Lewis B. *The Incarnation: Trends in Modern Anglican Thought.* J. H. Kok N.V., Kampen, 1953.

Smith, Ronald Gregor. *Collected Papers of Ronald Gregor Smith.* University of Glasgow Library. References have been made to the following unpublished materials:

'History is Personal.' 19 pages. Ca. 1940-1944.

'Introduction to Theology―Outline to the Course.' Ca. 1966.

'Lectures on Apologetics.' Ca. 1957.

'Preparing For the Ministry.' 3 pages. Ca. 1938.

'Princeton Lecture Notes.' 1968.

'Turning Point.' Ca. 1944.

'Untitled Autobiographical Reflections.' Ca. 1944-1946.

―― *The Doctrine of God.* Collins, London, 1970.

―― *The Free Man.* Collins, London, 1969.

―― *J. G. Hamann―A Study in Christian Existence.* Collins, London, 1960.

―― 'J. G. Hamann and the Princess Gallitzin.' *Philomathes.* 'Studies and Essays in the Humanities in Memory of Philip Merlan.' Robert Palmer and Robert Hammerton-Kelly eds. Martinus Nijhoff, The Hague.

―― *Martin Buber* (Makers of Contemporary Theology). The Carey Kingsgate Press, London, 1966.

―― *The New Man.* SCM Press, London, 1956. The Alexander Love Lectures of 1955.

―― *Secular Christianity.* Collins, London, 1966.

―― editor. *World Come of Age.* Collins, London, 1967.

Stallman, Martin, *Was ist Säkularisierung?* J. C. B. Mohr (Paul Siebeck), Tübingen, 1960.

Stevenson, Leslie, 'Immanent Transcendence' (Variations on a Logical Theme). *Religious Studies* (March, 1970), pp. 89-97.

Thomas, Thomas A., 'The Kenosis Question.' *The Evangelical Quarterly,* vol. 42 (1970), pp. 142-151.

Thompson, Francis, *Selected Poems of Francis Thompson.* Burns and Oates, London, 1907.

Thornton, Lionel, *The Incarnate Lord.* Longmans Green and Co., London, 1928.

Tillich, Paul, *Biblical Religion and the Search for Ultimate Reality.* James Nisbet and Co., London, 1955.
—— *The Courage to Be.* Collins, London, 1962.
—— *Systematic Theology,* vol. I. University of Chicago Press, Chicago, 1951.
Torrance, James B. 'The Place of Jesus Christ in Worship.' *Church Service Society Annual,* no. 40 (May, 1970), pp. 41-62.
Torrance, Thomas F., *God and Rationality.* Oxford University Press, London, 1971.
—— 'Service in Jesus Christ.' *Service in Christ* 'Essays Presented to Karl Barth on his 80th Birthday'. James I. McCord and T. H. L. Parker, eds. Epworth Press, London, 1966.
—— *Space, Time and Incarnation.* Oxford University Press, London, 1969.
—— *Theological Science.* Oxford University Press, London, 1969.
—— *Theology in Reconstruction.* Eerdmans Publishing Co., Grand Rapids, 1965.
Turner, Geoffrey. 'Wolfhart Pannenberg and the Hermeneutical Problem.' *The Irish Theological Quarterly,* vol. 39, no. 2 (April, 1972), pp. 107-129.
Turner, H. E. W., 'Under-estimated Theological Books—Frank Weston's "The One Christ".' *The Expository Times,* 72 (1960-61), pp. 277-279.
Versényi, Laszlo, *Heidegger, Being, and Truth.* Yale University Press, New Haven, 1965.
Vriezen, T. C., *An Outline of Old Testament Theology.* Second, revised edition, Basil Blackwell, Oxford, 1970. Trans. from *Hoofdlijnen der theologie van het Oude Testament* (1949), 3rd edition, 1966, pub. H. Veenman and Zonen N.V., Wageningen, the Netherlands, by S. Neuijen.
Wallace, David, 'A Note on μορφή.' *Theologische Zeitschrift,* 22 (1966), pp. 19-25.
Ward, Wayne E., 'The Person of Christ: The Kenotic Theory.' *Christianity Today,* vol. 6, no. 2 (October 27, 1961), pp. 18-19.
Ware, Timothy, *The Orthodox Church.* Penguin Books, Middlesex, England, 1963.
Welch, Claude, ed., *God and Incarnation in Mid-nineteenth Century German Theology.* Oxford University Press, New York, 1965.
Weston, Frank, *The One Christ.* Longmans Green and Co., London, 1914.
Whitehead, A. N., *Process and Reality.* Macmillan, New York, 1929.
Whitehouse, W. A., 'Christ and Creation.' *Essays in Christology.* T. H. L. Parker, ed. Lutterworth Press, London, 1956.
Wingren, Gustaf, *Man and the Incarnation.* Oliver and Boyd, Edinburgh/London, 1959.
Wittgenstein, Ludwig, *Philosophical Investigations.* Basil Blackwell, Oxford, 1953.
Wolfe, Thomas, *Look Homeward, Angel!* Charles Scribner's Sons, New York, 1930.
Woods, G. F., 'The Idea of the Transcendent.' *Soundings.* A. R. Vidler, ed. Cambridge University Press, Cambridge (1962), 1966, pp. 45-65.
Wright, G. Ernest, and Fuller, Reginald, *The Book of the Acts of God.* Penguin Books, Middlesex, England, 1965.

Wright, G. Ernest, and Fuller, Reginald, *The Old Testament and Theology*. Harper & Row, New York, 1969.

—— 'Reflections Concerning Old Testament Theology' *Studia Biblica et Semitica*. H. Veenman and Zonen N.V., Wageningen, 1966, pp. 376-388.

Zizioulas, John, 'Human Capacity and Human Incapacity.' Unpublished essay presented at the *Society for the Study of Theology*, Oxford University (April, 1972).

Index of Names

Abraham, 121, 124f
Adolfs, Robert, 231n
Albrecktson, Bertil, 113n
Altizer, Thomas J. J., 37n, 52n
Anderson, R. S., 132n, 168n
Aquinas, xvii, 41n, 55
Aristotle, xvii, xxiin, 14, 15, 41n, 152n
Athanasius, 57, 157
Augustine, 55, 220, 244

Baelz, Peter, xvin
Bandstra, Andrew J., 163n
Barr, James, 106n, 109n, 110n, 113n
Barth, Karl, 17, 22n, 40n, 70, 75, 91, 93n, 94, 117f, 119, 121, 127, 129n, 130n, 131n, 134, 140n, 147n, 148n, 150n, 160n, 178, 179n, 184n, 208n, 214n, 218, 220, 222n, 226, 242, 243n, 249n, 253n, 254, 263n, 275n, 278f, 288, 294
Beare, F. W., 164n
Berger, P. L., 6n, 7n, 8, 53n
Bethge, Eberhard, 72n, 73n, 74n, 76n, 86n, 95, 96n, 97n, 104, 184n, 219n, 245
Blaikie, Robert J., xixn, 41n, 56n
Boccaccio, 41, 50n
Bonhoeffer, Dietrich, xivf, xixf, 37, 53n, 55n, 56f, 58, 61, 66, 68, 72f, 74f, 77f, 79f, 83f, 87f, 90f, 93f, 96f, 104f, 108, 129, 137, 158, 162, 165n, 167n, 172n, 179n, 184n, 211n, 216-220, 228, 230, 236n, 245, 247-249, 252, 255-258, 265, 285, 294-295, 298n
Braun, Herbert, 46
Bruce, A. B., 149n
Brunner, Emil, 16, 17, 247-249, 273n
Bruno, Giordano, 104
Buber, Martin, xviiin, 44, 92, 128, 135n, 202n, 248, 273n
Bultmann, Rudolf, 5, 30f, 49n, 51, 68, 86, 106, 141n, 169, 212n, 222n, 284

Buren, Paul van, xiiin, xiv, 5n, 11, 21, 37n, 44n, 49n, 68n, 172n
Buri, Fritz, 44f
Buss, Martin J., 287

Cairns, David, 13n, 16, 17
Calvin, John, 149n, 161n
Campenhausen, Hans F. von, 288
Carnell, Edward John, 206n, 213n
Clayton, J. P., 231n
Cox, Harvey, 37n,
Cullman, Oscar, 161n, 163n

Dawes, Donald G., 150n, 159n
Descartes, xvii, 15, 41, 47, 152, 191
Diem, Hermann, 214
Dilthey, 218
Dodd, C. H., 161n, 268, 282n
Dumas, André, 96n

Ebeling, Gerhard, 222n
Ebner, F., 248
Erasmus, 41

Farley, Edward, 16n, 41n
Feuerbach, Ludwig, 154
Flew, A. and MacIntyre, A., ed., 10
Florovsky, George, 282n
Frege, 24n
Fry, Christopher, 103n, 187n
Fuller, Daniel P., 288-292

Galloway, Allan, xvin
Gess, W. F., 149n, 169n
Gibbs, John G., 161n, 162n, 163n
Gibran, K., 252n
Gogarten, Friedrich, 53n, 92
Gollwitzer, Helmut, 42n, 46f, 48n, 50, 69f
Gore, Charles, 149n, 150n
Graft, G. van der, 121n
Grass, Hans, 288

Index of Subjects

Act,
  as being, 17
  of God, see God, as agent
  as relation, 17
  as transcendence, 38
Adam,
  174n.85, 296
  'second Adam', 161n.51, 175
Agnosticism, 49, 152
Anthropomorphism, 12, 47, 114f, 116f
Apollinarianism, 171

Baptism, 281f
Being,
  authentic, 30
  being-itself, 28
  'holy being', 29f, 31, 37
  social, 77
  theology of, 92
Body,
  of Christ, see Church, as body of
    Christ
  as community of spirit, 79
  as existence form of spirit, 79, 129,
    183
Boundary mentality, 271f

Capitalism, 241n.31
Cartesian thought, 33n, 41f, 46, 47, 152,
  191, 290
Chalcedon,
  council of, 83, 165
Charismatic,
  community, 242, 243, 272
Christian,
  as eschaton of kenotic community,
    282
  evangelical, 265f
  incarnational, 260f, 263f
  as 'new man', 254
  in solidarity with world, 254, 265
  without faith in Christ, 265

  religionless, see Religionless Christi-
    anity
  worldliness of, 93
Christology, 84, 154, 158, 164, 229, 258
  D. Bonhoeffer's, 68, 75f, 85, 89, 91, 93,
    95f, 184, 218
  kenotic, 149, 155, 162, 169, 171, 175
  Lutheran, 179n.94, 180n.97, 218
Church,
  as body of Christ, 223, 256f, 261f,
    269f, 276
  boundaries of, 260f
  as 'boundary-less', 261f, 265, 267f, 274
  as 'community of Christ', 75, 82, 216,
    256
  as concrete form of Christ, 81n.36
  'confessing church', 75
  as *diakonia*, 275f
  doctrine of, 229ff, 237, 244f, 256f
  domesticity of, 237
  as *ekklesia*, 273
  as ek-static community, 238-251
  as 'household of faith', 237
  as kenotic community, 229-238
  koinonia of, 299f
  marks of, 82
  as 'non-institutional', 272f
  as 'place' of God's presence, 304
  renewal of, 231n.12, 232, 246n.43
  solidarity with world, 259f, 274
  as truthful, 274.50
  unity of, 55
  visible and invisible, 236n.22
Collective person, 75
Community,
  as Christ, 75f, 82, 93, 96, 182
  of covenant response, 185
  as 'incapacity', 249
  kenotic, *see* Kenotic community
  as religion, 201ff
  as social being, 77
  and society, 197, 247ff

Inner logic—*cont.*
  of the humanity of God, 127
  of incarnation, 105, 107, 113n.23,
    114, 116, 118, 124, 126ff, 138, 142f,
    150f, 169f, 171, 172, 175, 228, 293
  of Israel, 110, 145, 172
  of Scripture, 212
  of transcendence, 20, 39, 87, 93, 99
Israel,
  as a boundary religion, 271
  as covenant response, 142, 171
  election of, 119
  as the Logos of God, 130, 144, 164
  as organic with Christ, *see* Jesus
    Christ, organic connection with
    Israel
  as pre-history of incarnation, 109,
    130f, 172
  secularity of, 120
  as the 'suffering servant', 130, 144
  and the word of God, 220n.85
I-Thou relation, 17, 44, 67, 78f, 84n.45,
  92, 202, 248, 261, 273n.48

Jesus Christ,
  as 'anti-Logos', 167
  atonement of, 157, 175
  authority of, 165f
  body of, *see* Church, as body of
    Christ
  as 'boundary-less', 268
  clothed with his gospel, 275
  as covenant response, 142f, 181, 183
  cross of, 168, 172, 174, 182, 216, 279
  divinity of, 156, 169
  as the eschaton, 175, 281
  as the form of a servant, 167, 169
  form of in the world, 228
  forsakenness of, 168f, 175f, 177f
  growth of, 174
  humanity of, 70, 144, 148, 166, 169,
    252
  humiliation of, 156f, 159, 160, 162,
    178, 184ff
  law of, 258
  Logos of, 98, 104
  Lordship of, 55, 166
  as 'man for others', 172f
  meekness of, 166
  mind of, 184
  obedience of, 174, 176
  as the 'one Israelite', 130, 172f
  oneness with Father, 262
  organic connection with Israel, 105,

  108, 124, 142, 145
  person of, 162, 165, 173, 210, 218,
    233, 239
  reality of, 94
  resurrection of, *see* Resurrection of
    Jesus Christ
  self renunciation of, 156ff, 159ff
  sinlessness of, 233
  solidarity with man, 252f, 264
  as the way of transcendence, 36
Judaism, 166

Kenosis, xx, 99, 129n.64, 143, 145, 146f,
  149, 151, 156f, 160f, 162f, 169, 216,
  218, 229, 231, 259f, 280
  law of, 183f
  as loss of transcendence, 169
  as trinitarian act, 177f, 179, 180, 184,
    209
  as the way to the cross, 182
Kenotic community, 182, 229-238, 241,
  245f, 253f, 269, 281
  definition of, 259
  as *diakonia*, 275f
  secularity of, 255
  in solidarity with world, 269f
  in tension with world, 253f

Language, 123, 215n.72
  human and divine, 266n.36
  problematic of, 12, 39
  religious, 12f, 13n.43, 136
Lived transcendence, 227ff, 253f, 294f
  as a community of spirit, 183
  as difference in solidarity, 261f
  as ek-stasis of the body, 298ff
  as eschatological, 279f, 281f
  as kenotic community, 185, 231ff, 253
  as presence in absence, 302f
  as the reality of forgiveness, 300ff
  as the reality of God, 185
  as the recovery of the tragic, 296f
  thresholds of, 294f
Logos,
  see Jesus Christ, Logos of and God,
    Logos of
Love,
  as belonging-in-community, 206
  as ek-stasis of spirit, 242
  as incapacity, 297
  introversion of, 241
  as rationality, 50n.43, 188, 199
  as reality of personhood, 234f
  as self-renunciation, 179, 232

Transcendence—*cont.*
  264, 275
  crisis of, 10, 35, 37, 71, 151, 153, 279f
  definition of, 13, 147, 190
  as *diakonia*, 275f
  as difference in solidarity, 260, 264
  as eschaton, 279f
  as future, 207f, 212, 222, 279
  of God, *see* God, transcendence of
  as ground of being, 15
  as hiddenness, 18n, 20, 131, 143, 154, 164
  historical, *see* Historical transcendence
  as 'holy being', 29
  immanent, 24f, 27f, 30f, 34f, 37
  inner logic of, xv, 39, 52
  intra-divine, 180f, 183, 209, 232f, 242f
  as *kenosis*, 165ff, 208f, 223, 252f
  kerygmatic, 16n
  language of, 11, 22, 38, 40, 52
  as limit for man, 136f, 144, 165, 171, 177, 181
  lived, *see* Lived transcendence
  loss of, 3, 6ff, 10, 22, 37, 52, 148, 155, 296
  of man with God, 135
  models of, 13ff
  as otherness, 33
  'out and out', 21ff, 24, 29, 31, 34f
  as 'place', 183n.107, 237
  as reality of God, 32, 123
  secular, 36, 62n.82

  self, 201
  as self consciousness, 19
  as spirit, 40, 66
  this worldly, 68, 73
  visibility of, 235f
Trinity, 160, 177f, 179f, 185, 209, 246, 249, 293
Truth, 80
  coherence of, 103
  and disillusionment, 188
  non-formalizable, 116, 125
  placed into, 80, 82, 85, 86, 90, 92, 210, 216
  as 'unconcealingment', 215n.72
  as will to belong, 206

Ultimate concern, 35f
Universalism, 177n.89

Word of God,
  see God, word of
World, 55f
  desacralization of, 120
  as profane, 51f, 53, 56, 59f, 71, 87, 98f, 189
  as sacramental, 61
  as sacred, 52
World come of age, 73f, 86, 89, 96
Worship, 210, 245f, 246f, 304
  as celebration of presence in absence, 304